TEACHING NINETEENTH-CENTURY RUSSIAN LITERATURE

Essays in Honor of Robert L. Belknap

Ars Rossica

Series Editor: David M. BETHEA
(University of Wisconsin — Madison)

**ACADEMIC
STUDIES
PRESS**

TEACHING
NINETEENTH-CENTURY
RUSSIAN LITERATURE

Essays in Honor of Robert L. Belknap

Edited by
Deborah MARTINSEN
Cathy POPKIN
Irina REYFMAN

BOSTON
2014

Library of Congress Cataloging-in-Publication Data:
A catalog reference for this title is available from the Library
of Congress.

ISBN 978-1-618113-49-8 (hardback)
ISBN 978-1-618113-60-3 (electronic)
ISBN 978-1-618113-86-3 (paperback)

Cover design by Ivan Grave
On the cover: *Portrait of Adelaida Simonovich*, by Valentin Serov, 1889.

Published by Academic Studies Press in 2014
28 Montfern Avenue
Brighton, MA 02135, USA
press@academicstudiespress.com
www.academicstudiespress.com

Robert L. Belknap,
photo courtesy of The University Seminars at Columbia University,
photographer Alice Newton

Contents

ACKNOWLEDGMENTS

The editors would like first and foremost to thank Bob Belknap for being a master teacher and a great colleague, a model for us all. Bob's teaching, the basis of this collection, derives from his generosity, a virtue, to quote the philosopher Simon Blackburn, "that may be simply the exercise of an abundance, an overflow of good will or benevolence." Every contributor to this volume and countless Slavists in the United States and abroad have benefited from Bob's academic insight, teaching acumen, good will, and benevolence.

We are very grateful to our distinguished contributors for their conference papers, polished articles, good will, and great patience. We would also like to acknowledge the very generous support we received for both the original conference and the resulting publication from the Harriman Institute, especially its Publication Committee, from The Columbia University Seminar on Slavic History and Culture, and from the Columbia Slavic Department. We are particularly grateful to Liza Knapp for her invaluable help with the conference and her collaboration at earlier stages of the publication project. We owe a special debt to Alice Newton of The University Seminars at Columbia University for her indispensable aid throughout this period and for permission to use her photograph of Bob Belknap. Special thanks go to Kirsten Painter for her expert editing. We thank Mike Levine and the manuscript's initial readers. We would also like to thank Igor Nemirovsky and the team at Academic Studies Press for their enthusiasm and expertise.

Note on Transliteration

This volume uses a dual system of transliteration, following the guidelines in J. Thomas Shaw's *Transliteration of Modern Russian for English-Language Publications*:

> In the text and in all discursive parts of the endnotes, we use Shaw's "System I," which omits soft signs and anglicizes Russian proper names. It also uses the familiar spelling of well-known names (e.g., Herzen).
>
> Any transliteration in English-language quotations remains in the style used by the original author.
>
> When citing Russian sources in the bibliography and notes, we use the Library of Congress system without diacritics (Shaw's "System II").

Notes on Contributors

Robert L. Belknap is Professor Emeritus of Russian at Columbia. He was educated at Princeton University, The University of Paris, Columbia University, and Leningrad (now St. Petersburg) State University, and is the author of *The Structure of "The Brothers Karamazov"* (1967, 1989, in Russian 1997), *The Genesis of "The Brothers Karamazov"* (1990), and other studies of Russian literature and of university education. He has taught courses in general education, literary theory, and Russian and comparative literature, and has served as Dean of Students, Dean of the College, Director of the Russian (now Harriman) Institute, and Director of University Seminars at Columbia.

Elizabeth Klosty Beaujour holds a B.A. from Vassar and an M.A., Certificate of the Russian Institute, and Ph.D. from Columbia. She teaches at Hunter College and in the Doctoral Program in Comparative Literature at the CUNY Graduate Center. The author of *Alien Tongues: Bilingual Russian Writers of the "First" Emigration* (1989), and *The Invisible Land: A Study of the Artistic Imagination of Iurii Olesha* (1970), she has also contributed chapters to a variety of edited volumes and has written numerous articles on the relationship between architecture and Russian literature and on the interaction of French and Russian literature.

Ksana Blank, a senior lecturer in the Department of Slavic Languages and Literatures at Princeton University (Ph.D. in Russian literature from Columbia University), has been teaching Russian language and literature at Princeton since 2000. The author of *Dostoevsky's Dialectics and the Problem of Sin* (2010) and over two dozen articles on Russian literature in English and Russian, she is completing a book tentatively entitled *Unmarked Intersections: Essays on Russian Literature* (forthcoming, 2014).

Ellen Chances is Professor of Russian literature at Princeton University. Her publications include the books *Conformity's Children: An Approach to the Superfluous Man in Russian Literature* (1978) and *Andrei Bitov: The Ecology of Inspiration* (1993; in Russian 2006), as well as many articles on Russian literature and culture from the nineteenth century to the present. Her specialties include the Russian novel, Dostoevsky, Chekhov, Andrei Bitov, Russian journalism, the ethical dimensions of contemporary Russian cinema, and Russian literature and the arts.

Nicholas Dames is Theodore Kahan Professor of Humanities at Columbia University. A specialist in nineteenth-century British and European fiction, he is the author of *Amnesiac Selves: Nostalgia, Forgetting, and British Fiction, 1810-1870* (2001) and *The Physiology of the Novel: Reading, Neural Science, and the Form of Victorian Fiction* (2007).

Andrew R. Durkin was a member of the Department of Slavic Languages and Literatures at Indiana University from 1975 until his retirement in 2010. His research and publications have included topics in Russian literature (Sergei Aksakov, Turgenev, Chekhov, Andrei Sinyavskii, Iurii Trifonov, and others) as well as comparative topics (Czech and Russian literature, Russian literature and British literature, and Kurosawa's treatment of *The Idiot*).

Jefferson J. A. Gatrall is Associate Professor of Russian at Montclair State University. He is the co-editor, with Douglas Greenfield, of *Alter Icons: The Russian Icon and Modernity* (2010) as well as, with Angela Esterhammer, a special issue of the journal *arcadia* (2008) on Identity and Community. His publications include articles on Dostoevsky, Chekhov,

Tolstoy, Proust, Nikolai Ge, and Lew Wallace. His book *The Real and the Sacred: Picturing Jesus in Nineteenth-Century Fiction* is forthcoming in 2014. He is currently working on a book about representations of the historical Jesus in European and American fiction.

Svetlana Slavskaya Grenier is Associate Professor at Georgetown University. She is the author of *Representing the Marginal Woman in 19th-century Russian Literature: Personalism, Feminism, and Polyphony* (2001) and articles on Pushkin, Herzen, Tolstoy, Dostoevsky, and Maria Zhukova. She is currently completing a manuscript entitled *Beyond* Anna Karenina: *Russian Narratives of Adultery and the Freedom of Faithfulness*.

Robert Louis Jackson, B.E. Bensinger Professor (Emeritus) of Slavic Languages and Literatures at Yale University, has published widely on Dostoevsky, Tolstoy, Turgenev, Chekhov, and other writers of the nineteenth and twentieth centuries. Among his books are *Dostoevsky's Quest for Form: A Study of His Philosophy of Art* (1966) and *Dialogues with Dostoevsky: The Overwhelming Questions* (1993).

Liza Knapp is Associate Professor at Columbia University. She is the author of *The Annihilation of Inertia: Dostoevsky and Metaphysics* (1996), the editor of a critical companion to Dostoevsky's *The Idiot* (1998), and the co-editor of *Approaches to Teaching* Anna Karenina (2003).

Deborah A. Martinsen is Dean of Alumni Education at Columbia University, where she teaches courses in the Core Curriculum, the Slavic Department, and the Department of English and Comparative Literature. She is the author of *Surprised by Shame: Dostoevsky's Liars and Narratives of Exposure* (2003; in Russian 2011) as well as articles on Dostoevsky, Tolstoy, and Nabokov. She is the editor of *Literary Journals in Imperial Russia* (1997; in paper 2010) and is currently co-editing *Dostoevsky in Context*. She was President of the International Dostoevsky Society from 2007-2013.

Olga Meerson is Professor of Russian at Georgetown University and the author of several books, including *Dostoevsky's Taboos* (1998), *Svobodnaia veshch'. Poetika neostraneniia u Andreia Platonova* (1997; in Russia 2001), and *Personalizm kak poetika. Literaturnyi mir glazami ego obitatelei* (2009).

Maude Meisel taught Russian and humanities at Columbia University, Middlebury College, SUNY Stony Brook, and UC Riverside before becoming Associate Director of The Challenge to Achievement Program at Pace University in Pleasantville, where she also teaches courses in English, Russian, and drama. In 2005-2006, as a Fulbright Scholar, she taught Shakespeare at The University of Culture and the Arts in St. Petersburg (Russia).

Robin Feuer Miller is Edytha Macy Gross Professor of Humanities at Brandeis University and Guggenheim Fellow, 2013-14. Her books include *Dostoevsky and* The Idiot: *Author, Narrator and Reader* (1981), The Brothers Karamazov: *Worlds of the Novel* (1992, 2008), *Dostoevsky's Unfinished Journey* (2007), and numerous edited and co-edited volumes. She is currently working on a book entitled *Dostoevsky, Tolstoy, and the Small of This World* and editing a volume of letters tentatively entitled *Kazuko's Letters from Japan*. Her primary scholarly work has focused on various nineteenth-century writers.

Marcia A. Morris is Professor of Slavic Languages at Georgetown University. Her previous publications include *Saints and Revolutionaries: The Ascetic Hero in Russian Literature* (1993) and *The Literature of Roguery in Seventeenth- and Eighteenth-Century Russia* (2000). She is currently working on a study of historical fictions of Russian familial regicide.

Gary Saul Morson, Frances Hooper Professor at Northwestern University, has held simultaneous endowed chairs in teaching and research. He has won best-book awards from the American Association of Teachers of Slavic and East European Languages and the American Comparative Literature Association, as well as a career scholarly achievement award from AATSEEL.

Catharine Theimer Nepomnyashchy is Ann Whitney Olin Professor and Chair of the Slavic Department at Barnard College and former Director of the Harriman Institute. She is the author of *Abram Tertz and the Poetics of Crime* (1995), translator of *Strolls with Pushkin* (1993), and co-editor of *Under the Sky of My Africa: Alexander Pushkin and Blackness* (2006) and *Mapping the Feminine: Russian Women and Cultural Difference* (2008). She has published extensively on Soviet and post-Soviet literature and popular culture, Pushkin, Russian ballet, and the future of regional studies. She is currently working on a book titled *Nabokov and His Enemies: The Terms of Engagement*.

Cathy Popkin is the Jesse and George Siegel Professor in the Humanities and Professor of Russian at Columbia University. She is the author of *The Pragmatics of Insignificance: Chekhov, Zoshchenko, Gogol* (1993) and the editor and one of the translators of the new Norton Critical Edition of *Anton Chekhov's Selected Stories*. She is currently completing a book on the disciplinary practices and documentary forms that shape Chekhov's narrative prose and continuing an ongoing project on Turgenev and metaphor.

Irina Reyfman is Professor of Russian Literature at Columbia University. In her studies, Reyfman focuses on the interaction of literature and culture. Reyfman is the author of *Vasilii Trediakovsky: The Fool of the 'New' Russian Literature* (1990), *Ritualized Violence Russian Style: The Duel in Russian*

Culture and Literature (1999; in Russian 2002), and *Rank and Style: Russians in State Service, Life, and Literature* (2012). She is also a co-editor of *Mapping the Feminine: Russian Women and Cultural Difference* (2008). She is currently completing a book on the interaction of writing and state service in Russian literature of the imperial period.

Rebecca Stanton is Assistant Professor of Russian at Barnard College and the author of *Isaac Babel and the Self-Invention of Odessan Modernism* (2012). A specialist in Soviet literature and culture, she has also published scholarly articles on Gogol, Tolstoy, and Dostoevsky. She is currently working on a book examining the role of magic and the supernatural in Soviet fiction.

William Mills Todd III was educated at Dartmouth College, the University of Oxford, Columbia University, Leningrad State University, and around kitchen tables in Moscow and Petersburg. His books include *The Familiar Letter as a Literary Genre in the Age of Pushkin* (1976), *Literature and Society in Imperial Russia: 1800-1914* (edited, 1978), *Fiction and Society in the Age of Pushkin: Ideology, Institutions, and Narrative* (1986), and *Sovremennoe amerikanskoe pushkinovedenie* (edited, 1999). He is Harry Tuchman Levin Professor of Literature and Professor of Comparative Literature at Harvard University.

Nancy Workman is an adjunct of the Columbia University Slavic Department. She has been teaching Columbia College's Core Curriculum since 1999, and has had an appointment as Core Lecturer there.

INTRODUCTION

Cathy Popkin, Deborah Martinsen, Irina Reyfman

The essays in this volume present concrete strategies for teaching the works of some of Russia's best known writers: Pushkin, Lermontov, Gogol, Turgenev, Saltykov-Shchedrin, Dostoevsky, Tolstoy, and Chekhov. All are central to the Russian literary canon, but some have become part of the global literary heritage as well. Like many masterpieces of world literature, these nineteenth-century Russian literary texts have become required reading in a wide spectrum of courses, and the essays assembled here consider a correspondingly wide range of teaching contexts: from basic surveys of nineteenth-century Russian literature to topic-based courses with works from diverse traditions; from a course for advanced language students in a Russian program to a course sponsored by an English department for its majors and other readers; from advanced seminars on a single author to general education courses in both literature and social science. Most of the essays collected here address teaching these iconic works of nineteenth-century Russian literature in English translation because that is how they are most often taught, at least at the undergraduate level; as anyone in the Russian field knows from experience, it takes years for students of Russian to be able to read these classics in the original. In the meantime, the guidance of skilled teachers who are proficient in Russian is essential.

The teaching experience collected in this volume was first shared at a conference held at Columbia University in February 2010, to honor Robert L. Belknap. The conference, "Formulations: Teaching Nineteenth-Century Russian Literature," was motivated by and organized around Bob Belknap's trademark ability to

Cathy Popkin, Deborah Martinsen, Irina Reyfman

challenge students to assume the project of sense-making, to take the material in hand and figure out what to do with it, what to say about it. The object, Bob has always maintained, is to activate students to formulate productive questions and develop strategies for detecting meaning in the works they read. Thus we asked conference participants—former students and current colleagues of Belknap's—to suggest ways they have developed of doing this in their own teaching. The results exceeded our expectations. Not only were the individual papers exceptionally insightful and suggestive, but what emerged from the aggregate was a colloquy that gave those involved, both the presenters and the audience, a sense of being engaged in a common literary project in teaching the classics of nineteenth-century Russian literature. Not that the papers and the ideas they presented are all alike—teaching, after all, is a very individual process, and the approaches exemplified here are as varied as their contributors. Nonetheless, what unified the conference presentations was their shared commitment to the project of actively tracking down meaning in the classroom.

Not coincidentally, more than one of the essays in this Belknap-inspired volume frames the work of the classroom as a process of tracking down clues, pursuing leads, sifting through evidence, approaching the text with the painstaking scrutiny required in detective work. In her keynote essay "The Teacher and the Text: The Pragmatic Sleuth in the Classroom," Robin Feuer Miller explicitly likens Robert Belknap to *Crime and Punishment*'s super sleuth Porfiry Petrovich, famous for his instinctive ability "to sleuth, to pare away, to bare structure while simultaneously remaining alive to the influence of affective networks of associations."[1] No less canny an investigator herself, Miller conducts class as a careful examination of the textual evidence, working through the intellectual puzzles at hand, attending to plot-induced anxieties, moving backwards and forwards as the classroom situation or the evidence demands. Obviously, what Miller describes is no solo performance; the

---

[1]   Pp. 16-31 in this volume. All subsequent references to this volume are given in the text.

Cathy Popkin, Deborah Martinsen, Irina Reyfman

anxieties, the puzzling, and the movements in response presuppose active participation on the students' part, and Miller asks them specifically to track how they read, what they skip, what they turn back to. Nor is this keeping track solely in the interest of a lively classroom; rather, to become astute readers themselves, students must learn to monitor—and trust—their own responses. That primary reading, the moment when the novel is in private play with the reader, is too precious an experience and too important a source to squander. In order to safeguard students' intimate, direct encounters with a novel, Miller suggests, one may urge them to read scholarly introductions as afterwords, to immerse themselves in the critical or theoretical material only once they have become experts on the work.

Two things are immediately apparent in this model of literary forensics: the literary text remains the primary object of scrutiny, and the students' access to it is unimpeded. Yet what kind of "experts" are students positioned to become, untutored in anything other than their own responses? Even when, in class discussion, they are brought face-to-face with the equally unmediated responses of others, how are they to accommodate the diverse and potentially incompatible possibilities? Here the teacher's ability to work in real time with live response is key to modeling the transformation of raw reaction into meaningful observation, ideally imparting to students the skills they need to perform this operation on their own. All the essays collected here suggest that their authors, as teachers, recognize that their paramount duty is to guide their students through the text in this way, teaching them to read with the utmost intellectual rigor and honesty. The ideal classroom becomes the setting for fruitful collaboration among text, student reader, and more experienced reader—the teacher.

But surely not even the most perfect synergy generates everything students will need to engage the text with rigor and honesty. Doesn't their ignorance of the author's biography, the cultural and historical context, the conditions of production, the conventions of the genre, the era's philosophical debates, the works that precede this one, even the language it was written in constitute a formidable impediment to genuine understanding?

Indeed, teachers often face a dilemma as they determine how much background information and cultural context students need to read a work of literature adequately, particularly one from long ago and far away. Much will depend on the nature of the course, the constituency of students, and the constraints on time. But even in classroom situations where cultural context *per se* is not a major concern, such material can become integral to in-class discussion and provide the framework for scholarship; it might be argued that context is essential to read anything adequately, let alone well.

Needless to say, painstaking attention to text does not preclude diligent contextualization; even with the primary material center stage, Belknap himself makes no bones about his conviction that that stage must be set. "We should always investigate and always teach everything in its context, biographical, psychological, historical, political, economic, literary, linguistic, religious, etc.," he affirms in "Teaching Contexts," his essay in this volume (32). But art is long and class short, and too much context can also divert our attention from the matter at hand, especially when the matter at hand is elusive. "Context," Belknap notes, "can shield us from the text" (33). The challenge is to make sure that doesn't happen.

Significantly, as Ellen Chances reminds us in her essay, while Belknap made a name for himself with *The Structure of "The Brothers Karamazov"* (1968), his famous study of that novel's constituent elements, he is equally the author of *The Genesis of "The Brothers Karamazov"* (1990), his magisterial account of the novel's sources and precursors. The trick, it seems, is to approach the text from both the inside and the outside, ideally in a continuous loop, less like a hermeneutic circle and more like a moebius strip.

How much extra-textual material is warranted, and what sort should it be? How might the opacity of text be illuminated by a skillfully deployed flashlight? What contours might be delineated by a postcard from the edge? What else, in short, do students need to know to appreciate the texts they study, and what kind of extra-textual materials should we who teach them provide to enable them to put two and two—and two and two and two—together? It takes a hundred pairs of eyes to know another person, muses Virginia Woolf's narrator about Mrs. Ramsay, the enigmatic center

Cathy Popkin, Deborah Martinsen, Irina Reyfman

of *To the Lighthouse*. Each essay in this volume is likewise devoted to the classroom analysis of the aesthetic object at its center. But each also combines its determined focus on the workings of the text with a conscious inquiry about what *else*, in addition to the primary source, might make those workings maximally perceptible—and meaningful—to the students themselves. This overt concern with the primacy of text and the signifying potential of context in its innumerable forms lends a strong internal coherence to the twenty-two formulations presented here, as they negotiate ways for us to have our cake and eat it too.

Robert Belknap, in his essay, poses a slightly different question, focusing less on what students need to know by way of context than on how faculty can possibly supply it, and how much we need to know in order to provide it in anything beyond amateurish terms, given our finite lifetimes and the limits these necessarily impose on our expertise. In "Teaching Contexts," Belknap describes an experience of team-teaching in an experimental curriculum on the 1860s with colleagues from the French and English departments who provided expert contextualization from their respective arenas for students whose entire course load revolved around that decade and those cultures. The results were stunning, not to mention enviable, but, not surprisingly, the experiment proved unsustainable for practical reasons. Belknap's account of what was possible under those extraordinary circumstances places the constraints under which we normally operate into even starker relief. Many of the essays that follow offer strategies for achieving the effect, if not the extent, of the historical, cultural, and disciplinary contextualization facilitated by the bevy of experts and the generous contact hours in the 1860s experiment.

And yet we mustn't put the contextual cart before the horse, cautions Olga Meerson. What students need first, she argues in "Theorizing vs. Teaching Literary Theory: What Is to Be Done with *Crime and Punishment?*," is unmediated access to the text itself, the opportunity to stumble and experience firsthand the need for a helpful frame of reference before turning to anything that might mitigate their confusion. Thus, in Meerson's detailed lesson plan, students begin by reading the assigned section of Dostoevsky's novel closely, wrestling with its specific riddles, and focusing on what trips them up. Only once the students have begun to formulate their own questions does Meerson introduce some of the theoretical approaches that can help them cope with the work's complexity and empower them to detect the polyphony of Dostoevsky's prose. Her essay offers a model for the productive use of Bakhtin in the undergraduate classroom. Theories are valuable interpretive tools, Meerson avers, and they ought to be taught. Yet like Robin Miller and other literary detectives before her (she cites Sherlock Holmes and Lord Peter Wimsey), Meerson is alert to the danger of theorizing in advance of the facts.

Stumbling and interpretive missteps play a productive role in Irina Reyfman's classroom as well, above all in her courses conceived to introduce non-native speakers to the art of reading literary works in the original Russian. Her essay on "Literature in the Original for the Defective Detective, or Teaching Suspect Grammar to Unsuspecting Students" offers expert advice on training students with less than optimal control of the target language to develop a feel for where the trouble spots lie, to pursue their own intuitions about things like word play and tense changes, and to relate these observations to the text's possible meanings. The obstacles are daunting, especially when nonstandard usage requires that students with an imperfect sense of grammatical, syntactic, or stylistic norms recognize deviations from those norms. Reyfman begins by preparing students for the kinds of irregularities they might encounter, instructing them not to gloss over difficulties but to make them an explicit object of attention and to speculate on the effects they produce. Taking Chekhov's "The New Dacha" as her case study, Reyfman vividly demonstrates the instructional value of misunderstanding a story about people who can't understand one another.

If Meerson is wary of putting anything ahead of the novel lest the reading be unduly shaped by what precedes it, Ksana Blank emphasizes the value of the novel's own leading edge—its epigraph—as an interpretive key to everything that follows. In "'The Way of the Grain': Teaching *The Brothers Karamazov* through the Novel's Epigraph," Blank demonstrates how teachers can use what comes first—the passage from the Gospel of John about seeds dying and bearing fruit—to reveal patterns of meaning that inform the novel as a whole. Starting small, with the seed itself, offers students a productive way of expanding toward the big picture. Blank detects the biblical seed in less and less accessible contexts with broader and broader associations—from the Russian literary and historical to the broadly mythological—thereby revealing how a humble introductory image can structure a long and complex novel and reveal the vastness of its truth. By practicing this kind of reading, working from the inside out rather than imposing a reading or a theory from the outside in, Blank reveals that Dostoevsky's "realism" in *The Brothers Karamazov* is rooted, to an even greater degree than in his other novels, in the workings of a deep structure of allusions, both symbolic and real.

Liza Knapp's "Teaching Raskolnikov's Dream: Regarding the Pain of Others in the Classroom" takes not an epigraph but a single episode in *Crime and Punishment*—Raskolnikov's dream about the beating of a cart horse—as a springboard to discussing a question at the heart of the novel and at the center of human experience: "What does the pain of others have to do with us?" She shows students not only how the dream reconfigures and reappears in other episodes in the novel, but how the episode's biblical subtext—the story of the Good Samaritan—draws the gospel world and the novelistic world together for an exploration of the question of who our neighbors are, how this question reverberates in Dostoevsky's and Tolstoy's later works, and how it fits into the nineteenth-century European literary tradition. Knapp shows how this evocative scene can activate the moral imagination: because the pain and suffering depicted are so immediately accessible and students respond so viscerally to reading the scene, it enacts its own argument, for the scene is less about what the peasant is doing to the poor horse than about how we respond to the suffering of another being. By asking students to identify with characters or situations and thus to do the moral work required by the text, Knapp creates the opportunity for students to expand their capacities for empathy.

Instead of juxtaposing text and subtext, Andrew Durkin's "Chekhov's 'In Exile' and 'The Student': Text/Countertext as

Cathy Popkin, Deborah Martinsen, Irina Reyfman

Strategy" demonstrates how one story by Chekhov becomes far more resonant when ricocheted off another one, illustrating the way that the meaning of the part illuminates the meaning of the whole. As Durkin observes in his essay, syllabi are organized around "text sets" designed to help students appreciate particular features of those texts. While we often play authors, media, and cultural traditions off each other, the experience is different, as Durkin shows, when all the texts in a set are by the same author. As students' familiarity with a given author and his work grows, they learn to read him differently. Careful attention to parallels and equivalences in text sets leads students first to an increased awareness of the relevance of a given element or *modus operandi*, then to remarkable revelations about the stories' meanings that would never have been visible had they been read in isolation. Teaching students to perceive the connections between "In Exile" and "The Student," Durkin helps them to read the latter story as mitigating the former's dogmatic and oppressive message. Furthermore, Durkin suggests that being a student—that is, making connections and "mastering the past in order to engage the future"—is what we should strive for not only as readers but also as human beings living in a cultural tradition and interacting with it.

If Durkin works wonders by reading two stories by Chekhov against each other, Robert Jackson ups the ante by increasing the set to three texts ("Enemies," "Kashtanka," and "In the Ravine"). A master class in the best kind of close reading, Jackson's "Three Deaths: A Boy, a Goose, and an Infant" demonstrates how to detect, in the fabric of Chekhov's text, and especially in the resonance of each text with the others, semantically marked words and phrases. Jackson's reading of these three episodes involving death thus detects far more than just Chekhov's ongoing meditation on mortality. By juxtaposing and sequencing these three stories, Jackson helps students understand Chekhov's spiritual materialism, which he locates in the synthesis of tenderness, understanding, and truth that is achieved by Chekhov himself.

In Nicholas Dames's "Turgenev's Preoccupations," the emphasis shifts from the confrontation of text with other text to the encounter between text and reader. Drawing attention to the

Cathy Popkin, Deborah Martinsen, Irina Reyfman

ways in which *Fathers and Sons* forces readers to think about the presuppositions they bring to the act of reading, Dames challenges students to observe both the cognitive and the social dimensions involved in the reading of novels. Dames explores Turgenev's continual recourse to moments of *pensiveness*—abstracted thought, reverie, preoccupation rather than occupation—in his descriptions of characters, particularly at the ends of episodes and chapters, where we ourselves encounter the blank space between the end of one chapter and the beginning of the next. Thinking alone, in retreat, the characters model a pensiveness that we, as solitary readers, may experience—if we permit ourselves the distraction that the focused nature of the classroom generally precludes. What, Dames wonders, if daydreaming is not only natural but also essential to reading well? If so, how do we as teachers reconcile the need for moments of daydreaming with our demands for rigorously attentive reading? Dames's essay suggests some fruitful ways of dealing with this dilemma.

The blanks that loom large in Gary Saul Morson's consideration of reading don't come in the breaks between chapters, but operate as constituent parts of the work itself. In "This Page Left Intentionally Blank: Absences in *Anna Karenina*," Morson addresses that novel's deliberate omissions. Making sense of these textual "absences" requires deep moral engagement and attention. Readers must plunge into the world of the novel to figure out what's missing—what moral qualities a character lacks, for instance—in order to understand what causes him or her to act or react in a particular manner. Morson argues that novelistic ethics demand that the readers identify with characters and situations as a means of expanding their moral imagination. He asks us to consider why Tolstoy would take such pains for us to feel Anna's experience from within if he did not mean for readers to identify with her. Literary characters, he argues, are possible people and their ethical and psychological problems are ones that we may have faced, or may yet face in the future. We've *got* to care in order to apprehend all aspects of the characters' psychology, including the reasons for their moral lapses as well as the reasons for our reluctance to see them. Morson uses a lesson in close reading to teach awareness of both our tendency to engage in self-deception and our unwillingness to see inconvenient truths that are implied but not articulated in the text.

In "Getting Away with Murder: Teaching *Crime and Punishment*," Deborah Martinsen works explicitly with this kind of reader engagement and response to catch students in the act of focusing so intently on the murder of the pawnbroker that they tend to forget the more brutal attack on the defenseless Lizaveta. What can we learn about the reactive emotions of shame and guilt by attending to—or forgetting—one or the other victim? Martinsen's essay on *Crime and Punishment* poses four big questions—including Belknap's question of whether the reader wants Raskolnikov to get away—that draw on reader response and the problem of identification to get to the novel's most vexed and eternal questions.

Nancy Workman too asks students whether they identify with Dostoevsky's irritable underground man. Once they do, she explains in her "Notes from a Cave: Teaching *Notes from Underground* in a Philosophy Course," she can discuss Dostoevsky's narrative strategy for plunging readers into the consciousness of a complex and contradictory mind in ways that get us to recognize parts of ourselves. She thus demonstrates how Dostoevsky's literary strategy exposes the inadequacy of any account of human nature that does not consider perversity. Like Morson, she shows that sympathetic imagination can lead to a deep understanding of what it is to be human.

And yet Workman writes about her experience teaching *Notes from Underground* in a course devoted to the great works of the Western political and philosophical tradition. What happens when a work by an author whose genius is by nature literary takes on philosophy? By placing the underground man's dialogic and paradoxical monologue into conversation with Plato's Socratic dialogue *The Republic*, Workman demonstrates that when readers try on the persona of the underground man and recognize him as a person resistant to logic, they are forced to dismiss any idea of Utopia or Republic. While Plato uses the techniques of fiction to promote philosophy and condemn fiction, Workman demonstrates how Dostoevsky uses the techniques of fiction to condemn or cast suspicion on philosophy.

Cathy Popkin, Deborah Martinsen, Irina Reyfman

In her essay "Dostoevsky's *Notes from Underground* Revisited, Plus a Few Thoughts about Winnie-the-Pooh," Ellen Chances grapples with this same problematic text and argues that students will *need* background information if they are to get a grip on Dostoevsky's narrator, the underground man. Drawing on her own expertise, Chances elucidates for her students a spectrum of topics she deems essential: Dostoevsky's concept of *pochvennichestvo* (native soil), the print culture and ideological polemics of the early sixties, Dostoevsky's biography, his journalism, and his *Notes from the House of the Dead*. Although she provides indispensable context, other scholars' insights, and her own set of questions, Chances involves students in every step of the process, asking them to generate their own questions even as she challenges them to explain how the information provided shapes their understanding of the underground man and the work's reverse chronology. Discussion veers off in unexpected directions, but she finds that this non-linear pedagogical process reflects Dostoevsky's *modus operandi* as well as life itself.

William Mills Todd III, in "The Birth of a Novel from the Work of Journalism: Teaching Saltykov-Shchedrin's *Golovlevs*," presents several strategies to help students build a sense of the novel inductively: by working to establish "what Robert Belknap has called 'inherent relationships,' i.e., recurring persons, places, things, thoughts, and emotions that echo through the work, inviting readers to compare and contrast situations in the novel, to see change and development, or lack thereof, and to feel the working of relentless, destructive fate" (204). The essay also illustrates the macro-literary patterns in *The Golovlevs* by looking at how its author parodies works by Rousseau, Aksakov, and Dostoevsky. Most importantly, Todd's essay on teaching Saltykov-Shchedrin's novel shows how familiarizing students with the Russian literary context—in particular its literary institutions—can be used to complement the search for patterns in a literary work. Todd's work here reminds us of the importance of taking into account, as we teach nineteenth-century Russian literature, the specifics of Russian print culture, particularly the nature of the Russian "thick journals," the "pragmatics" of serialization, and debates about current events and accursed questions.

Jefferson Gatrall's essay "An Inconvenient Footnote: Lermontov's 'Bela' and the Circassian Expulsion" deals head-on with the fundamental question raised by Todd and Chances and faced by every one of us: how can we teach nineteenth-century literature to students with little or no knowledge of Russian history, especially in general education courses? Can unabashed "informing" lead to fruitful discussion? Gatrall concludes that in teaching Lermontov's treatment of the Circassian question in "Bela," the responsible thing to do is to educate students about the Tsarist expulsion of the Circassians, even though these events postdate Lermontov's novel—and his lifetime—by ten to twenty years. Despite the fact that this requires lecturing to the class, which he is loath to do, Gatrall argues that the alternative—silence on this issue—is not acceptable. Nor is the problem unique to Lermontov or the Caucasus; many of the works we teach raise the specter of inconvenient truths.

Cathy Popkin's essay, "Teaching 'Literature and Empire': The Case for *Anna Karenina*," addresses the opposite configuration: a thematically organized course in which empire is the given. What happens, she asks, if you put *Anna Karenina* on the syllabus for a course on "Literature and Empire"? Do students read the work differently in a course concerned with imperialism? What features of the novel does the paradigm of empire bring into sharp relief? What does a "domestic" novel have to do with foreign affairs? Does a work have to be explicitly *about* the topic to have something to say about it? Speculating on what's at stake in constructing a syllabus, Popkin demonstrates how productive it can be to teach a known and familiar text in a new context. In the case of *Anna Karenina*, the new frame crystallizes the novel's concern not with patent cultural difference but with the nuances of cultural similarity, demonstrating how Tolstoy draws parallels between Russia's search for national identity and his characters' search for identity in a world of relatedness. Recontextualization, as she shows, allows us to recognize our own silent assumptions, to see what lurks in texts we readily embrace as our own.

Cathy Popkin, Deborah Martinsen, Irina Reyfman

In her course "The Discourse of Self in Russia and the West," Rebecca Stanton similarly resituates Lermontov's *A Hero of Our Time* from its usual berth between *Eugene Onegin* and *Dead Souls* in surveys of nineteenth-century Russian literature to the broader context of European autobiography. Her essay, "Reading for the Self: Unwrapping the Nested Autobiographies in Lermontov's *A Hero of Our Time*," reveals the ways in which Lermontov's novel, takes on new life when read alongside "a wide variety of first-person narratives, from that of Odysseus in Homer's *Odyssey* to that of Rigoberta Menchú in her controversial memoir" (246). This examination reveals more "selves" than just the "self" of Pechorin on which our reading usually focuses. By problematizing the notions of both "hero" and "time" so prominently brought to our attention by the novel's title, Stanton teaches students both to pay attention to titles and to consider their validity. Furthermore, by regarding the novel as a set of nested autobiographies, Stanton encourages students to reconsider its genre.

Marcia Morris's essay offers genre itself as an interpretive lens for Gogol's problematic novel. "Unsettling Students: Road Rage and the Quest for Fixity in *Dead Souls*" introduces a broad range of Russian and Western life-as-journey works to establish a "horizon of expectations" as one frame for discussing Gogol's *poema* in prose. Morris argues that using genre as an interpretive tool in the discussion of *Dead Souls* helps undergraduate students cope with this complex and often exasperating work. By situating Chichikov in the company of Odysseus, Dante's pilgrim, Western rogues, such as Lazarillo de Tormes, and rogues from the Russian tradition, such as the title characters in the anonymous seventeenth-century *Tale of Ruff, Son of Ruff* or Faddei Bulgarin's *Ivan Vyzhigin*, Morris offers students a field of possibilities against which to evaluate the actions of Gogol's picaresque yet sedentary hero.

Svetlana Grenier's essay "Searching for Freedom in *Eugene Onegin*" also draws on generic expectations to contend with confusing texts. By invoking the novel of adultery to re-examine Pushkin's *Eugene Onegin*, Grenier raises an important question: does viewing a literary work through a specific lens—whether generic or thematic—impinge on interpretive freedom? Or might this interpretive dilemma be harnessed to focus students' attention on questions of personal freedom, free will, and responsibility? Grenier argues that her approach encourages students to detect and confront such moral issues embedded in Pushkin's novel. Indeed, Grenier's essay works by deconstructing Pushkin's text as a novel of adultery, thereby revealing its generic indiscretions. Grenier also offers strategies for reading Pushkin's novel alongside its Western counterparts. What happens, she asks, when Pushkin's novel, which culminates in the heroine just saying no to adultery (for reasons that readers from Belinsky to Dostoevsky to Tsvetaeva to today's students have disagreed on) is read together with novels that follow the dominant masterplot and end with the adulterous heroine taking poison, drowning herself, or throwing herself under a train?

Catharine Nepomnyashchy, in her essay "Examining Lensky's Body: Forensic Pedagogy," also stacks *Eugene Onegin* up against Western counterparts. What happens, she asks, if we consider *Eugene Onegin* as a Russian variant of *Pride and Prejudice*: not as a novel of adultery, that is, but as a novel of manners? If we do, does Lensky's corpse, which confronts readers mid-novel, change this potential Russian novel of manners into a tragedy? As Nepomnyashchy scrutinizes that tragedy, she moves students from considering the language of a specific scene in Pushkin's *Eugene Onegin* to exploring the moral content of language, and ultimately to contemplating the ethical experience of reading itself.

In "The Power of Pedagogy: Dispelling the Darkness in Tolstoy's Drama," Maude Meisel models ways of envisioning a play's three-dimensional aspects using *The Power of Darkness*, Tolstoy's first full-length dramatic work, as her example. In exploring the play's conception, structure, innovative use of peasant language, staging, and themes, Meisel particularly focuses on what she calls Dostoevskian devices of "reaching-right-inside" (302) to affect readers and viewers alike. As she and her students closely examine the two versions of the play's fourth act, Meisel demonstrates how the censored and revised versions move the audience in different but equally powerful ways. Tolstoy, she argues, reaches inside of us, changes our perceptions, and teaches us, thereby filling "the void

Cathy Popkin, Deborah Martinsen, Irina Reyfman

he perceived under the ritual surface of his contemporary theater" (312).

Elizabeth Klosty Beaujour, in "'Visible Only in Very Clear Weather': Teaching Chekhov's Second Acts," describes what happens if one asks students to concretize elements of a play that cannot be performed simply because they are not part of the dialogue. How do readers deal with non-dialogic elements of the play, such as stage directions? How do silences, pauses, sounds, and light create an atmosphere that may or may not be captured by a stage director? In her essay on Chekhov's dramatic work, Elizabeth Beaujour focuses on second acts, where mood predominates over action, where changes in light are every bit as important as dialogue, if not more so. Beaujour continually draws her students' attention to Chekhov's stage directions, which most readers skip over, and which, for the most part, resist precise interpretation and unambiguous staging. By leaving mood-creating directions to the students' imaginations, Beaujour hopes to give them "a fuller sense of the extraordinary balance of elements that create mood than seeing an actual performance" would provide (325).

* * *

Classrooms are intimate places, their proceedings privileged communications. We recognize the rare opportunity conferred by these behind-the-scenes glimpses into classrooms where nineteenth-century Russian literature is taught well, and we thank our contributors for their generosity and candor. We trust that the pedagogical insights gathered here will inspire other teachers in their classrooms, whether their discipline is literature, history, or philosophy.

1

TEXT AND TEACHER

The Teacher and the Text:
The Pragmatic Sleuth in the Classroom

Robin Feuer Miller

This essay explores questions of pedagogy and critical influence, two subjects that seem dry—even unfashionable—but which lie at the heart of how generations evolve and how received ideas migrate and change over time. Although the observations here center on one teacher-critic and one canonical writer, they are a kind of marker for thinking about pedagogy and critical influence generally. An effort to appraise and characterize effective pedagogy or to mark major influence often arises slowly. "The truth is that one cannot adequately evaluate a teacher until years after one has sat in his classroom, except in cases of inept or egregiously shoddy teachers. Proper evaluation can perhaps only be made after the spell of a powerful teacher has worn off, in the former student's maturity, when in tranquility he can recollect influence. Influence is subtle, sometimes accidental, often mysterious. It cannot generally be analyzed on a computer form in the last ten minutes of the last class of a course."[1] The intellectual, moral, and aesthetic growth that some teacher-critics can inspire may occasionally rival the parent-child relationship, or other basic family ties.

What are some practical goals for those of us engaged in similar pursuits of teaching and writing? If one has had the experience of being the student of a master teacher and critic, how can one translate that into one's own endeavors in the classroom? How can one adapt another's honesty, directness, energy, freshness

---

[1] Joseph Epstein, introduction to *Portraits of Great Teachers* (New York: Basic Books, 1981), xiii.

of vision, and playfulness—an intellectual essence—to the ongoing effort to dredge up the same qualities within oneself? A great teacher wastes no time with the nugatory (although he can distinguish between important trifles and unimportant ones, unlike Dostoevsky's Raskolnikov), nor does he hesitate to upturn received notions of any kind. In the classroom a teacher should continuously convey to students a sense of the importance—even the urgency— of our collective enterprise and urge students to tease out their own readings of any particular text well before they get bogged down in the secondary material.

A teacher who is single-mindedly committed to unpacking the complexities of a particular text to her students may eventually come to seem to them to be indelibly and weirdly associated with it, in almost as intimate a way as Kugelmass is with *Madame Bovary* in the Woody Allen story "The Kugelmass Episode," in which students and professors for a time find the unlikely Kugelmass lurking in the novel with its eponymous heroine. The ridiculous and annoying Kugelmass briefly changed the experience of reading for them by literally showing up in the novel as a minor character. Such a teacher or critic enters into the work at hand and becomes indelibly associated with it even while striving against imposing her own biases and preconceptions upon it.

Likewise, the insights a successful teacher imparts through his engagement in the classroom with the text, no matter how local or particular they seem to be, embody some insight that is transferable, universal, and often surprising. If we are doing our job well, we teach the arts of detection, how to be open to the impact of large or small units of plot or narrative as well as to passing shards of detail. These details can attain an unexpected quality of pragmatic portability. If students experience either recognition ("How true!") or surprise ("How new!") in classroom discussions of a text, we have not failed. The ability to engender in students transferable (because universal) insights or ways of thinking transferable in their universality, as well as a readiness to engage with the surprising, constitutes the quiddity of our enterprise. A master teacher allows herself to be as open as possible to the text and finds questions to ask about it that are either morally, aesthetically, or philosophically portable and thus important. In this sense she is a pragmatist.

To illustrate these points about openness to the text, engendering surprise or recognition, and striving for portability, I focus here on a short essay in a 1982 volume entitled *Actualité de Dostoevskij*, "The Didactic Plot: The Lesson about Suffering in *Poor Folk*," by Robert L. Belknap, a master teacher and critic who has inspired most of the contributors to this volume. No paraphrase can do justice to this incisive essay, which begins by exploding some cherished and long-held notions about Dostoevsky's views on suffering as an essential part of the process of salvation. Belknap's task in this essay is to pursue meaning, even if that may seem an unfashionable enterprise. How does he do it? "As a didactic instrument, plot can offer an inherent unsubtlety that bypasses the Bakhtinian caveats and may even permit us to talk without apology about authorial intent."[2] A master teacher follows the clues.

Like the detective in *Crime and Punishment*, Porfiry Petrovich, the teacher-critic strives to be a sly and playful practitioner of deduction who relies on evidence, while understanding that any piece of evidence can have several even contradictory applications, can be downright irrelevant, or can serve as a linchpin. The trick is to know the difference. In this essay on *Poor Folk*, Belknap uses general but sharp observations about plot as surgical tools to unpack larger, portable meanings. One would think that illuminating the elements of a plot would be a relatively simple activity, bordering on summary. Belknap quickly demonstrates how elusive, complex, and mystifying something as simple as describing a plot, any plot, can be. "Literary plots, of course, have many functions that are more sophisticated than the didactic one. They inspire terror and pity, as Aristotle noted in the *Poetics*; they reveal character, as James observed in his prefaces; they refer to earlier works of literature in the ways Bloom and Riffaterre describe, and also in other ways, and

---

2   Robert L. Belknap, "The Didactic Plot: The Lesson about Suffering in *Poor Folk*," in *Actualité de Dostoevskij*, ed. Nina Kauchtschischwili (Genoa: La Quercia Edizioni, 1982), 66. Subsequent references to this essay will appear in parentheses in the text.

they control the reader's interest by structuring the experience of a work, as Shklovsky has shown.… Dostoevsky himself was thinking seriously about the function and the nature of a literary plot while he was writing *Poor Folk*.… A plot organizes units of action not only in chronological and causal sequences but also in networks of emotional and moral value" ("The Didactic Plot," 67, 73). Although plots function both chronologically and in larger spatial units, what is most significant in this story's plot and possibly in plots generally tends, as in a mystery novel before the puzzle is solved, to remain hidden in the background.

How many of us, for example, while reading *Poor Folk*, notice that in it (as in Pushkin's "Stationmaster," which figures, like Gogol's "Overcoat," prominently in the riddle of Dostoevsky's story) "the emotion gathers about the abandonment of the pathetic old government employee who is the protector, but the action [read, plot] carries the battle of the sexes to its ultimate conclusion, the subjection of the seducer" ("The Didactic Plot," 75). "To the reader's surprise, both seducers get the ultimate comeuppance for a literary seducer: they become enslaved by their victim. In both stories, the victorious woman spends a great deal of her conquered man's money, and weeps sincere tears for her former protector, who is left as the only real victim in the story" ("The Didactic Plot," 74-75). The real point, of course, is that most readers will miss all this, even though it is featured prominently in the plot. It is hidden but supremely evident. A master teacher-critic teaches us to sleuth, to pare away, to bare structure, while simultaneously remaining alive to the influence of affective networks of association.

The argument in Belknap's short essay does not stop there; it goes deeper. By comparing the different plots depicting suffering in this work (Varvara's, along with her "three companion sufferers, the two Pokrovskys … and Makar"), Belknap concludes that "Dostoevsky's lesson is unmistakable [though we, of course, have probably mistaken it]: *Not one of these characters is evil, but the more one has suffered, the worse one is*" ("The Didactic Plot," 76, emphasis added). There it is. Our received notion of the inherent value of suffering in Dostoevsky topples over. The assertion made at the outset has been demonstrated.

And as if that is not enough, Belknap quietly expands his argument, transferring it to other works: "Dostoevsky's later plots often teach the same lesson when they give a clear picture of characters before and after suffering. Marmeladov's wife ... had been a silly, pretty, provincial girl before she suffered. Afterwards, she was a vicious hag who dragged her husband about the room by his hair, beating his head against the floor, drove one child to prostitution and the others to beg on the street, spent the tiny sum of money that came her way on a horrible funeral banquet, and never abated in her ridiculously genteel social pretensions." And Sonya, he argues, was "astonishingly good even before she suffered" ("The Didactic Plot," 76-77). This short essay exerts a wiry force and alters the landscape for understanding Dostoevsky's ideas about the potential value of suffering.

How many of us teach *Crime and Punishment* or any novel with these irresistible but discomfiting truths in mind? Are we ready to separate our reading of a particular work and our students' readings of it from the heavy baggage of received wisdom, from the many past readings that are considered "authoritative" in one way or another? A master teacher or critic, however knowledgeable, retains a profound openness to the primary text itself. If this openness takes her in surprising directions, she does not resist or hesitate to explore their ramifications.

Such a teacher resembles the little child in a fairy tale willing to cry out, "But the emperor has no clothes!" The words of the master teacher-critic describe honestly, clearly, simply what is observed and implied—no more, no less. Yet that obligation, when taken seriously, is significant.

In the project of teaching works of literature, especially the "big novels," a determination to stick to what is important, to use the arts of detection and face up to the implications of what one actually sees, is primary. Even though class time is precious, when teaching a "big novel"—and *The Brothers Karamazov* is definitely a primary marker of the genre—it is generally worthwhile to spend quite a bit of that time on its first page or so. That is, at least at the outset, approach any big novel as you would a short story or a poem. Take its first lines seriously—not to discover in them the main themes of the work, but as the gateway into the narrator's landscape. What Helen Vendler, in her book *The Art of Shakespeare's Sonnets*, cautions against in reading a sonnet can guide us on how not to read the first paragraphs of a big novel: "The chief defect in critical readings of the *Sonnets* has been the critics' propensity to take the first line of a sonnet as a 'topic sentence' which the rest of the poem merely illustrates and reiterates."[3] The first sentence of *The Brothers Karamazov* reads: "Alexey Fyodorovich Karamazov was the third son of Fyodor Pavlovich Karamazov, a landowner well-known in our district in his own day (and still remembered among us) owing to his tragic and obscure death, which happened exactly thirteen years ago, and which I shall describe in its proper place."[4] This sentence offers a wealth of entrances into the novel, but does not hint at its most important themes or ideas, although it may seem to.

Even when encouraging students from the very outset to pace their reading of a big novel in the ways their fancies and attention naturally direct them—sometimes rapidly, sometimes even very rapidly skimming across them like a bug across water, sometimes skipping pages altogether, and sometimes reading very slowly indeed, it is still worthwhile to suggest that they give that first page deep attention—their best attentiveness. Ask them to keep track of how they read, what they skip, what they turn back to. In her best seller *The Suspicions of Mr. Whicher or The Murder at Road Hill House*, Kate Summerscale suggests that "the purpose of detective investigations, real and fictional[, is] to transform sensation, horror and grief into a puzzle and then to solve the puzzle to make it go

---

[3] Helen Vendler, *The Art of Shakespeare's Sonnets* (Cambridge, MA: Harvard University Press, 1997), 22-23.

[4] F. M. Dostoevskii, *Polnoe sobranie sochinenii v tridtsati tomakh*, ed. G. M. Fridlender, V. E. Vetlovskaia, E. I. Kiiko, et al. (Leningrad: Nauka, 1972-90), 14:7, and Fyodor Dostoevsky, *The Brothers Karamazov*, trans. Constance Garnett, ed. and rev. Ralph E. Matlaw (New York: W. W. Norton, 1976), 2. Subsequent references to the novel will appear in parentheses, with the page number in Russian appearing first.

away."[5] Quoting Raymond Chandler, she says, "'The detective story is a tragedy with a happy ending.' A storybook detective starts by confronting us with a murder and ends by absolving us of it. He clears us of guilt. He relieves us of uncertainty. He removes us from the presence of death" (*The Suspicions of Mr. Whicher*, 304).[6] Both Summerscale and Chandler focus on the reader's activity—the situational anxiety and story's uncertainty are counterbalanced by the pleasure of solving the plot's puzzle. The two work together. As students track the process of their reading, they inevitably navigate between emotive uncertainties and intellectual pleasure. Dostoevsky, an avid reader of the Gothic novels of Radcliffe, Lewis, and Maturin, as well as of the work of Poe and De Quincey, strove to create all possible varieties of anxiety in his readers, while at the same time presenting them with satisfying intellectual riddles and puzzles to decipher or ponder. Even those that remain unsolved counterbalance and to some extent relieve the prevalent atmosphere of anxiety.[7]

In reading a novel, one follows temporally the deliberate traces left by the novelist, but this temporal process gradually transforms into an expanding mental space in the reader's mind. Consider how Dostoevsky worked over the beginnings of his novels, think about Tolstoy and his many drafts and beginnings for *War and Peace* and *Anna Karenina*. It is instructive to expose students to the labyrinth of conundrums one necessarily enters when trying to talk about the genesis of any particular novel, in this case *The Brothers Karamazov*. Once students understand about the Intentional Fallacy, it is acceptable to commit it, at least briefly. Belknap has probed the question of the genesis of *The Brothers Karamazov* from a variety of

---

5   Kate Summerscale, *The Suspicions of Mr. Whicher or The Murder at Road Hill House* (London: Bloomsbury Publishing, 2008), 303. Subsequent references will occur in parentheses in the text.

6   Summerscale is quoting a letter of June 1949 by Chandler to James Sandoe, in *The Raymond Chandler Papers: Selected Letters and Non-Fiction, 1909-1959*, ed. Tom Hiney and Frank MacShane (New York: Atlantic Monthly, 2000).

7   For a fuller treatment of these issues, see my *Dostoevsky's Unfinished Journey* (New Haven, CT: Yale University Press, 2007), 109-11, 128-48, 159-60.

angles, including Dostoevsky's habits of mind, his reading, and his conscious and unconscious transformations of other materials into his novel. He writes:

> The beginnings of *The Brothers Karamazov* are hard to date…. Every novel or story he published contains elements that emerge again in *The Brothers Karamazov*…. Each of Dostoevsky's surviving notebooks has been published in association with the novel closest to it, but all of the notebooks also contain leftovers that went into later novels, including *The Brothers Karamazov*. Consider the 196th item of the 500 convict sayings that he wrote down in Siberia in the first of his notebooks that survives: "Hello!" "Well, hello, if you're not joking" (*Pss:* 4: 240). No information survives about the circumstances of this interchange, or about whether it was recorded in the notes a helpful orderly in the prison hospital kept for Dostoevsky or whether he wrote it down himself from memory after his release from the camp.[8]

What we do know is that this exchange reappears decades later, in expanded form, in a scene between Kolya Krasotkin and the schoolboys. The evidence is compelling, but no amount of literary sleuthing can account for why it remained in Dostoevsky's memory for all those years, ready to resurface at "the needed moment."

It can also be instructive to point out to students the first lines of Dostoevsky's notebooks for the novel:

> Memento (about the novel)
>
> -Find out whether it is possible to lie between the rails under a railway car when it passes over you at full speed.
>
> -Find out whether the wife *of a prisoner* can marry someone else immediately.
>
> -Does the Idiot have the right to take care of such a horde of adopted kids, to have a school, etc.?[9]

---

[8] Robert L. Belknap, *The Genesis of "The Brothers Karamazov": The Aesthetics, Ideology, and Psychology of Making a Text* (Evanston, IL: Northwestern University Press, 1990), 46.

[9] Dostoevskii, *Polnoe sobranie sochinenii*, 15:199; and Dostoevsky, *The Notebooks*

The early notes for the novel continue in this vein. They recreate vividly for students the hum and buzz that were in Dostoevsky's brain as he began to write; students can reflect later upon which of these striking items make it into this particular novel and which might have eventually found themselves in some other future (unwritten) work. Readers of Dostoevsky's novels encounter thrilling plots and well-developed characters. Readers of his notebooks enter an unstable, surreal world where the trivial detail often seems privileged and the significant one submerged.

The beginnings of a novel—what we find in notebooks and drafts—differ qualitatively from the beginning of a novel, "the point at which," as Edward Said has succinctly described it, "in a given work, the writer departs from all other works; a beginning immediately establishes relationships with works already existing, relationships of either continuity or antagonism or some mixture of both."[10] Any beginning, that is, already starts to establish its context, pretexts, and limits. The created world contained in a novel always, in Said's understanding, exists in opposition to the larger world outside it. "Each piece of fiction, therefore, excludes a larger truth than it contains, even though it is the novelist's task to make his readers see active relationships among various orders of reality or truth both inside and outside the text" (*Beginnings*, 100). The novel bobs as a kind of bubble; its fragile surface or skin—its narrative structure—encloses a defined, self-contained spherical world, a world composed of the same air inside as out. It floats and is sustained, a discrete entity, in the very element against which it defines itself.

So to go back the beginning again, what about the first short chapter (some four paragraphs) of *The Brothers Karamazov*, with its surprise ending in which Fyodor, upon hearing of the death of his first wife, is reported to have both wept and shouted with joy? As the students struggle with those simultaneous tears and laughter,

---

for *"The Brothers Karamazov,"* ed. and trans. Edward Wasiolek (Chicago: University of Chicago Press, 1971), 22.

[10] Edward W. Said, *Beginnings: Intention and Method* (Baltimore, MD: Johns Hopkins University Press, 1975), 3.

fast upon them comes the narrator-chronicler's sudden intrusion into the text: "As a general rule, people, even the wicked, are much more naïve and simple-hearted than we suppose. And we ourselves are too" (14:10; *The Brothers Karamazov*, 4). Are we, they wonder?

At this point, just as students expect you might move on into the rest of the material assigned for the day, surprise them by taking a step even further back, to "From the Author." As we old-fogey teachers know, "From the Author" itself has generated interesting debate. In whose voice is it written? The narrator-chronicler's? The author's? Could this be Dostoevsky himself? This novel, perhaps more than all of Dostoevsky's other novels, is concerned with matters of narrative voice, with layers of narration, with inserted stories of many varieties, with the interplay between omniscience and downright deception.

From there, one can go back even further to the novel's epigraph, from John 12:24. Even the briefest discussion of this passage, without reference to the many ways in which it will subsequently reverberate in the plot and the hearts of the major characters, will most likely bring one abruptly to the end of a first class on *The Brothers Karamazov*. Little has been accomplished, yet one hopes the students' minds are engaged, both with Dostoevsky's artistic process and with a readiness to absorb what the novel might be about. But the moment when the novel actually begins remains somewhat ambiguous. Does the beginning lie in the epigraph, the preface, the first sentence?

From looking only at these first few paragraphs of chapter 1, what themes might the students guess will be important? What elements can they find from other kinds of narratives they have already encountered? Are the fairy-tale elements significant? What expectations do the students think are already being put upon them as they read?

It is worthwhile to encourage students to keep tabs not only on the pacing of their reading, but also on as many other aspects of their readerly responses as possible. What passages did they like? What did they skip? Do the reading experiences of the class form a collective pattern, or do they vary widely? For example, when teaching *War and Peace* I tend to assume that first-time readers of the novel will skip the history passages in order to pursue the exciting plot, but I am frequently proven wrong. To my surprise, many students immediately prefer those sections devoted to history at first reading. A novel exists in as many shapes as there are readers in part because each reader, through her own idiosyncratic pattern of reading the words on the page, through moments of inattention, distraction, and association, reads a different novel.

Writers want their readers to read and not to put their books down. They want clever close readers, of course. However, at the same time they count upon—they need—the reader's inattentiveness. A writer like Dostoevsky, who is writing a thriller, albeit a metaphysical thriller, particularly needs to divert his reader's attention and to hide an important detail amidst others that seem to be of more significance. As the students skim and sweep along, what clues are they missing? When they go back in the text to retrieve what they have missed, are they surprised?

In the novel, some clues become irrelevant, others important—e.g., at the time of the murder, was the door of the gate at Fyodor Karamazov's house open or closed? What were the things Mitya did before he went to Mokroe? Why are such things important? How does the author succeed in distracting and misleading his reader? Or is it the narrator-chronicler who is trying to distract the reader? Does the difference between them matter?

Most important is for students to trust their own responses, to allow themselves to have a first encounter with the novel that is unimpeded by the massive amount of criticism on it, or by reading even a brief introduction to it. The primary reading, the moment when the novel is in private play with the reader, is too precious an experience to squander. In the classroom, ideally, students can find a shared way of keeping the work in play, although such an experience may be somewhat intimidating, even when it is heady. In order to promote students' intimate, direct encounter with a novel, one may urge them to read all introductions as afterwords and to immerse themselves in the critical or theoretical material only after they have themselves become their own experts on the work.

Let the novel also come alive through that now-endangered commodity, face-to-face conversation and discussion. Not class emails, not twitter droppings about the work, though those might come later, but conversation and debate in the classroom, that protected yet risky space where we all make eye-contact with each other, where words and sometimes awkward silences exist in time, where sudden changes in volume can be heard and voices interrupt each other. That is when the novel is in play and when, perhaps with the exception of the most private and intense moments of reading, it is most alive.

In a different context I wrote, "These conversations and discussions, while not real performances of the novel per se, do contain aspects of the performative in that the novel, for the duration of the time it is under discussion, lives a life in the words and the gestures of its several simultaneous readers. At these moments [the novel] is literally 'in play'; in 'the air,' much like the many conversations in which Raskolnikov partakes or the snatches of conversations that he overhears. Works of imaginative literature have a public as well as a private existence."[11] As Martha Nussbaum has written, "The literary imagination is a part of public rationality … it seems … an essential ingredient of an ethical stance that asks us to concern ourselves with the good of other people whose lives are distant from our own."[12] Such emphasis on the more public aspects of reading may surprise students, but they may gravitate to the practice, through class discussions, of interpreting values and engaging imaginatively with distant other people, in this case characters whose fictional lives are both similar to and distant from their own.

Ask who in the class may have read the novel before. Several students usually have. The question offers us an opportunity to discuss the experience of reading and subsequent rereading. Our students are, for the most part, just leaving adolescence. If they have read a novel assigned in one of our classes before, they have read it either in late childhood or earlier in adolescence. How has the novel

---

[11] Miller, *Dostoevsky's Unfinished Journey*, 45.

[12] Martha C. Nussbaum, *Poetic Justice: The Literary Imagination and Public Life* (Boston: Beacon Press, 1995), xiv.

changed for them? Consider, for example, the extreme difference for George Orwell between his first and subsequent readings of Dickens's *David Copperfield:*

> I must have been about nine years old when I first read *David Copperfield.* The mental atmosphere of the opening chapters was so immediately intelligible to me that I vaguely imagined they had been written *by a child.* And yet when one rereads the book as an adult and sees the Murdstones, for instance, dwindle from gigantic figures of doom into semi-comic monsters, these passages lose nothing. Dickens has been able to stand both inside and outside the child's mind, in such a way that the same scene can be wild burlesque or sinister reality, according to the age at which one reads it.[13]

Likewise, students may move from a kind of horror of Fyodor Pavlovich to finding him wildly comic; they may find their understanding of any character subject to dramatic change.

The Brothers Karamazov can produce precise discussions about the relationship of the part to the whole, especially since this novel, more than most, is one in which some parts—usually "The Legend of the Grand Inquisitor"—are excerpted into other kinds of texts. Students who read those texts rarely go on to read the whole novel. How important, one can ask the students, is the basic flow of the novel from which these parts are drawn? For them it is not old hat to talk about "the hermeneutic journey"—which presupposes a happy choice between the part and the whole, where an excursion to one becomes an excursion to the other and vice versa. What is the effect if one speaks only about the part, out of its context? Once students have read even slightly beyond "The Legend" we can ask them other questions related to this. For example, "Where does one 'part' end and become another 'part'?" Alyosha prepares us to ask such questions by his own questions to Ivan: "'How does your poem end?' he asked, suddenly looking down. 'Or was it the end?'"

---

13   George Orwell, "Charles Dickens," in *A Collection of Essays* (New York: Harcourt Brace Jovanovic, 1946), 60.

Ivan suddenly hedges, "I meant to end it like this." He meant to. But does he? "Like this"?—not, "Here is how it ends." The actual ending of Ivan's story becomes increasingly dialogic, as Alyosha's questions and gestures become more frequent and intrusive into what is left of Ivan's narrative. The precise moment when "The Legend" ends is unclear. The part bleeds into the whole.

If the matter of the beginning or beginnings is obscure and complicated, the matter of the ending and endings may be more so. In fact, the question of the ending of *The Brothers Karamazov*, or rather the question of whether or not Dostoevsky actually completed it or intended a sequel or sequels, has reemerged as a subject recently, especially in the work of James Rice, who argues forcefully that Dostoevsky did intend such a continuation. Belknap's final chapter in *The Structure of "The Brothers Karamazov"* had, some decades ago, already offered impressive suppositions, deductions, and facts to argue convincingly that Dostoevsky had completed the novel. He carefully considered both the internal and the external evidence that the novel is unfinished and marshaled strong evidence, both concrete and aesthetic, to demonstrate the contrary view. Particularly compelling is his discussion of the uses of the artistic convention of incompleteness, demonstrated through analogies to the work of Schubert, Michelangelo, Sterne, and others. In other words, Dostoevsky, like many other nineteenth-century novelists, recognized the pragmatic value of suggesting a sequel long before any filmmaker. Moreover, he had already done so at the end of *Crime and Punishment*, and, though he had ample time to carry out the project of continuing that novel, he never chose to, even though the suggestion had been usefully planted in the minds of his reading public. It is a truism that to hint at a sequel keeps the reader's interest whetted and the author's options open. The suggestion of a sequel is a strategy, not an intention or a promise.

In a 1927 review of detective fiction in the *Times Literary Supplement*, T. S. Eliot wrote that "The detective story, as created by Poe, is something as specialized and intellectual as a chess problem, whereas the best English detective fiction has relied less on the beauty of the mathematical problem and much more on the intangible human element."[14] A teacher, whether in the classroom or on the page, should strive to deliver on both fronts: our goal in the classroom is to harness the human capacity for hardwired analysis and deductions about structure to our other capacities for experiencing the less tangible but equally powerful inferential evidence of aesthetic perception. For readers of Dostoevsky, a compelling example of this kind of critical hybrid, where tangible analysis combines with the more inferential and experiential, occurs in *The Structure of "The Brothers Karamazov"* in a passage well-known in the critical literature. Here Belknap analyzes three passages from the novel that display a similar cluster of associations about divine grace and concludes:

> In these passages, a power at work in the causal structure of the novel has a parallel in the structure of inherent relationship, where sunlight, lamplight, candlelight, tears, kneeling, embracing, dedicating, mothers and children, silence, guilt, and benedictions merge with birds, trees, meadows, the earth, growth, unjudgingess, angelic uniqueness, and seeds that die and grow to generate the mystical presence of grace.[15]

The detection and articulation of the importance of this constellation of details, as well as of many other such constellations, readers of Dostoevsky now see as evident, transparent, and simply given, but they were initially, when first identified by the critic, surprising. Literature has the power to generate endless new readings that first surprise, then become familiar, and eventually become self-evident.

When we consider the challenges of teaching *The Brothers Karamazov*, we are grappling with the specifics of introducing our students to this complex work, but we are also, in a larger sense, addressing the question of how to teach any big novel. To this

---

14   See T. S. Eliot, "Wilkie Collins and Dickens," *Times Literary Supplement*, no. 1331 (August 4, 1927): 525. I first saw reference to this essay by Eliot in Summerscale's *The Suspicions of Mr. Whicher or The Murder at Road Hill House*, 269, 348.

15   Robert L. Belknap, *The Structure of "The Brothers Karamazov"* (1967; repr., Evanston, IL: Northwestern University Press, 1989), 42.

degree *The Brothers Karamazov* is a place marker for a different kind of discussion. The truth is that although literacy is up, the practice of reading big novels in the United States is down, at least according to the report entitled *Reading at Risk* and its updates, issued by the NEA in 2004 and subsequently.[16] Moreover, the number of demands made on our students' time is complex, and they now usually respond more fluently to visual images than to the subtleties of the written word.

In a time of multi-tasking it is an act almost of spiritual meditation, certainly of impressive time-management, to find the time to sit down with a novel, without a computer or a tablet in hand or the sounds of an iPhone trilling in one's ears. Asking students to undertake an extended private commitment of time in their busily connected lives can seem to them taxing and strange, the paths they are to tread through this or any large novel may seem daunting, but the immediate dual pay-offs—for having undertaken the reading and for the subsequent experience they potentially can have in the classroom when they talk to each other without any aids or devices except their own minds in the moment and the book lying on the table—will offer them, we hope, a suitable reward. The rewards to be reaped later in their lives for these acts of reading are of course immense and utterly incalculable.

---

[16] For a more complete discussion of this report, its weaknesses, and its ramifications, see Miller, *Dostoevsky's Unfinished Journey*, 46-47, 200-201.

2

TEXT AND CONTEXT I

Teaching Contexts

Robert L. Belknap

Let me begin with the warmest thanks for this volume, and for the conference that generated it, one of the high points of my life. I loved it not only because so many students, friends, and colleagues came together, with me and with one another, but also because it was a concentrated moment of something I have rejoiced in all my life: learning from my students and my interlocutors. My six decades of studying and teaching nineteenth-century Russian literature and other matters at Columbia have shown me a variety of structures for this kind of learning that deserve discussion.

In American academia, teaching competes with scholarship for our time. European systems sometimes place their good scholars at the universities, and their great scholars in the Academy of Science for pure research. But even the Academy sometimes insists on teaching students too, just as the Rockefeller Institute felt it had to turn into Rockefeller University. The students were cheap labor, of course, but these most rarified scholars also recognized them as a pretext for encounters beyond one's specialty. Rigor demands specialization, but students demand context, and even the purest virologist, econometrician, or Slavist cannot stand alone, apart from intersecting fields.

We should always investigate and always teach everything in its context, biographical, psychological, historical, political, economic, literary, linguistic, religious, etc., in our Russian literature, and, equally, in other subjects. And yet life is too short for any of us to know most of these contexts with scholarly expertise. Marc Raeff used to say that we could have a monographic control of one or maybe two fields, and only a textbook knowledge of anything else. Our scholarly or pedagogical use of context is therefore either amateurish or dependent on the expertise of others. Universities exist to enable scholars to use each other's brains, but often they do not make it easy.

In the field of literature, context threatens rigor in a special way. A text is a fearsome thing, emotionally and intellectually. Like the most benighted savages in some colonial accounts, when shot at it shoots back, and any serious literary scholar has had formulations pierced by literary fact. In self-defense we may therefore prefer to discuss more obedient matters, like the Marxism we absorbed as freshmen, or the Freudian doctrine we picked up from our shrinks, or other fields made simple by our lack of mature study. Context can shield us from the text.

The New Critics responded to this risk in times when literary criticism often took the form of "The Life and Works of..." or "... in My Life." They wrote manifestos demanding concentration on a text and ignoring the author's biography, the reader's reaction, the background, and such, but when they wrote practical criticism, as opposed to *Practical Criticism,* they often divulged the breadth of their curiosity and waded into deep waters from the safe ground of their technical task. In the same way, the Russian Formalists had positivistic dreams of studying not literature but *literaturnost',* in all its purity, but their later careers displayed them as broadly learned philologists.

In my own Proseminar for beginning Columbia graduate students, I usually stole a pedagogical trick from I. A. Richards to minimize context at the start. I picked a fairly obscure short story and asked the students to write a Freudian or Marxian or Feminist or Semiotic or other kind of paper on it, without knowing the author or even the title of the story. One author blew his cover when a careful student found that the story's title was cited as the dictionary's example of a rare word. Nowadays computer searches make anonymity harder. One time an angry Soviet émigré refused to write the first paper without knowing the author's name. I didn't know her yet and secretly suspected that I was making plagiarism too difficult, or terrifying someone who had never expressed an opinion not ratified by an encyclopedia, but I had to admit that she was right to be angry. Even an American could understand that books are social, economic, and political products. But this course was not real life. It was like training a boxer with one hand tied behind his back. She had to learn tough ways to bob and weave and prepare for an uppercut, but half-way through the course would be allowed to meet the onslaught of a text with a fuller sense of its context.

The amateurishness inherent in context and the narrowness that rigor demands of finite humans temper each other in three great academic inventions made at Columbia in the first half of the nineteenth century: the Core Curriculum, the Regional Studies Institute, and the University Seminars. The first two serve the students directly, but all three serve them indirectly, by educating their professors. I learned a great deal in college and graduate school, but far more through my teaching at Columbia. Dostoevsky lives in many contexts, but for most Columbia undergraduates, *Crime and Punishment* exists not in the company of Pushkin, Gogol, Tolstoy, Turgenev, and Chekhov, but in that of Homer, Plato, Aristotle, Aeschylus, Sophocles, Euripides, Aristophanes, Virgil, Genesis, Matthew, St. Augustine, Boccaccio, Shakespeare, Montaigne, Cervantes, Goethe, Austen, Woolf, and the other figures all Columbia College students read and discuss in the required Humanities course. A thousand students read each one of these books the same week every year in the residence halls. As their fifty teachers moved through this same list of readings, some of us treated it as a course in Plato and his footnoters, others as Homer and his imitators, others as Goethe and his sources. For Slavists it can become a course on the two thousand years' work it took to produce Dostoevsky.

But first-year college students rarely care about *quellenforschung*. More tellingly, the family structures in the *Oresteia, Oedipus, The Bacchae,* or *Don Quixote* gave them fresh ways to see the presence and the absence of families in *Crime and Punishment*, the step-by-step extermination of the married couples, the Svidrigailovs, the Marmeladovs, and the Raskolnikov parents, leaving only the explosive lieutenant whom Raskolnikov inexplicably selects for his final, proper confession, after rehearsals with the single people, Zametov, Porfiry, Razumikhin, and Sonia. The readings in Plato, Augustine, Dante, and the Bible enable the Humanities staff to show how that confession was the means to, not the result of, Raskolnikov's repentance, and how his secular pilgrimage moves in steps, like the mystical experiences encountered in the course. I know most of the people who have taught this course since 1956, but even if I did not, it is easy to recognize the scholarship of anyone who has had to discuss this list of books for several hours each with a roomful of disrespectful Columbia students. The intimacy and unforeseeability of reference is different, and *Crime and Punishment* is different for them.

Columbia invented this kind of course for social studies almost a century ago, and expanded it to include the humanities in the thirties, the arts in the fifties, and the natural sciences very recently. St. John's College expanded the model to include most of its curriculum, and Chicago, Harvard, and many other universities tried out versions of it, though most made students select among a variety of more specialized courses, sacrificing the dormitory discussions to faculty fears of overwork or lack of rigor. For students, such programs can be valuable, but they let professors wall themselves inside their specialties in ways that may advance careers while delaying the advancement of knowledge that often occurs in the fields between established specialties.

The Russian Institute was the first of its kind, and still very young when I became a graduate student in 1952. For a certificate, I had to get an MA in Slavic for rigor, but also take courses in politics, international affairs, economics, and history, for context. The courses were not amateurish. John Hazard taught Soviet law and politics with the practicality of an American lawyer who had graduated from a Soviet law school in the 1930s. Abe Bergson was one of the inventors of matrix economics. He used the fact that each car required a knowable amount of steel, and that this amount of steel, in turn, required a knowable amount of coal, and so on, to figure out from incomplete, inaccurate, and sometimes falsified data what was actually going on in the Soviet economy. I had never taken an economics course before; it is weird and wonderful to jump into a field at the graduate level. My basic ignorance was spectacular and my learning curve high; the experience prepared me to teach an economist or a law school student in the Russian Institute that a Soviet farce about having to share a room with one's ex-spouse was part of a tradition going back beyond Menander, as well as a reflection on Soviet property rights and on the political allocation of economic resources. The Institute kept me doing that all my life. I ran it while Marshall Shulman was serving in Washington, and still profit from my encounters with colleagues and visitors doing all sorts of thing involving Russia and its empire.

Columbia's third great contextualizing invention is the University Seminars, for professors and other experts from Columbia or elsewhere. The eighty groups meet every month either to solve some problem that falls outside any one department or to listen politely to a speaker who claims to have solved it, but may or may not be able to answer the Seminar's questioning. Academic departments should try to hire masters of the latest intellectual approaches and subjects. Ideally, departments should also be thinking of the next way of thinking, but that is unknowable, and hiring a brilliant young scholar exploring a dead end may cost a department millions of dollars over a lifetime. University Seminars pay no salaries and can take intellectual risks that departments should avoid.

I first learned about the Seminars at a weekly luncheon of the Humanities staff at which Susan Sontag and Walter Sokel happened to discuss an argument at the Hermeneutics Seminar the night before between Hannah Arendt and Hans Jonas, a wonderful philosopher at the New School, who earlier had been a lieutenant general in the Israeli army. They invited me to attend, and I continued to educate myself there until the Seminar split in two: one on religion and one on literary theory. Both interested me, but I spent more time in the latter, and also in the Seminar on Slavic History and Culture. These Seminars changed with the times, but they offered the chance to interact with experts of all sorts who wanted to exploit the intellectual riches of New York. The Russian Formalists had ideas that could only be systematized by the French Structuralists, and the Seminar on Literary Theory brought us together. When Edward

Said chaired it, I began to see the Soviet handling of Ukrainian language and literature, or translations of central Asian literatures, in the light of imperialism and orientalism, though some members of the Seminar rejected those terms when applied to the Great Socialist Experiment.

The first two of these Columbia inventions have spread around the country, modified to match the needs, resources, and cultures of many universities, for in the academic world, at least, practices thrive only if they are invented or reinvented by the faculty that will use them. The University Seminars remain unique, partly because Frank Tannenbaum endowed them, and no one has made similar endowments elsewhere, and partly because New York is probably the only area in which there are three thousand people who want that kind of interdepartmental excitement.

But I want to talk about a fourth academic adventure at Columbia, one that never spread or even continued, but was the finest teaching experience I ever had, the most contextual and among the most rigorous. I sat down with Michael Rengstorf, a semiotician in the French Department, and David Robertson, a major expert on Victorian literature and art, to invent a course that would use the often wasted final college semester to continue the general education most Columbia students interrupt to concentrate on their major. By the end of senior year, they relax; they feel informed about their field, and at the time this experiment was performed they were usually already placed in a graduate school or a job. We conceived a twelve-point course on European prose of the 1860s. This would be considered a full program for a Columbia senior, though one more course might be allowed.

We decided to spend all day on Tuesdays and Thursdays with the students. One of us would lecture from 9:00 to 11:00 on that week's book, with the other two attending and learning. Then we would split the students into three groups of ten to discuss it. Around 1:00, we would move to a different room for lunch, and ask a colleague to give a lecture on a topic beyond our expertise (none refused, unless they were absent from the city), and in the afternoon, we would break up again into groups of ten, but this time according to our specialty: the French-speakers with Rengstorf, the English majors with Robertson, and the couple of Russian majors, together with the historians, mathematicians, and the others, with me. Each afternoon session had its own additional assignments and oral reports from the students, culminating in a week with no lectures during which each student wrote a thirty-page paper emerging from the reports. The English, French, Russian, and History Departments accepted the course as satisfying their major requirements for a seminar and one additional course. We put together a fat book with a chronology, a list identifying political, religious, scholarly, and literary figures in our three countries who would appear in our texts, a table of currency values, a bibliography, and the texts of assignments that were out of print.

Our reading list scared even us. We admitted students after vetting their records and interviewing them, so that we could warn them to read *War and Peace* over Christmas vacation, since they would have to discuss it in a group of ten for four hours in the first week of the course. That week, Istvan Deak lectured at lunch on the Crimean War, and Elizabeth Valkenier on the collision between the *Peredvizhniki* and the more academic Russian art establishment. The English group concentrated on the historical background, and the French group on the doctrines of realism, while the Russian group had an additional assignment, Tolstoy's *Sevastopol Stories* (for us, the 1860s actually began in the 1850s). For me, these texts offered a sense of the continuities and the evolution in Tolstoy's attitude toward war, and his capacity to see the slogging soldier in his international context. I have taught *Anna Karenina* and many other Tolstoy works quite often, but this was my only chance to teach *War and Peace*. My teaching of Borodino had to prepare the students for Victor Hugo's "Waterloo," which they would read about during their next vacation. Most of us have done comparisons of battle scenes in class, but this time I had to do half of a comparison, and it was an entrancing exercise. With this first reading, I also had to mark the picture of political life for comparison with that of Trollope, whom Tolstoy admired so highly, and map the seductions to prepare the students for Flaubert. For the students, Tolstoy also offered a historical context for the rest of the course, in the Napoleonic period and the Crimean War.

The next week, we jumped to England and read *Our Mutual Friend*, with a separate assignment for the Russian group, Aksakov's *Family Chronicle*. The Russian authors had adored Dickens, but in this course the undergraduates were more interested in comparing the plotting of family structures and relationships, or the handling of suspense, than in the actual literary influences. That week at lunch, Karl-Ludwig Selig, a German expert on the Spanish Renaissance, talked about the novella as it was developed all over Europe, in a tradition going back to his beloved Boccaccio. Robert Paxton, whose specialty is twentieth-century French history, discussed the 1860s in France.

We pressed on into France with *Madame Bovary*, and back to Russia the next week with Goncharov's *Oblomov*. The Russian afternoon group read Chernyshevsky's *What Is to Be Done?*, a novel with a very different take on marriage and society than Flaubert's, and the critique of *Oblomov* by Dobrolyubov, another radical. The juxtaposition was wild, and the Russian adultery novel came to life far better than it ever had for me when I had taught it in the immediate glare of Dostoevsky's attack in the *Notes from Underground*. A lunchtime lecture on opera by Hubert Doris gave us a context for both novels, as did one by Leopold Haimson on the emergence of a Russian working class among the peasants laboring winters in the Petersburg textile mills. Both lectures were brilliant set pieces from which the three professors learned as much as the students did. Haimson's talk was bracketed intellectually by that of Edward Malefakis, a colleague of his in the History Department, on the European peasantry, and that of the sociologist, Allan Silver, on social classes.

For the next two weeks, we read intellectual history for our morning sessions—John Stuart Mill's *On Liberty* and some Huxley essays on Darwin the first week, and religious writers the second week: George Eliot's translation of Strauss's *Life of Jesus*, Renan's *Vie de Jesus* (for one afternoon group in the original), a Jowett essay, and Cardinal Newman's *Apologia pro Vita Sua*. Our lunch-time lecturers included Samuel Devons discussing physics in the 1860s and Maxwell's achievements, and Donald Ritchie discussing Darwin. For a lunch considering the closely-related religious controversies and anxieties of the period, Canon Edward West invited us to the Cathedral of St. John the Divine and explained how unthreatening some of Darwin teachings were to a congregation that loved to sing "A thousand ages in Thy sight are like an evening gone," while others seemed to threaten their faith. Allan Silver used his background as a sociologist for a lecture on the European social classes, and David Robertson, whose expertise included alpinism and who had climbed and trekked a good deal in the Himalayas, spoke on the Great Game, discussing Britain and Russia in Central Asia.

The last week before spring vacation, we all read Turgenev's *Fathers and Sons* and the section of Herzen's *Past and Thoughts* dealing with his life in Europe in the 1850s and 1860s. We had neither the expertise nor the time to deal with many literatures, but that week Gertrud Sakrawa outlined the chief events in the German literatures of the period, and Olga Ragusa did the same for the Italian. The Russian section in these weeks concentrated on the literature reflecting this period, which produced institutional changes that may have been greater and more rapid than those of any others from Peter the Great to Gorbachev: Pisarev's "Destruction of Aesthetics" and short stories by Sleptsov, Levitov, Naumov, Uspensky, and Reshetnikov.

The next week, most students left Columbia, but not those taking this course. They all read *Les Misérables*, partly in French, for one group, and the Russian group read Pisemsky's *A Thousand Souls*, too. That week, our lunchtime lectures dealt with French too: Michael Riffaterre discussed Lautréamont, and LeRoy Breunig Baudelaire. We followed this huge immersion with a week on each of our central literatures, Trollope's *Phineas Finn*, Zola's *Thérèse Raquin*, and Dostoevsky's *Crime and Punishment*. The Russian group read Pavlova's *A Double Life*, a selection from Saltykov-Shchedrin's *Fables*, and Dostoevsky's *Notes from Underground*. In those weeks, Anne Prescott spoke on Lewis Carroll, Allen Staley on English painting, Joan Rosasco on French painting, and Richard Kuhns on the aesthetic doctrines of the time.

In our final three weeks, our lunchtime talks continued to consider the arts, with Mary McLeod treating Haussmann's architectural activities in Paris, Richard Taruskin Russian music, and Theodore Reff French painting. In addition, Paula Hyman discussed the Jews in Europe, and Fritz Stern the subject of his major study, Bismarck. In two of those weeks, our readings returned to intellectual history and literary criticism, considering Matthew Arnold, Ruskin, Mill, Sainte-Beuve, the Goncourts, Baudelaire, Taine, Dmitry Pisarev, and Apollon Grigoriev. Few scholars had ever encountered the Russians in this company, who seemed as intelligent as the European masters, but far less universal in their concerns. Our Russian group read Leskov's *Enigmatic Man*, which, like the Dostoevsky readings in this course, attacked and ridiculed the social upheaval that inspired Pisarev and the "Men of the Sixties." These deliberations over what we had been surveying throughout much of Europe helped to organize the wild array of half-processed experiences we were still reeling from.

The penultimate week of the course did this job better than any reading could. We had no lectures or class meetings, though we stayed available in our offices while the students worked day and night on the thirty-page papers that grew out of the reports they had given in their afternoon sessions. These were undergraduate papers, not research scholarship but thirty serious tunnelings into one or another corner of the texts we had read, illuminated by the intense experience of all the other texts and the way they reached out to one another and beyond.

Those students are scattered now, doctors, lawyers, merchants—maybe a thief or two!—and when they stop me on the street or in a theatre (as still happens), they have forgotten most of our lectures and much of their readings but clearly remember what they said in their papers. More important, we all go on exploring things that seized our minds in those three months during which the thirty-three of us drenched ourselves in one embayment of a mighty ocean.

We only taught this course twice. It needed imitators to attract enough students from other courses that could then be closed, and thus liberate their professors for such an adventure. Some universities concentrate their energies on a single topic every term, but for Columbia the last semester seemed best. It may never happen here again. The pressure for stellar careers has led the Columbia faculty to yield the governance of the university to administrators with other priorities. However, maybe this account will provoke other teaching experiments that also teach professors to maintain their rigor in the huge complexity of the world.

3

TEXT, THEN THEORY

Theorizing vs. Teaching Literary Theory: What Is to Be Done with *Crime and Punishment*?

Olga Meerson

"It is a capital mistake to theorize in advance of the facts," says Sherlock Holmes in Sir Arthur Conan Doyle's "The Adventure of the Second Stain." Porfiry Petrovich couldn't have said it better himself. Dorothy Sayers even has her detective, Lord Peter Wimsey, quote Holmes verbatim several times. To be sure, when it comes to solving crimes (or, for that matter, *committing* them, if Raskolnikov's experience is any indication), putting the theory first can go very, very wrong. Thus, when Dorothy Sayers, who wrote both detective fiction and literary criticism, has her detective repeat Holmes's cautionary remark in the academic setting of *Gaudy Night*, it may be a hermeneutic lead worth pursuing.

Indeed, theorizing ahead of the data can have just as dire consequences for unraveling literary texts as it does for solving murders. When theory is frontloaded, the literary "data" serve principally to confirm or deny the theoretical proposition. If, on the other hand, the goal is to detect meaning in a work of art, theories have the most to offer *after* an encounter with the work itself. Only by trying to solve *specific* riddles in the works of this or that particular writer, riddles unique and peculiar to each author's poetics, can our students—or anyone else—approach an understanding of what this or that particular work is all about.

Literary theories must be taught; they are necessary *tools* for interpreting literature. But no theory should be introduced "ahead of the data." I never discuss any theory or any critical or theoretical school until and unless the students have encountered the problems this theory may help address in the actual primary literary text they are reading and trying to understand. It is useless to read Bakhtin before reading Dostoevsky, or to read Shklovsky before reading Tolstoy. It also would be nice to read Pushkin, and even Khlebnikov, Mayakovsky, and Edgar Allan Poe, before reading Roman Jakobson. Any other way would be "theorizing ahead of the data." Then the worst happens: the students begin to use "big words" without ever having experienced any need for their true meaning. This need can come only from first savoring the reading of *actual books*.

So much for the theory. How does all this translate into teaching? Problems should be encountered first in the primary text itself. Then students will approach close readings of texts in a manner independent of any external influence, mine or anyone else's; the goal is to teach them how to combine freedom with precision in close readings.

What follows is intended as a demonstration of this process. My example will be the close reading of a text that requires several theoretical approaches in order to be understood adequately, a text many of us teach, not merely in Russian but also in translation, in the context of many basic literature or humanities courses: *Crime and Punishment*. The lesson that follows consists of interconnected excerpts from two consecutive chapters. The goal is to make students "stumble" over the text itself, and only afterward go on to consider some theoretical approaches and notions that may help them cope with its complexity, and recognize some important functions of that complexity for Dostoevsky's poetics as a whole. The main condition of this method is to avoid letting students discover any theory before they read the primary text. In this presentation, the footnotes contain assignments for the next class. They should *not* be considered by students before encountering the relevant problems in the text to be read in class. I may give them as endnotes, thereby concluding the class with the next assignment.

The lesson I will use here to illustrate my point applies three different lenses to the same set of textual passages: the Bakhtinian lens,[1]

---

1   Note to students (most of these are): For *the next* class, read *Problems of Dostoevsky's Poetics*, finding what pertains to "the double-voiced word" and all the forms of dialogue to which the word usually does not refer.

the semiotic one,[2] and the narrower semiotic one that focuses on deixis.[3] These three different lenses form a rather eclectic theoretical approach but, provided the students encounter the actual hermeneutic problems in the actual text first, "ahead of theorizing," this combination may prove useful—precisely because each lens corrects or complements the other two.

Before we start the lesson, I assign my students the following reading of the primary text alone: *Crime and Punishment*, part 1, chapters 3 and 4. I ask them to find all the parallel passages in Pulkheriya Alexandrovna's letter in chapter 3 and Raskolnikov's internal monologue on it in chapter 4, taking note of what Raskolnikov changes as he quotes from his mother's letter, and what remains unchanged. This preliminary preparation enables the students to answer the following questions:

(1) List all the pronouns and pronominal words (personal, like "s/he" or "you," but also pronominal adverbs like "much/many," "everything," etc.). Judging by the context, what do they actually refer to?

(2) Why does Raskolnikov refer to his mother and sister, and even to Luzhin, sometimes in the third person, sometimes in the second, and sometimes even in first person plural? Discuss each form of reference, or address, separately. What changes in the tone every time?

(3) According to his mother's letter, what do she and her daughter omit in conversation that Raskolnikov dwells

---

[2] For next class, find information on Charles Sanders Peirce, Ferdinand de Saussure, and their respective understandings of the sign as the signifier, the signified, and the referent. Pay special attention to the difference between the latter two.

[3] Read about "deixis" in the Merriam-Webster Dictionary, e.g., online: http://www.merriam-webster.com/dictionary/DEIXIS

Etymology: Greek, literally, display, from *deiknynai*, to show.

deixis: the pointing or specifying function of some words (such as definite articles and demonstrative pronouns) whose denotation changes from one discourse to another.

on? Why do they omit these themes, and why does Raskolnikov dwell on them?

(4)   When he dwells on what they omit, do you expect him to use their words or his own? If the former, how is that possible if they actually do not talk about what he "quotes"?

(5)   As he reads and reacts, is he more concerned about them or himself? Why do you think so?

Students are required to email me their responses to these questions before the next class and also to print out a copy for themselves so that we can start class discussion with their observations about the text they thus initially encountered on their own, not through the lens of any critic's or theoretician's assertions, protestations, or refutations of what the assigned passages might possibly mean. As I am also a critic and a theoretician, I may ask questions, but at this stage may not provide any of my own possible answers. The questions aim to make the students initially clash against the primary text head-on.

After they come up with their own examples, I choose some of the more graphic ones to be discussed in class. For example, we may examine how Pulkheriya Alexandrovna paraphrases a message she seems to get from Luzhin, her prospective son-in-law, whom she is desperately trying to like but nonetheless deeply distrusts, and with good reason:

> муж ничем не должен быть обязан своей жене, а гораздо лучше, если жена считает мужа за своего благодетеля.[4]

> The husband should owe nothing to his wife; rather, it is better when the wife regards her husband as her benefactor.

---

[4]   F. M. Dostoevskii, *Polnoe sobranie sochinenii v tridtsati tomakh* (Leningrad: Nauka, 1972-90), 6:32. All subsequent page references are listed in the text. All translations from Dostoevsky are my own.

Pulkheriya Alexandrovna then interprets not only these words but her own subjective interpretation of them:

> Прибавляю, что он **выразился несколько мягче и ласковее, чем я написала**, потому что я забыла настоящее выражение, а помню одну только мысль, и, кроме того, сказал он это отнюдь не преднамеренно, а, очевидно, **проговорившись, в пылу разговора, так что даже старался потом поправиться и смягчить; но мне все-таки показалось это немного как бы резко**. (6:32)

> Let me add that he **expressed himself more mildly and tenderly than what I have written here, because I have forgotten his actual expression, and all I remember is the thought alone**; besides, he said that with no intent at all but rather **let it slip, in the heat of the moment in conversation—so that, later, he even tried to correct himself and alleviate [his expression]; but nonetheless, it all seemed rather somewhat harsh to me, in a sense.**

Pulkheriya Alexandrovna then narrates Dunya's interpretation of her own interpretation:

> и я сообщила об этом Дуне. Но Дуня даже с досадой отвечала мне, что "слова еще не дело", и это, конечно, справедливо. **Пред тем, как решиться, Дунечка не спала всю ночь и, полагая, что я уже сплю, встала с постели и всю ночь ходила взад и вперед по комнате; наконец стала на колени и долго и горячо молилась пред образом, а наутро объявила мне, что она решилась.** (6:32)

> So I shared [all] that with Dunya. But Dunya responded, even somewhat vexed, that "words were not the same as deeds yet," and she is right, of course. **Before she was finally resolved, Dunechka didn't sleep all night; thinking I was asleep, she rose from her bed and then paced back and forth in our room; in the end, she knelt and prayed, for a long time and fervently, in front of the icon [of the Mother of God]; and the next morning she told me she was resolved.**

This latter narrative is Pulkheriya Alexandrovna's interpretation of Dunya's interpretation of both Pulkheriya Alexandrovna's reaction, as well as, directly, of Luzhin's words. Dunya's implied hermeneutic[5] is both parallel and consecutive to Pulkheriya Alexandrovna's. So is Raskolnikov's. As he cites the words of both his mother and his sister, he tints them with his own interpretation, as well as tinting the interpretation of each by the other with his own interpretation. He thereby polyphonizes[6] Pulkheriya Alexandrovna's letter even more: because of the pain he perceives in what Pulkheriya Alexandrovna and Dunya say or do not say to each other, he *re-accentuates* their words, adding his own interpreting voice to their utterances. Interestingly, his need to do so is accompanied by an attempt to imagine them as addressees in an actual dialogue. In the section from which the next passage comes, Raskolnikov addresses his mother and sister in the second person. It is also significant that he talks around what both he and his sister would understand without words:

---

[5] What is relevant for us about hermeneutics is that it focuses on the prism of perception relevant for the perceiver, a prism conditioned by the context relevant for him or her—a context that may be cultural or personal, depending on the perceiver's sore spots or points of reference, etc. Thus Dunya sees both her mother and her prospective fiancé in a very specific way, as these two people obviously concern her more than the reader. Unless and until the readers assume her perspective, they cannot make any sense at all of Luzhin or Pulkheriya Alexandrovna: neither means anything to us before they begin to mean anything to her. In order to interpret the significance of her behavior, we first have to appreciate what significance the events she is reacting to have for her personally. Unless we consider her subjective prism, we have no way to understand what we read about. Similarly, since she means a lot to her brother, unless and until we see her reaction through the eyes of her brother, we cannot appreciate her tragedy or sacrifice.

[6] Polyphony here is understood as superimposing different, sometimes conflicting, meanings on the same sentence, phrase, or at times single word. The same utterance may contain a whole dialogue, depending on who is speaking and who is listening. After class, at home, read about "another's word" in Bakhtin's *Problems of Dostoevsky's Poetics*.

> Нет, Дунечка, все вижу и знаю, о чем **ты** со мной **много-то** говорить собираешься; знаю и то, о чем ты всю ночь продумала, ходя по комнате, и о чем молилась перед Казанскою Божией Матерью, которая у мамаши в спальне стоит. (6:35; bold face in quotations is mine. O.M.)

> O, no, Dunechka, I see it all and I do know what it is **you** are set to talk to me about, to talk *so much*, that is [*много-то*]; I also know what you thought about for the whole night while pacing the room, and what you prayed for in front of the Kazan Mother of God, the one in Maman's bedroom. [*or: "who stands in Maman's bedroom"—as if the Mother of God were actually present there, in the guise of that specific icon. O.M.*]

Unless they notice these shifts themselves, I draw my students' attention to the unexpected "you" Raskolnikov uses to address Dunya and the deictic word "a lot/so much/*много*," which also stands out. What is "a lot" for one may be little for another, and *what is to be said or talked about* matters "a lot." Who says these words— "to talk *a lot*"? In her letter, Pulkheriya Alexandrovna quotes them as something said by her daughter Dunya. Does Raskolnikov quote Dunya or his mother while he seems to address Dunya? He is interested in the way in which his mother quotes Dunya—i.e., interprets or fails to interpret her—like someone trying to avoid mentioning a sore spot, rather than explicating it. The less the direct referent of this deictically functioning word ("a lot"/*много*) means outside of any specified context, the more charged it is with the potential ominous or painful meaning in its present context. This is the function of pronouns, or deictic words in general, especially in Dostoevsky.

Here, the semiotics of a work of art can be seen in action. This is the time to show my students what may be relevant about such fancy terms as "the signifier," "the signified," and "the referent." In normal speech, we usually ignore the difference between the *signified* and its obvious *referent*. In marked speech, especially in poetic or rhetorical usage, tropes or rhetorical devices often tear the referent and the signified apart. Pointing at things can be more charged than naming them. For this reason, pronouns matter very much. As pronouns lose direct referents, their "signifieds" become ever more important. In Dostoevsky, pronouns often pretend to euphemize, while they actually refer to the ineffable—the pangs of the murderer's conscience or a sore spot of another character, a sinner or a victim, or both. I have written about the murderer's conscience elsewhere,[7] but here it is important for my students to see how italicized pronouns in Dostoevsky function as what Bakhtin called "another's speech," "polyphonizing" the whole narrative.

> На Голгофу-то тяжело всходить. Гм... Так, значит, решено уж окончательно: за делового и рационального человека **изволите** выходить, Авдотья Романовна, **имеющего свой капитал** (*уже* **имеющего свой капитал**, это солиднее, внушительнее), служащего в двух местах и **разделяющего убеждения новейших наших поколений** (как пишет мамаша) и, *"кажется, доброго"*, как замечает сама Дунечка. Это *кажется* всего великолепнее! И эта же Дунечка за это же *кажется* замуж идет!.. Великолепно! Великолепно!.. (6:35)

> After all, it is not easy to ascend Golgotha. Hmm… So it is—decided finally: you, Avdotya Romanovna, are **so good as to [изволите]** marry a business-like and rational man who has **his own/independent capital (who** *already* **has his own capital**—this sounds more impressive), a man holding office in two places **and sharing the principles of our newest generations** (as maman has put it), and one who, *"it seems, is kind"*—as Dunechka herself notes. This *"it seems"* is the most magnificent part of all! So this very same Dunechka is about to marry this very *seems*!.. Magnificent! Magnificent!..

---

7   If interested, for the next class read Olga Meerson, *Dostoevsky's Taboos*, Studies of the Harriman Institute (Dresden: Dresden University Press, 1998), 53-81. Do not, however, read that chapter until you have finished your first reading of the whole novel.

Polyphony, by this time, may also stop being a fancy word, having gained unexpected urgency and relevance from the students' emotionally charged direct encounter with this text. It is only because Raskolnikov re-processes others' words—Dunya's "it seems," their mother's and Luzhin's own "business-like and rational man," "*already* having capital of his own," "sharing the convictions of our new generations"— that we, the readers, suddenly realize how significant the choice of these words is—not because of their straightforward, pedestrian referents, but because of their very failure to signify anything they would signify in real life, pointing instead to the characters' very personal sore spots. Without Raskolnikov's interpretation of his mother's letter, we would be clueless about its significance. The letter signifies only in terms of his own sore spots, which, in turn, consist of his sensitivity to others' sore spots, which, in turn, are his mother's and sister's concern about what ails him!

The result of the lesson is that:

Students begin to see that, for Dostoevsky, truth can be obtained by *attending* to the various subjective prisms—rather than by trying to remove them for direct access to seemingly objective content. Style and tone may reveal themselves to the students as instruments for conveying truth more reliably than any allegedly objective and dispassionate accounts of facts and events. This will be a revelation about both "fictional truth"[8] (yes, there is such a thing!) and the unexpected unreliability of texts and documents presumed to be objective, such as some allegedly dispassionate or unengaged historical accounts and testimonies. The students will see not only that objective discourse is less reliable than they may have initially believed, but also that the subjective narrative and discursive prisms may actually touch upon a truth more palpably than expected. This revelation is particularly striking when, for example, a student majoring in history stumbles upon it, or it may even prove to be

---

[8] Cf. Michael Riffaterre, *Fictional Truth* (Baltimore, MD: Johns Hopkins University Press, 1990).

an eye-opener for a physics or economics major. (Incidentally, close readings are particularly popular with math majors.)

Thus, even my practical-minded students can be taught about the relevance of literary studies—as long as they, and I myself, do not attempt to "theorize ahead of the facts." In fact, I might have to concede (to them) that, unless we read *Gaudy Night* first, we don't really know what Lord Peter Wimsey meant to do with Sherlock Holmes's words.

4

TEXT AND LANGUAGE

Literature in the Original for the Defective Detective, or Teaching Suspect Grammar to Unsuspecting Students

Irina Reyfman

Writers of a given language write for native speakers (or, rather, readers). Furthermore, their imagined reader is nearly always a sophisticated reader of the given language, not only thoroughly versed in its standard, grammatically correct forms, but also familiar with its vernacular, regional, slang, and other nonstandard variants. This reader understands the grandiloquence in Lermontov's "On the Poet's Death," the deceptive simplicity of Pushkin's "Insomnia," the subtle play on linguistic norms in Gogol's "Overcoat," and the regional peasant speech in Turgenev's *Notes of a Hunter* or Tolstoy's *The Power of Darkness*, as well as the collage effect of Leskov's *skaz* and the syntactical manipulation that allows him to seem to say one thing but to mean something completely different.

Of necessity, we teach our students standard Russian. We occasionally teach them the vernacular, mostly to prepare them for trips to Russia, and we teach them some of Russian's stranger features, such as the Church Slavonicisms that writers use for a variety of stylistic effects. But we must always keep in mind that students develop linguistic competence slowly, over several years, which means that when we first introduce them to literary texts, their grasp of the language (spelling, grammar, syntax, and style) is still shaky. Using a good dictionary, they can get through literary texts that avoid linguistic experimentation. When facing less transparent literary texts, they are bound to miss subtle linguistic play; they can be completely derailed by more complex writerly tricks.

So what is a teacher of literature in the original to do? One obvious (and tempting) technique is to provide students with a list of the linguistic deviations present in a particular work. This would help them get through this one text efficiently, leaving more class time for discussion of these deviations' significance. This kind of helpful list, however, will not train the students themselves to uncover places where a writer deliberately uses faulty grammar to create a particular effect. It is therefore worth spending some time teaching them to expect all kinds of deviations from the linguistic norm in a literary text, coaching them to detect the obvious ones, and finally training them to see the ones that they are inclined to expect the least, namely deliberate anomalous usage.

When teaching Russian literature in the original, I devote my first class to discussing how different the process of reading a literary text is from that of reading a non-literary one. Most students already know that language is used differently in a literary work, that its function is not necessarily to deliver information in the most efficient way, and that its grammatical neutrality is not a given. We collectively agree that we will pay attention not only to *what* is told in the story we are reading, but also (and even more vigorously) to *how* it is told linguistically, particularly if this *how* deviates from standard Russian.

I then give my students an overview of standard departures from the linguistic norm they may expect in a literary work: syntactical irregularities (such as inversions, ellipses, or incomplete sentences); unexpected use of tenses (such as the "historical present" or switching from past to present and back); the likely presence of exotic and nonstandard words (Church Slavonicisms, archaisms, regional words, slang); and the text's possible unusual phonetic organization, most often in poetry, but frequently in prose as well. I point out the importance of figurative language. Finally, I stress that it is essential to detect deviations from the norm in all kinds of usage frequency, suggesting that increased or decreased frequency often points to the work's "message."

Course requirements include creating discussion questions (or observations that may facilitate class discussion), which I use to train students to pay attention to language, particularly irregularities. To illustrate the results of my approach, I will provide three examples of such discussion questions or observations without reproducing students' egregious grammatical errors, but otherwise retaining the basic structure of their sentences.[1] One example comes from a student reacting to Nikolai Karamzin's "Poor Liza":

> Когда рассказчик рассказывает о *Лизе*, он использует прошедшее время. Но когда *Лиза* и *Эраст* имеют сексуальные отношения первый раз, я заметила, что рассказчик использует настоящее время в двух строчках: "— Эраст чувствует в себе трепет — *Лиза* также, не зная, отчего — не зная, что с нею делается... Ах Лиза, Лиза! Где ангел-хранитель твой? Где — твоя невинность?" Рассказчик также использует интересную пунктуацию в этот момент. Он вставляет многоточие, и кажется, что действие происходит там, в тишине. Кажется, что рассказчик использует настоящее время, чтобы подчеркнуть этот момент.

> When the narrator tells us about Liza, he uses past tense. But I have noticed that when Liza and Erast have sex for the first time, the narrator uses present tense in two lines: "—Erast feels a quiver—Liza as well, not knowing why—not knowing what is happening to her... Ah, Liza, Liza! Where is your guardian angel? Where is your innocence?" The narrator also uses punctuation in an interesting way at this moment. He inserts elision marks, and it seems that the action takes place there, in silence. It seems that the narrator uses present tense to emphasize this moment.

The student rightly interprets the change of tense from past to present as a narrative strategy that brings the reader closer to the event and signals its crucial importance for the story. The student's astute interpretation of the ellipsis also demonstrates that even readers with imperfect control of the language can be taught to pay attention to non-standard linguistic features. (It is regrettable that the student did not comment on the overuse of dashes in the passage.)

---

[1]   I have received permission to use these examples from the students involved. All originals are in Russian.

In another example, a student points out the narrator's famously "bad" style in Fyodor Dostoevsky's "fantastic story" "Bobok":

> Когда я прочитала разговор мертвых — "Бобок", очевидно, Петербургская повесть — я подумала, что опять рассказчик окажется просто рамкой для действия рассказа. Но у нашего рассказчика такой странный стиль письма, что мне кажется, что у него бо́льшая роль. Он неудачный писатель, который пишет незаконченными предложениями — например, он часто не употребляет местоимения, и это имеет странный эффект. ... Сцена с бутербродом особенно смешная и интересная — как рассказчик манипулирует словами, чтобы значение совпадало с его действиями или мнениями.

> When I read the conversation of the dead—"Bobok," obviously, is a "Petersburg tale"—I thought that the narrator would again turn out to be just a frame for the story's action. But our narrator has such a strange written style that it seems to me that his role is larger. He is an unsuccessful writer whose sentences are unfinished; for instance, he frequently skips pronouns, and this has a strange effect. ... The scene with the sandwich is especially funny: the narrator manipulates words so that their meanings coincide with his actions and thoughts.

The student observes and correctly interprets the narrator's awkward and ungrammatical language as an important feature of his characterization. The student also detects and appreciates the verbal play: "It is not bread, but just a sandwich" that illustrates the narrator's penchant (early in the story) for manipulating facts to his advantage.

The last example, a reaction to Mikhail Lermontov's "Bela," illustrates a student's ability to see how both repetitions and phonetic play can convey meaning:

> Я заметила, что Лермонтов использует каламбур в последней части рассказа. Когда Печорин и Максим Максимович возвращаются домой после охоты, они видят

всадника. До того, как они узнали, что этот всадник — Казбич с Бэлой, Максим Максимович говорит, что он "держит что-то белое на седле". Оказалось, что это "что-то белое" была Бэла. "Белое" не пишется, как "Бэла", но эти слова звучат подобным образом. Кажется, что Лермонтов выбирает слово "белое", чтобы показать, что это Бэла с Казбичем. В конце новеллы слово "белое" опять появляется по отношению к Бэле: "кругом ее могилки теперь разрослись кусты белой акации и бузины".

I have noticed that Lermontov uses a pun in the last part of the story. When Pechorin and Maksim Maksimovich return home from hunting, they see a rider. Even before they learn that this rider is Kazbich with Bela, Maksim Maksimovich says that he "holds something white on his saddle." It turned out that this "something white [белое]" was Bela. "Beloe" is not spelled like "Bela," but these words sound alike. It seems that Lermontov chooses the word "beloe" to point out that it was Bela who was with Kazbich. At the end of the story the word "beloe" appears again in relation to Bela: "[A]round her grave grow bushes of acacia [*belaia akatsiia*] and elder."

The student's analysis shows attention to the novella's language and sophistication in interpreting her observations. My examples demonstrate that rather early in their study of language students are capable of appreciating stylistic play (including incorrect language) in literary works, and should be further encouraged to do so.

I will now describe how I guide my students through Anton Chekhov's 1899 story "The New Dacha" ("Novaia dacha"), which is a particularly apt choice for my pedagogical task. In this story Chekhov embodies the failure of his characters to connect in their differing linguistic competence: though all the characters speak some form of Russian, they nevertheless do not speak each other's language.

Like many of Chekhov's works, "The New Dacha" is about the difficulty of establishing connections and understanding between people: the Kucherovs, a family of newcomers, build a summer house in the picturesque countryside, but have a hard time being accepted by the local peasants. Despite the newcomers' efforts to be neighborly, they fail not only to befriend the locals but even to attain a state of neutral coexistence with them. Eventually the family leaves, selling the house. The peasants' hostility remains unexplained. The reader is told, however, that the dacha's new owner maintains peace with the peasants but has absolutely no relations with them: he does not even return their greetings, information which suggests that it was the Kucherovs' very attempt to establish communication that caused the conflict.

The themes of division, disruption, disagreement, discord, and separation abound in the story and can be easily detected even by students with little experience of reading Russian literature in the original. The contrast between the seemingly joyful life at the New Dacha and the clearly hard existence in the village is obvious, as are the discord and violence within most of the peasant families. Likewise, the peasants' openly hostile actions toward the newcomers (such as their disregard for the Kucherovs' property) do not require much detective work on the readers' part. To comprehend and interpret these episodes, all students need is a basic understanding of Russian grammar and a good dictionary.

Other instances of disharmony are less apparent but eventually made available for detection and analysis by the students. Thus, in an attempt to establish friendly and more equal relations with the peasants, the mistress of the new house, Elena Ivanovna, tells them about her own non-noble origin and about the discord this causes in her family:

> Я не дворянка. Дед мой был простой крестьянин, отец торговал в Москве и тоже был простой человек. А у моего мужа родители знатные и богатые. Они не хотели, чтобы он женился на мне, но он ослушался, поссорился с ними, и вот они до сих пор не прощают нас. Это беспокоит мужа, волнует, держит в постоянной тревоге....[2]

---

[2] A. P. Chekhov, *Polnoe sobranie sochinenii v tridtsati tomakh* (Moscow: Nauka, 1977), 10:122. All subsequent references to Chekhov's story are given in parentheses.

> I am not a gentlewoman. My grandfather was a simple peasant, my father was a merchant in Moscow and was also a simple man. But my husband's parents are socially prominent and rich. They didn't want him to marry me, but he disobeyed them, quarreled with them, and now they still won't forgive us. This upsets my husband, worries him, keeps him perpetually anxious....

Neither syntax nor grammar present much difficulty here: Elena Ivanovna speaks standard and cultured Russian, making it easy for inexperienced readers of Russian to follow what she is saying. Paradoxically (and importantly for my argument), the students are actually in a better position to decipher what Elena Ivanovna is saying than her listeners in the story are. Several times during her lengthy monologue to the peasants Chekhov's narrator makes it clear that they do not understand her. This makes them suspect a hidden agenda in her kind offers of help, which they rudely reject in verbal forms I will later discuss in detail.

Other signs of the disruption and disagreement that plague life in the countryside are presented emblematically. One such emblem, a railroad bridge being built nearby, explains Kucherov's presence in the countryside, as he is an engineer overseeing the construction. The peasants' utter hostility to the bridge intended to connect them to the larger world—"Жили мы без моста ... не просили, зачем нам мост? Не желаем!" ("We have lived without a bridge ... we haven't asked for it, why do we need a bridge? We don't want it!"; 10:118)—emblematizes their stubborn refusal to interact with the wider world and, perhaps, explains their enmity toward Kucherov, the builder. The ditch the peasants dig across the road that the engineer uses to get to work likewise emblematizes the troubled relations between the peasants and the newcomers. The peasants not only resent the idea of connectedness with the rest of the world, but make it more difficult for the engineer building this connection to do his job by forcing him to take a three-mile detour, thereby physically separating him from the bridge. In both cases, nothing precludes students, diligently consulting their dictionaries, from understanding Chekhov's emblematic images of discord.

Another emblem of connection and separation, this one ironic, can be found in the name of the village where the hostile peasants live, Obruchanovo, which derives either from the word *obruch* (hoop, band) or from the word *obruchenie* (engagement). Either way, the name points to the idea of unity, and thus highlights both the disunity plaguing village life and the peasants' obstinate isolationism. Unless students are properly trained to heed random proper names, they are likely to miss this subtle message and will need help in deciphering Chekhov's play on words.

The most important and effective illustration of failed communication between the newcomers and the local peasants is their linguistic separation: the Kucherov family doesn't understand the language of the peasants, and the peasants don't understand the language of the Kucherovs. Their inability to understand each other escalates their mutual hostility. Here the students get doubly confused, because they are not fully equipped to understand either party.

In one of the two direct confrontations between Kucherov and the peasants, Kucherov makes a sincere attempt to establish communication. He reasons with the peasants:

> Я и жена изо всех сил стараемся жить с вами в мире и согласии, мы помогаем крестьянам, как можем. Жена моя добрая, сердечная женщина, она не отказывает в помощи, это ее мечта быть полезной вам и вашим детям. Вы же за добро платите нам злом. Вы несправедливы, братцы. ... Мы относимся к вам по-человечески, платите и вы нам тою же монетою. (10:119)

> My wife and I try with all our might and main to live in peace and harmony with you, we help the peasants any way we can. My wife is a kind, warm-hearted woman, she doesn't refuse to help, it is her dream to be useful to you and your children. And you repay our kindness with evil. You are not just, dear fellows. ... We treat you humanely, pay us in our own coin.

In his attempt to convince the peasants to treat him and his family justly, Kucherov uses an idiom, which, translated word for word, is "pay us with the same coin." English, of course, has a similar idiom, "to pay back in the same coin." The meanings of the two idioms differ, however: while the English idiom almost always has a negative meaning, the Russian may also be used positively, as in my example. Later I will discuss the implications of this false similarity for the students' understanding of the story.

If students are likely to misunderstand the Russian idiom due to their native language interference, the peasants make a different kind of error. The expression is figurative, but they understand it literally: "Родион, который понимал то, что ему говорили, не так, как нужно, а всегда как-то по-своему, вздохнул и сказал: 'Платить надо. Платите, говорит, братцы, монетой...'" ("Rodion, who understood what was told to him not as it was proper but always in his own way, sighed and said: 'We should pay. Pay, he says, dear fellows, with a coin...'"; 10:119). In his naïve iteration Rodion deconstructs the idiomatic expression, destroying its figurative meaning. Returning home, he retells the incident to his wife: "Платить, говорит, надо... Монетой, говорит... Монетой не монетой, а уж по гривеннику со двора надо бы" ("We should pay, he says... With a coin, he says... Well, with a coin or not with a coin, but ten kopecks from every household we should come up with.") Characteristically, his son, Volodka, one of the most hostile peasants, retorts: "Жили мы без моста ... и не желаем" ("We lived [well] without the bridge ... and we don't want [it]"; 10:120). Volodka's words are unclear: is he protesting the building of the bridge (of which the engineer is an obvious representative) or the idea of paying the person who is building it? Either way, his remarks represent a refusal to accept any kind of human connection.

In his second confrontation with the peasants, Kucherov is openly angry, even aggressive. Significantly, he attributes his anger to the total impossibility of communicating his message to the peasants:

> Я просил не собирать грибов у меня в парке и около двора, оставлять моей жене и детям, но ваши девушки приходят чуть свет, и потом не остается ни одного гриба. Проси вас или не проси – это все равно. Просьба, и ласки, и убеждение, вижу, всё бесполезно. (10:125)

I asked you not to pick mushrooms in my park and near the backyard, to leave them for my wife and children, but your girls come at dawn, and then there is not a single mushroom left. Well, whether we ask you or not, it's all the same. Entreaties, kindness, persuasion—I see that everything is useless.

In the last sentence, Kucherov lists all the means that he believes he has used to convey his message to the peasants, and he angrily acknowledges defeat. He continues to rebuke the peasants: "Я и жена относились к вам, как к людям [this expression does not sound as demeaning in Russian as it is in English], как к равным, а вы? Э, да что говорить! Кончится, вероятно, тем, что мы будем вас презирать. Больше ничего не остается!" ("My wife and I treated you like human beings, like equals, and you? All the same, there is no use talking! It is likely that we will begin to despise you. There is nothing left for us to do!" 10:125). Once again, Rodion acts as interpreter of Kucherov's speech, and once again his interpretation is erroneous. This time he misinterprets Kucherov's words both as a demand for donations of goods (mushrooms) and, surprisingly, as a promise of help. He reports to his wife:

Да... ... Идем сейчас, а барин Кучеров навстречу... Да... Девок чуть свет видел... Отчего, говорит, грибов не несут... жене, говорит, и детям. А потом глядит на меня и говорит: я, говорит, с женой тебя призирать буду. Хотел я ему в ноги поклониться, да сробел... Дай бог здоровья... Пошли им, господи.... (10:125)

So... ... we are walking, and master Kucherov [comes] toward us... So... He saw our girls at dawn... Why, he says, don't they bring mushrooms... to his wife, he says, and children? And then he looks at me and says: I, he says, and my wife will take care of you. I wanted to bow low to him but lost courage... God bless [him]... Send to them [blessings], Lord....

The Russian verbs *prezirat'* (to despise) and *prizirat'* (to take care) sound the same, of course, but nothing in Kucherov's rebukes to the peasants suggests Rodion's proposal. Moreover, he misinterprets not only Kucherov's words, but also his gestures: he registers Kucherov's stare at him, but does not notice that the stare is an angry one. Rodion seems to detect some incongruity in Kucherov's promise to take care of him, but he ascribes it to Kucherov's kindness and simplemindedness: "Господа добрые, простоватые... ... 'Призирать будем...' – при всех обещал. На старости лет и... оно бы ничего. Вечно бы за них бога молил..." ("The master and mistress are kind, a bit simpleminded... ... 'We will take care of you...' he promised, and everybody heard it. In our old age... it would be good... I would pray for them forever..."; 10:125-26).

Significantly, the misunderstanding goes both ways: Elena Ivanovna also fails to grasp fully the meaning of the peasants' responses to her promise to help them. She assures the peasants: "Если все будет благополучно, то мы, обещаю вам, сделаем все, что в наших силах; ... мы построим вашим детям школу. Обещаю вам" ("If everything goes well, then we, I promise you, will do everything in our power; ... we will build a school for your children. I promise you"; 10:123). Her promises are met with mistrust: the peasants fear that the offered help will cost them financially, as happened with the peasants in a neighboring village, where one rich peasant, Voronov, began building a school but eventually forced the other peasants to pay a thousand rubles for its completion. The peasants state their suspicions and then make a derisive and somewhat enigmatic comment: "То был ворон, а теперь грач налетел" ("That was a raven, and now a rook has descended"; 10:123). *Voron*, of course, refers to the false benefactor Voronov's last name, but *grach* seems not to make much sense. The comment's form, however, implies a proverb articulating a popular wisdom. While no such proverb exists, the comment obviously invokes the Slavic popular belief that all birds from the genus *corvus* are "evil, predatory, and impure."[3] The peasants, for whom the implied meaning of the newly-coined proverb is clear, laugh. Characteristically, at this point Volodka voices his opposition to the

---

[3] See entry for *Voron* in *Slavianskaia mifologiia: Entsiklopedicheskii slovar'* (Moscow: Ellis Lak, 1995), 116.

new school in the same words that he uses to protest the bridge—
the source, it seems, of all conflicts: "Не надо нам школы. … Наши
ребята ходят в Покровское, и пускай. Не желаем" ("We don't
need a school. … Our children go to Pokrovskoe, and let them [keep
doing it]. We don't want it"; 10:123).

Elena Ivanovna neither expects nor understands the
peasants' reply. She responds with silence and withdrawal: "Елена
Ивановна как-то оробела вдруг. Она побледнела, осунулась, вся
сжалась, точно к ней прикоснулись чем-то грубым, и пошла,
не сказав больше ни слова. И шла всё быстрей и быстрей, не
оглядываясь." ("Elena Ivanovna somehow suddenly lost courage.
She grew pale, thin, completely shrunk, as if touched by something
rough, and walked away, not having said a single word. And she
walked faster and faster, not looking back"; 10:123). Her behavior
seems to suggest she has concluded that communication is indeed
impossible.

Remarkably, it is Rodion—who, as we know, has the most
trouble understanding the Kucherovs—who tries to restore communication. He follows Elena Ivanovna, calling after her, "Барыня,
погоди-ка, что я тебе скажу" ("Mistress, wait, I'll tell you something"; 10:123; and again, verbatim, 10:124). It is crucial to observe
that Rodion is the only person in the village capable of cordial relations with another human being. In particular, his marriage to
Stepanida is portrayed as exceedingly loving: "Он и Степанида,
когда были дома, всегда сидели рядом и по улице всегда ходи-
ли рядом, ели, пили и спали вместе, и чем старше становились,
тем сильнее любили друг друга" ("He and Stepanida, when they
were at home, would always sit next to each other; they would also
always walk next to each other along the street; they would eat,
drink, and sleep always together, and the older they got, the more
they loved each other"; 10:119). Rodion also seems to understand
that the peasants' inability to communicate causes the conflict. He
explains to Elena Ivanovna: "Иной, знаешь, и рад бы слово сказать по совести, вступиться, значит, да не может. И душа есть,
и совесть есть, да языка в нем нет" ("Some [person], you know,
would be glad to say a just word, to intercede, you know, but cannot. He has a soul, he has a conscience, but doesn't have a language/

tongue in himself"; 10:124). Rodion strains but fails to explain to Elena Ivanovna how to close the communication gap. His awkward attempt to console Elena Ivanovna's frightened daughter is also inappropriate: "'Ну, ну…' забормотал он, хмурясь сурово. … 'Плакать не годится, маменька прибьет… дома отцу пожалится… Ну, ну…'" ("'Now, now…,' he muttered, frowning sternly. … 'Crying is no good, your mama will beat you up… she'll tell your daddy at home… Now, now…'"; 10:124). All his efforts to improve things fail, and mother and daughter depart without a word. Rodion follows for a while, still hoping to restore communication ("А он все шел позади них, желая сказать им что-нибудь ласковое и убедительное"; "And he kept walking after them, wanting to tell them something kind and convincing"; 10:124), but he eventually realizes the futility of his endeavor.

In the episodes that describe failed attempts at communication, the students may have difficulties in understanding Chekhov's linguistic devices. The passage depicting Kucherov's first meeting with the peasants is tricky because the negativity levels in the similar English and Russian idioms differ: the students are likely to recognize the idiomatic expression "to pay with the same coin" as meaning essentially the same thing as the English "to pay someone back in their own coin." As a result, they may understand the general meaning of Kucherov's plea (be kind to us), but his use of an idiom that seemingly invites negative action may perplex them. They need some help in grasping the correct meaning of Kucherov's speech. At the same time, the similarity between the Russian and the English idioms allows the students to appreciate the humor when Rodion takes Kucherov's words literally and urges his fellow peasants to repay Kucherov in real money.

In the second episode, Rodion's misinterpretation of Kucherov's displeasure over the missing mushrooms should not present much difficulty to the students, but Rodion's expectation that Kucherov will take care of him in his old age will perplex them, unless they are very careful readers, detect the spelling difference between the Russian verbs for "to despise" and "to take care," and check the dictionary for their meanings. Even though the verbs are separated by just a few short paragraphs, this still is not very likely to happen, and it is up to the instructor to point out the pun and help the students figure out its function in the story.

It is important for the instructor teaching "The New Dacha" to keep in mind that student readers may at times be in an even worse situation than the story's warring parties, because they may have difficulties understanding both. Kucherov uses expressions that Rodion misunderstands and that students are likely to misunderstand too. Rodion, grasping the general meaning of Kucherov's reproaches, does not question his word choice. In contrast, students may require explanations when confronted with Kucherov's seemingly illogical choice of the "pay back" idiom and, especially, with the "to despise/to take care" pair. Rodion does not know the abstract verb презирать but recognizes призирать, perhaps having heard the expression дом призрения, "alms house." Students, however, probably do not know either verb and are thus likely to miss the meaning of Chekhov's verbal play completely. The students share Elena Ivanovna's perplexity over the peasants' reaction to her offer of help. The raven/rook insult will be as obscure to them as it is to Elena Ivanovna. During her last scene with Rodion, the students will probably understand less than she does: most of them will not notice or comprehend Rodion's inappropriate tone and poor word choice as he attempts to console Elena Ivanovna's crying daughter.

Many language learners in my classes are sophisticated readers in their native language. My job as an instructor is to provide them with the tools to transfer their reading skills to a text in a language that is still fairly new to them. I need to make them aware that a literary text is likely to present them with unfamiliar non-standard language. Even more importantly, I also help them develop both a sense of where the trouble spots lie and the skills to work through those spots. Students' difficulties while reading "The New Dacha" provide the instructor with opportunities not only to expand the students' knowledge of Russian, but also to allow them to experience what the characters in the story face, namely the inability to understand and thus to connect. Thanks to this experience, language learners may get more out of the story than their native-reader counterparts.

5

Text and Epigraph

"The Way of the Grain": Teaching *The Brothers Karamazov* through the Novel's Epigraph

Ksana Blank

Most epigraphs serve as useful lenses through which a novel, story, or poem can be read and interpreted, for their very purpose is to bring things into focus and to shed light on the authors' stances toward their subject matter. The epigraph to *The Brothers Karamazov*—"Verily, verily, I say unto you, Except a corn of wheat fall into the ground and die, it abideth alone: but if it die, it bringeth forth much fruit" (John 12:24)—is a particularly useful tool for teaching the novel.

First, its rhetoric is emblematic of Dostoevsky's artistic style. Constructed as a double antithesis, with two "if" clauses that denote two possibilities (one of eternal solitude and the other of abundant new life), the epigraph gives rise to a series of bifurcations, inviting the reader to proceed along them in multiple directions. These bifurcations create an overarching system of references and meanings, all tied up in one single whole—the hypertext of *The Brothers Karamazov*. As Robin Feuer Miller comments, "The epigraph, in the many guises we see it assuming through the novel, becomes a kind of standard-bearer for these weighty, metaphysical themes, themes the modern reader tends to avoid."[1] Inscribed on Dostoevsky's tombstone in Aleksandro-Nevskaya Lavra, the grain parable stands as an epitaph to the writer's creative career.

Secondly, the epigraph is useful because of its imagery. A universal symbol of potentiality, in Dostoevsky the grain stands

---

[1]   Robin Feuer Miller, *"The Brothers Karamazov": Worlds of the Novel* (New York: Twayne Publishers, 1992), 14.

as a symbol of a moral renewal. The Christian understanding of death as the gateway to new life is figuratively realized in *The Brothers Karamazov* as the idea of fallen man's regeneration. Here organic growth becomes a metaphor for spiritual growth: the death of the grain and the emerged fruit metaphorically suggest the dying of an old self and the emergence of a new spiritual identity. The image of the earth/soil is also emblematic because of Dostoevsky's involvement in *pochvennichestvo*—the movement that derived its name from the Russian word for soil, *pochva*, and, being tied to Slavophile ideology, launched an appeal to return to national sources.

Finally, the epigraph to *The Brothers Karamazov* has the quality of an opening statement. To borrow the imagery from John 12:24, the relationship between the epigraph and the main body of the text may be compared to that of the grain and the soil: the ideas expressed in the epigraph take root, spring up, and grow abundantly in the novel's various layers, reaching out to most of its characters—Dmitry, Ivan and his Grand Inquisitor, Grushenka, Ilyusha, Smerdyakov, and the elder Zosima—taking a new form and acquiring a new meaning for each.

The Christian Layer

In my experience of teaching *The Brothers Karamazov*, it has been helpful to draw the students' attention to the fact that, according to the novel, planting a seed can lead to either good or bad results, depending on two major factors—the "quality of the grain" (for man is capable of sowing seeds of both good and evil) and "the quality of the soil" (the condition of a person's heart and his susceptibility to influences of all sorts). Both possibilities are emphasized by the elder Zosima.

By quoting John 12:24, first when he explains to Alyosha the symbolic meaning of his bow to Dmitry and later when he tells the story of the mysterious visitor Mikhail, Zosima seems to suggest that the way of the grain may be understood as the way of a sinner toward moral resurrection. This scenario is most fully exemplified in Dmitry's spiritual metamorphosis, predicted by the elder, from "a brute of an officer who drinks cognac and goes whoring" (as Dmitry describes himself to Alyosha at the novel's beginning), to the "new man" he senses himself to be at its end. Symbolically representing a progression from sin through repentance to renewal, the epigraph thus connects two detective stories: Dmitry's unrealized parricide and Mikhail's perfect crime. Although very different, both stories exemplify what Robert Belknap calls the "insemination of grace": "The delay in the operation of grace is a central theme of the novel. The whole imagery of seeds in the earth is united with this causal mechanism by the epigraph of the novel."[2] Despite the tragic outcomes—Mikhail's delirium and early death and Dmitry's long-term verdict, their "moral dying to their old selves" brings forth good fruit, regenerative for their souls.

Unlike Dmitry, Grushenka "does not die to herself" and does not resurrect, but her name connects her to the epigraph's fertility imagery in a positive way: her full name, Agraphena, derives from the root *agra*, which means "earth" in Greek; her affectionate diminutive Grushenka in Russian means "little pear." Moreover, the folk tale of the "little onion" (луковка) that she tells Alyosha enhances her association with agrarian images. Grushenka's onion story featuring an old peasant woman is linked to the epigraph through the biblical parable of the mustard seed, in which the kingdom of heaven is compared to "the smallest of all seeds" which grows into "the largest of garden plants" (Matt. 13:31-32). This parable exemplifies the philosophical idea established in the epigraph: just as a little grain has the potential to bring forth much fruit, so does a single virtuous act contain enough power to outweigh a person's wickedness and thus to lead him or her to salvation. As Gary Saul Morson comments on the onion story, "Small things may have great consequences; that is also the logic of the novel's epigraph."[3]

---

[2]   Robert Belknap, *The Structure of "The Brothers Karamazov"* (Evanston, IL: Northwestern University Press, 1989), 66.

[3]   Gary Saul Morson, "The God of Onions: *The Brothers Karamazov* and the Mythic Prosaic," in *A New Word on "The Brothers Karamazov,"* ed. Robert Louis Jackson, Studies in Russian Literature and Theory series (Evanston, IL: Northwestern University Press, 2004), 115.

This story proves that potentiality is not necessarily realized: a tiny virtue may initiate a significant change and may be sufficient for salvation, but the change is not automatically guaranteed. Because she acts selfishly, the peasant woman loses her chance. The epigraph reminds us that in order to bring fruit, the grain must die to itself.

Zosima reminds us about the danger of planting the seeds of evil when he alludes to the biblical parable of the weeds (Matt. 13:24-30)—the story of good and bad seeds, sown in the same field, both bearing fruits. The elder cautions against planting a bad seed in that most virgin soil—the soul of an innocent child:

> See, here you have passed by a small child, passed by in anger, with a foul word, with a wrathful soul; you perhaps did not notice the child, but he saw you, and your unsightly and impious image has remained in his defenseless heart. You did not know it, but you may thereby have planted a bad seed in him, and it may grow, and all because you did not restrain yourself before the child, because you did not nurture in yourself a heedful, active love.[4]

Zosima's warning about planting bad seeds is dramatized in at least three episodes in the novel. In the first, Dmitry insults and humiliates Captain Snegiryov, thus planting a seed of violence in his little son Ilyusha. From that moment on, the boy's heart fills with shame and anger, exacerbating his already fragile health. Next, Smerdyakov plants a seed of violence in Ilyusha's heart when he induces him to place a pin in the bread he gives to the dog Zhuchka. Finally, Ivan shares his theories with Smerdyakov, indirectly planting the idea of murdering Fyodor Karamazov in Smerdyakov's mind. In all of these cases, the grains of evil prove to be dangerous because of their ability for expansion and growth.

---

[4]   Fyodor Dostoevsky, *The Brothers Karamazov*, trans. Richard Pevear and Larissa Volokhonsky (New York: Farrar, Straus and Giroux, 1990), 319. Further references are given in the text.

In Zosima's homily, reminiscent of the Parable of the Sower (Matt. 13:1-9), the grain imagery acquires cosmological dimensions:

> Much on earth is concealed from us, but in place of it we have been granted a secret, mysterious sense of our living bond with the other world, with the higher heavenly world, and the roots of our thoughts and feelings are not here but in other worlds. That is why philosophers say it is impossible on earth to conceive the essence of things. God took seeds from other worlds and sowed them on this earth, and raised up his garden; and everything that could sprout sprouted, but it lives and grows only through its sense of being in touch with other mysterious worlds; if this sense is weakened or destroyed in you, that which has grown up in you dies.[5]

By way of an implicit reference to the story of the Garden of Eden, this passage touches upon the issue of man's moral responsibility, so central to the novel. Creatively infused with multiple meanings, the insemination metaphors thus provide organic illustrations to the core of Zosima's philosophy: *one is responsible for all*. Good and evil alike grow from microscopic particles. Through an indirect reference to Adam and Eve's partaking of the forbidden fruit, the concept of the world's "organic" creation connects to the problem of good and evil and Ivan Karamazov's painful attempt to understand their coexistence.

Dmitry and the Myth of Demeter

The idea that the dying grain brings forth much fruit predates Christianity. Significantly, Christ's parable is addressed to the Greeks who gathered to hear his preaching (John 12:20-23). For the Greeks of the time, grain imagery must have been associated with their own religious experience—the Eleusinian Mysteries celebrating the rebirth of the grain and the cult of Demeter, goddess

---

5   Ibid., 320.

of earth and harvest.[6] Although many ancient cults assumed the existence of an afterlife, the Eleusinian sacraments stand out because of their particular closeness to Christianity. Demeter's gift—the grain—held a double significance for the Greeks: it symbolized not only practical knowledge (the science of tillage and sowing) but also esoteric knowledge (the mystery of death turning into life). Initiates were prohibited from disclosing the secret of light revealed in the Kingdom of the Dead. According to Aristotle, Aeschylus— a citizen of Eleusis by birth—nearly paid with his life for supposedly revealing the secrets of these Mysteries in his tragedies.[7]

Elsewhere I have argued that Dmitry Karamazov's recitation of "The Eleusinian Festival" as part of his confession to Alyosha reinforces Dmitry's eponymous connection to the Greek goddess Demeter.[8] The poem's myth links the novel's epigraph and Dmitry's three-stage journey to the underworld: 1) his trip to Mokroe, which he himself perceives as a descent into hell; 2) his journey to the Kingdom of the Dead—in Russian мытарства; and 3) his upcoming descent into the literal underworld—a descent to the mines. Dmitry's eagerness to embark upon this last, and most difficult, stage, signals the "dying of his old self" and gives rise to Dmitry's new conviction that an encounter with God is possible not only in the "higher abyss," but also in the "lower depths": "If God is driven

---

[6]   The biblical scholar Aleksandr Lopukhin has noted that, "If the pagans also began to heed the words of Christ, then it means that even they were able to comprehend their meaning somewhat, since—just as in their Mysteries— grain served as a symbol of life." *Tolkovaia Bibliia ili Kommentarii na vse knigi sv. Pisaniia Vetkhogo i Novogo Zaveta*, 2nd ed. (1904-13; repr., Stockholm: Institut perevoda Biblii, 1987), 432. Some modern scholars also suggest that John's Hellenistic readers would be aware of the grain symbolism in mystery religions as the symbolism of death and rebirth. See R. G. Bury, *The Logos Doctrine and the Fourth Gospel* (Cambridge: Cambridge University Press, 1940), 56, and C. H. Dodd, *The Interpretation of the Fourth Gospel* (repr.; Cambridge: Cambridge University Press, 1980), 372.

[7]   See N. J. Richardson, ed., *The Homeric Hymn to Demeter* (Oxford: Clarendon Press, 1974), 76.

[8]   Ksana Blank, *Dostoevsky's Dialectics and the Problem of Sin* (Evanston, IL: Northwestern University Press, 2010), 40-51.

from the earth, we'll meet him underground [мы под землей его сретим]! It's impossible for a convict to be without God, even more impossible than for a non-convict! And then from the depths of the earth, we, the men underground, will start singing a tragic hymn to God, in whom there is joy! Hail to God and his joy! I love him!" (592). The Church Slavonic term сретим (here translated simply as "we'll meet") adds an unmistakable biblical pathos to Dmitry's new belief.

Students in comparative literature and comparative religion may find the mythological subtext of *The Brothers Karamazov* especially inspirational. The earliest mention of the Demeter myth and Eleusinian Mysteries appears in what is known as the "Homeric Hymn to Demeter," a text that describes how the young goddess Persephone was abducted by Hades, ruler of the Kingdom of the Dead, and later rescued by her mother Demeter.[9] This myth captured the imagination of many poets and writers in classical antiquity.[10]

It made its way into Russian literature rather circuitously: through the sensational discovery of the oldest surviving manuscript of the "Hymn to Demeter" in the archives of the Moscow Imperial Library in 1777. This discovery sparked interest in the ancient myth, first among German poets and then among the Russians. The theme of the Eleusinian Mysteries was developed in one of Goethe's "Roman Elegies" ("Römische Elegien," 12, 1795). This

---

[9] The title "Homeric Hymn" does not indicate that the author of this hymn is Homer. Myths designated as Homeric are generally considered to date from the seventh to sixth centuries BCE and are now regarded as a largely anonymous collection of works. Some scholars believe that they were written by Hesiod, but this proposition is disputed. Homeric hymns are distinguished from Orphic hymns, which were composed in either the late Hellenistic or the early Roman era and were of special importance for Orphism and its mystery cult.

[10] This myth appears in Aristophanes, Euripides, Pindar, Sophocles, Aristotle, Plutarch, and Pausanias. Ovid recounts the tale of Persephone's abduction in his *Metamorphoses* and "Fasti." See *The Homeric Hymn to Demeter*, 68–86, as well as Diether Lauenstein, *Die Mysterien von Eleusis* (Stuttgart: Urachhaus, 1988).

elegy was translated into Russian by Ivan Turgenev and published in Nekrasov's *Petersburg Collection* (*Peterburgskii sbornik*, 1846), the same volume in which the young Dostoevsky had his literary debut with the novella *Poor Folk*. The theme was also developed in Schiller's poems "The Plaint of Ceres" ("Klage der Ceres," 1796) and "The Eleusinian Festival" ("Das Eleusische Fest," 1798), which were translated into Russian by Vasily Zhukovsky in the 1830s. Fifty years later, Dostoevsky employed the Eleusinian motif in Dmitry's confession to Alyosha in book 3 of *The Brothers Karamazov*.

It is important to emphasize that tracing such mythological connections throughout *The Brothers Karamazov* does not undermine the Christian dimension of the novel. On the contrary, it lends it support. Unlike Sigmund Freud's dark use of the Oedipus myth in his essay "Dostoevsky and Parricide," the Demeter myth enhances the novel's bright aspect by rendering Dmitry's spiritual evolution positive and artistically expressive.

Dmitry's journey to the underworld brings up the issue of Dostoevsky's own spiritual quest. In keeping with the future he predicts for his fictional character, the novelist arrived at his mature faith as a result of imprisonment and hard labor, which played a mystical role in his own spiritual evolution. Dostoevsky took the path of the dying and resurrected grain and experienced a "second birth" after his Siberian exile. For him, these years represented a journey to the underworld, similar to that in the Eleusinian Mysteries. The renewal did not occur suddenly. Having returned from exile, Dostoevsky wrote to his brother, "Well, how can I impart my mind to you, my understanding, everything that I lived through, what I became convinced of and what I dwelt on all of that time? I will not undertake that. Such work is positively impossible.... What happened with my soul, with my beliefs, with my mind and heart in those four years—I will not tell you. It would take a long time to tell."[11] Akin to the participants in the Eleusinian Mysteries,

---

[11] Fyodor Dostoevsky to Mikhail Dostoevsky, letter 29, written between January 30 and February 22, 1854, *Polnoe sobranie sochinenii v tridtsati tomakh* (Leningrad: Nauka, 1972–90), vol. 28, bk. 1, 167, 171.

Dostoevsky did not disclose, at least in this letter, the secret of the light revealed to him in the underworld.

Seeds of Freedom and Earthly Bread: The Ideological Perspective

The grain theme in the novel's epigraph enables us to place the legend of the Grand Inquisitor in the context of nineteenth-century Russian literature by tracing its connections with a special literary tradition, within which the grain imagery represented a conventional metaphor for political freedom. Pushkin launched this tradition in 1823 with his poem "The Sower of Freedom in the Wilderness" (*Svobody seiatel' pustynnyi*). In his note to Alexander Turgenev, Pushkin comments that this poem was written as "an imitation of a parable of the moderate democrat J<esus> C<hrist>" (подражание басне умеренного демократа И<исуса> Х<риста>).[12] Because of its provocatively negative tone, the poem could not be published during Pushkin's lifetime. It first appeared in 1856 in Herzen's *Polar Star*, published in London, together with several additional political poems by Pushkin that had been banned by the censorship: "Liberty" (*Volnost'*), "To Chaadaev" (*K Chaadaevu*), and "In the depths of Siberian mines" (*Vo glubine sibirskikh rud*), among others. In Russia it was published only in 1866, in the historico-literary journal *Russian Archive*.

Pushkin's poem conveys the idea that freedom does not grow in the wilderness; the life-giving seed does not bring forth any fruit in the desert's rocky soil:

Изыде сеятель сеяти семена своя.

Свободы сеятель пустынный,
Я вышел рано, до звезды;
Рукою чистой и безвинной
В порабощенные бразды

---

[12] Pushkin's letter to Alexander Turgenev from December 1, 1823, in Pushkin's *Polnoe sobranie sochinenii v shestnadtsati tomakh* (Moscow: Izdatel'stvo Akademii Nauk SSSR, 1937-49), 13:79.

Бросал живительное семя —
Но потерял я только время,
Благие мысли и труды.....

Паситесь, мирные народы!
Вас не разбудит чести клич.
К чему стадам дары свободы?
Их должно резать или стричь.
Наследство их из рода в роды
Ярмо с гремушками да бич.

A sower went out to sow his seed

A sower of freedom in the wilderness,
I came out early, before the morning star;
With my pure and innocent hand
Into the impoverished furrows
I scattered the life-giving seed—
But I only wasted my time,
My noble thoughts and deeds.

Graze, o peaceful nations!
The call of honor will not awaken you.
What good are gifts of freedom for the herd?
They should be sheared or slaughtered.
From generation to generation they inherit
Only the bell of the yoke and the whip.[13]

Even though its epigraph is taken from the biblical parable of the sower, the poem tells us far more about Pushkin's political and artistic views than about his religious worldview. According to Vadim Stark's commentary, it alludes to the repression of revolutionary events that took place in France, Italy, Spain, and Portugal in the early 1820s. In a more general sense, of course, Pushkin elaborates on the theme of the crowd incapable of hearing, understanding, and receiving the poet/prophet's Word. The Sower

---

[13]   I thank Michael Wachtel for his translation of this poem.

is pessimistic because he senses a gap between noble ideas and the possibility of their realization.[14]

Recently, Sergei Bocharov has pointed to striking similarities between Pushkin's "Sower" and the legend of the Grand Inquisitor. As he notes, Pushkin's phraseology—порабощенные бразды (enslaved/impoverished furrows), стадо (herd), дары свободы (the gifts of freedom), and ярмо с гремушками да бич (the bell of the yoke and the whip)—are echoed almost literally in the Grand Inquisitor's speech. Bocharov further argues that the Sower's monologue bifurcates into the Grand Inquisitor's passionate speech and Christ's silent response.[15]

These parallels between Pushkin's "Sower" and the Grand Inquisitor poem do not surprise us if we recall that in the second half of the nineteenth century grain imagery became a popular metaphor for enlightenment and political freedom among Russian liberal circles. In the poem "V. G. Belinsky" (1855), dedicated to the critic's memory, Nikolai Nekrasov calls Belinsky "an honest sower of Goodness" (честный сеятель Добра). In "The Parable" ("*Pritcha*," 1869), Nekrasov bestows the epithet "the sower of austere truth" (сеятель правды суровой) upon Nikolai Chernyshevsky. His poem "To the Sowers" ("*Seiateliam*," 1876) concludes with lines that later became a slogan among the Russian intelligentsia: "Сейте разумное, доброе, вечное,/Сейте! Спасибо вам скажет сердечное/Русский народ" ("Sow what is reasonable, what is good, what is eternal,/ Sow! The Russian people will thank you with all their heart"). In his best-known work, *Who Can Be Happy and Free in Russia?* (1873-77), Nekrasov, concerned with social injustice, expresses his empathy for the poor and oppressed and compares the soul of the Russian people as a whole to fertile soil awaiting its sower ("такая почва добрая—/душа народа русского.../О, сеятель, приди"—"such

---

[14] See V. P. Stark, "Pritcha o seiatele i tema poeta-proroka v lirike Pushkina," in *Pushkin: Issledovaniia i materialy*, ed. V. E. Vatsuro et al., AN SSSR, Institut russkoi literatury (Pushkinskii dom) (Leningrad: Nauka, 1991), 14:53.

[15] S. G. Bocharov, "Pustynnyi seiatel' i velikii inkvizitor," *Roman F. M. Dostoevskogo "Brat'ia Karamazovy": Sovremennoe sostoianie izucheniia* (Moscow: Nauka, 2007), 70-97.

good soil—/the Russian people's soul.../O, sower, come"). Many of Nekrasov's compatriots perceived his fervent exhortations as a guide for action.

The ideological leader of the Russian revolutionaries, Nikolai Chernyshevsky, also elaborates on grain and soil imagery. In his novel *What Is to Be Done?* (1862-63), as if alluding to Pushkin's "Sower of Freedom in the Wilderness," Chernyshevsky launches a grandiose utopian project meant to transform a "fruitless desert" into a "most fruitful land" through scientific innovations. In the chapter "The Second Dream of Vera Pavlovna," Vera imagines a conversation between Lopukhov and Mertsalov about various conditions for growing wheat. In the spirit of Justus von Liebig (1803–73), a German chemist whose ideas were influential in Russian radical circles, Lopukhov speaks about chemical agriculture, whereas his friend Mertsalov translates agricultural metaphors into the language of philosophy, differentiating between the "real, healthy dirt" that produces white, pure wheat and "the rotting, black soil," the "fantastic dirt," which does not bear any fruit.[16] Chernyshevsky thus extends the agricultural imagery to man's social condition: just as unhealthy soil can be transformed into healthy soil, so can the idle, parasitic life of the ruling class give way to the joyous labor of the "new people." The transformation of the earth thus symbolizes the radical transformation of society, the enlightenment of the masses, and their transition to a new future life in which freedom and happiness would be guaranteed.

Chernyshevsky reveals the abundant fruits of this socio-agrarian enterprise in the most radical, most famous part of his novel: "The Fourth Dream of Vera Pavlovna." She dreams of an edifice built of cast-iron and glass—a symbol of social justice and equality modeled on Fourier's phalansteries—which "stands amid fields of grain, meadows, gardens, and groves. The fields of grain— this is our grain—they are not such as we have now but rich, rich,

---

[16] Nikolai Chernyshevsky, *What Is to Be Done?*, trans. N. Dole and S. S. Skidelsky, intro. Kathryn Feuer (Ann Arbor, MI: Ardis, 1986), 163-64.

abundant, abundant."[17] Amazed by the abundance of this growing vegetation, she exclaims, "Is it wheat? Who ever saw such heads? Who ever saw such grain?"[18] And she immediately answers these questions: "Only in forcing-houses [оранжерей] is it possible to make such heads of wheat, such royal grain! The meadows are our meadows; but such flowers as these are now found only in flower-gardens."[19] Vera Pavlovna admires the workers in the field who are harvesting grain by machines, singing happily, celebrating the victory of the miraculous transformation of bad soil into good: "That a fruitless desert became a most fruitful land, where almost all of us spend two-thirds of our year. How has this happened? Is there anything miraculous in it?"[20] The transformation indeed resembles a miracle, although not a Christian one. Irina Paperno remarks that in *What Is to Be Done?*, Chernyshevsky reinterprets Christian mysteries in a rational, positivist key, hinting at the possibility of a scientific explanation for the miracles.[21]

In the legend of the Grand Inquisitor, Dostoevsky continues the theme launched by Pushkin and subsequently taken up by Chernyshevsky. By combining the pessimism of the one with the idealism of the other, he creates a sullen, anti-utopian society of a Socialist sort, where people cultivate bread while singing happily, unaware that their freedom has given way to slavery:

> Receiving bread from us, they will see clearly, of course, that we take from them the bread they have procured with their own hands, in order to distribute it among them, without any miracle; they will see that we have not turned stones into bread; but, indeed, more than over the bread itself, they will rejoice over taking it from our hands! ... But the flock [стадо]

---

17 Ibid., 378.

18 Ibid.

19 Ibid.

20 Ibid., 384.

21 Irina Paperno, *Chernshevsky and the Age of Realism: A Study in the Semiotics of Behavior* (Stanford, CA: Stanford University Press, 1988), 215–18.

will gather again, and again submit, and this time once and for all. Then we shall give them quiet, humble happiness, the happiness of feeble creatures, such as they were created.... Yes, we will make them work, but in the hours free from labor we will arrange their lives like a children's game, with children's songs, choruses, and innocent dancing.[22]

The question raised in Pushkin's "Sower"—"What good are gifts of freedom for the herd?"—still sounds pessimistic decades later, after Chernyshevsky's agrarian utopia in *What Is to Be Done?*, for it receives no positive answer in *The Brothers Karamazov*.

In *Notes from Underground* Dostoevsky challenges the idea of the Crystal Palace, a "forever indestructible" edifice. In his Grand Inquisitor he undermines its agrarian version: a socialist Eden, planted by the radical sowers of materialist goodness and truth— Belinsky, Chernyshevsky, and Nekrasov. In this way the epigraph functions not only on the novel's spiritual level but also on its ideological level. Entering into a polemic with Chernyshevsky, Dostoevsky revisits Pushkin's "Sower of Freedom in the Wilderness," re-accenting the poem's phraseology and imagery and providing a new and terrible authoritarian variant on its idea that the best intentions do not always bring forth the best results.

The epigraph to *The Brothers Karamazov* epitomizes Dostoevsky's way of dealing with polarities. The paradox it offers— endless life is fruitless whereas death is fruitful—accentuates the writer's fondness for reversals of all sorts. The idea of the reversibility of opposites expressed in John 12:24 is universal. It recalls the dialectics of Heraclitus, who advocates the interdependence of opposites: "Immortals are mortal, mortals immortal";[23] "The

---

22 Dostoevsky, *The Brothers Karamazov*, 258–59.

23 Charles H. Kahn, *The Art and Thought of Heraclitus: An Edition of the Fragments with Translation and Commentary* (Cambridge: Cambridge University Press, 1979), 71, Fragment 92.

beginning and the end are shared in the circumference of a circle."[24] It is also consonant with the ancient Chinese philosophy of change illustrated by the harmonious interaction of Yin and Yang, each of which already contains the seed of its opposite (a black dot on a white background and a white one on black), a graphic model that illustrates Dostoevsky's dialectics.[25] The epigraph to *The Brothers Karamazov* exemplifies the same idea of the inseparability and reversibility of opposites, but with organic imagery. The maxim from St. John suggests that life and death constitute two parts of a single whole, their flowing into each other being two sides of a single process.[26] And thus it establishes a paradigm for many other oppositions in Dostoevsky, introducing the reader to the dualities of his world—in which good and evil, faith and disbelief, and freedom and slavery are dynamic and interdependent.

---

[24] Ibid., 75, Fragment 99.

[25] See Ksana Blank, *Dostoevsky's Dialectics and the Problem of Sin*, 3-26.

[26] The idea of the reversibility of life and death is doubled in the verse that follows the grain parable: "He that loveth his life shall lose it; and he that hateth his life in this world shall keep it unto life eternal" (John 12:25).

TEXT AND BIBLICAL TEXT

Teaching Raskolnikov's Dream:
Regarding the Pain of Others in the Classroom

Liza Knapp

One of the many things that I have learned about Dostoevsky from Robert Belknap is that for every literary source you find for a passage in Dostoevsky's fiction, there will be a dozen more. This textual polygeny is beautifully illustrated by Raskolnikov's dream of the beaten mare in *Crime and Punishment.* Dostoevsky scholars have had a heyday identifying its sources, starting with Victor Hugo and Nikolai Nekrasov,[1] as well as antecedents in Dostoevsky's real-life experience.[2] Fractured and reconstituted versions of the dream recur in Dostoevsky's works. Dostoevsky's treatment of this material, with its archetypal feel, seems, in turn, to have spawned copycat scenes in novels by others[3]—not to mention the special case that occurred in Turin, on January 3, 1889, when Nietzsche, sobbing, threw his arms around a horse that was being beaten by a brutal driver, an act eerily familiar from Raskolnikov's dream.[4] In this one

---

[1] For discussion, see Nathalie Babel Brown, *Dostoevsky and Hugo* (Ann Arbor, MI: Ardis, 1978).

[2] See notes in F. M. Dostoevskii, *Polnoe sobranie sochinenii v tridtsati tomakh* (Leningrad: Nauka, 1972-90), 7:368-69.

[3] In *Literature and the Taste of Knowledge,* Michael Wood cites an example of a copycat scene in Joseph Conrad's *The Secret Agent* (Cambridge: Cambridge University Press, 2005), 165n11.

[4] My wording of the description of Nietzsche's embrace of the horse is taken from Lesley Chamberlain, *Nietzsche in Turin* (London: Quartet Books, 1996), 208, as quoted in Wood, *Literature and the Taste of Knowledge,* 163-64. See also Chamberlain, "The Right Attitude to Horses," *TLS,* March 1, 1996. Chamberlain suggests that Nietzsche's encounter with the horse was in some way influenced by his internalization of Raskolnikov's dream. Wood

act Nietszche seems to recant and repent for all the pity-bashing of *The Antichrist* (1888) and other works. He lived the rest of his life in what is often referred to as a state of madness—with his arms around that horse.[5]

What makes Raskolnikov's dream work so well in the classroom may be what made Dostoevsky choose it when he gave public readings. You don't actually need subtexts or even context for this passage to raise a question at the heart of the human experience: what does the pain of others have to do with us? When I teach *Crime and Punishment* in the Columbia "great books" course, I find that this scene hits hard, in part because works that precede it on the syllabus (Augustine's *Confession*, Dante's *Inferno*) take a hard line on compassion, or show random acts of compassion going awry (Cervantes's *Don Quixote*).[6] And Raskolnikov's dream is also part of

---

also discusses responses to Nietzsche's embrace of the horse by Kundera, Barthes, and others. (Given the influence of Dostoevsky on Nietzsche, these twentieth-century responses also go back, via Dostoevsky, to Nekrasov and Hugo.)

5   Chamberlain and other biographers of Nietzsche suggest that this event marks the onset of the madness that lasted until his death (Wood, *Literature and the Taste of Knowledge*, 163).

6   In Dante's *Inferno*, Virgil discourages Dante the traveler from feeling pity because the suffering he responds to is that of sinners who are, according to Christian theology, getting their just deserts. To feel pity for those suffering in hell thus amounts to challenging the Divine Judgment. As Virgil tells Dante, "Piety lives when pity is quite dead."

Augustine's *Confessions* also offer insights to students on this subject. Given his Platonist leanings, it's not surprising that Augustine objects to watching suffering in the theater, where the audience is called on "to grieve" but "not to help." As Paul M. Blowers ("Pity, Empathy, and the Tragic Spectacle of Human Suffering: Exploring the Emotional Culture of Compassion in Late Ancient Christianity," *Journal of Early Christian Studies* 18, no. 1 [Spring 2010]) has argued, Augustine, conscious of how "empathy in another's tragedy ever risks becoming a kind of emotional voyeurism," nevertheless sought to develop ways of encouraging empathy. However, the *Confessions* don't seem to focus on Augustine responding to the *real* suffering of others. Thus, for example, Augustine's revelatory encounter with a drunken beggar involves Augustine coming to a new understanding of the emptiness of his own striving rather than inspiring him to love the beggar as a neighbor. Of course, this was before Augustine's conversion, but from the *Confessions*

why *Crime and Punishment* falls like an axe on the "little bit of ivory, two inches wide, on which [she] worked with … a fine brush"[7] that is Jane Austen's *Pride and Prejudice*, the work students read just before. *Crime and Punishment* introduces students to the "Russian point of view" on what the suffering of fellow human beings has to do with us: this, as Virginia Woolf famously argued, is the "cloud that broods over" Russian literature. The students, who read *To the Lighthouse* next, see that Virginia Woolf found this "Russian point of view" kindred to the extent that Mrs. Ramsay can't get "suffering, death, and the poor" out of her mind—although she doesn't delude herself about her charity, acknowledging that it's "half a sop to her own indignation" or worse.[8]

The following proposes that instructors use Raskolnikov's dream as an entrance into the questions about the pain of others and neighborly love that are at the heart of *Crime and Punishment* and Dostoevsky's work in general. It also offers suggestions for using this nightmare as a point of reference for classroom exploration of

---

students often get the impression that for Augustine what matters is finding God in an inner space and cultivating his own self. (For this feature, see Philip Carey, *Augustine's Invention of the Inner Self* [Oxford: Oxford University Press, 2003].)

Don Quixote responds with compassion to the suffering of others, but his attempts to help often fail and even lead to further violence. Especially relevant in view of Raskolnikov's dream and the parable of the loving Samaritan is the early episode (pt. 1, ch. 4) in which, as he is riding along, Don Quixote hears what sounds like a fellow human being in pain; he follows the cries to find a peasant farmer beating a fifteen-year-old boy. Don Quixote intercedes to stop the beating. However, when Don Quixote encounters the shepherd boy again we learn that the boy ended up nearly dead because his master had renewed the beatings even more harshly after Don Quixote had left. The victim in this case wishes that Don Quixote had not gotten involved. We see the good intentions of Don Quixote, but on the other hand, what are we to make of the fact that his intercession for a neighbor in pain doesn't seem to help?

7   Letter to J. Edward Austen (1816-12-16), *Letters of Jane Austen: Brabourne Edition* (1884).

8   Virginia Woolf, "The Russian Point of View," *The Common Reader* (1925; repr., New York: Harcourt, 1953), 173-85. Virginia Woolf, *To the Lighthouse* (1927; repr., New York: Harcourt, 1955), 9, 64.

these same questions as they arise in different forms in the novels of Tolstoy, so often taught with those of Dostoevsky. Both novelists were haunted by the call to love their neighbors. The same cloud broods over them, as Virginia Woolf has argued, but it's important to remind our students that these Russians were part of a widespread movement in the mid-nineteenth century, which also included Harriet Beecher Stowe, Elizabeth Gaskell, Charles Dickens, George Eliot, and Victor Hugo. These novelists all ask readers to use their moral imaginations to consider the question of who our neighbor is, really, and what his misery has to do with us.[9] The questions posed in these novels anticipate those formulated by recent thinkers like Susan Sontag in her essay *Regarding the Pain of Others* as being central to our (post)modernity, with the contemporary twist brought by greater, graphic exposure to this misery and pain.[10] As Sontag observes, compassion is an "unstable emotion," which can easily run amok. That Dostoevsky understood this, too, can be seen from Ivan Karamazov's collection of newspaper clippings about the pain of under-age others, as well as from Raskolnikov's dream of the beaten horse. But if Sontag considered Dostoevsky's art "a turning point in the history of moral feeling and of sorrow" (44-45), it was because he, too, challenges us to find the right ways of regarding the pain of others, instead of simply turning our backs or, worse, enjoying the spectacle.

Let us first look at the dream itself (pt. 1, ch. 5). Since the territory is familiar, I will focus on a few points in the dream, leaving aside the question of its genesis and its function in the

---

[9] Lionel Trilling, in "On Manners, Morals, and the Novel," in *The Liberal Imagination* (New York: *New York Review of Books*, 2008), 221, writes about the moral imagination and the dangers of making others in pain "the objects of our pity, then of our wisdom, ultimately of our coercion."

[10] See Susan Sontag, *Regarding the Pain of Others* (New York: Farrar, Straus and Giroux, 2003). Certainly photography, television, and computers have increased our exposure to the pain of others and resulted in the possibility of our becoming inured to suffering, as Sontag argues. Also relevant is the "compassion fatigue" others have documented.

buildup to the murder.[11] The dream takes Raskolnikov back to his childhood in the provinces, as he and his father walk by a tavern on a feast day when everyone is drunk. A peasant named Mikolka starts urging all comers to hop into a cart to which an old mare is harnessed. People tell him that the horse is too old to pull them all. But Mikolka viciously beats the mare to make her go, declaring: "I might as well kill her, she's not worth her feed" (Or: "It's a waste to feed her" [Даром хлеб ест]) (pt. 1, ch. 5, 56).[12] Mikolka's declaration recalls what Luzhin calls "economic truth," presented as an English invention and import, which determines who lives and who dies in the Russian childhood of Raskolnikov's dream world.[13] The beating of the horse continues while Mikolka justifies himself by saying, "It's my property."

This nightmare, however, is ultimately not about Mikolka and what he is doing to the horse, terrible as that is. It's about how others respond: many join in, and others are mesmerized by the spectacle, which becomes, in the words of Robert Louis Jackson, "an orgy of violence": watching becomes "a form of vicarious and corrupt participation."[14] At first only one peasant, with a gray beard, protests, warning that this isn't Christian behavior. But the

---

[11] See Ruth Mortimer, "Dostoevski and the Dream," *Modern Philology* (November 1956): 106-16, and Thomas Shaw, "Raskol'nikov's Dreams," *SEEJ* 17, no. 2 (1973): 131-45, as well as the notes to the PSS and commentary in Boris Tikhomirov, *"Lazar'! Griadi von": Roman F. M. Dostoevskogo "Prestuplenie i nakazanie" v sovremennom prochtenii* (St. Petersburg: Serebriannyi vek, 2005).

[12] For citations from *Crime and Punishment,* I use the Pevear/Volokhonsky translation (New York: Vintage, 1993). Page numbers to this translation are given after the part and chapter numbers.

[13] Luzhin expounds on "economic truth" in pt. 2, ch. 5 (149); Marmeladov reports to Raskolnikov that a scientific movement forbidding compassion has gained a foothold in England in pt. 2, ch. 2 (14).

[14] Robert Louis Jackson, *Dialogues with Dostoevsky* (Stanford, CA: Stanford University Press, 1996), 46. In his discussion of "the ethics of vision," Jackson focuses on how Russian writers address the question of whether and how to look at scenes of execution and other forms of violence and suffering. As Jackson points out in reference to Raskolnikov's dream, the parameters differ for a child.

real drama occurs between father and son, as little Rodya is initiated into this world of violence. Looking to his father, he asks, "Papa [папочка], papa, papa, what are they doing? Papa, they're beating the horse...." He expects his father (the embodiment of wisdom, authority, manhood, the way of the world?) to answer his questions about this cruelty and suffering.

How does Raskolnikov's father react? He tells him to "Come along, come along! They're drunk, they're playing pranks, the fools—come along, don't look!" The father's final word, later, as they leave, is more disturbing: "It's not our business!" (Не наше дело!). In the symbolic world of the dream, little Rodya looked up to his father as an authority who will restore order, make peace, bring about justice, eliminate suffering, express outrage, and perhaps punish the wrong-doer, or, at the very least, protest. The child wants his father to do something.

Raskolnikov breaks free from his father, and, as he heads to the horse, is grazed by Mikolka's whip. Then he finds the gray-bearded godly man, the voice of protest, who shakes his head in solemn judgment at the continuing abuse. Finally, a woman from the crowd "takes him by the hand and tries to lead him away."[15] Again, Raskolnikov breaks free and makes his way through the crowd to the horse, throws his arms around her, and kisses her eyes and bloody mouth. When his father finally catches hold of him, Raskolnikov embraces him, asking him, through hysterical cries, "What did they... kill... the poor horse for!" At this point he wakes up.

Raskolnikov's hysterical response contains intimations of the metaphysical protest that Dostoevsky is known for. His hysteria is a form of protest, against the suffering that permeates the world and against the ethos that tells him it is none of his business. (The victim in the dream is a horse, not a human being, but in Raskolnikov's psyche and in the symbolic web of the novel, the suffering horse is

---

[15] The woman's actions recall those of Raskolnikov's mother, as she would bring him away from the window when he would "feel so sorry, so sorry" and "almost weep" as he would watch horses being beaten as they were driven by his house in pt. 1, ch. 5 (55).

closely identified with suffering women.) Little Raskolnikov of the dream rebels against a world built on suffering, thereby anticipating Ivan Karamazov and others.

Little Rodya and his father had been on a mission, to go to the cemetery to pray for their dead. [16] Dostoevsky incorporates into the dream all of the trappings of Orthodox piety, including a green-cupolaed church, the sweet kutya bedecked with a cross of raisins, the requiems for Rodya's grandmother, the icons, and so forth. Raskolnikov's father performs the blessed parental role of bringing his son into communion with Orthodox life.[17] But what message is conveyed to the child when, on their way to carry out this act of Christian piety, Raskolnikov's father tells him that this scene of suffering outside the tavern is "not [their] business"?

In the parable of the loving Samaritan in the gospel of Luke (10:30-35), Jesus addresses the question that looms large in Raskolnikov's dream, a question that also echoes in other works by Dostoevsky: What does other people's suffering have to do with us? The loving Samaritan makes another's pain his business. Given Dostoevsky's direct use of the raising of Lazarus from the gospel of John, it is instructive for students to contemplate other, less overt, ways that biblical subtexts add to the novel's gospel-like aura.[18] At the very least, it's important to remind a class of

---

[16] Dostoevsky scholars suggest that Raskolnikov is dreaming about *"roditel'skaia subbota,"* one of the special days for remembering the dead, starting with one's own dead ancestors and family members (Tikhomirov, *"Lazar'! Griadi von,"* 109). This enforces the tension between the love for one's own kin and the love of one's neighbor. In the parable of the Samaritan, the Samaritan's "otherness" emphasizes the fact that one's neighbor is whoever one meets on the road from Jerusalem to Jericho.

[17] For Dostoevsky, tending to religious upbringing can redeem even a delinquent father like Marmeladov: Raskolnikov, in one link in the chain of events that is symbolically linked to this dream, learns from Polechka that Marmeladov (her stepfather) has taught her to read the catechism.

[18] As Robert Belknap notes (in this volume), "First-year college students rarely care about *quellenforschung."* But students in the Columbia Literature Humanities are trained to put one text "in conversation" with another. Since they've read the gospels of both John and of Luke, they're ready to tackle the biblical subtexts of Dostoevsky's novel.

Dostoevsky enthusiasts that the gospel of John, showcased in *Crime and Punishment* and often cited as Dostoevsky's favorite, was not the only gospel in the book under his pillow during those long years in Siberia. Dostoevsky marked Luke 10:27-29 with his nail and dog-eared the bottom of the page that contains the parable itself.[19] And allusions to this passage in his fiction suggest that it was firmly engrained in his religious imagination.[20]

In Luke's gospel, the only one of the four gospels to include it, Jesus tells the parable of the loving Samaritan when he is "tested" ("tempted" in Russian) by a lawyer who demands to know what he should do to inherit eternal life. Jesus responds by telling him to do what is written in the law. The lawyer replies that the law tells him to love his God with all his heart, with all his soul, and with all his might, *and to love his neighbor as himself*. The lawyer, "wanting to justify himself," asks one further question, namely, "And who is my neighbor?" Jesus tells the parable to respond to this challenge.

On the road between Jerusalem and Jericho, thieves have stripped a man of his raiment, beaten him, and left him for dead. A priest and then a Levite see him there but pass him by. A Samaritan comes along, sees him, has compassion, dresses his wounds, and takes care of him. For Jesus, thus, your neighbor is that suffering other or stranger that you pass on the road from Jerusalem to Jericho.

---

19   This parable of the Samaritan, like the parable of the prodigal son, is unique to the gospel of Luke. Both parables, according to John Drury, "are honored by historical critics as Jesus' own work" ("The Gospel of Luke," in *Literary Guide to the Bible*, ed. Robert Alter and Frank Kermode [Cambridge, MA: Belknap Press of Harvard University Press, 1987], 432).

20   In "Motifs of Compassion in Dostoevskii's Novels," in *Cultural Discontinuity and Reconstruction: The Byzanto-Slav Heritage and the Creation of a Russian National Literature in the Nineteenth Century*, ed. Jostein Bortnes and Ingunn Lunder (Oslo: Solum Forlag, 1997), 185-201, Diane Oenning Thompson finds "outlines" of the parable of the good Samaritan in Raskolnikov's interactions with Marmeladov, both at their initial meeting in the tavern and later when he finds him nearly dead in the street and takes him home (189-90). For further discussion of Raskolnikov's acts of charity, see Lyudmilla Parts, "Christianity as Active Pity in *Crime and Punishment*," *Dostoevsky Studies* 13 (2008): 61-91.

How do these gospel lessons relate to Dostoevsky's novel? As mentioned above, the mare in the symbology of the dream and the novel is closely associated with the suffering women Raskolnikov encounters. In simple terms, the novel asks how Raskolnikov will respond: will he join Mikolka in perpetuating the brutality?; will he "come along" with his father, leaving for dead the victims, telling himself that their suffering isn't "our business"?; will he protest hysterically, like his childish self?; or will he somehow, miraculously, love his neighbor, like the Samaritan?

Dostoevsky brings the gospel world into his novel not only through direct references to the raising of Lazarus, but also through the many ways in which he evokes neighborly love in the spirit of the Samaritan. Students can be invited to find fractured versions of Raskolnikov's nightmare and the gospel parable elsewhere in the novel. Thus, for example, Dostoevsky reconfigures the elements of both in a scene that occurs soon after the murder when the action picks up again. Walking in a daze in the middle of the road, Raskolnikov gets in the way of a carriage and is "stoutly lashed on the back with a whip by the driver of the carriage" (pt. 2, ch. 2; 113).[21] Whereas the crowd mocks him, a mother and daughter witness his pain, and respond by giving him alms, saying, "Take it, *batiushka*, in the name of Christ."[22] Dostoevsky thus conflates dream and parable to provide a variation: as in the dream, a parent and child respond to a beating with a horse whip. Raskolnikov here is in the

---

[21] The carriage driver, sounding a bit like Mikolka with his rationalizations for violence, suggests that he was only protecting his own interests by lashing Raskolnikov to get him out of the way. He complains that Raskolnikov was just pretending to be drunk and getting under the wheels on purpose, so that he would get hit and the driver would be liable. Some passerby agrees that "They live from it, my good sir, they live from it…"

[22] "He suddenly felt someone put money in his hand. He looked; it was an elderly merchant's wife in a kerchief and goatskin shoes, with a girl beside her in a little hat and holding a green parasol, probably her daughter. 'Take it, my dear, in Christ's name.' He took it, and they went on. It was a twenty-kopeck piece. From his clothes and appearance, they could well have taken him for a beggar, for a real collector of half kopecks in the street, and the offering of so much as twenty kopecks he doubtless owed to the stroke of the whip's having moved them to pity" (pt. 2, ch. 2; 113-14).

position of the mare in his dream and of the victim of thieves in the parable, but whereas Raskolnikov's papa told him it was "none of their business"—like the priest and the Levite in the parable—this mother and daughter show compassion as they, like the Samaritan, respond to a body in pain on the side of the road. Even though Raskolnikov casts their coin into the river, this episode breaks the spell of the nightmare.

A few chapters later (pt. 2, ch. 7), Dostoevsky again reworks the nightmare and reenacts the parable. Raskolnikov comes across a man run over by a carriage and, like the loving Samaritan, shows compassion for his neighbor in pain and takes him home. This man dying on the side of the road is Marmeladov. At this point, he is not a stranger, since Raskolnikov had met him once before. In their first encounter, Marmeladov had cried out for compassion, noting that it had, as Lebezyatnikov informed him, been outlawed in England (where, presumably, political economy prevailed over the gospel ethos). Raskolnikov, acting like the Samaritan, takes the suffering Marmeladov home to his family, where he, as in the parable, leaves money. [23] When he encounters Marmeladov for the second time— half-dead in the road, like the victim in the parable—Raskolnikov acts on his compassion as he brings him home to die. Dostoevsky's narrator notes that Raskolnikov responds "as if it were a matter of his own father" (pt. 2, ch. 7; 175-76), thereby evoking the dream. If taken to heart, the figure of speech—that Raskolnikov acted as if he

---

[23] Just before the dream of the horse, Raskolnikov intercedes on behalf of the young girl who had been violated (pt. 1, ch. 4; 46-50); in his behavior he shows an impulse like that of the Samaritan in the parable that Jesus uses to define the love of neighbor that, along with love of God, brings about eternal life. Raskolnikov, after involving the policeman and providing money for the cab—much as the Samaritan leaves money with the innkeeper to whom he delivers the man he rescues from the ditch—reverts back to his hard-hearted rationalizations, relying on Quetelet's social percentages.

Diane Thompson comments on Raskolnikov behaving like a "good Samaritan" in this scene. See her "Dostoevsky and Science," in *The Cambridge Companion to Dostoevsky*, ed. W. J. Leatherbarrow (Cambridge: Cambridge University Press, 2002), 202. Ruth Mortimer notes that Raskolnikov's encounter with this girl provides part of the inspiration for his nightmare about the horse.

were caring for his own father—suggests that Raskolnikov loves his neighbor Marmeladov as his kin. That this is possible is nothing short of miraculous within the context of Dostoevsky's gospel-inspired world.[24]

Elsewhere in his work Dostoevsky affirms the definition of our neighbor as any human being whose pain is brought to our knowledge.[25] But his heroes, from Ivan Karamazov to Zosima, show that loving one's neighbor in pain is hard. Dostoevsky was well aware that compassion is, as Susan Sontag would put it, an "unstable emotion," and that regarding the pain of others can easily go wrong. We need only remember the scene in *The Brothers Karamazov* where Lise Khoklakova wants to watch a child tortured while she (Lise) eats pineapple compote.

"Who is my neighbor?"—the question that prompts Jesus to tell the parable of the loving Samaritan—lies at the heart of Tolstoy's *Anna Karenina*, at least as Dostoevsky reads it in *Diary of a Writer* (July-August 1877). Bringing Dostoevsky's wisdom (or bias) to bear on *Anna Karenina* illuminates an aspect of Tolstoy's novel that students may not otherwise notice and helps students see that while the same cloud broods over these two writers, there are significant differences in how each handles the tension between the call to love your neighbor and the self-interested pursuit of family happiness.

Throughout *Anna Karenina*, Levin wants to know who his neighbor is and what his neighbor has to do with him.[26] Levin's final revelation about "loving your neighbor" ultimately gives him the faith to carry on through the crisis in the novel's last part. In the *Diary*

---

[24] We learn in the epilogue that before the murder, Raskolnikov had—in the spirit of the loving Samaritan—performed spontaneous acts of charity to his neighbors, that is, to strangers encountered on his way around Petersburg: he had rescued two children from a fire, and he had cared for the paralytic father of a friend who had died (Epilogue, 537). These form an important Dostoevskian web and on some level figure into the miracle of Raskolnikov's eventual rebirth.

[25] This definition is modified from that of Catharine Beecher in her explanation of the parable of the Samaritan in *The American Woman's Home* (1870).

[26] For discussion, see my work-in-progress, *"Anna Karenina" and Others*.

of a Writer, Dostoevsky demands to know at what distance Levin's love for his neighbor ("near one" in Russian) kicks in. Dostoevsky's harangue attempts to prove that love for his neighbor (his Slavic brethren, in particular) ought to make Levin want to go fight a war, a war that Tolstoy, like his hero Levin, wanted nothing to do with.[27] These differences allow us to draw further distinctions between Dostoevsky and Tolstoy. The questions Dostoevsky asks about Levin and neighborly love offer an insight into Levin and *Anna Karenina* because, in fact, the anxieties dramatized in Raskolnikov's nightmare haunt Levin, too.

At the birth of his son, Levin experiences fatherhood as "the consciousness of a new sphere of liability to pain" (Garnett translation of "сознание новой области уязвимости," which could be more literally translated as "consciousness of a new sphere of vulnerability"; pt. 7, ch. 16). Tolstoy times it so that establishing this new zone of vulnerability to his son Mitya's suffering coincides with Levin's making himself at least outwardly impervious to the pain of more distant others. Whereas Dostoevsky takes Levin to task for lack of concern for his Slavic brethren, perhaps the more

---

[27]   In "A Question: Does Distance Have an Influence on Love for Humankind?," Dostoevsky complains that Levin doesn't *feel* any compassion for his Slavic brethren. Dostoevsky wants to know at what distance or what proximity Levin will start to react to the pain of others. He starts by asking whether we would feel any compassion for infants whose eyes were being pierced on Mars, then gets closer to home and wonders what Levin would feel if the atrocities in the Balkans were happening under his nose. To make his point, Dostoevsky describes a Turk piercing the eyes of a two-year-old while his sister watched. As he lambasts Levin for not wanting to jump to the aid of his Slavic brethren suffering under the Turks, Dostoevsky wants to present Levin's refusal as a failure in Levin's capacity to love his neighbor. What the warmongering Dostoevsky was up to is clear as he regales readers with narratives, fit for Ivan Karamazov's collection, about the suffering of Orthodox women and children at the hands of the Turks. Levin really ought to want, Dostoevsky reasons, to help this other in pain, to stop the suffering, to join the war effort, and go to the Balkans and kill Turks. Dostoevsky presents it as Levin's duty, if he professes neighborly love, to go to the aid of his Slavic brethren. Levin (or Tolstoy), however, also appealed to Christ's law, citing it as a rationale for *not* waging war. Thus, both camps claimed Christ to be on their side.

interesting question is where this puts Anna Karenina: within the zone of Levin's neighborly love or outside it? Levin comes home from his one and only meeting with Anna full of a volatile mixture of feelings that seems to include true compassion for her suffering (pt. 7, chs. 10 and 11). At home, however, he fights and makes up with Kitty, who suspects that there was too much eros in that mix. Once Kitty goes into labor the next morning, Levin is entrenched in the new sphere of vulnerability to his son's pain, leaving unspoken the message that Anna's suffering is "none of his business."

If at the end of *Anna Karenina* Levin seems to set the boundaries of Pokrovskoe (his estate) as the outer limit of neighborly love, it is not only out of concern with family first (as suggested by the bath "experiment" in which it's proven that baby Mitya recognizes "his" people, i.e., those in his circle of love) or a simple desire to exclude unsavory elements:[28] it's a matter of survival. For Levin, to contemplate the pain of others, from that of his "Slavic brethren" (described by Dostoevsky in *Diary of a Writer*) to that also of Anna Karenina, would be more than he could bear. The drafts of the novel inspire and corroborate this suggestion that Levin protects himself from the pain of others out of desperation: drawing from his own experience of seeing the corpse of his (actual) neighbor's mistress, who had thrown herself on the tracks, Tolstoy originally intended to have Levin behold the corpse of Anna after her brutal suicide. How was it to affect him? Levin would not, little-Rodya-like (or mad-Nietzsche-like), fling himself on the body in a gesture of compassion, but the sight of Anna's suffering would trigger his own suicidal crisis, in a way that suggests that Levin is, in fact, very vulnerable to the suffering of others. In the final version of the novel, the suicidal onset is more complicated but still related to his "consciousness of zones of liability to suffering." His solution is to cordon off his neighborhood.

---

[28] See Gina Kovarsky on how this "experiment" has the indirect effect of excluding Anna Karenina from the human family. Gina Kovarsky, "The Moral Education of the Reader," in *Approaches to Teaching "Anna Karenina,"* ed. Liza Knapp and Amy Mandelker (New York: Modern Language Association of America, 2003), 166-72.

Another case, this one from *War and Peace*, helps students understand how the Tolstoyan hero is haunted by anxieties about the pain of others. As a prisoner of war, Pierre Bezukhov, at a spiritual low, meets Platon Karataev, whose loving kindness returns him to life. Platon, however, practices the kind of love that Jesus celebrated in the parable of the loving Samaritan. Pierre learns that Platon regards as his neighbor whoever is near him, regardless of class, nationality, or creed. As Pierre, Platon, and the other prisoners are forced to march along with their retreating French captors, Pierre is aware that those who lag behind are being shot. He also knows that Platon is in pain and near death. As the convoy of prisoners stops to rest, Pierre notices that Platon wants him to approach: Platon, "with his kind, round eyes, now veiled with tears, ... was evidently calling him over, wanting to say something. But Pierre was too afraid for himself. He pretended that he had not seen his look and hurriedly walked away." Pierre soon thereafter hears "the shot clearly." (And when Platon's dog, back with the body, starts howling, Pierre thinks to himself, "What a fool, what is it howling about?").[29] In order to survive, Pierre fails to love his neighbor Platon Karataev just before he is shot dead. This is a more pointed version of what happens to Levin in *Anna Karenina*, when he must purge his compassion for Anna and cease to regard her as a neighbor in pain. To survive, the Tolstoyan hero must leave for dead the suffering bodies on the way from Jerusalem to Jericho.

This focus on the suffering of one's fellow human beings, according to Virginia Woolf, is the distinctive feature of the Russian point of view. Dostoevsky's novels record countless failures to love neighbors, with occasional intimations of a success story, usually with a gospel aura about it. However, this concern with loving your neighbor is not a phenomenon unique to the Russian novel. George Eliot is, every bit as much as Tolstoy and Dostoevsky, a novelist of neighborly love, but she has a more literal and territorial understanding of neighborliness—neighbors ought to

---

[29] Leo Tolstoy, *War and Peace*, vol. 4, pt. 3, ch. 13-15. Citations are from the Pevear/Volokhonsky translation (New York: Knopf, 2007), 1063-64.

be responsible for neighbors in Middlemarch, and this feeds into that novel's construction. Similarly, significant differences in the poetics and ethics of Dostoevsky and Tolstoy derive directly from their respective approaches to the suffering of others and to the call to love your neighbor. The worlds of Tolstoy's novels are haunted by the same problems of who is my neighbor, and what does his pain have to do with me, but his novels are about circumscribing the spheres of liability to pain. In contrast, for Dostoevsky, in whose novels random encounters with strangers are central, your neighbor is the body in pain on the road between Jerusalem and Jericho. Dostoevsky's heroes are always on that road, as students will see when they read beyond Raskolnikov's nightmare.

7

TEXT PLUS TEXT

Chekhov's "In Exile" and "The Student": Text/Countertext as Strategy

Andrew R. Durkin

One of the most useful strategies for helping students perceive specific features of works of literature (or of other arts) is the use of a text and countertext(s) or a text set, that is, a pair or group of texts that can be related in terms of theme, plot, narrative devices, or other elements. The mere selection of works for most course syllabi, even for courses of a survey nature, implicitly involves a certain amount of selection on the basis of similarity among the works chosen for inclusion, but the deliberate "seeding" of syllabi with groups of texts with clear interrelations can provide for an illuminating contrast and comparison (that beloved duo of the essay question) of two or more texts. Text sets can, for example, comprise works of a given genre and theme (e.g., love lyrics) or a single narrative in differing media (*War and Peace* and its film treatments). Teachers of Russian literature have particularly rich possibilities for this sort of instruction in that Russian authors have perhaps been more cognizant than writers in other literatures of preceding texts and more explicit in their references to such works. Additional possibilities for defining a text set include their having a common theme (the fate of the *intelligent* in the post-Revolutionary period) or plot element (the duel from Pushkin's "The Shot" through Lermontov, Turgenev, Chekhov, and Kuprin to Nabokov's "An Affair of Honor"), as well as being works that can be treated as "aftershocks" to a cataclysmic literary event. For instance, Chekhov's "The Lady with the Little Dog," Bunin's "Sunstroke," and Nabokov's "Spring in Fialta" all restage the meeting between Anna and Vronsky in *Anna Karenina* in order to rewrite, in various ways, the ethical and social implications of that event. (Even if the originating text, in this case Tolstoy's novel, is not included in the text set, students who have read it can usually be counted on to summarize the key plot elements to their peers, or a brief synopsis can be provided.)

Of course all the works of a given author can be classified as members of a text set that is usually designated *The Collected Works of...*, but within that larger category, especially for a prolific author such as Chekhov, smaller (and pedagogically more manageable) subsets can be selected to elucidate crucial aspects of the given author's technique and themes more apparent to students. Close reading of a series of Chekhov stories focusing on children or featuring letters (with an intersection of the two sets in the story "Vanka") can enhance students' attentiveness to detail and difference as they come to perceive some of Chekhov's enduring preoccupations. In the present paper, I would like to examine a text set that consists of two texts from which students can arrive at some notion of one of Chekhov's central concerns, the nature and adequacy of verbal communication.

The stories "In Exile" ("V ssylke," 1892) and "The Student" ("Student," 1894) have received considerable critical attention, but with few exceptions[1] they have not been considered in relation to each other, leaving space for a fruitful juxtaposition of the two texts, which do seem to be closely linked in at least one respect: they both investigate problems of discourse and communication. I would suggest that the two stories jointly explore questions of communicative mode and aesthetic orientation that are expressed primarily in the speech of their respective principal characters, and careful attention to this aspect of the stories can lead students to an increased awareness of the relevance of such linguistic modeling not only in Chekhov but in other authors as well.

Beginning with "In Exile," the earlier of the two stories, it is perhaps helpful to have students first consider aspects of the story that seem to be purposely reduced to a minimum (although that

---

[1]   Richard Peace, "'In Exile' and Russian Fatalism," in *Reading Chekhov's Text*, ed. Robert Louis Jackson (Evanston, IL: Northwestern University Press, 1993), 137-44.

reduction itself may be significant). Most importantly, the setting is presented in an extremely laconic or schematic fashion, its minimal, abstract, or elemental quality an ultimate, existential landscape. In "In Exile," each element of the setting reinforces the stark significance of every other: the bank of a Siberian river opposite a small settlement, the nearest human space; the flat and featureless terrain, with only the clay banks of the river providing relief; in all, a barren boundary zone, with intimations of the meaning-less flow of time and of life devoid of human significance. The situation is liminal, on a geographic and human boundary. Time, too, is at a boundary, between the cold of winter and an uncertain spring.

Like the setting, the cast of characters within this empty space is minimal, consisting of a group of oarsmen for a ferry that crosses the river. The focus of human activity is a small fire; beside it sit the two central characters, whose conflicting visions and versions of human existence form the central issue of the story. On the one hand is Semyon Tolkovyi (a nickname meaning "he who makes sense" or "he who explains"), sixty, a long-term convict, strong and hale, totally adjusted to his environment and his situation, and seemingly indifferent to others; on the other is a young, even childish-looking Tartar, nameless, recently and unjustly sentenced. The Tartar is ill, in rags, shivering, repulsed by the setting in which he finds himself, beset by fears, and haunted by memories of his young wife back in Simbirsk.

Given the deliberate restriction of elements, such as setting, characters, and physical action, that often figure prominently in fiction, readers are faced with the possibility that in this story speech in large part takes on the functions of character and action, with contrast between the two main characters played out primarily on the level of their respective speech or discourse. What each character says and, even more importantly, the manner in which he says it, the relation between what he says and the context, and the contrastive interaction between the two discourses, together give rise to the "real" meaning of the story, which is perhaps not so much about philosophies of life as it is about the modes of perception and communication that give rise to one's philosophy of life. Esthetics underlies ethics; how one speaks or tells a story becomes a metaphor for how one lives.

With this new focus, readers are able to look beyond what the characters say (although that is significant too) to the manner in which they say it, and what the implicit view of existence of a given mode of expression might be. Semyon speaks explicitly and at length of how to live; true to his nickname, he does explain to the Tartar what life in Siberia, and by implication everywhere, is or should be. His first statement, "Оно, конечно, тут не рай" ("It's true, it's no paradise here"),[2] is the first quoted speech in the story and in large measure sums up Semyon's vision of life, just as his second statement, "привыкнешь" ("You'll get used to it") expresses the core of his ethics. It may be pointed out to students that Semyon's position in fact has distant philosophical antecedents. He espouses a radical Stoicism, or rather a provincial Cynicism, since Chekhov, who read Marcus Aurelius closely, doubtless recognized the strong altruistic dimension in Stoicism. A Siberian Diogenes, Semyon boasts of his hard-won indifference to all that is external to himself, whether it is social or physical. His appeal to animals as models of self-sufficiency may echo the Cynics' recourse to such analogies, as the name given to their school, from a Greek word for dog, reflects.

> Щука и нельма под водой, а я над водой. И слава богу. Ничего мне не надо. Дай бог всякому такой жизни. ... А теперь довел себя до такой точки, что могу голый на земле спать и траву жрать. И дай бог всякому такой жизни. Ничего мне не надо и никого я не боюсь, и так себя понимаю, что богаче и вольнее меня человека нет. (8:43)

> The pike and the nel'ma [a Siberian fish] are under the water and I am above the water. And thanks be to God. I don't need anything. God grant everyone such a life. ... Now I have gotten myself to the point that I can sleep naked on the

---

2   Anton Pavlovich Chekhov, *Polnoe sobranie sochinenii i pisem v tridtsati tomakh* (Moscow: Nauka, 1974-83), part 1: *Sochineniia*, 8:42. All subsequent page references are listed in the text.

ground and feed on grass. And God grant everyone this sort of life. I don't need anything and I'm not afraid of anyone, and I understand myself so well that a person richer or freer than I am doesn't exist.

Semyon then illustrates his argument through an extended account of the tribulations of Vasily Sergeevich, a *barin* (gentleman) who has been exiled to the region. At first Vasily Sergeevich's wife joins him, but then she runs off with a local official, abandoning her husband and daughter. The daughter has fallen ill with tuberculosis, and the father now spends his time seeking medical treatment for her, probably in vain. Vasily Sergeevich's life of striving and dashed hopes emerges onto the level of action toward the end of the story, when he himself calls for the ferry from the opposite shore; he is on his way to fetch a new doctor for his daughter, and Semyon taunts him by repeating the words that Vasily Sergeevich himself had uttered to Semyon years before about the possibility of happiness in exile in Siberia:

"И в Сибири люди живут. Живу-ут!"
На лице у Толкового было торжествующее выражение, как будто он что-то доказал и будто радовался, что вышло именно так, как он предполагал. (8:49)

"Even in Siberia people live. They li–i–ve!"
There was a triumphant expression on Tolkovyi's face as if he had proven something and was rejoicing that things had come out just as he had assumed.

Semyon's ironic appropriation and recontextualization of Vasily Sergeevich's words seems to cap the inexorable logic of his argument against the value of the life of the feelings. He parodically turns the speech of another into a component of his own attempt at authoritative discourse, which permits no alternative statement the right to autonomous existence.[3]

---

[3]   Mikhail Mikhailovich Bakhtin, "Slovo v romane," in *Voprosy literatury i*

Given Semyon's rhetorical barrage and his appeal to a confirming instance, students often initially take Semyon's position to be as convincing as he himself does. (It may be useful to stress the vocabulary of logical proof ["он что-то доказал ... что вышло именно так, как он предполагал"] surrounding Semyon's statements, but also the qualification of that proof ["как будто"] by the narrator.) In apparent confirmation of the rightness of Semyon's principles, his predictions of the collapse of the *barin's* hopes have become unfortunate truth, and the Tartar's dreams of his wife joining him seem equally doomed to failure.

Students might be asked to consider, or even debate, how convincing these arguments in fact are; even if they are morally repugnant, are they nevertheless persuasive? Is the author implicitly endorsing them, or are they implicitly undercut and/or countered by other elements in the text? While head-on refutation does not seem to be provided, could there be other, less direct, means of refutation in operation? Upon consideration, students often recognize that there are significant intrinsic flaws in Semyon's position and by implication in his argument. Most obviously, Semyon is nothing if not verbose; his tale concerning Vasily Sergeevich occupies over two pages— that is, twenty-five per cent of the entire text of the final version of the story. Semyon's interminable, if relentlessly logical, argument unintentionally exposes his emotional closedness, but his extended diatribe also reveals deeper flaws in his discourse, both in its style and in its relation to the context. Semyon's boast of his need for no man, his entire "wisdom" of self-isolation and imperviousness, is undercut by his very loquacity, which indicates a suppressed desire to communicate, a need for others to impress (or oppress) with his own truth. (His nickname may suggest that this verbal behavior is in fact habitual.) Semyon is not truly content in his isolation, but lies in wait, eager to enter into dialogue (or rather directed monologue) in a decidedly aggressive manner. With both of the people to whom he speaks, the Tartar and Vasily Sergeevich, his objective is to prove

---

estetiki: Issledovaniia raznykh let (Moscow: Khudozhestvennaia literatura, 1975), 156.

his own view of life and mode of existence correct and theirs wrong. But Semyon's very act of speaking undercuts the central point of his "doctrine" and "unproves" Semyon. In terms of Roman Jakobson's classic analysis of the elements and functions involved in an act of communication, Semyon seeks to establish contact with a listener in order to convey a message denying the very need for contact.[4] The need to communicate the lack of a need to communicate ultimately communicates a need to communicate.

Second, there is the question of the sort of story Semyon tells—what are its merits as a story, and should we accept it as esthetically adequate? The continuation of the "back-story" of the *barin* into the present would at first glance seem to prove Semyon's point that striving for connection beyond the self is doomed to failure, but this apparent inevitability is in a sense a weakness of his story specifically as story: it is so closely linked to its initial premise, so completely a demonstration of it, that it is redundant, more a geometrical proof inexorably derived from axioms than a story that reveals something new about human beings or about life in its variability. In other words, Semyon is no Chekhov; Semyon's story leaves no room for inference or discovery by the reader.

The redundancy of Semyon's story and the weakness of his whole argument are underscored stylistically by his numerous repetitions. He throws back in Vasily Sergeevich's face words with which he had taunted him on previous occasions. His final comment in the story, "привыкнет" ("[The Tartar will] get used to it") is the third time he uses the word to or about the Tartar and repeats one of his initial statements ("привыкнешь"/"You'll get used to it"). Along with his ironic use of "People can live here!" to the *barin*, the word sums up his philosophy of life; the repetitions suggest the static, dead quality of such accommodation to the status quo. Significantly, unlike the *barin*, whom we see in motion, or the Tartar, who imagines himself in other settings and circumstances, or even the other ferrymen, who will move on after the spring flood

---

[4]   Roman Jakobson, "Closing Statement: Linguistics and Poetics," in *Style in Language*, ed. Thomas A. Sebeok (Cambridge, MA: MIT Press, 1960), 353ff.

subsides, Semyon will remain where he is, guiding a cable ferry back and forth across the river, as he apparently has done for some years. Of all the characters, Semyon is the most rooted to a single spot, the least capable of movement in any sense, physical or psychological.

In his opening statement, Semyon boasts that, unlike others, he has gained self-understanding: "I understand myself"/ "Я ... себя понимаю." Unwittingly, he claims to have fulfilled the command of the Delphic Oracle ("Know thyself"/*gnothi sauton*), in some ways the point of departure for all Greek and later Western philosophy. The flaws in his discourse suggest, on the contrary, that Semyon knows not himself, but a false version of himself that he has constructed and invested in rather heavily.

Readers who resist the seemingly inexorable force of Semyon's argument for egotistical isolation can find an emotional ally, if not an entirely adequate counter-argument, in the Tartar's response. The weakness of Semyon's philosophy of negation and the repulsiveness of his mode of life are readily perceived by the Tartar, who responds at last with an outburst, in his broken Russian, that equates Semyon with his dead surroundings:

> Он хорошо... хорошо, а ты — худо! Ты худо! Барин хоро-
> шая душа, отличный, а ты зверь, ты худо! Барин живой,
> а ты дохлый... Бог создал человека, чтоб живой был, чтоб
> и радость была, и тоска была, и горе было, а ты хочешь
> ничего, значит, ты не живой, а камень, глина! Камню надо
> ничего и тебе ничего... Ты камень — и бог тебя не любит,
> а барина любит! (8:49-50)

> He [Vasily Sergeevich] good... good, but you bad! You bad!
> *Barin* a good soul, excellent man, but you beast, you bad! *Barin*
> alive, but you croaked... God made man for to be alive, for to
> be joy, and be longing, and be grief, but you want nothing,
> means you not alive, but stone, clay! Stone need nothing and
> you nothing... You stone—and God doesn't love you, but
> loves *barin*!

By appropriating some of Semyon's concepts and words (зверь as a more generic term for the animals Semyon claims to emulate; тебе ничего [не надо]—you need nothing) and reversing their moral significance, the Tartar guilelessly plays his interlocutor's own game with the *barin*, appropriating Semyon's words and reaccenting them. The Tartar offers the essential ethical criticism of the bestial quality of Semyon's suppression of feeling for others. The Tartar certainly elicits greater sympathy from the reader (as does his moral ally, Vasily Sergeevich): he is young, suffering from fever, in an alien environment, unjustly convicted, and in love with his young wife. Most of all, he is alive, physically and emotionally: he is sensitive to the cold, the wind pierces him through the holes in his rags, and he feeds the campfire, which serves as a correlative to his own self-consumption in emotion. His suffering proves the intensity of his view of life. Like many of Chekhov's characters, the Tartar is a "pathetic" in the root sense, a sufferer for whom experience, even with attendant anguish, serves as the guarantee of life and humanity. He transcends time and space, at least subjectively; escaping this alien, inhuman place, he transports himself in dreams back to his home in Simbirsk. All times and places are not equivalent and therefore meaningless for him as they are for Semyon. Like Vasily Sergeevich, the Tartar may be fated to disillusionment and suffering, even to early death, but at least his feelings endow his fate with value and fill the void of empty existence.

The Tartar is at a great disadvantage in speaking with the rhetorically adept Semyon, partly because Russian is not the Tartar's native language and he speaks only a broken version of it; in fact, his linguistic vulnerability may well be a reason for Semyon's picking on him as an audience in the first place. His "voice" is muted in another sense as well; his few attempts at extended discourse, mainly concerning his wife and the manner in which he was framed, are summarized by the narrator, while Semyon's redundancies are quoted at length, in apparent contradiction to the norms of the Chekhov (and the modern) short story. In all, the Tartar has only one speech other than the one already quoted that is longer than a few words, an earlier outburst of protest against Semyon's patently unfair story about Vasily Sergeevich (although the relevance of the story to himself may account in part for his vehemence):

Жена, дочка... Пускай каторга и пускай тоска, зато он видал и жену и дочку... Ты говоришь, ничего не надо. Но ничего — худо! Жена прожила с ним три года — это ему бог подарил. Ничего — худо, а три года — хорошо. Как не понимай? (8:46)

Wife, daughter... Let prison and let longing, for that he saw both wife and daughter... You say nothing is needed. But nothing—bad! Wife lived with him three years—that God granted him. Nothing—bad, but three years—good. How not understand?

The Tartar's rhetorical question ("How not understand?"/"Как не понимай?") echoes Semyon's boast of understanding himself ("Я себя так понимаю"), but transforms Semyon's assertion into a challenge. The Tartar incorrectly uses an imperative form in his question, but his grammatical error may suggest a moral imperative: how can we *not* carry out the obligation to understand? But paradoxically, understanding is dialogic; it comes through experience, especially shared experience, and we understand ourselves only by first understanding others, their joys and sorrows. The Delphic command to comprehend the self may in fact be a dead end if the self is taken as an isolated entity; we cannot understand our self without reference to and interaction with others.

At this juncture, some students may feel the "point" of the story has been discovered, the argument settled. However, given the doubts that the story raises about the validity of Semyon's argument (as well as the questioning of certitudes typical of Chekhov's outlook as a whole), one might confront students with the possibility that the story itself ultimately rejects such a neat apportioning of "correct" and "incorrect." More specifically, even given that the Tartar's outbursts expose the fundamental flaws in Semyon's ethical position, could the Tartar's own discourse be, in turn, not without weaknesses of its own? As the Tartar's broken but meaningful speech suggests, his characteristic "genre" is not extended realistic narrative, Semyon's *forte*. Rather it is the lyric, imagistic, associative, and non-discursive. Significantly, the Tartar does not tell tales, he dreams dreams. The Tartar at one point dozes off and imagines himself back in Simbirsk province (8:47-48). He is uncertain whether this is a dream, and, when he is awakened again, he isn't sure whether he is home on the Volga or on the bank of the unnamed river in Siberia. The insubstantial and evanescent quality of dreams points to the central problem or flaw in the Tartar's position of maximal emotional intensity. In dreams, the possibility of ordering or controlling subjective experience is reduced; the creator of dreams and their symbols becomes their helpless victim. Analogously, the Tartar's inarticulate speech takes on the qualities of lyric, the genre perhaps closest to dream in its subjective quality. As Yury Lotman points out, the lexicon of a poetic text, particularly a lyric, forms the entire "language" of the text and constitutes its semantic universe.[5] The Tartar's restricted vocabulary in Russian and the ungrammatical and asyntactic quality of his speech create a discourse in which, because of lexical and grammatical reduction, each element takes on heightened significance, but that significance becomes increasingly less definable or communicable. As the Tartar's frequent silence, the narrator's paraphrase of much of his speech, and his few broken direct utterances all suggest, subjective, lyrical experience becomes, in proportion to its intensity, private and idiosyncratic. The antinomy of Chekhovian private symbols, as each of the Tartar's words becomes, lies in the fact that the more strongly they are felt by the individual, the greater their power to isolate the individual in a world of purely subjective meanings. (As early as 1884, in "Oysters" ["Ustritsy"], Chekhov was investigating the antinomies of words as symbols vs. words as signs.)

The impossibility of ordering and controlling experience through symbols, the danger of unchecked emotional intensity leading to non-communication and isolation, is summed up in the concluding image of the Tartar refusing to leave his fire to sleep with the other ferrymen in the minimal shelter and society of their hut (as even the self-proclaimed isolationist Semyon does at the end of the story, again suggesting the implicit contradiction of his

---

5   Iu. M. Lotman, *Analiz poeticheskogo teksta: Struktura stikha* (Leningrad: Prosveshchenie, 1972), 86.

position). Instead, he continues his metaphoric self-immolation, alone at the fire. The others, in the hut, hear him crying:

> Со двора послышались звуки, похожие на собачий вой.
> — Что это? Кто это там?
> — Это татарин плачет.
> — Ишь ты... Чудак!
> — Привы-ыкнет! — сказал Семен и тотчас же заснул.
> Скоро заснули и остальные. А дверь так и осталась не затворенной. (8:50)

> From outside there were heard sounds resembling the howling of a dog.
> "What's that? Who's there?"
> "That's the Tartar crying."
> "Well now... He's crazy!"
> "He'll get u-used to it!" said Semyon and fell asleep at once.
> The others fell asleep too. And the door remained open.

The Tartar's dog-like howling (собачий вой), pure, formless emotive expression, its full meaning incommunicable, reveals an unexpected parallel with the cynical Semyon, the beast (зверь) who can sleep naked on the ground and eat grass. Taken to their limit, the positions of *both* characters lead to isolation, as well as to self-contradiction and paradox. On the level of discourse, like on the ethical level, the story seems to end in non-resolution.[6] On the one hand, excessively referential discourse is marshaled in support of a predetermined position, which in turn undermines the purported objectivity of that referential discourse. On the other, discourse approaches pure lyric in its symbolic intensity, but the greater the intensity, the more the boundary between poetic and purely emotive language is erased and effective communication becomes problematic.[7] A possible means of resolving this dilemma and

---

[6] V. B. Kataev, "'V ssylke': spor o schast'e i asketizme," in *Chekhov i Lev Tolstoi* (Moscow: Nauka, 1980), 224.

[7] Jakobson, "Closing Statement," 357-58.

offering a truly effective method of communication is absent. The final image of the door left open (literally, left unclosed) suggests the lack of a resolution but also hints at the possibility of one; however, that resolution lies outside that door, beyond the limits of the story itself. Perhaps the story's final suggestion is that neither figure's position is adequate, and that only the overall narrative, which can encompass both the realistic and the lyric, the logical and the irrational, provides a valid form of narrative.

The indeterminate ending of "In Exile" finds, if not full resolution, at least a possible alternative in a brief but subtly powerful story, "The Student" (1894). The inclusion of the two stories in a single set can enhance the significance of each text for readers by highlighting the multiplicity of possible resolutions of a single question, namely what constitutes adequate communication. "The Student" describes an incident that at first seems even more trivial than the dialogue by the river in "In Exile": on Good Friday, a seminary student retells to two peasant women the Gospel account of Peter's denial of Christ. Even on a single reading, students can readily discern many of the story's affinities with "In Exile," as well as possibly significant differences. As in the earlier story, the setting is a barren landscape, although now in the Russian heartland. The season is again an uncertain spring; however, the hesitation between the dead of winter and the rebirth of spring is more prominent, as befits a story in which the central character wavers between doubt and faith. As in "In Exile," an embedded narrative occupies close to a quarter of the total text, and in this case this sub-narrative is one well-known to the central character, the seminary student Ivan Velikopolsky, to his pious audience of two, and of course to the Russian reader of 1894 as well. However, it is precisely the embedded narrative's apparent lack of "newness" that helps to foreground it as a paradigm of discourse. While Velikopolsky's narrative does not seem to have overt ethical import in the manner of the statements of either Semyon or the Tartar in "In Exile," it nevertheless relates to them as yet another model of discourse, and one that may resolve the complementary defects of the two modes of speech in "In Exile."

As with the discourse in "In Exile," there are clear links drawn between the story told and the context in which it is told. A fire at which the two women are standing provides a focus for the central dialogue, as in "In Exile," but this fire also generates the initial metaphoric link between the immediate reality and the situation in the Gospel; Velikopolsky's perception of this similarity prompts him to tell the story of Peter's denials. The women, the widow Vasilisa and her daughter Lukerya, also come to perceive these relations, as suggested by their reactions to Velikopolsky's story (profound attention and tears), and they presumably make an emotional identification between the Gospel account and their own situation, specifically the intensity of Peter's anguish and remorse and their own emotional experiences. Thus the three characters come to share in a process of making metaphors, linking themselves in a creative or poetic community, in a marked difference from the radical separation between the characters in "In Exile" and their opposing discourses. This miniature community, however transitory it may be, is able to form because at its core lies a different sort of discourse, one that attracts agreement rather than demanding assent (Semyon's relentless story) or precluding full comprehension (the Tartar's symbols and visions). Velikopolsky's narrative is neither cognitive didacticism nor symbolic lyricism, but to a large extent corrects the deficiencies of both. Instead, it tends toward the revelation of the mythic, not a statement of logical fact or an expression of individual emotion; it depends for its efficacy on the re-actualization of a text that is preserved in cultural memory and that in a new context is capable of generating new meanings.[8] As a mythic text, it makes manifest a culturally persistent paradigm renewed in specific re-tellings or re-performances that connect the structuring events that occurred *in illo tempore* with the here and now, replacing profane time with sacred time and full existence. In Velikopolsky's actualization, the interaction of these two phases of

---

[8] Iu. M. Lotman, "Pamiat' v kul'turologicheskom osveshchenii," in *Izbrannye stat'i v 3 tomakh*, vol. 1: *Stat'i po semiotike i tipologii kul'tury* (Tallinn: Aleksandra, 1992), 200-202.

time finds expression on the stylistic level, with citation from the Gospel, with its archaic forms ("исшед," "плакася") juxtaposed to colloquial Russian ("горько-горько," "тихий-тихий, темный-темный сад"). (Although the contrasts of archaic and modern forms are perhaps greater with the Church Slavonic and modern Russian forms that Velikopolsky interweaves, students might get some sense of the mix of stylistic registers by comparing the King James versions of the relevant passages [Luke 22:54-62 and Matt. 26:69-75] with their own retelling of the incident.) The operation of "translating" between the fixed forms of sacred text and contemporary colloquial forms ("исшед вон"/"вышел со двора"; "плакася горько"/"горько-горько заплакал") provides a figure of the overall function of Velikopolsky's narrative:

> [Петр] Вспомнил, очнулся, пошел со двора и горько-горько заплакал. В евангелии сказано: "И исшед вон, плакася горько". Воображаю: тихий-тихий, темный-темный сад, и в тишине едва слышатся глухие рыдания.... (8:308)

> [Peter] remembered, came to his senses, left the courtyard, and began to weep so bitterly. In the Gospel it is said: "He went out, and wept bitterly" [Matt. 26:75]. I imagine it: the garden so dark and so quiet, and in the stillness there can be barely heard muffled sobs....

It is the fusion of the permanent and the contingent that frees Velikopolsky's narrative from the falsely authoritative on the one hand and the entirely subjective on the other. The combination of enduring structure and present freedom makes his account both communicable and accessible to his audience. The gospel text functions as a template or paradigm that, like a folkloric text,[9] is actualized in the specific moment, taking on full existence and

---

9   Roman Jakobson and Petr Bogatyrev, "K probleme razmezhevaniia fol'kloristiki i literaturovedeniia," in Roman Jakobson, *Selected Writings*, vol. 4: *Slavic Epic Studies* (The Hague: Mouton, 1966), 16-18.

meaning only in a particular context and only (at least in this particular way) for the immediate participants. At least in the moment of telling his story, Velikopolsky is an artist or a priest, capable of fusing past and present, universal and particular; he is performing on the level of discourse alone what he will accomplish through full ritual (language fused with representative action) in the profession for which he is in fact preparing. This interpenetration of times and existential levels makes the renewed mythic story an effective work of art. Others are able to bring their own meaning to it, but with neither the story nor an interpretation of it being imposed on them. The myth thus transcends the individual, linking people in the present, and also transcends time, connecting past and present both metaphorically (the fires are similar) and metonymically (the story itself has survived until now and is being transmitted once again). In a valid form of art, which Chekhov is outlining here, discourse overcomes the limits of self and of historical moment. Art indeed redeems man from his betrayals of himself. The text that Velikopolsky selects is significant in this regard: Peter uses language, or abuses it through lying, to deny his relation with Jesus, to reject interconnection and responsibility, although repentance and reconnection triumph at the end. Language can potentially both sever and create connection. Similarly, the full story that we read moves from disjunction and meaninglessness to conjunction and meaningfulness.[10] Velikopolsky's act of narration functions as a model of the narrative as a whole—through the mythic dimension of art, the student touches his audience and creates a community, just as the narrator, through the story he tells (with its embedded story), touches the reader.

Velikopolsky's recreation of mythic connection (отношение — "relation"—in the text) and his recognition of that connection in terms of a chain of linkages are mirrored by interconnections on the textual level with prior works of fiction, in particular

[10] Robert Louis Jackson, "Chekhov's 'The Student,'" in *Reading Chekhov's Text*, ed. Robert Louis Jackson (Evanston, IL: Northwestern University Press, 1993), 127-33.

Dostoevsky's *The Brothers Karamazov*. (Students may recall the image of the interlinkage of all existence in Zosima's teachings; if not, the passage can be provided.) It is not the character himself but rather the narrator and the reader who are capable of drawing these literary connections, of creating a further metaphorical relation between the immediate text and cultural memory. The reader is thus placed in a position with regard to the full text analogous to that of Velikopolsky to his spoken text within the world of the story: to perceive connections, to make metaphors, to create meaning where meaning has been absent. Some have questioned the validity and permanence of Velikopolsky's final perception of the connectedness and "sense" ("смысл," 309, the final word of the story) of existence.[11] Velikopolsky's vision of coherence may well be transitory for him, especially given the dynamic quality of many of Chekhov's characters, but this does not automatically lead to the conclusion that that vision is invalidated from the perspective of the reader, who has perceived meaningful connections encoded in the text beyond Velikopolsky's own horizon of perception. While characters and readers both have their limitations, the knowledge of readers, provided with the information of the entire text, may exceed that of characters.

If we return to the notion of a text set that consists of "In Exile" and "The Student," students can in retrospect consider the implications of reading the two stories one against the other as stories about stories and about the possibility of effective communication. If "In Exile" ends with the unresolved alternatives of either a "realistic" story with a clear, accessible, but ultimately oppressive message ("Live as I do, want nothing"), a mode hardly unfamiliar in the Russian nineteenth-century tradition, or an emotional vision, expressed in lyrical but dangerously personal symbols ("You are clay"), "The Student" offers the mediating example of a narrative that is both personal and social, realistic and lyrical, resolving such

---

[11] Vol'f Shmid [Wolf Schmidt], "Mnimoe prozrenie Ivana Velikopol'skogo ('Student')," in *Proza kak poeziia: Stat'i o povestvovanii v russkoi literature* (St. Petersburg: Gumanitarnoe agentstvo "Akademicheskii proekt," 1994), 167-83.

polarities in a mythic discourse that is grounded in cultural tradition and permits valid communication. Significantly, in this story — which, according to the memoirs of his contemporaries, Chekhov considered his favorite and referred to as a counter-statement to critics who accused him of pessimism (8:507) — the central character is in fact a student, someone who is diligent or striving (from Latin *studere*). The project of being a student, mastering the past in order to engage the future, can be seen as paradigmatic of the situation of the reader and of the general dynamic of culture. In some sense we are all students, extending from past to future the human cultural chain that Velikopolsky briefly envisions.

8

TEXT PLUS TEXT PLUS TEXT

Three Deaths:
A Boy, a Goose, and an Infant

Robert Louis Jackson

I focus here on episodes involving death within three of Chekhov's stories: "Enemies" (*Vragi*, 1887), "Kashtanka" (1887), and "In the Ravine" (*V ovrage*, 1900).[1] In each of these episodes, to one degree or another, the spiritualization and sometimes estheticization of the experience of death contrasts with a starkly naturalistic, even clinical depiction of it as a happening. The episodes, however, evince no movement on Chekhov's part toward any religious resolution of the questions of mortality. Rather, they suggest that the "soul" of the individual human being, his mind, his living life, is earth-bound and at one with his entire material being and the life of nature. Death extinguishes this "soul." Chekhov appears to deny any conventional religious notion of an after-life. "I am now without

---

[1]   I have written essays on each of these stories individually. See my essay "'The Enemies': A Story at War with Itself," in *Reading Chekhov's Text*, ed. Robert Louis Jackson (Evanston, IL: Northwestern University Press, 1993), 63-73; "Chekhov and Proust: A Posing of the Problem," in *The Supernatural in Slavic and Baltic Literature: Essays in Honor of Victor Terras*, ed. Amy Mandelker and Roberta Reeder (Columbus, OH: Slavica, 1988), 200-13; the essay appears in Russian under the title, "Chekhov i Prust: Postanovka problemy," in *Chekhoviana: Chekhov i Frantsiia* (Moscow: Nauka, 1992), 129-40; "Requiem in Chekhov's 'Ravine': Lipa and the Death of Nikifor," in *Itinera Slavica: Studien zu Literatur und Kultur der Slaven; Festschrift für Rolf-Dieter Kluge zum 65. Geburtstag*, ed. Heide Willich-Lederbogen et al. (Munich: Verlag Otto Sagner, 2002), 113-22. The first two parts of my discussion in this essay focus on material I did *not* discuss, or passed over briefly, in the above-mentioned essays. The third part of the present essay is a condensed and revised version of parts of my earlier discussion of "In the Ravine" (see above).

religion," he writes on March 9, 1892, to I. L. Leontiev (Shcheglov) in connection with his own religious upbringing.[2]

His comments in his correspondence and notebook on the questions of death provide ample evidence of his materialist orientation; at the same time they speak of a highly spiritualized materialism. "We talked about immortality," Chekhov wrote in his notebook shortly after Tolstoy visited him in 1897 at the clinic where he was recovering from serious tuberculosis-based hemorrhaging.[3] He wrote further about this visit in a letter of April 16, 1897 to M. O. Menshikov:

> [Tolstoy] accepts immortality in the Kantian sense; he presumes that all of us (people and animals) will live in an elemental way (reason, love), the essence and goals of which remain a secret to us. To me this element or force presents itself in the aspect of a formless bitter cold mass; my "I," my individuality, my consciousness will merge with this mass— [now] this kind of immortality I don't need, and I don't understand it, and Lev Nikolaevich is amazed that I don't understand it.[4]

A short time later, according to his friend and publisher, A. S. Suvorin, Chekhov spoke bluntly about death as

> Cruelty—a revolting punishment. If individuality is annihilated after death, then there is no life. I can't console myself with the fact that I will merge with sighs and pains in a universal life which has a purpose. I don't even know this purpose. Death arouses something more than horror. But when you live, you think little of it. At least I don't. And when I die I'll find out what it's all about. It's terrible to become nothing. They carry you off to the cemetery, come back home

2   A. P. Chekhov, *Polnoe sobranie sochinenii i pisem v tridtsati tomakh* (Moscow: Nauka, 1974-83), part 2: *Pis'ma*, 5:20. The works (*sochineniia*) and letters (*pis'ma*) are numbered separately. All translations are my own.

3   Ibid., part 1: *Sochineniia*, 17:225.

4   Ibid., *Pis'ma*, 6:332.

and start drinking tea and saying hypocritical things. It's revolting to think of this.[5]

Revolting as the thought may have been, it turns up in his notebook: "Looking out the window at a dead person who is being carried off: 'You've died, they're taking you to the cemetery, but I'm going out for breakfast.'"[6]

As for what non-being, or the void of death, is all about, Chekhov a few pages later in his notebook observes: "There is no possible mortal standpoint for judging non-being, what it means not to be a human being."[7]

According to the Russian writer Ivan Bunin (1870-1953), Chekhov frequently argued that immortality, any kind of life after death, was "absolute rubbish," a "superstition," and that "every superstition is horrible. One must think clearly and boldly." Bunin records Chekhov as saying, "I can prove to you as twice two is four that immortality is rubbish." At other times, however, Bunin maintains Chekhov would insist even more emphatically that "we can in no way disappear after death. For a certainty we will live after death. Immortality is a fact. Just wait and I'll prove it to you."[8] These comments suggest, perhaps, a certain playfulness and

---

[5] *Dnevnik A. S. Suvorina*, ed. Mikhail Krichevskii (Moscow-Petrograd: I. D. Frenkel', 1923), 165. The entry is dated July 23, 1897. In a letter to his sister, Masha, dated November 13, 1898, Chekhov writes more gently and philosophically about death. He remarks on the cyclical character of all nature and life, then adds (asking Masha to pass this idea on to their mother): "Man cannot be happy and joyful his entire life, losses always await him, he cannot save himself from death, even if he be Alexander the Macedonian, — and one must be ready for everything and relate to everything as to something inevitably necessary, however sad that may be. One should do one's duty as far as possible, however — and that's that" (Chekhov, *Pis'ma*, 7:32).

[6] Chekhov, *Sochineniia*, 17:95.

[7] "Ни одна наша смертная мерка не годится для суждения о небытии, о том, что не есть человек." Ibid., 101.

[8] Ivan A. Bunin, *O Chekhove: Nezakonchennaia rukopis'*, introd. M. A. Aldanov (New York: Chekhov Publishing House, 1955), 98-99.

provocation on Chekhov's part. Viewed out of context, in any case, they are difficult to evaluate.

"Twice two is four" turns up again in Chekhov's letter of December 30, 1902, to the Russian ballet impresario, Sergei Diaghilev. Present-day culture, he remarks, is the beginning of work that will continue for tens of thousands of years as a result of which "mankind will come to know the truth of the real God" ("познало истину настоящего Бога"), that is, not simply make guesses or seek him out in Dostoevsky, but know him as clearly as one knows that "twice two is four."[9] What Chekhov had in mind here is not clear. His "truth about the real God" does not seem connected with personal immortality or anything resembling religion as we know it.

The idea expressed to Bunin that "we can in no way disappear after death" finds a more concrete formulation in Chekhov's story *My Life* (*Moia zhizn'*, 1896): "If I had wanted to order a ring for myself," the narrator remarks, "I should have chosen an inscription like this: 'Nothing passes.' I believe nothing passes without leaving a trace, and that even our slightest step has significance for our present and future life" (9:279).

In a letter to Suvorin dated May 7, 1889, Chekhov adamantly defends his materialist convictions. "Everything that lives on earth is by necessity materialistic…. To forbid man a materialist orientation is tantamount to blocking the search for truth. Outside of matter there is no experience, no knowledge, in other words, no truth…. It seems to me that when a corpse is being dissected," Chekhov writes again, "even the most inveterate spiritualist must *necessarily* confront the question: where is the soul here?" Chekhov is not saying that soul or spirit is a fiction, but that "one cannot separate soul from the body,"[10] as one cannot separate life from nature.[11] The

---

9   Chekhov, *Pis'ma*, 11:106.

10   Chekhov, *Pis'ma*, 3:208.

11   "Goethe the poet," Chekhov remarked in a letter of May 15, 1889, to Aleksei
     Suvorin, "coexisted splendidly with Goethe the naturalist" (*Pis'ma*, 3:216).
     As the late Boris Christa noted, for both Chekhov and Goethe the "human
     mind and spirit and, in fact, all the metaphysical dimension of existence,
     is not a separable abstract identity but an essential ingredient of nature.

dead body, we might sum up, is soul-less, while the living body is soul-full.[12] This thought finds signal expression in a brief episode in "Enemies."

The Death of a Boy

In the opening two lines of "Enemies," the reader learns that the son of Dr. Kirilov, a boy of six, has just died of diphtheria. In the second line, the doctor's wife is pictured on her knees at her dead son's bedside, overwhelmed with despair. Several paragraphs later, the narrator contrasts the stark, clinical image of the dead boy's face with the image of an anguished mother at her son's bedside.

As the exhausted and stunned Dr. Kirilov walks from his office toward the bedroom where but moments before he had fought and lost the battle to save his son, a "broad swath of light, together with the heavy, stale smell of carbolic acid and ether … emerged from a slightly opened door leading from the office to the bedroom." Kirilov enters a brightly-lit room where his son lies dead and his wife is kneeling beside the boy's bed. The narrator speaks of a "dead silence" (мертвый покой) prevailing in a room that but a short while ago was a scene of desperation and turmoil:

> Here in the bedroom there reigned a peace like the dead …
> a large lamp on the table brightly illuminated the whole
> room. On the bed by the window lay the boy with open eyes
> and an expression of wonder on his face. He did not move,

Spirit is immutable and permanent and finds expression in all facets of life." See Boris Christa, "The Semiotic Expression of *Weltanschauung* in Čechov's Major Plays," in Anton P. Čechov, *Philosophische und religiöse Dimensionen im Leben und im Werk: Vorträge des Zweiten Internationalen Čechov-Symposiums, Badenweiler, 20-24. Oktober 1994,* ed. Vladimir B. Kataev, Rolf-Dieger Kluge, Regine Nohejl (Munich: Verlag Otto Sagner, 1997), 520.

[12] It is no accident that in setting forth what would be sacred to him as a "great writer," what he calls his "program," Chekhov puts the human body in the first place: "My holy of holies," he wrote in a letter to A. N. Pleshcheev, on October 4, 1888, "is the human body, health, mind, talent, inspiration, love, and the most absolute freedom, freedom from violence and lies, whatever form the latter may take." *Pis'ma,* 3:11.

but it seemed that his open eyes with every moment became darker and darker as they receded into his skull (уходили во внутрь черепа). (6:33)

Chekhov limits himself to three details about the boy: his facial expression, the eyes, and the skull. At first sight, the boy's face almost suggests proverbial evangelical wonder or surprise, but this expression is a reflex of rigor mortis. That impression is confirmed by Chekhov's description of the boy's open eyes (typically the locus of light and spirit) becoming "darker and darker as they receded into his skull." A line from Chekhov's letter to Suvorin, cited above, comes to mind: "It seems to me that when a corpse is being dissected even the most inveterate spiritualist must *necessarily* confront the question: where is the soul here?"

Chekhov's verbal painting of this scene, however, is incomplete. In the next paragraph his attention shifts from the dead boy to the grieving mother.

> Hands laid on the body [of her son], her face hidden in the folds of the bed-clothes, the mother kneeled beside the bed. Like the boy she did not stir, but how much living movement was felt in the winding lines of her body and in her hands! She pressed against the bed with all her being, powerfully and possessively, as though she were afraid to violate the restful and comfortable pose which she had found at last for her exhausted body. Blankets, rags, basins, puddles on the floor, brushes, and spoons, a white bottle with lime water, the air, heavy and suffocating—everything was at a standstill [все замерло—literally, everything was dead] and seemed sunk in rest. (6:33)

Everything seems at rest, lifeless. In fact, the body and hands of the exhausted and anguished mother, her whole physical and spiritual being, almost in defiance of her stillness, are alive with "living movement." Chekhov punctuates this observation with an exclamation mark (!)—the traditional sign signifying amazement, astonishment, wonder. Indeed, he has executed a remarkable reversal of perspective on the semantic plane of narration. The "wonder" on the face of the *dead* boy, a visual exclamation, was a delusion. By contrast, the movements and harmonies of the mother's anguished but *living* body and being are a matter of genuine wonder and amazement, an incarnation of spiritual beauty. In a single stroke (!), Chekhov reminds his reader *where the soul is*.

Powerful as this scene is, Chekhov felt a need to underscore its aesthetic and spiritual beauty; that is, to tell the reader what he had already expressed in imagery. "That repulsive horror which people think of when they speak of death was absent in the bedroom," the narrator writes. "In the general numbness everywhere, in the attitude [поза] of the mother, and in the expression of indifference on Dr. Kirilov's face, there was something compelling, touching the heart: precisely that subtle, barely perceptible beauty of human sorrow which people will not soon learn to understand and describe, and which it seems only music can convey" (6:33-34).

Was Chekhov uncertain as to whether the aesthetic and spiritual image of the mother at her dead child's bedside, his representation of the "beauty of human sorrow," his Russian Pietà, constituted a sufficient counterweight to the devastating image of physical death and the general impression of defeat and desperation in the child's bedroom? Whatever the answer, Chekhov continues to emphasize the dance of beauty and death. He calls attention to the "beauty in the gloomy quiet," to the Kirilovs' own awareness of the "lyricism of their situation," one in which their youth had passed and their "right to have children had forever *passed into eternity*" (уходило в вечность). Not lost on the reader is the parallel Chekhov establishes between the preceding image and his earlier view of the dead boy's eyes *"passing into the skull"* (уходили во внутрь черепа), that is, into the void of eternity. If the sensuous materialism of man and nature is the source of a rich aestheticism and spirituality, then the obverse side of that materialism is a revolting horror. "Death," as Chekhov had said to Suvorin, "arouses something more than horror. But when you live, you think little of it."

The Death of Ivan Ivanych

"Primitive dread," the French philosopher, Paul Ricoeur, writes in *Symbols of Evil*, "deserves to be interrogated as our earliest memory."[13] Dr. Dorn in *The Seagull* (act 4) declares to Anna Arkadyevna's anxious brother, Pyotr Sorin, that "fear of death is an animal fear." He goes on to assert, jocularly, that the "only people who consciously fear death are those who believe in eternal life and who are terribly concerned with their sins." Chekhov appears to mark out an area of unconscious, primordial, or animal fear of death, one detached from any conceptual apprehension of death, that is, from any awareness of time and mortality. In any case, he explores this animal dread of death in "An Anxious Night" ("Беспокойная ночь"), the sixth and penultimate chapter of his fantasy tale "Kashtanka" (1887). "An Anxious Night" is not a treatise on animal cognition, any more than is the larger story, "Kashtanka"; rather it imaginatively posits a world of primordial sub-mind and myth where the boundaries of animal and human consciousness appear to meet—a realm of fear and dread (страх), of the uncanny, or *"unheimliche,"* as Freud defined the phenomenon in an essay of 1908.[14]

The story "Kashtanka" focuses as a whole on a dog of the same name who gets separated from her owner on the street one day, is picked up shivering on a doorstep by a circus trainer and performer, and is forthwith integrated into his animal team. "Auntie," or Tetka, as Kashtanka is known in her new circus life, gradually loses all memory of her past. At story's end her old owner and his son recognize her in a circus act and call out her old name, "Kashtanka!" Her memory restored, Kashtanka leaps joyfully and

---

[13] Paul Ricoeur, *The Symbolism of Evil*, trans. Emerson Buchanan (Boston: Beacon Press, 1969), 20.

[14] The "uncanny," in Freud's definition, incarnates a sense of the mysterious and dangerous, of "something" that is normally repressed, something (Freud quotes the German nineteenth-century philosopher, F. W. J. Schelling) "that should have remained hidden and has come into the open." See Sigmund Freud, *The Uncanny*, trans. David McLintock, intro. Hugh Haughton (New York: Penguin, 2003), 132 (originally published as *Psychologie des Unheimlichen*, 1908). Later on Heidegger attributes "angst" (dread, anxiety) to the human being, to *Dasein*, when it becomes aware that it is not "at home." Authentic awareness is a realm of intuition that Heidegger reserves for human beings, but not for animals who are "poor in world." The dread that Chekhov's Kashtanka experiences, whatever its relation to Heidegger's philosophical concepts, certainly is *rich in world*.

dashes over to her old masters. On leaving the circus "she rejoiced that there had not been a moment's break in her life." In a Proustian sense, the past has been recaptured. Prior to this happy event, however, Kashtanka, or "Auntie," as she has been named by her animal trainer, experiences a traumatic night ("An Anxious Night"). The cause of her terrifying anxiety is the dying and death of the grey circus goose who, earlier in the day, had been trampled and mortally wounded by a horse. Ivan Ivanych, as the goose is called, makes his condition known that night by fearful shrieks.[15]

Chekhov describes dying and death in naturalistic detail. His focus, however, is on others' responses to that death: first that of Kashtanka, who recoils in terror and dread from the death agonies of Ivan Ivanych, and second that of the circus master, who knows death, and responds to the death of his beloved goose with grief and pain.

"An Anxious Night" begins ominously for Kashtanka. She was "dreaming a doggy dream in which the janitor seemed to be chasing her with a broom, and she awoke with terror." As a rule she did not fear darkness, but now "for some reason" she felt alarmed and wanted to bark.

> Suddenly not far from her rang out a strange cry that made Auntie shudder and leap on all four paws. It was Ivan Ivanych who was crying out, but his cry was not chatty and confident, as it usually was, but somehow wild, piercing and unnatural, like the screeching of gates opening up. Discerning nothing in the darkness and understanding nothing, she felt even greater terror and growled: "Rrrrr...." (6:441)

---

[15] The analogue to "An Anxious Night" in which the death of Ivan Ivanych plays a pivotal role is Tolstoy's *Death of Ivan Ilych* (1886). This work appeared a year before Chekhov's "Kashtanka." "An Anxious Night" and Tolstoy's story are linked chiefly on the moral-philosophical plane (the themes of dread in the face of death and the triumph over it through love). Both stories have epiphanic endings. The accident that caused Ivan Ivanych's illness and death echoes Ivan Ilych's accidental (though psychologically complex) fall from a ladder.

Kashtanka is unaware that *what* terrifies her is death and dying. Yet she has an intuition of something strange and uncanny. She draws upon canine experience and dreams to make doggy sense of what, to her, is literally inconceivable and unimaginable, and therefore dread-full and awe-full. She dozes again; this time she dreams of eating from a trough and being attacked by two fierce black dogs. A peasant drives them off with a knout, but as soon as he "goes away from the gates," the two dogs again rush upon Kashtanka. And suddenly she again hears a wild screech that causes her to leap up and howl. "It seemed to her that the scream came not from Ivan Ivanych, but from somebody else, a stranger" (посторонний—also outsider, alien one, foreigner) (6:441).

Gates and wild dogs are part of Kashtanka's everyday life, but in the mythopoetic world they represent the gates of Hades and the hellhounds of death that sit between the worlds of life and death, like Hecate's dog, Cerberus, watchdog to the entrance to Hades. The screeching of opening gates, the widening jaws of death, portend the approach of the intruder, death. Kashtanka associates the fearful screaming of Ivan Ivanych with the "посторонний"—the dreaded stranger. Throughout this scene Kashtanka, or "Auntie," anthropomorphizes death.

When the circus master appears with his candlelight, Kashtanka "saw that there was no stranger in the room" (6:441). The light that banishes darkness reveals the dying Ivan Ivanych; he is sprawled strangely on the floor, wings stretched out, beak open, looking "as though he was quite exhausted and wanted something to drink." When the circus master leaves, taking with him the candlelight, Kashtanka again fancies "someone alien" (кто-то чужой) in the darkness: "The most dreadful thing of all was that one could not bite this alien one, since he was invisible and without form [невидим и не имел формы]."[16]

---

[16] The words "invisible and without form" echo Genesis 1:2: "And the earth was invisible and without form" ("Земля же бѣ невидима и неустроена," in the Slavonic Bible Chekhov would have used); these words underscore Kashtanka's inability to conceptualize the dreadful "alien" presence of death. She cannot "bite" it, literally and figuratively. So, too, Augustine of

When he returns to the room a second time, the circus master perceives the dying Ivan Ivanych in the candle's light. That light, however, in Chekhov's use, not only discloses death in all its disfiguring reality but may be said to symbolize the circus master's simple humanity, his tenderness and love for his animals, especially for Ivan Ivanych. "Ivan Ivanych!" he calls out to the motionless goose, "what's this all about, are you dying or something?" And he remembers with despair the accident with the horse (6:442). "Yes, yes, he's dying!" the circus trainer says to Kashtanka, adding, as though to clarify to her the abstract idea of dying: "Death has entered your room."

"'Drink, Ivan Ivanych' he said tenderly, offering a little dish to Ivan Ivanych. 'Drink, my love' [Пей, голубчик]." "'It's no longer possible to do anything!' sighs the master. 'It's all over. Ivan Ivanych is done for!'" At this point, in a picture seen partially from the perspective of Kashtanka and the cat, Chekhov writes: "And brilliant drops inched down his cheeks, such as are on windows when it rains. Not understanding what was the matter, Auntie and Fyodor Timofeich pressed up against him and looked with horror at the goose" (6:443).

The matter in this moment is not only the mystery and horror of death for Kashtanka and the cat, but the reality of grief and love, and the beauty of human sorrow—a beauty that only music can convey, as Chekhov puts it in "Enemies."

The circus master's final words to his beloved Ivan Ivanych are noteworthy:

> "Poor Ivan Ivanych!" said the master, sadly and again with
> a sigh. "And I had been looking forward so much to taking
> you to my dacha in spring, and we would roam together

Hippo (354-430 AD) in his early analysis of Genesis 1:2 struggles vainly to perceive the "formlessness of matter." "My mind turned over forms, foul and horrid in confused array, but still forms. I called it formless *not* because it lacked all form, but because it had such form that, if it ever showed itself, my senses would have turned away from it as from something strange and improper, and man's frail powers would be disturbed by it." See *The Confessions of St. Augustine*, trans. and ed. John K. Ryan (New York: Doubleday, 1960), bk. 12 (Form and Matter), chap. 6, 307.

through the green grass. Dearest animal, my good comrade, you've gone! Now how shall I manage without you!" (6:443)

Touching is the circus trainer's addressing Ivan Ivanych as his *"miloe zhivotnoe"* (dearest animal). Chekhov's symbolic use of the word *"zhivotnoe"* should not be overlooked, for the Church Slavonic root of *"zhivotnoe"* is *"zhivot"* — "life," a word that in Russian may also refer to the belly. The circus trainer's hope had been to wander about through the "green fields" with Ivan Ivanych at his dacha in the spring. The delicate allusion here to the classical green fields of Elysium — in classical mythology the haven of the dead for those who are blessed or brave — evokes the poetry of memory and loss, while at the same time underscoring the fact that for the circus trainer (and for Chekhov) Elysium is not a heavenly place or dream, but an earthly reality.

"Dawn came," the narrator writes, "and the invisible alien one that so frightened Kashtanka was no longer in the little room." "Primitive dread," what Paul Ricoeur had called "our earliest memory," has retreated into Kashtanka's depths. She returns to her everyday life of food, boredom, and oblivion. The janitor, meanwhile, unceremoniously takes the "goose by the paws and carries him away somewhere" (6:444). This "somewhere" is not Elysium.

The brief and matter-of-fact mention of the disposal of Ivan Ivanych's corpse is a jarring but calculated detail on Chekhov's part. Here is the stark materialism of death. The action, however, reminds the reader again that one cannot separate soul from living body: that for the circus trainer the beauty and magic of Ivan Ivanych the goose, his soul or spirit, if you will, is inseparable from the *zhivotnoe* (animal), from *zhivot* (life), from nature, and from the primitive, mysterious, and tender understanding that draws together the circus trainer and his grey goose. Here *is* Elysium.

Lipa's Journey Home

Chekhov again takes up the challenge of conveying the "elusive beauty of sorrow" in his characterization of the peasant girl

Lipa's response to the death of her baby, Nikifor (chapter 8, "In the Ravine"). The immediate cause of her suffering is Aksinya's horrendous scalding of Nikifor. "After that," comments the narrator, "there was heard a scream of a kind that had never been heard in Ukleevo, and nobody believed that such a small and weak creature as Lipa was capable of screaming that way" (10:172). That scream, in its visceral power, echoes Ivan Karamazov's "rebellion" over the suffering and victimization of innocent children. Ivan responds to the suffering of children by returning his "ticket" to world harmony, choosing to remain with his "unrequited suffering and unquenched indignation." Though Ivan's questions will later arise in Lipa's consciousness, she will not remain with her questions and suffering, but will sublimate them in a hosanna to life, holding her ticket to world harmony.

Chekhov's portrayal of Lipa, at the beginning of chapter 8, as she descends the hill from the hospital where her child has died, invokes the theme of the Madonna and child.[17] The interacting words, "*gora*," hill or mountain, and "*gore*," misery, and the verb "*goret'*," to burn, define the moment and its spiritual and religious implications. In the face of the setting sun, we are told, the large, gleaming windows of the hospital on the hill (*na gore*) look as though there was a fire within (*gorela vnutri*) (10:173). "Burning" (*gorela*) here alludes both to Lipa's own grief (*gore*), the burning at the center of her being, and the burning of her child.

"*Gora*," mountain, though unconnected etymologically with "*gore*," suffering, is not only the literal site of the hospital where Lipa watches her son suffer a cruel death, but is also, in a symbolic sense, Calvary, the place of Jesus's suffering. Chekhov earlier has suggested in the vagary of relationships involving Nikifor's paternity a parodic parallel to the biblical Mary, her husband Joseph, and the virgin birth. The baby's name, "Nikifor," is rooted in the

---

17 "Here is the countenance of the Virgin Mother, although Lipa is married and has a baby…," wrote Boris Zaitsev. "It was given to Chekhov to delineate in Lipa with child a vision of an almost evangelical character." See Zaitsev, *Chekhov: Literaturnaia biografiia* (New York: Chekhov Publishing House, 1954), 200, 203.

Greek word for the triumphant or victorious one. The image of the setting sun, royal in its colors and sinking to rest, quietly deepens the Christian symbolism, even as the image of a horse refusing, despite all urging, to drink water signals the engagement and empathy of nature for Lipa and her dead baby.

On her journey home Lipa interacts with surrounding nature in a way that suggests she is both creature and creator of myth. She walks through a spring night of awakening life. The hollow melancholy sound of a bittern is seemingly a reminder of the inappropriateness of celebration in the face of misfortune. Yet nature insists on her rights; the power of life over death asserts itself in the cacophonous excitement of birds and other animate beings. It seems, the narrator writes, that "all these creatures were singing and shouting on purpose... so that all, even the angry frogs, might appreciate and enjoy every minute: after all, life is given only once!" Nature's intoxication with life anticipates the affirmative outlook of the old peasant whom Lipa will shortly encounter, as well as her own singing and exhilaration at story's end. For the present, the grieving Lipa, a child of nature, looks at the sky and wonders where her baby's soul is now: "Was it following her, or floating aloft yonder among the stars and thinking nothing now of his mother."

On her lonely, sorrowful journey home, Lipa passes momentarily through a dark night of the soul. Her longing for people and communication is answered by the sounds of horses, a dog, and an old man calling out: "Hitch up" (запрягай)—words that Pierre Bezukhov (*War and Peace*), alone at night in a field, hears when his coachman wakes him up from a dream—a call that coalesces with Pierre's desire to unite all his thoughts and energies. These same words in Chekhov's story would seem to signify that only by "hitching up" with life, only by moving on, can one cope with, and transcend, sorrow. Lipa encounters an old peasant and tells him of her grief. Ill at ease with her sorrow, his initial response is a conventional, fatalistic one: "No matter, my dear. It's God's will" (Это ничего, милая. Божья воля), but "his glance expresses tenderness and compassion," and Lipa is moved (10:174). While the old peasant evokes memories of Platon Karataev of *War and*

Peace, Chekhov's peasant has a more dynamic, indeed voluntaristic, outlook than his literary ancestor.

Lipa again speaks of her trials, concluding with questions that seem drawn from Ivan Karamazov's "rebellion": "And tell me, grandfather," asks Lipa, "why should a little one be tormented before his death... why a little one, when he has no sins?" "Why?" asks Lipa simply and quietly, repeating the word three times. "Who knows!" (А кто ж его знает!), answers the old peasant. "They drove on for half an hour in silence," the narrator remarks. This half-hour of silence—it resembles one of Chekhov's dramatic "pauses" in his plays—perfectly expresses the peasant's difficulty with the intractable question of theodicy, the justification of evil and suffering in God's world. In the end, however, he dismisses the whole realm of philosophical and theological inquiry, and declares:

> One can't know everything, why or how. It's ordained for a bird not to have four wings, but two, because it is capable of flying with two wings. In the same way man is not ordained to know everything, but only a half or a quarter. As much as he needs to know in order to live, so much he knows. (10:175)

The peasant at this point appears to echo the fatalism, resignation, and passivity of Lipa's mother. Earlier in the story, in answer to her daughter's sorrowful question of why she, Lipa, had had to marry into the Tsybukin family, the mother had replied, "One must marry, daughter. It was not us who ordained it." (At that moment Lipa and her mother are humbly huddled together, like innocent sheep, trusting in "God's world" and his "truth and justice," waiting for "everything on earth" to "blend with truth") (10:165-66). The old peasant's assertion that "man is not ordained to know everything" is not a plea for resignation, however, but a call to life. We cannot know everything, but we can and must live in the face of all mysteries. In his story of his life, the peasant speaks of his ups and downs. "Life is long, there will be good and bad," he emphasizes. "There will be everything." And, echoing the Karamazov thirst for life, he says that he wants to live another twenty years, "which means," he adds, that "there's more of the good [than the bad in the world]" (10:175).

Here the will to live emerges as an ethical act, one that creates a preponderance of good over evil. The questions of good and evil, of life and death, do not lend themselves to finite solutions; they can only be lived through in the infinity of life and living. The peasant, in short, offers Lipa the open road: life in the place of epistemology.

In some casual lines at the end of a note to Lydia A. Avilova, dated February 14, 1904, some months before his death, Chekhov appears to echo the peasant's advice to Lipa:

> All the best to you, chiefly—be cheerful, do not look on life in such a complicated way; probably things really are far more simple. Indeed, does it deserve, [this] life which we do not know, all the tormenting reflections on which our Russian minds wear themselves out—that's still a question.[18]

The paths of Lipa and the old peasant merge in their ultimate choice of life over the meaning of life. At the story's end, in an episode of great symbolic importance, Chekhov depicts Lipa coming home from work with a group of women and girls: "They were singing. Ahead of them all was Lipa singing in a high voice, looking up at the sky, pouring out her song as though triumphant and ecstatic that the day, thank God, had ended, and she could rest" (10:180).

The Lipa of these lines may be found in embryo in the earlier Lipa, but this Lipa is a stronger, empowered being. She is *leading* a group of working peasant women and girls, *leading* a chorus of singers in song. Characteristically, her eyes look up at the sky, yet her ecstatic and triumphant song celebrates both heaven and

---

[18] Chekhov, *Pis'ma*, 12:34-35. Chekhov's artistic-philosophical engagement in his belles-lettres with the questions that "torment" the Russian literary and philosophical mind, such as those revolving around the question of "knowing," is exceedingly complex. His remark to Lydia Avilova, taken as a whole, nonetheless is interesting for its disclosure of certain tensions in his thinking. Not without reason did Sergei Bulgakov more than one hundred years ago assert that after Tolstoy and Dostoevsky, writers who took as their chief theme "the basic questions of human life and spirit," Chekhov is "*the* writer of greatest philosophical significance." See Sergei N. Bulgakov, *Chekhov kak myslitel'* (Kiev, 1910 [orig. pub. 1904]), 8.

earth, work and rest, all of creation. This epiphanic moment is psychologically distant from the time when, huddled with her mother, she was waiting for "everything on earth" to "blend with truth" (10:165-66); Lipa is now celebrating and participating in that truth. Lipa with the childlike and "sad, timid smile" (10:149); Lipa, the iconic suffering Mother with dead child; Lipa, the innocent Joban quester, now emerges as a Madonna "without grief"—as the root meaning of the name Lipa suggests;[19] that is, she comes forth as a person who has spiritually triumphed over sorrow and death. The final lines of "In the Ravine" return Lipa to the tragic world to which she belongs—and transcends:

> The sun had already set; its glow had vanished even on the road above. It had become dark and cool. Lipa and Praskovya walked on, and for a long time kept crossing themselves. (10:180)

Chekhov's image of Lipa in "In the Ravine" is manifold and in movement: a composite of elements of the highest spiritual beauty and sentiment that has migrated down through centuries of Christian art and liturgy, and at the same time a Russian figure of nature, of moral instinct and natural intellect, of peasant power (her "mannish hands... like two big claws" [10:150], her capacity for work, her endurance, her scream), and of resounding song. Lipa is a Russian-universal type.

In his Pushkin speech in 1880, Dostoevsky extolled the Russian poet Alexander Pushkin (1799-1837) and his work, citing his "faith in Russian character, faith in its spiritual might."[20] Those

---

[19]   The name "Lipa," from the Russian "Alipiya," derives from the Greek "alypos" — "free from pain or grief," literally, "no grief, no pain."

[20]   See F. M. Dostoevskii, *Polnoe sobranie sochinenii v tridtsati tomakh* (Leningrad: Nauka, 1972-90), 26:144. As an iconic Russian peasant type, spiritually triumphant in her Christian and pantheistic apprehension of life and nature, Lipa is a descendant of the afflicted peasant girl, Lukeriya, in Ivan Turgenev's stupendous story, "Live Relics" ("Живые мощи," 1874). The story was included in Turgenev's earlier collection of tales, *Notes of a Hunter*

words certainly could be applied to Chekhov and his thaumaturgic creation, Lipa, one of the greatest embodiments of his spiritual materialism.

The synthesis Chekhov achieves in all three episodes involving death is not a religious one, not one based on faith, and not one premised on a belief in resurrection and immortality. What binds the episodes, and what constitutes the unique character of Chekhov's spiritual materialism, is his synthesis of *tenderness and truth*. "You have no tenderness, you have only truth—therefore you are unjust," remarks one of Dostoevsky's characters in *The Idiot*.[21] Chekhov is one of the most *just* among writers: the motif of tenderness, of understanding, pervades his art, as does his unrelenting truth.

(*Записки охотника*, 1847-74). See Ivan Turgenev, *Polnoe sobranie sochinenii i pisem v dvadtsati vos'mi tomakh* (Moscow: Nauka, 1960-68), 4:352-65.

[21] Ibid., 8:354. Dostoevsky's line reads, in Russian,"У нас нежности нет: одна правда, стало быть—несправедливо."

9

TEXT AND READER I
Turgenev's Preoccupations

Nicholas Dames

Teaching *Fathers and Sons* can be an uncomfortably enlightening experience, for the same reason that Freud found great therapeutic potential in transference: it forces you to think about the presuppositions you bring to the activity in which you are engaged. Which is to say that Turgenev's novel, seen in one way, obliges its reader—and even more so the reader's teacher—to think about the cognitive and social aspects of reading novels. Against our presuppositions, it depicts, and even counsels, a state of mind that novel-reading, as we normally hope, cuts through: the hazily self-directed mental abstraction that we call "reverie" or "daydreaming." These reveries are sometimes linked to reading, although more often described as a withdrawn reaction to any demand to account for oneself and one's thoughts; thus the reveries of Turgenev produce a potentially troubling friction when rubbed against the pedagogical rationales for reading imaginative literature.

Those rationales are so deeply embedded in the history of literary criticism in the twentieth century that they are rarely even made explicit, except at the franker edges of critical theory. But one might usefully turn to the seminal example of I. A. Richards, whose *Practical Criticism* (1929) warns about modes of reading-response characterized by mental drift. Richards's terms for this less-than-attentive kind of reading vary, but are characterized by a family resemblance: readers engaging in "swoon reading"; readers "content to loll at ease swinging softly in the hammock of the rhythm"; readers who follow "accidents of the individual reader's mood or history or temperament"; readers who avoid strenuous thinking in favor of pursuing "*momentary* tendencies, desires, and impulses."[1] This cognitive bias in favor of an outer-directed attentive focus is standard across any number of critical schools, although it has slipped from its status in Richards—as a prerequisite to any effective engagement with questions of literary value—to, in more recent critical theory, a prerequisite for effective democratic citizenship. Martha Nussbaum is one of many recent voices who have described rigorously attentive reading, something that combines "one's own absorbed imagining with periods of more detached (and interactive) critical scrutiny," as the training-ground for "public reasoning in a democratic society."[2] And yet the novel, as a form and a familiar cultural touchstone for how reading works, has never been an easy fit with these ideas and ideals. Its amplitude, which means that continuous reading must be occasionally interrupted, and which makes memorization largely impossible, strains attentive scrutiny to its breaking point. The matter is, at best, the subject of somewhat embarrassed asides. In the words of D. A. Miller, "Another open secret that everyone knows and no one wants to: the immense amount of daydreaming that accompanies the ordinary reading of a novel."[3]

This is rarely more evident than it is in *Fathers and Sons*, a novel that begins with a character falling into a daydream. Nikolai Petrovich Kirsanov, waiting anxiously for the delayed arrival of his university-graduate son Arkady, sits down on the bench of a post-station, thereby performing the novel's first action: an act of resignation. From here, his thoughts wander:

> His servant, out of a feeling of propriety and perhaps because he didn't want to remain under his master's gaze, had gone out of the gates and lit a pipe. Nikolai Petrovich bent his head and began studying the ancient verandah steps. A plump

---

[1]   See I. A. Richards, *Practical Criticism: A Study of Literary Judgment* (New York: Harcourt Brace, 1966), 154-55, 223, 225, 236.

[2]   Martha Nussbaum, *Poetic Justice: The Literary Imagination and Public Life* (Boston: Beacon Press, 1995), 4.

[3]   D. A. Miller, *The Novel and the Police* (Berkeley: University of California Press, 1988), 215.

young chicken in motley plumage strutted self-importantly along them, tapping away firmly with its large yellow claws. A bedraggled-looking cat, curled up foppishly against the railings, eyed it in an unfriendly way. The sun burned down. From the shadowy entrance to the post-station wafted the smell of hot rye bread. Nikolai Petrovich fell into a day-dream. "My son… graduated… my boy Arkady—a graduate…." He went over and over such thoughts in his mind. He tried to think about something else, but again and again his thoughts returned to the same thing.[4]

If a small gesture of resignation is the novel's first act, its first depiction of a mental process is encapsulated by the verb *zamechtat'sia*: to fall into, or give way to, a daydream. The daydream itself is perhaps best defined by its passivity and aimless drift, a kind of focus that isolates minute, chance details with only half a consciousness. Nikolai looks—at the verandah steps, a chicken, a cat—but doesn't see; sense-impressions, like the smell of baking bread, are registered just beneath the threshold of conscious attention. What constitutes "thought," in this mental state, is crucially a series of vaguely connected terms, where no syntax, or causal relations, are present ("My son… graduated… my boy Arkady"). Nikolai is immobile, obviously thinking of something, not available for social interaction, but equally obviously not thinking *hard*; he is, one might say, preoccupied.

What it means to daydream, then, is not to occupy oneself with a concern—that is, to work it through in some ratiocinative fashion—but to be preoccupied by it, to circle around it tentatively, to let it float free of any firm definition and to resist the urge to master it. Daydreaming, admittedly, is not a mental state that has any particular dignity. It is similar to a host of minor affects and cognitive processes whose perceived lack of strenuousness gives them little purchase on major theories of mind, such as worry, or

---

[4]   Ivan Turgenev, *Fathers and Sons*, trans. Richard Freeborn (Oxford: Oxford University Press, 1991), 5. Subsequent references will be given in parentheses.

regret, or irritation—states of mind, in Adam Phillips's phrase, that seem "to lack metaphysical ambition."[5] Unlike attentive thought, it will not produce conclusions (Nikolai's mind simply goes "over and over"); unlike desire, it will not issue in the dramatic binary of repression or fulfillment. It is at once pervasive and fragile, easy to slip into and easily broken (as it will be, in this opening scene, by the sound of the wheels of Arkady's approaching troika). What it does, above all, is fill time.

Daydreams, or *mechtaniya*, do have a literary-historical significance in the 1860s, primarily deriving from the Germanic Romanticism of Vissarion Belinsky's 1834 *Literaturnye mechtaniia* ("Literary Reveries"), in which non-directed thought is linked to a vague organicism through which artworks can be both consumed and judged. Turgenev's *mechtaniya*, however, bear very little of this literary-philosophical burden: they are resolutely ordinary. Put another way, they permit a kind of half-attention to the ordinary world, and are the basis of what might be thought of as a theory of ordinary thinking. The plump chicken and bedraggled cat might be "organic" images, but their comic everydayness refuses any grandiose interpretations. Nikolai is closer to boredom than to some kind of poetic, or profound, apprehension. Rousseau to Schelling— the lineage that informs Belinsky's use of the term *mechtaniya*— matter less here than the sheer mundanity of Nikolai's mental state.

This does not necessarily mean that this mental state has no effect on the outside world. For all its minorness, preoccupation is eminently visible, and it carves out what we might call a space of subjectivity. Seeing Nikolai about to fall into his daydream, his servant Pyotr withdraws, compelled by a feeling of both respect (for his master's privacy) and shame (at possibly being caught by his master's preoccupied gaze). The gesture is minute but importantly characteristic: the abstracted look of the preoccupied

---

5   Adam Phillips, from the essay "Worrying and its Discontents," in *On Kissing, Tickling, and Being Bored: Psychoanalytic Essays on the Unexamined Life* (Cambridge, MA: Harvard University Press, 1993), 58. My thinking about minor affect is also indebted to Sianne Ngai, *Ugly Feelings* (Cambridge, MA: Harvard University Press, 2005).

person summons up, as if by a kind of ordinary magic, a zone of public solitude that warns off others. The zone is both mysterious, in the way it works without intention or speech, but also, it must be said, utterly banal. That is, what preoccupies Nikolai can scarcely be a mystery for anyone here. Affection for his son, regret at the passing of time, the feeling of encroaching age: these are the entirely understandable, and entirely expected, thoughts to have on such an occasion. There is no interpretive problem about Nikolai's thoughts; their content is exactly what one would imagine. But their banal content does not harm the effect they have, which is to signal, and enforce, the zone of an inaccessible, while still perfectly knowable, interiority.

This split between a perfectly knowable thought-content and a still-mysterious zone of privacy is encoded here, on a slightly larger level, in the relation between narrative voice and character. There is a strange, vaguely causal relationship between a character's withdrawal into preoccupation—here, Nikolai taking a seat and keeping himself company with his drifting thoughts—and the narrator's ability to provide background information. While Nikolai is poised on the edge of daydream, and immediately before Pyotr's respectful departure, Turgenev can fill in the details of Nikolai's past, including his social status, parentage, university career, happy if brief first marriage, and post-1848 dabbling in reformist estate management. These are necessary facts, of course, but the way in which their relation seems to depend upon the silence and preoccupation of their subject poses a link between narration and character similar to that between servant and master: we can only find the time and space to hear about Nikolai when he is himself too preoccupied to notice. The pause provided by characters' daydreams, in other words, can be filled with the contents of their lives, without harming the zone of privacy created by their only-partially-articulate preoccupations—perhaps, even, reaffirming it.

A later example of the same dynamic demonstrates, with even more force and explicitness, the way in which a character's falling into preoccupied thought creates an interiority effect in no way damaged by the predictability of what they are thinking.

A sudden, ostensibly unmotivated visit by the coldly aristocratic Pavel Petrovich to the rooms occupied by Fenechka, Nikolai's peasant mistress and the mother of his infant son, is followed by his equally sudden withdrawal. He takes himself to his own room and enfolds himself in a double solitude, behind a closed door and heavy curtains:

> But Pavel Petrovich returned to his elegant room, hung with fine dark-grey wallpaper and decorated with guns fixed on a colourful Persian rug, with walnut furniture upholstered in dark-green velveteen, a Renaissance-style bookcase in old dark oak, bronze statuettes on a magnificent desk and a fireplace. He flung himself on his sofa, folded his hands behind his head and remained there motionless, gazing almost with despair at the ceiling. Whether it was that he wanted to hide from the very walls themselves what was happening to his face, or for some other reason, he stood up, undid the loops holding the heavy window curtains and once again flung himself down on the sofa. (40-41)

These acts of retirement, and the preoccupied thoughts that occasion them, in no way prevent us from knowing, even naming, their source: a barely-suppressed attraction to Fenechka, envy for his fortunate brother, and regret for his old love, the enigmatic Princess R. We know, intuitively and without much uncertainty, what is going on here, but the narrator nonetheless maintains a discreet, respectful distance from Pavel, not only halting just short of specifying his thoughts but also breaking off the narration at the precise moment that Pavel draws the curtains. Just as Pyotr respects Nikolai's preoccupation, the narrator respects Pavel's by retreating.

What follows, crucially, is a chapter break. This is not the only time that moments of character-preoccupation are immediately followed by the implied pause of a chapter ending. The novel's fourth chapter, for instance, ends with multiple moments of drifting thought, as the day of Arkady's return ends with Nikolai "supporting his head on his hand," thinking "long thoughts"; Pavel Petrovich holding *Galignani* without reading it, gazing abstractedly into his fire ("God knows where his thoughts wandered"); and Fenechka sitting alone, "from time to time" listening to the breathing of her child (18). Chapter 25, to cite another, ends with Arkady alone in the garden of the Odintsova estate, "his chin resting on his clasped hands ... sitting lost in thought" (174). The coalescence of preoccupation *within* the diegesis, and a temporary break *to* the diegesis, suggests that preoccupation is not just a matter for representation but also for response: we watch characters withdraw into private thought, and then we ourselves are given the space with which to do so ourselves. The narrator retires from characters, and then retires from us. The blank between chapters, then, signifies and occasions the potential "blank" of our own thinking.

Preoccupation, in other words, like so many other minor affects—irritation or embarrassment most obviously—is contagious.[6] It "catches" so well that it breaks the barriers between represented action and readerly activity. Reading about preoccupation, that is, we stand a good chance of ourselves becoming preoccupied: thinking of ourselves, idly, in a circular or non-directed fashion, finding ourselves accompanied by our own hovering concerns. As a feature of novelistic closure, this contagion was perhaps first noted by Roland Barthes, who gave it the name "pensiveness" (*pensivité*): the pensive, argued Barthes, "is the signifier of the inexpressible," the sign for an expressiveness that nonetheless refuses to speak itself. "At its discreet urging," Barthes writes, "we want to ask the classic text: *What are you thinking about?* but the text, wilier than all those who try to escape by answering: *about nothing*, does not reply, giving meaning its last closure: suspension."[7]

---

[6]   Although scarcely a "minor" affect in his account—since it is virtually constitutive of selfhood—shame or embarrassment is nonetheless contagious in the affect theory of Silvan Tomkins, and in the recent return to Tomkins's work by Eve Kosofsky Sedgwick. See Tomkins, *Affect, Imagery, Consciousness*, 2 vols. (New York: Springer, 1963), and Sedgwick, *Touching Feeling: Affect, Pedagogy, Performativity* (Durham, NC: Duke University Press, 2003). For an account of the contagion of shame rooted in the Russian literary tradition, see Deborah Martinsen, *Surprised by Shame: Dostoevsky's Liars and Narrative Exposure* (Columbus: Ohio State University Press, 2003).

[7]   Roland Barthes, *S/Z: An Essay*, trans. Richard Howard (New York: Hill and Wang, 1974), 216-17.

A repletion of possible meanings masking the obviousness of actual meanings, pensiveness, in Barthes's account, produces the very zone of interiority that is so evident from the withdrawals of Turgenev's preoccupied characters.

One crucial difference between Turgenev's daydreams and the pensive ending of Balzac's *Sarrasine*, out of which Barthes elaborates his theory, is encapsulated in the difference between chapter-break and actual ending: Turgenev's preoccupations, or pensiveness, is rhythmic; its state is temporary, if repeated; his characters, just like his implied readers, fall into and out of daydreams repeatedly. This, perhaps, is the rhythm of novel-reading offered us by *Fathers and Sons*: retreats, withdrawals, submergences into preoccupied drift, followed by sudden awakenings or interruptions, as we resume a more alert, outwardly-focused attention. Something, inevitably, will end our drift, and the world (or the text we are reading) will reassert its claim on us, but we also know that more preoccupation is always possible, indeed inevitable.

Daydreaming, in other words, is not only a particular kind of mental process, but also stands for a particular temporal rhythm: the oscillation of attention and distraction, or the way in which the outside world moves in and out of focus. Logical, ratiocinative thought endures in Turgenev no longer than drifting preoccupation—or, perhaps, is frequently aerated by pervasive distractions. Arkady, driving from the post-house to his father's estate, first notices the signs of rural poverty and dilapidation that bring his new reformist politics to mind: "It can't, just can't stay like this," he thinks. "Reforms are essential. But how to go about them, how to start?" (12). Then, abruptly, this train of thought pivots, or dissipates into pure sensation: "Those were Arkady's thoughts, but while he was thinking them spring began to come into its own ... Arkady gazed and gazed and his thoughts, gradually diminishing, finally vanished completely" (13). States of consciousness associated with will or intellect—with some kind of purposiveness—are continually set against a kind of perceptual acuity that produces something less than full attention. Odintsova's thoughts might "be filled with sudden boldness and bubble with noble aspirations, but a draught would come from an open window and Anna Sergeevna would shrink into herself" (88). The rhythm of conscious thought and vague distraction is too general in Turgenev to be characterological; it is simply a property of his psychological realism per se. And that realism, which dictates that our mental processes are at least half composed of preoccupied, dreamy, "pensive" drift, extends inevitably to the assumed processes of reading itself.

I say "assumed"—or, to use the language of much twentieth-century narratology, "implied"—not only because the rhythm of chapter breaks and character withdrawals in *Fathers and Sons* permits us our own space for inattention and drift, but also because the act of reading, as depicted within the novel, is always partial or even failed: the book or text, in Turgenev, may be open, but it is rarely being consumed raptly. Instead, text in Turgenev seems more like a prop that permits private drift. It occasions detachment from the social more than engagement with the virtual. There is, of course, Pavel's *Galignani*, held on his lap while he stares into space, but also Arkady and Katya being mutually silent while Arkady "held in his hand a half-opened book" (165), and Odintsova, avoiding thinking about her attraction to Bazarov as she "ran her eyes over a couple of pages of a French novel, dropped the book and fell asleep" (89). "When you read, the tip of your nose wiggles very charmingly," Bazarov tells Fenechka, confirming that reading is less strenuous intellection than an opportunity for other kinds of vaguely pleasurable derelictions (145). The "half-opened book" is exemplary in the way it mirrors the half-attentive mind that reads it.[8]

---

[8] Here I am pursuing a line of thought that has been of great interest recently to scholars of British fiction: the question, as David Kurnick has put it, of "how to characterize the readerly disposition encouraged by fiction." See Kurnick, "An Erotics of Detachment: *Middlemarch* and Novel-Reading as Critical Practice," *English Literary History* 74 (2007): 586. As many of these critics have argued, total immersion in a book is never quite the ideal, or even the practice, imagined by nineteenth-century fiction. In extending these insights to Russian fiction I am implicitly wondering if this is true, in a larger sense, of realist fiction as a whole, regardless of national peculiarities—or even, perhaps, fiction outside of the realist mode. See also Leah Price, *The Anthology and the Rise of the Novel: From Richardson to George Eliot* (Cambridge: Cambridge University Press, 2000), and Price's "Reader's Block: Response," *Victorian Studies* 46, no. 2 (Winter 2004): 231-42.

The fact—an uncomfortable one for someone charged with instructing students in the novel—is that reading in Turgenev is an adjunct to distraction. To make the discomfort sharper, alongside these examples of reading as, at best, a desultory pursuit, what we might call assigned reading receives little respect. Bazarov's recommendations of textbooks like T. J. Pelouse and E. Frémy's 1853 *Notions générales de chimie* are politely ignored; within the frame of Turgenev's novel such applied study is difficult to imagine. Which is to say that *Fathers and Sons* is inimical in spirit to the situations in which it is taught, and to the theories of criticism—dependent as they habitually are on a notion of rapt attention as a virtue—that inform its teaching. What Turgenev offers us is a picture of what we can only recognize ruefully as Bad Reading: self-preoccupied, only sporadically attentive, time-killing drift. (It is a drift, it should be noted, figured at another level by the directionless, aleatory, almost picaresque movements of Arkady and Bazarov themselves, who veer from locale to locale without firm itineraries in mind, deflected as they are by vague promptings that are acted on without being precisely understood.)

But is that the only thing we can do—recognize the ironic divide between the novel's depiction of mental processing and our own desires to foster, in the classroom, something entirely different? Or, conversely, praise ourselves for having successfully smuggled into the classroom a guide to those slightly asocial affects—whether we call them preoccupation, distraction, pensiveness, or *mechtaniya*—that work subtly against the grain of our own pedagogies? There is, perhaps, another possibility, neither discomfiting nor self-congratulatory: that *Fathers and Sons* gives us an alternate model for novel-reading that might suggest a reconfigured relation between models of mental processing and models of correctly responsive (or responsible) reading. What if what looks like Bad Reading is, in various ways, Good? If, that is, the vague self-concern that is so evident in Turgenev's novel is not just the abject Other of correctly attentive reading, but its necessary complement, the stage on which, occasionally and fortuitously, attention might actually occur? Recognizing the imperfections of preoccupied consciousness—its solipsism, its way of thinking around rather than thinking through—

is also a way of recognizing its importance for the kind of selfhood that, in Turgenev, has the potential for actual connectedness. Those who are most adept at and fond of solitary daydreams, after all—Arkady and Katya most notably—are also best at the communions with others that have always been claimed as the intellectual and ethical work of novel-reading.

Preoccupation, then, is the flawed value of Turgenev's novel, its humble alternative to more strenuous ideals of mental functioning. Here we might be reminded of the allegorical statues ordered by Odintsova's late husband, which were to have represented "Solitariness, Silence, Contemplation, Melancholy, Modesty, and Sensitivity" (175). Of these virtues only "the Goddess of Silence" in fact arrived, "with a finger to her lips," and it was subsequently defaced by boys from the manor house who struck off her nose; as a result, Odintsov had her removed to a corner of the threshing barn where, we are told, "she stood for many years, giving rise to superstitious horror among the peasant women" (175). A less dignified allegory could scarcely be imagined, but the secret of the durability of this statue, and of Silence itself, could in fact be its degradation. We may, that is, not give much respect to preoccupation, to daydreams, or to the silence that so often signals its presence, but it survives, while its more august companions remain only notional. What Turgenev continually suggests is the stubborn presence, and importance to our fragile subjectivities, of the abstracted thinking that silent reading—even, perhaps, the reading of *Fathers and Sons* itself—frees us to experience.

10

TEXTS WITH BLANKS

This Page Left Intentionally Blank: Absences in *Anna Karenina*

Gary Saul Morson

Why Read Literature?

Over the years, I have met countless students who do not see the point of reading masterpieces. Given how literature is usually taught, their attitude makes sense: teachers often engage in the consoling practice of judging writers "progressive" or "conservative," depending on today's proper opinions. But if this is the case, how can literature teach people anything they don't already know?

Today, many college literature courses do not teach much great literature at all. Specialists in what for some reason is called "cultural" studies maintain that judgments of literary value reduce to nothing more than hegemonic power relations. "Such critics," Belknap observes, "resemble the zealots in Lucretius who commit suicide upon realizing that they are not immortal."[1]

In his book on *The Genesis of "The Brothers Karamazov,"* Belknap boldly goes against the consensus. Genesis, of course, has long been a banned topic for sophisticated theorists, either because it individualistically attributes too much power to the writer or because it directs attention away from the text. For Belknap, tracing genesis offers a way to investigate creative greatness:

> If one accepts distortion as a part of the human condition and not a new discovery, Dostoevsky's particular ways of distorting may offer probes into the workings of a creative mind. Such

---

[1] Robert L. Belknap, *The Genesis of "The Brothers Karamazov": The Aesthetics, Ideology, and Psychology of Making a Text* (Evanston, IL: Northwestern University Press, 1990), 3.

a postnihilist approach has not yet become fashionable, but it may prove to be one of the critically energetic alternatives to solipsism or epistemological despair when those doctrines come to seem old-fashioned again.[2]

Most Slavists, trained in the Jakobsonian tradition and its successors, have learned to focus on what has come to be called "the text." This tradition has bequeathed to many scholars the unspoken assumption that "the text" is simply a more sophisticated synonym for what used to be called "the work." I cannot insist too strongly that *the text is not the work*, and if one is to teach students to be good readers, one must keep in mind the difference.

Text and Work

A number of years ago, I gave a series of lectures on *Anna Karenina* to a group of Scandinavian Slavists, many of whom were avowed Jakobsonians. One remarked that, "All my career I have been telling students not to do what you have done, that is, treat characters as real people with real problems and real human psychology. Characters in a novel are so many formal features, nothing more than words on a page. It is primitive to treat fictional people as real, as primitive as the spectator who rushed on stage to stay the hand of Judas." It is just such a position that drives students away.

Why in God's name should students care about the well-being of formal features? This approach reaffirms what they were taught in high school literature classes: literature is about its clever techniques. When you read a novel, you need to look for devices, allusions, foreshadowing, and—above all—*symbols*. Students learn mechanical ways of writing papers guaranteed to earn an A and eventually, if they choose, tenure.

But does anyone seriously believe that Tolstoy, Milton, and Dante composed their works so that professors could discover devices? Of course not, because these authors were composing not texts but works. The distinction between the two is the same

---

[2]   Ibid.

as that which Bakhtin drew between "sentences" and "utterances." Someone has to *say* an utterance, try to accomplish something by it, and take responsibility for ("sign") it. The sentence provides material for the utterance but is not itself the utterance.

In much the same way, the text provides material for the work. The text is the words on the page, the work is the experience they produce in a sensitive reader. And just as an understanding of utterances requires much more than grammar and vocabulary, so an understanding of works requires understanding of much that the text does not contain.

Writers use the text to create a certain experience in the reader. But critics often bypass the work and go straight to the text, which means that they have missed the entire point of reading.

Textualism has led critics to regard a number of activities that readers routinely do, that writers keep in mind, and that are absolutely necessary for experiencing the work as somehow philistine. My colleagues wince when I tell them that I ask students whether they *like* a character or were able to identify with him or her. *Identification* is out. But why would Tolstoy have taken such pains for us to feel Anna's experience from within if he did not mean for us to identify with her?

I would answer my Scandinavian friend by saying that she has allowed for only two possibilities, but great novels demand a third. Literary characters are neither textual features nor real people. Rather, they are *possible* people. By the same token, their ethical and psychological problems are possible problems, ones that in some form we have faced or might face. That is why we care.

If you present literature to students this way, they may see the point of reading. But if you instruct them that the more they love or hate a character, the more childish they are—then, if they have any brains, they will probably take courses with more human content, like accounting.

Two Kinds of Absence

If one analyzes a text, one sees what is there. One can also detect what is not there if the text leads one to expect it, like a missing final rhyme. But great novels often depend on our detecting an absence that is not textual in this sense. It requires attention not to formal patterning but to deep moral engagement. We may say that such absences are not from the text but from the work.

Two sorts of absences particularly concerned the author of *Anna Karenina*. First, some important psychological lack may explain immoral behavior. In that case, the person who inflicts harm will regard himself as entirely guiltless for the same reason that he inflicts the harm in the first place. He cannot see that he isn't seeing something.

Second, most harm in the world is negative: it derives from what we do *not* do. A good forgettory, like Stiva's, helps: he manages to forget everything it would be unpleasant to remember, including the operations of his forgettory.

Tolstoy leads us to reflect on what the work has significantly omitted and what we ourselves easily overlook, or overlooked on a first reading. Of course, one must attend to the text to discover what is significantly absent from the work. But one must not attend to the text as if that is all there is.

It Has Still Not Crossed My Mind That...

Reflecting on Vronsky's attentiveness to Kitty, her mother concludes that he will propose. "Vronsky openly flirted with Kitty at balls, danced with her, and came continually to the house; consequently there could be no doubt of the seriousness of his intentions."[3] This is one of those third-person passages that in fact traces a character's thoughts. The "consequently" belongs to Kitty's mother, but we hear along with her use of it the author's commentary on her explanatory leap.

Kitty and her mother have overlooked the possibility of Vronsky's *not* knowing what, in their view, everyone knows: that

---

[3]   Leo Tolstoy, *Anna Karenina*, trans. Constance Garnett, rev. and ed. Leonard J. Kent and Nina Berberova (New York: Modern Library, 1965), 48. The translation has been modified where necessary. Further references are given in the text.

a young man who behaves as Vronsky does is toying with a girl's feelings and compromising her future chances.

Right after Kitty's parents argue about Vronsky's intentions, Tolstoy explains him in terms of what he has not experienced:

> Vronsky had never had a real family life. His mother had been in her youth a brilliant society woman, who had during her married life, and especially afterward, many love affairs notorious in all society. His father he scarcely remembered, and he had been educated in the Corps of Pages. (AK, 62)

Family life develops countless assumptions, values, and habits which come to seem obvious. But Vronsky remains ignorant of all that family life teaches. He is also ignorant that he is ignorant. He knows that Kitty is becoming ever more attached to him, but he sincerely does not see the moral implications of his behavior:

> He did not know that this mode of behavior in relation to Kitty had a definite character, that it is courting young girls with no intention of marriage, and that such courtship is one of the evil actions common among brilliant young men such as he was. It seemed to him that he was the first who had discovered this pleasure, and he was enjoying his discovery. (AK, 63)

Unlike the third-person paraphrase of Kitty's mother's thoughts, this one could not be from the character's point of view. Sometimes a passage can be read either way, but this one cannot, because we are told what the character does *not* know. The character could not be thinking that he is not thinking something or that some consideration has not even dawned on him. Statements describing such an absence must belong to the author. So important is it to Tolstoy to tell us of such non-thoughts that he often uses his characteristic didactic tone to do so.

If Vronsky imagines that he is the first to discover this pleasure, he must not have asked himself the obvious question: how could this not have happened to someone before? But such a question demands moral self-scrutiny of a sort not encouraged in the Corps of Pages.

Exploring the difference between what the Shcherbatskys and Vronsky take for granted, Tolstoy next imagines something that could not happen, a revealing negative possibility:

> If he could have heard what her parents were saying that evening, if he could have put himself in the position of her family and would have heard that Kitty would be unhappy if he did not marry her, he would not have believed it. He could not believe that what gave such great and delicate pleasure to him, and above all to her, could be wrong. (AK, 62)

Tolstoy imagines Vronsky eavesdropping on the Shcherbatskys and not believing what he hears. By and large, Vronsky lacks the imagination to see matters from any perspective much different from his own. He has not been taught such identification with another, and so has not practiced it. Since the book appeals to and encourages such imagination on the part of readers, they are bound to feel their difference from Vronsky.

Tolstoy's novel tries to cultivate in us the habits Vronsky lacks.

The Novel Reader's Privilege, Extended

"If he could have heard": Tolstoy often extends an invitation to eavesdrop. Of course, readers eavesdrop whenever Tolstoy gives a character's thoughts in free indirect discourse or direct quotation. But, as in this case, readers may also be asked to imagine the reaction of another character if she could overhear the first character's thoughts.

Realist novels offer readers the ability to understand other people from within, as we cannot do in real life. Let us call this ability "the novel reader's privilege."

If Characters Enjoyed the Novel Reader's Privilege...

Tolstoy goes beyond allowing us to eavesdrop. He also invites us to imagine the reactions of characters if they could enjoy the novel's reader's privilege with respect to each other. If Vronsky could have heard Kitty's thoughts, how would he have reacted? In one remarkable scene, Levin wonders how Sviyazhsky thinks, but is rebuffed at the start.

Anna Karenina often takes the form of a drama of looking and listening at looking and listening. Extending the novel reader's privilege by asking us to imagine what a character would think if she enjoyed it intensifies this drama.

Karenin keeps trying to understand what Anna is thinking, but she conceals everything "with a barrier … made up of a sort of amused perplexity" (AK, 57). As Anna expertly blocks signs of what her thoughts might be, she also "betrays" them, as if unawares. As with her willful tendril, she plans displays of "spontaneity." It is as if her audience could listen in on the beatings of her heart and the trepidations of her soul. In so doing, she creates a seductive sense of intimacy, as she does with Levin.

The recipient of such "unwitting" revelation feels as if he enjoys something like the reader's privilege. That is another way in which Anna acts as if she were the heroine of a novel. Because other characters sense her with an intimacy almost like that usually reserved for readers, their experience resembles ours, and so we more easily identify with them.

As If

Just as people in real life cannot eavesdrop on each other's thoughts, neither can characters in novels. But by extending the novel reader's privilege hypothetically, the author can create an "as if" experience. Readers who accept the author's invitation to guess what one character *would* think of another's thoughts may arrive at *a part of the work that is absent from the text*—or, more accurately, that is present in the text as an absence to fill. So long as a critic regards the work as nothing more than a text, he will not even notice such an invitation.

To really understand a character, one has to imagine "might-have-beens," what a character might have done or felt had circumstances differed. Suppose Anna had accepted Karenin's offer of a divorce with custody of both children. What then? How would she have acted and felt, how would remarriage and Seryozha's presence have affected her relationship with Vronsky? Does the answer to these questions tell us something about why she refuses Karenin's offer?

In life, we try to understand other people and ourselves by imagining hypothetical situations. To know who a person is requires guessing what he did not do, but might have done.

Novelistic Ethics

From the perspective of the realist novel, ethics demands that before condemning another person, we ask what we would have done in his or her place. Levin constantly does so, and discovers that he is unsure of the answer.

One can state as an implicit novelistic ethical precept: do not condemn others for something one might well have done oneself. As this novel's epigraph tells us, such condemnation belongs not to us but to God. Novels teach us that "There but for the grace of God go I."

What If Dolly Heard Stiva's Thoughts As We Do?

Let us consider an example of an invitation to extend the novel author's privilege to a character. As the book begins, Stiva wakes from a delightful dream. Dolly, of course, has been grieving all night. We listen to his thoughts:

> Stepan Arkadyevich was a truthful man with himself. He was incapable of deceiving himself and persuading himself that he repented of his conduct. He could not at this date feel repentant that he, a handsome, susceptible man of thirty-four, was not in love with his wife, the mother of five living and two dead children … Possibly he might have managed to conceal his sins better from his wife if he had anticipated the effect on her should she discover them. He had never clearly thought out the subject, but he had vaguely conceived that his wife must long ago have suspected him of being unfaithful to her, and shut her eyes to the fact. He had even supposed that she, a worn-out woman no longer young or good-looking, and in no way remarkable or interesting, merely a good

mother, ought from a sense of fairness to take an indulgent
view. It had turned out quite the other way. (AK, 6)

It is, of course, Stiva, not the author, who offers the remarkable
comment that he is truthful because he cannot regret an affair,
only its discovery. As we follow Stiva's thoughts, we hear him
mentioning the one thing that he has done wrong: not anticipating
Dolly's reaction to his infidelity.

What if Dolly could overhear these thoughts? Later in part
1, Anna will tell her that Stiva is "weighed down by remorse,"
dwells obsessively on how much he has hurt her, and loves her
"beyond anything in the world" (AK, 74). All of these comments are
contradicted by the waking scene, but they enable reconciliation by
soothing Dolly's injured self-esteem. Anna allows Dolly the superior
position of forgiving. But what if Dolly could have listened in and
known, as we do, that Stiva is not in the least repentant?

And how would Dolly have responded to Stiva's unconflicted
comment that he is not in love with her, or to his reference to her
as the mother of "five living and two dead children"? How much
imagination does it take to guess that Dolly cannot think of those
dead children without deep pain? Surely, she might think, these
two dead children ought to mean more to Stiva than their effect on
her attractiveness?

As the passage continues, Dolly would next hear that Stiva
has long vaguely imagined that she knew about the affairs, which
means that there have been many. And how would she react to
Stiva's expectation that she would shut her eyes? Might she wonder:
Does he think I would shut my eyes to what I don't want to see
because that is what he routinely does? In fact, Stiva is a master of
not seeing the unpleasant.

If she could listen in, Dolly would next hear herself described
as "a worn-out woman no longer young and good-looking, and in
no way remarkable or interesting, merely a good mother" (AK, 6).
One can imagine her hearing, one after the other, each insulting
phrase, their effect mounting. But she might react most strongly to
Stiva's characterization of her as "merely a good mother." Merely?
For Dolly, and for Tolstoy, no activity could be more important

than being a good mother. Stiva's "merely" betrays his mistaken values.

At last, Dolly would confront Stiva's belief that her reaction to the discovery represents *her* unfairness! How selfish does one have to be to draw such a conclusion? She would realize—as she later does—that Stiva lacks any moral core.

In the passage's final sentence—"it had turned out quite the other way"—we hear not only Stiva's wistful sigh but also the author's irony. That much is obvious, but if we leave it at that—at the interaction of two speakers—we miss a deeper source of complexity, the possible listener. As there are what Bakhtin calls "double-voiced words," there are also "double-listened words." We listen not only to Stiva, but also to Dolly's potential listening to Stiva.

Textualism and More Novelistic Ethics

None of this is in the text, but it is there for us to find. We find it if we ask the sort of questions that might occur to a morally sensitive observer. What would Dolly think if she overheard?—this question does not arise from textualism, no matter how rigorous. And yet to miss it is to miss something truly important to that dense humanness we sense in the book.

Novelistic ethics implies that, perhaps in life as well, we should consider how others might react to our thoughts about them. Could the habit of doing so constitute an intrinsic element of what we call "conscience"—literally, a "with-knowing"?

Missing in Action

From an ethical perspective, the key to Stiva's meditations lies in that mention of something that did *not* happen: "He had never clearly thought out the subject" of his wife's feelings.

Tolstoy's novel develops what I think of as "the Russian idea of evil." Evil need not be grand, Satanic, or dramatic, as we usually suppose and as literature usually represents it. Rather, it may primarily consist of and derive from a hundred million small actions we barely notice and assume to be without moral significance.

That is why *The Brothers Karamazov* describes the devil as ordinary and banal, and Chekhov located the source of most harm in daily neglect.[4]

For the author of *Anna Karenina*, evil does not require *any* action, not even small cruelties or evil wishes. It may be, and usually is, a matter of what one does *not* do or does not bother even to think about. It is closer to what we call criminal negligence. We have more to fear from genial forgetfulness than from active hatred.[5]

Stiva's mistreatment of his wife derives from no hostility. It is essentially negative, and consists of failing to put himself in her place. It is one thing to harm someone, but quite another to do so without even bothering to wonder what that person would feel. The first is morally problematic, the second borders on horrifying. It is not just an ethical lapse, it negates the very basis of ethics, which, for the realist novel, is empathy.

For years Stiva has had affairs. Can it be that he has never bothered to imagine what his wife would feel if she knew? Any serious consideration would have told him that she would not regard it as simple fairness to take an indulgent view. The humor of the passage's last line—"It had turned out quite the other way"— reflects how obvious that conclusion should have been.

"As If" Storytelling

How does an author show non-actions? Literature offers several ways to do so. The writer can employ various forms of "as if" story-telling, such as dreams, frustrated anticipations, misunderstandings, or false but plausible accusations. Dostoevsky uses all these forms of "as if" narration and more. His novels rely constantly on what

---

[4] I discuss Chekhov from this perspective in "Prosaic Chekhov: Metadrama, the Intelligentsia, and *Uncle Vanya*," in *TriQuarterly* (Winter 1990/91): 118-59.

[5] So I argue in my book *"Anna Karenina" in Our Time: Seeing More Wisely* (New Haven, CT: Yale University Press, 2007). I would add that Stiva apparently alludes to Dickens's Harold Skimpol, who raises similar moral problems.

I have elsewhere called "sideshadowing"—indications of what might have been.[6]

Is and As If: so close are Raskolnikov's dreams and feverish fears to reality that they almost blend in with his many actions that are themselves nightmarish and performed as if he were only dreaming about them, like the murders themselves. Since the unconscious mind does not easily distinguish fears and wishes from actualities, such mystery indicates a lot about how a character's mind works. Porfiry Petrovich grasps all of this and so can create an "as if" realm of suspicions that play on Raskolnikov's "as if" psychology. He is literature's great master of empathy.

Anna Karenina evokes nonactions in rather different ways, specifically designed to show the moral importance of neglect. These evocations of absence, and their textual traces, remain invisible unless one attends to more than the text.

Textualism does not come to grips with the text.

To notice what is important in the text, one needs to ask nontextualist questions and apply moral habits appropriate to real people.

For the First Time

Obviously, one cannot show what a character is not thinking about by having him think about what he is not thinking about. One can, however, have the character entertain thoughts that indicate a prior non-thinking. That Stiva "had never clearly thought out the subject" indicates actions not taken—actions that we might have expected him to take.

Consider the passage in which Karenin confronts Anna after meeting Vronsky in the doorway. Karenin has stipulated just one condition for tolerating the affair, for allowing her to live with Seryozha and in society as before, and for providing her with money: not seeing Vronsky at their house. It does not seem like

---

6   That is my argument in *Narrative and Freedom: The Shadows of Time* (New Haven, CT: Yale University Press, 1994).

much to ask. Karenin is therefore angry at having met Vronsky at home. Karenin is so overcome that, uncharacteristically, he loses the power to enunciate:

> "Yes, you think only of yourself! But the sufferings of a man who was your husband have no interest for you. You don't care that his whole life is ruined, that he is thuff... thuff... thuffering."
>
> Aleksey Aleksandrovich was speaking so quickly that he stammered, and was utterly unable to articulate the word "suffering," and pronounced it "thuffering" [пелестрадал]. She wanted to laugh, and was immediately ashamed that anything could amuse her at such a moment. And for the first time, for an instant, she felt for him, put herself in his place, and was sorry for him. (AK, 384)

"For the first time" she puts herself in his place: the affair has been going on for a long time, she is anticipating the birth of Vronsky's child, and yet she has not once bothered to put herself in Karenin's place. This omission damns her much more severely than the affair itself.

One might have an affair while regretting its effect on one's spouse; or one might have the affair and justify the suffering it inflicts. Altogether worse than either of these behaviors is the failure even to think about one's spouse's feelings at all. In any case, Anna immediately banishes the thought: "'No, it was my imagination,' she thought, recalling the expression of his face when he stumbled over the word 'suffering.' 'No, can a man with those dull eyes, with that self-satisfied complacency feel anything?'" If he cannot feel, then surely she need not consider his feelings.

Not Considering

Sometimes Tolstoy explicitly states that Anna has been monstrously unfair to Karenin because she has not even tried to guess what he might be feeling, or what she would feel in his place. At the races, she watches him in the least charitable way:

> "I'm a wicked woman, a lost woman," she thought; "but I don't like lying. I can't endure falsehood, while as for *him*"

(her husband) "it's the breath of his life—falsehood. He knows all about it, he sees it all; what does he care if he can talk so calmly?... No, all he wants is falsehood and propriety," Anna said to herself, not considering exactly what it was she wanted of her husband, and how she would have liked to see him behave. She did not understand either that his peculiar loquacity that day, so exasperating to her, was merely the expression of his inward distress and uneasiness. As a child that has been hurt skips about, putting all his muscles into movement to drown the pain, in the same way Aleksey Aleksandrovich needed mental exercise to drown the thoughts of his wife which in her presence and in Vronsky's, and with the continual iteration of his name, would force themselves on his attention. (AK, 220)

"Not considering" what she wanted of him or why he might be so peculiarly loquacious: what does it take to grasp that Karenin might be distressed at a spectacle in which the man he correctly suspects is his wife's lover, and whom she stares at with a fixity that attracts attention, is the focus of all eyes? She attributes his loquacity to his caring only for outward propriety—that is, not caring about the affair itself and not suffering jealousy. But surely if she had bothered to consider what he might be feeling, she would at least entertain the possibility that his peculiar loquacity reflects jealousy and real pain. That would be so even for someone who does not have Anna's amazing insight into people.

Tolstoy's authorial comment on Anna's thoughts speaks explicitly about what she was not doing but might have done. She was not doing what the very basis of novelistic morality demands, putting yourself in the other person's place.

Of course, her non-action recalls her brother's forgettory, and, of course, we hear the echo of Stiva's affirmation of his "truthfulness" when Anna, still concealing her affair, accuses Karenin of falsehood. She lies by stating that she hates lying. For Tolstoy, lying may consist not just of false speaking but also of false listening and false looking, that is, of *not paying attention* to whatever might contradict what one wants to believe.

A Loving Machine

Anyone who knows the film versions or criticism of the novel will acknowledge that most readers have accepted Anna's assertion that Karenin cares only about propriety. And that is strange, because the novel contains several explicit statements by the author about Karenin's jealousy and several representations of the pain it causes him. For example, book 2, chapter 8, dwells on Karenin's inner thoughts and follows his attempts to assure himself that he is *not* jealous, which is sure proof that he is jealous.

It is understandable that Anna would lie to herself about what she is doing, but why do so many critics believe her? After all, the author tells us repeatedly that Anna consciously lies, and even revels in falsehood. He tells us explicitly that she dehumanizes her husband:

> "He's not a man but a machine, and a spiteful machine when he's angry," she added, recalling Aleksey Aleksandrovich with all the peculiarities of his figure and manner of speaking and setting against him every defect she could find in him, softening nothing for the great wrong she was doing him. (AK, 201)

> Don't I know him, the lie in which he is utterly steeped?.. ... He's not a man, not a human being—he's a puppet! No one knows him; but I know him…. He's not a man, he's an official machine. (AK, 380)

Tolstoy not only calls such a statement unfair, he explicitly gives us a quite different explanation of Karenin's apparent coldness. As Anna will later admit, his problem is an inability to express feelings, not an inability to feel. Quite the contrary: we are told that he suffers so much at the sight of another person's tears and suffering that he cannot stand it. His conversion to Christian love in the childbirth scene takes place because, for once, in spite of Anna's and Vronsky's suffering and tears, he cannot banish them or leave. He must let his feelings, which he had always considered a weakness, predominate. A conversion to Christian love is not what we would expect of a machine. At this moment, Anna says that she alone knew his saintly capacity for forgiveness. "He sees her eyes gazing at him with such triumphant tenderness as he had never seen in them" (AK, 434). Even afterward, when she wants to justify going to Italy with Vronsky, she no longer calls Karenin a machine incapable of feeling but, on the contrary, a man so loving and saintly that his presence constitutes a kind of reproach.

Like Anna, We Forget What We Don't Want to See

Then why have so many adapters, readers, and critics missed these passages? Why is Karenin so often described as Anna teaches herself to see him? This time, I think, the mistake does not lie in paying attention only to the text and forgetting the work. After all, the text itself states over and over again that Anna is lying, dehumanizing, and overlooking the feelings Karenin clearly has. If one paid attention to the text, the usual view of Anna and Karenin would be impossible.

Like Anna's self-justifications, the usual view depends on not seeing what is right before one's eyes.

One reviewer of my book on *Anna Karenina* wrote that he could not believe that the passages I cited were actually in the text and had to go back and check. He was honest and conscientious enough to say so. If his surprise is representative, then the usual reading depends on omissions not noticed as such.

Anna tells us repeatedly that she has to choose between her son and her lover, and most readers believe her. That is also how film versions represent her "tragedy." And yet her statement is plainly false. At the end of part 4, Karenin explicitly offers her a divorce, with custody of both children, and he offers to plead guilty to adultery himself so that she can marry Vronsky. He offers her anything else that she might want. And yet Anna refuses. Why?

The text makes her reasons explicit. Anna feels that, precisely because Karenin's offer comes from genuine forgiveness and sincere Christian love, it establishes his moral superiority over her. She tells Stiva:

> "I have heard it said that women love men for their vices,"
> Anna began suddenly, "but I hate him for his virtues.... Would
> you believe it, that knowing he's a good man, a splendid man,
> that I'm not worth his little finger, still I hate him. I hate him
> for his generosity." (AK, 448)

She must have rehearsed this witty reversal of the maxim to get it so
perfectly. We usually associate this sort of feeling with Dostoevsky,
but at the time its most famous expression belonged to La
Rochefoucauld: "Our evildoing arouses less hate and persecution
than our good qualities."[7]

Tolstoy could hardly give more prominence to her refusal of
Karenin's offer of a divorce with custody of both children. The last
sentence of part 4 reads, "A month later Aleksey Aleksandrovich
was left alone with his son in the house at Petersburg, while Anna
and Vronsky had gone abroad, not having obtained a divorce, but
having absolutely refused one" (AK, 457).

How, then, is it possible that so many readers and critics have
believed Anna's palpably false statement that she had to choose
between her son and her lover?

I can only guess. Perhaps we are dealing with another
significant absence, a work that the text suggests we construct
precisely so that we can subsequently see its falsity. We construct
the story of a great romantic love and subsequent tragedy, as so
many readers have done—the story captured so well in the Garbo
version of the novel. If we recognize the falsity, we can ask ourselves
why it seemed plausible.

The Negative Work

Let us call this mistaken story the "negative work"—negative in
the sense of both a photographic negative inverting what is really
there and a significant absence. One clue that Tolstoy intends us to

---

7   *The Maxims of La Rochefoucauld*, trans. Louis Kronenberger (New York:
Modern Library, 1959), 38.

construct this negative work lies in the book's title. Why is it called *Anna Karenina* when only about forty percent of the text is devoted to the Anna story?

We can see why if we reflect that *Anna Karenina* is, in fact, the right title for the Garbo version. It is the story *as Anna herself would tell it*. Anna, of course, is a consummate narcissist and, if she were telling the story, would not only focus on herself but would also insist that she suffers from fate rather than from her own choices. "But I was not to blame," she tells Dolly. "Could it have been otherwise? ... Could it possibly happen that you didn't become the wife of Stiva?"

The usual reading accepts these justifications. Her story is routinely described as tragedy and her suffering as the inevitable result of the conflict of true love with hypocritical society. Karenin is represented as unfeeling, Anna as truthful, and her abandonment of Seryozha as inevitable.

That reading is really there. It gives us an *Anna Karenina*: Anna's *Anna*. It gives us a decoy. If we perceive it as such, and recognize the mistake we have made, we will do what Anna does in the childbirth scene: reflect on the self-deceptions in which we engaged in order to construct the work we wished were there.

If the negative work were not there at all, we would not be able to examine the ways in which we overlook counter-evidence to our prejudices.

11

Text and Reader II

**Getting Away with Murder:
Teaching *Crime and Punishment***

Deborah A. Martinsen

This paper will propose four big questions around which to structure classes on *Crime and Punishment*: 1) How do we read the novel?; 2) Do we want Raskolnikov to get away?; 3) Do we forget Lizaveta, and why does this matter?; and 4) Is the Epilogue organic or tacked on? The first and second questions point to the narrative strategy that plunges readers into Raskolnikov's head. The third demonstrates the effectiveness of that strategy: students see how closely we have come to identify with Raskolnikov and his thinking. By structuring discussion around his dreams and confessions, I help my students to see that Dostoevsky creates the expectation that the novel will follow a guilt script—crime, repentance, expiation, and redemption. Yet Dostoevsky thwarts that expectation by staying close to a protagonist who has developed a theory of crime in which guilt serves as a litmus test for strength/pride or weakness/shame. Once Raskolnikov commits murder, he opens a narcissistic wound: feeling guilt reveals shame at his identity. For the novel's duration, he denies guilt, because to admit that he was wrong to murder the pawnbroker would be to destroy his dream of greatness. We want Raskolnikov to get away, and we forget Lizaveta. Dostoevsky's narrative strategy makes us complicit, but also uneasy. The Epilogue provides the distance needed to evaluate the novel's action.

One can start class by providing some historical background about the 1860s and the nihilists, but I start with the opening pages to show students how Dostoevsky plunges us into the mind of his sympathetic hero-murderer. I ask students: How does the narrator involve us in the novel's action? We observe that in the third paragraph, the narrator moves from commentary to indirect discourse. Commentary: "He was so immersed in himself and had isolated himself so much from everyone that he was afraid not only of meeting his landlady but of meeting anyone at all." Indirect discourse: "As a matter of fact, he was not afraid of any landlady, whatever she might be plotting against him" (1.1.3).[1] By the fifth paragraph, the narrator has moved to direct discourse, reporting the young man's inner speech: "'I want to attempt such a thing, and at the same time I'm afraid of such trifles!' he thought with a strange smile." By teaching my students to observe not only the "what" of narration—time, place, character, circumstances, emotion— but also the "how" of narration—strategies such as reporting, indirect discourse, and direct discourse—I've helped them see how Dostoevsky's narrator progresses from outside to inside the young protagonist's head. I inform them that Dostoevsky started the novel in the first person but moved to the third person, and we use the first pages of the novel to discuss what he gains by the shift. Students see that by staying close to Raskolnikov, the narrator creates sympathy for him. As we go forward, we must ask whether the narrator—or we ourselves—can maintain critical distance from Raskolnikov's words and deeds.

I next leap to the end of part 1 and ask Belknap's question: Do we want Raskolnikov to get away? Yes, we all say. Why? I ask. Because he's not a murderer at heart, one student replies. How do we know that? By this time the whole class is providing textual clues to Raskolnikov's divided self, including his spontaneous charity, his response to his mother's letter, and his dream of the mare—evidence Olga Meerson and Liza Knapp discuss in their articles. Students who have read the novel before or who are studying Russian often know that Raskolnikov's name derives from the word for "schism" (which can provide the opportunity to talk about the Schism in the Orthodox Church). This discussion naturally leads to the question

---

[1]   Citations, with some modifications, come from Fyodor Dostoevsky, *Crime and Punishment*, trans. Richard Pevear and Larissa Volokhonsky (New York: Vintage Books, 1993). For students using the original or other translations, I cite part and chapter. Hereafter, citations in the text will follow this format: Part.Chapter.Page.

of Raskolnikov's motives, to which we return in all future sessions. Eventually, we will follow Robin Feuer Miller and see how the change to third-person narration keeps multiple motives in play[2] — a strategy Belknap calls Dostoevsky's "both/and."

In the meantime, we ask what Dostoevsky our author is up to. If we want Raskolnikov to escape, what does that say about us? Do we accept Raskolnikov's reasons for the crime? Now is the time to discuss Russia in 1865, and how Raskolnikov is not just a young man of any culture torn between desire for power and dominance on the one hand, and desire for love and community on the other, but also a nihilist, who believes that the superior individual not only has the right but also the obligation to act now, creating the future by tearing down existing beliefs and power structures. Following Belknap, I observe that Dostoevsky took the language and ideas for Raskolnikov's article "On Crime" (3.5.258) from *Russian Word*, the "thick" journal that was the Nihilists' organ. As Belknap notes, Dostoevsky made one significant addition: he uses variations on the word переступить—which means to overstep, cross over, transgress, commit a crime—seventeen times. Dostoevsky thus identifies Raskolnikov as a young nihilist whose ruthlessness is inspired by sympathy for the downtrodden and a desire to improve society. His internal division emblematizes the contradictions inherent in the nihilist movement.

In order to show students how we have come to see the world through Raskolnikov's eyes, I ask them first whether anyone remembers the pawnbroker's name and then to characterize her. Why do we refer to her as "the pawnbroker" or "the old crone"? We see that Dostoevsky's narrator has adopted Raskolnikov's language, objectifying her, using a label rather than her name, Alyona Ivanovna. It's easier to kill someone whom you see as a function ("pawnbroker"), a category ("old crone"), or a parasite ("louse"). We are not far from Auschwitz or skinheads here. Lizaveta, by contrast, we call by name: we feel sympathy for her. So why do

---

[2] Robin Feuer Miller, *Dostoevsky's Unfinished Journey* (New Haven, CT: Yale University Press, 2007), 59.

most of us, and the novel's characters, forget her? That, I argue, is Dostoevsky's challenge to us.

In order to get students to see that Dostoevsky the author creates the expectation of a guilt script (transgression, repentance, expiation, redemption), but frustrates that expectation by providing a shame script (no set pattern), I must get them to see that Lizaveta represents the guilt script and the pawnbroker the shame script. Because Dostoevsky's narrator stays so close to Raskolnikov that readers tend to identify with him,[3] and because Raskolnikov forgets Lizaveta, we do too. But why does Raskolnikov forget her?

I ask students to list the dreams in the novel. By this time we have read to part 3 or 4 of the text. We generate a list that I supplement and classify: 1) unconscious dreams (сны)—of the mare (1.5.54-60) and of beating the old crone (3.6.273-78); 2) semi-conscious dreams such as the daydreams (грёзы) of the oasis (1.6.67) and the Epilogue (Epilogue 2), as well as the auditory hallucination of Ilya Petrovich beating the landlady (2.2.115-17); 3) nightmares (кошмары)—Svidrigailov's (6.6.506-10); and 4) conscious dreams (мечты). We return to the novel's third page, where Raskolnikov thinks of his plan to murder Alyona Ivanovna as the "ugly" dream (мечта) he has been contemplating for months. We then contrast his conscious with his unconscious dreams. Students have already discussed the dream of the mare—how Raskolnikov identifies with the child and feels compassion for the mare and horror at the murderer. We revisit this dream briefly and find more evidence of Raskolnikov's moral self in the sense of guilt behind the relief he feels upon waking: "'Lord!' he pleaded, 'show me my way; I renounce this cursed … dream of mine!" (мечты моей; 1.5.60). With this dream, Dostoevsky prepares us to expect a guilt script.

---

[3]   Citing Gary Rosenshield's excellent monograph, I tell my students that while the narrator stays close to Raskolnikov's viewpoint, as the need arises he briefly jumps into other characters' consciousnesses: "He exposes the consciousness of Luzhin, Svidrigaylov, and Razumikhin, but rarely reveals the inner emotional and mental lives of Dunya, Pulkheria Alexandrovna, Marmeladov, Katerina Ivanovna, Sonya, and Porfiry Petrovich." Rosenshield, *Crime and Punishment: The Techniques of the Omniscient Narrator* (Lisse, UK: The Peter de Ridder Press, 1978), 29.

The dream of the crone remains a puzzle until we explore it as the novel's most concentrated shame scene. Shame relates broadly to human identity, i.e., who we are, whereas guilt relates more narrowly to human action, i.e., what we do. The two can be related, as they so clearly are in Raskolnikov, but they need not be. I cite the underground man's shame at his face, for instance, or Dmitry Karamazov's shame at his ugly feet. Shame arises when a person negatively evaluates him- or herself in relation to an idealized self, thereby arousing feelings of inferiority or inadequacy. Guilt arises when a self acts so as to transgress against personal, moral, social, or legal norms. As noted earlier, guilt follows a script: transgression, repentance, expiation, redemption. Shame has no set script, yet it always involves an unexpected and disorienting sense of exposure. Seeing and being seen are critical: the painful self-consciousness that accompanies shame derives from a sense of being exposed. Standard responses to shame are flight and paralysis. We find all of this in Raskolnikov's dream.

Before his dream of the old crone, Raskolnikov asks the question that I try to keep alive for students: "Poor Lizaveta! Why did she have to turn up there!.. Strange though; why is it that I almost never think of her, as if I hadn't killed her?.. Lizaveta! Sonya! Poor, meek ones, with meek eyes … Dear ones!" (3.6.275) This is the only time Raskolnikov thinks of the unintended consequence of his realized "dream." We also note that Raskolnikov links Lizaveta and Sonya using the biblical language of Marmeladov's drunken rant.

I ask students: what precipitates the dream of the crone? Raskolnikov encounters the tradesman who accuses him of murder. He returns to his room feeling vulnerable and exposed, and the narrator reports his agonized internal monologue. Raskolnikov bemoans the fact that his crime was petty and insignificant, not grand and earth-shattering: "Napoleons, pyramids, Waterloo—and a scraggly, repulsive registrar's widow, an old crone, a moneylender with a red trunk under her bed—so, how is someone like Porfiry Petrovich going to digest that!.." (3.6.274). His crime does not reflect his idealized, Napoleonic self-image. As he heaps scorn on himself, Raskolnikov identifies with his victim: "'That's why, that's why I am definitively a louse,' he added, grinding his teeth, 'because I am myself perhaps even more nasty and repulsive than the louse I killed, and I *sensed* beforehand that I would tell myself so *after* I killed her. Is there anything that can compare with such horror!'" (3.6.275). Raskolnikov is clearly not experiencing guilt or repentance here. In fact, he tells himself, "Oh, how I hate that little old crone now! If she recovered, I think I'd kill her again!" (3.6.275).

In the dream he has a moment later, Raskolnikov does exactly that. He revisits the murder scene and repeatedly hits his victim on the crown of her head. She does not stir, as though she were made of wood. The dream thus reflects his sense of impotence. He commits the crime, but he fails: "Then he bent completely down to the floor and peeked into her face from below, peeked and went dead [помертвел]: the little old crone was sitting and laughing—simply dissolving in soft, inaudible laughter, trying with all her might not to let him hear her" (3.6.277). As the victim lives and the murderer goes dead, Raskolnikov's worst fears are realized: he is not only impotent but ridiculous. Responding with the rage of the narcissistically injured, he renews his assault. Yet the harder he hits, the louder she laughs. Raskolnikov then hears laughter and whispering from the bedroom: "He started to run away, but the whole entryway is already full of people, the doors to the stairs are wide open, and on the landing, on the stairway, and farther down—there are people, head to head, all looking—but hidden, waiting, silent... His heart contracted, his feet refuse to move, they've become rooted... He wanted to cry out—and woke up" (3.6.277-78). This part of the dream magnifies his sense of exposure. He is caught red-handed, not as a murderer but as a failed murderer, an impotent killer. His unconscious exposes him as a failure.

By murdering the pawnbroker, Raskolnikov exposes himself to a humiliating self-examination. He is not the hero he wants to be. His crime has failed—not literally, but figuratively. He has killed his dream of greatness. Raskolnikov confesses to Sonya, "I killed myself, not the old crone!" (5.4.420). In his theory, Raskolnikov divides the world into the powerful and the powerless. We see his will to power as a defense against his sense of dependency and weakness. He is indebted to women, his landlady and his mother, yet he has incurred his debts by the choices he has made. After arriving in Petersburg, he lived above his income; more recently he has given up tutoring. If he proves to himself and others that he is extraordinary, he can overcome the shame of poverty and nonentity. Raskolnikov is seeking a new word, but students must understand that he is not only a literary cliché—a young man from the provinces who squanders his family's money in the city—he is also a derivative thinker who overhears other young men in a tavern discussing "his" theory. Raskolnikov has fallen victim to what Dostoevsky calls "ideas in the air."[4]

Significantly, the dream underscores Raskolnikov's obsession with the pawnbroker, and we come to see that she is associated with Raskolnikov's sense of identity and thus with the shame script. Lizaveta, on the other hand, represents the unintended consequence of his theory or "dream" and thus the guilt script. In order to take responsibility for Lizaveta's murder, he must acknowledge it. But Lizaveta does not figure in this disturbing dream. Viewing this as a shame dream helps us see that Raskolnikov must get past his shame in order to acknowledge his guilt.

The three methods of ridding oneself of shame—denial/forgetting, laughter, and confession—all involve distancing the self from pain by pushing it out of consciousness or by changing one's position, viewing one's self from the witness perspective. Now is the time to ask students to list the confessions and near-confessions in the novel. They usually generate all of them: in the Crystal Palace, Raskolnikov taunts Zamyotov with hints (2.6.159-66); in the corridor, he tells Razumikhin with his eyes (4.3.314); in Sonya's room, he promises to tell her next time (4.4.330); in Porfiry's quarters, he comes close (4.5.331-50); in what is usually called "the confession" scene, he comes to Sonya and conveys his guilt but never accepts responsibility for it (5.4.409-22); in his room he acknowledges his crime to Dunya when he realizes she knows,

---

[4] F. M. Dostoevskii, *Polnoe sobranie sochinenii v tridtsati tomakh* (Leningrad: Nauka, 1972-90), vol. 28, bk. 2, 136. See also Miller, *Dostoevsky's Unfinished Journey*, 58.

but he does not voice repentance (6.7.517-20); and finally, at the police station, he confesses to Ilya Petrovich (6.8.531). We get many confessions, but no sense of guilt.

Then we examine the big "confession" (5.4.405-22). Like Sonya, one of the novel's moral agents, we are primed for a guilt script. But Raskolnikov never actually says that he killed the two women. He conveys this information with a look. On the other hand, he provides torrents of explanations, all focusing on the pawnbroker, all of which Sonya rejects. When Raskolnikov offers Sonya the Napoleonic scenario, arguing that he has the right to transgress, she rejects it because it does not make moral sense. Likewise, she rejects his arguments of poverty and desire to help his family. We are with her here because Dostoevsky has provided us with a control to refute the positivist doctrine that poverty necessarily leads to crime. Razumikhin is even poorer than Raskolnikov; he also lives in a "closet"; he has also left the university; but he works. He views poverty as a temporary setback. Razumikhin shows us that Raskolnikov's crime does not necessarily derive from his poverty. Once Sonya rejects the explanation of poverty, Raskolnikov returns to his superman theory and his desire to prove something to himself. Sonya again dismisses his arguments on moral grounds. First she rejects the label he attaches to Alyona Ivanovna, the pawnbroker: "A human being—a louse!" (5.4.416). Then she challenges the act itself: "To kill? The right to kill?" (5.4.419). Finally, Sonya proposes that Raskolnikov accept the guilt script: "Accept suffering and redeem yourself by it, that's what you must do" (5.4.420). I ask the students to note his responses: Raskolnikov projects blame, accuses others of evildoing, and expresses contempt. He refuses the guilt script and clings to the grandiosity that protects him from shame: "How am I guilty before them? Why should I go? What should I tell them? ... They'll just laugh at me; ... They won't understand a thing, Sonya, not a thing—and they're not worthy to understand" (5.4.420-21). Dostoevsky the author keeps us waiting.

As we can see, Raskolnikov forgets Lizaveta, because she does not figure in his theory. Sonya, on the other hand, considers Lizaveta the more important victim, because she was her friend. Sonya has Lizaveta's Bible and her cross. She keeps the memory of

Lizaveta alive. For Raskolnikov, Sonya represents an "implacable sentence" (6.3.463): accept the guilt script and rejoin the community. Where are we now? Have we put one foot into Sonya's camp?

Separation from community is the real punishment for Raskolnikov's crime. During his early visit to the police station, Raskolnikov experiences a "dark sensation of infinite isolation and estrangement" (2.1.103). His crime has cut him off from his family, from human community, and, as we will realize at novel's end, from God. Zossimov the doctor offers him Delphic advice: "Your complete recovery now depends chiefly on you yourself.... I do not know these original causes, but they must be known to you. You are an intelligent man and, of course, have observed yourself. It seems to me that the beginning of your disorder partially coincides with your leaving the university" (3.3.223). He thus articulates one of the best reasons for staying in school: university as community.

Raskolnikov confirms this diagnosis by acknowledging the dangers of isolation. During his first visit to Sonya, he tells her, "If you remain *alone*, you'll lose your mind, like I did" (4.4.329). During his second visit, Raskolnikov emphasizes the consequences of his choice to isolate himself by using the language of the underground man: "I *turned spiteful*" (Я *озлился*; 5.4.417). Fortunately for Raskolnikov, Porfiry proves himself a moral diagnostician who recognizes the need for community. During their third encounter, this time in Raskolnikov's room, Porfiry diagnoses Raskolnikov's shame: "He came up with a theory and became ashamed because it did not work, because it did not come out originally! It did come out meanly, that's true, but even so you're not a hopeless scoundrel. Not such a scoundrel at all" (6.2.459-60). Like Sonya and my students, Porfiry differentiates between Raskolnikov's act and his self. He urges Raskolnikov to find himself: "It's not a matter of time, but of you yourself. Become a sun and everyone will see you. The sun must above all be the sun" (6.2.460). Porfiry thus urges positive agency on Raskolnikov. He also predicts Raskolnikov's need for community: "Run away, and you'll come back on your own. You cannot get along without us" (6.2.461). Although Porfiry forgets Lizaveta, he articulates the Orthodox view of human interdependency. He also displays an acute understanding of shame dynamics: shame alienates, but it also reminds us of our connection to others. As Vladimir Solovyov, the philosopher who both influenced and was influenced by Dostoevsky, observes, even though shame is experienced as a negative self-assessment, the very fact that shame is experienced speaks of a positive self-assessment. Only if we feel ourselves capable of something better can we experience the pain of falling short.

Shame is critical to understanding why Sonya becomes Raskolnikov's vehicle for return to community. I ask my students why he had been drawn to her from the first time he heard about her. Somewhere along the way, we have discussed the parallels between the Marmeladovs and the Raskolnikovs: daughters who are willing to sell themselves for their families; mothers who consent and go mad; self-tormenting men who are dependent on women's financial support. Raskolnikov identifies with Sonya because, like him, she has deep knowledge of both shame and guilt. Like Raskolnikov, Sonya is isolated and self-divided: she experiences Dunya's politeness and attention as burdensome and tormenting (3.4.239) and feels relief at being alone (3.4.243). Like Raskolnikov, when alone, Sonya is pensive and distracted: Svidrigailov notices Sonya's pensiveness (3.4.244) just as Dunya notices Raskolnikov's (6.5.486). Raskolnikov asks her: "Haven't you done the same thing?" (4.4.329). He may have murdered others, but he sees Sonya as someone who has murdered part of herself. Raskolnikov diagnoses similar alternatives for her: madness, suicide, depravity. Like Raskolnikov, Sonya is a divided self: her profession does not reflect her beliefs. She has also experienced shame and banishment from community. As Raskolnikov says, "We're cursed together, so let's go together" (4.4.329).

After "confessing" to Sonya in 5.4.405-22, Raskolnikov starts his three-step return to community. First, he bows down and embraces his mother (6.6.515). Next, he bows down and kisses the earth (6.7.525). Finally, at the very end of the Epilogue, he bows down and embraces Sonya (Epilogue 2.529). He thus returns to himself, the human community, and God. The biblical imagery of the heart softening used in his confession to Sonya dominates the first two bowing scenes. With his mother, "As though making up for that whole terrible time his heart softened all at once. He fell down before her, he kissed her feet, and they both, embracing each other, wept" (6.6.515). In the Haymarket Square, "Everything in him softened all at once, and the tears flowed. He fell to the earth where he stood... He knelt in the middle of the square, bowed to the earth, and kissed that dirty earth with pleasure and happiness" (6.7.525). Both these moments represent a breaking down of Raskolnikov's defenses, an opening of self. Both contain imagery of bowing. The imagery of conversion dominates the third scene. Whereas St. Paul on the road to Damascus sees a light and falls to the ground, Raskolnikov is lifted up and flung down. The change has been long in coming, yet it arrives dramatically.

To understand this dramatic change, we return to Raskolnikov's semi-conscious—his daydreams of the trichinae, which reveal the twin dangers of rationality and emotional isolation. Conversion is possible only once he realizes that he loves Sonya. In the confession scene, we saw the dynamic of love dissolving barriers: "Here was love; his hatred vanished like a ghost" (5.4.409). After his daydreams, he looks out the hospital window and sees Sonya. Heart pierced, he steps back. Sonya disappears for two days. Raskolnikov starts to worry, a sign of the move from self-enclosure to love that culminates on the novel's final pages: "He remembered how he had constantly tormented her and torn her heart; he remembered her poor, thin little face; but these memories almost did not torment him now; he knew by what infinite love he would now redeem all her sufferings" (Epilogue.2.550).

Dostoevsky leaves readers to draw our own conclusions. In acknowledging his guilt to Sonya, Raskolnikov relinquishes his shame. Accepting that he has wronged her, he accepts himself as he is. He no longer needs to prove his superiority. Love releases him from the prison house of ego. When he thinks of Sonya, Raskolnikov forgets his "self." Whether or not students accept that the link between Sonya and Lizaveta means that he can expiate his guilt toward both with his love for one, they can see that this scene represents the end of Raskolnikov's personal, social, and spiritual alienation. Whether they think the ending is tacky and artificial is another matter.

Michael Holquist argues that the Epilogue represents another time frame, that of the wisdom tale, which transcends the historical time of the novel's detective action.[5] Gary Rosenshield observes that the narrative shift from indirect discourse to summarization allows Dostoevsky to convey authorial message and approval.[6] Although I agree partially with both, I try to get my students to see that the shift in the Epilogue's narration reflects the change in Raskolnikov. He has confessed and accepted external punishment. Exile to Siberia gives him the geographical and spiritual distance from his crime necessary to see his way clearly. Most importantly, I want my students to see that the Epilogue represents a recapitulation of the novel's major plot events with one big difference: no murder.

Epilogue part 1 summarizes the eighteen months following Raskolnikov's confession. Significantly, nine of them have been in Siberia—a sign that he is ready for rebirth. This part ends with the report that Raskolnikov is seriously ill. Part 2 focuses on Raskolnikov. I ask my students to comment on his spiritual state: he is still indifferent to his environment—doesn't even feel his chains (Epilogue 2.543). He is ill and has haunting dreams. He experiences emotional change and bows down to a woman.

Until the very end of Epilogue 2, we see the same old unrepentant Raskolnikov. The narrator comments: "But he was ashamed not of a shaved head and chains: his pride was badly wounded; and it was from wounded pride that he fell ill. Oh, how happy he would have been if he could have condemned himself! He could have endured everything then, even shame and disgrace. But he judged himself severely, and his hardened conscience did not find any especially terrible guilt in his past, except perhaps a simple *blunder* that could have happened to anyone. He was ashamed precisely because he, Raskolnikov, had perished so blindly, hopelessly, vainly, and stupidly, by some sort of decree of blind fate" (Epilogue 2.543). Here we realize that Raskolnikov

---

5   Michael Holquist, *Dostoevsky and the Novel* (Evanston, IL: Northwestern University Press, 1977), 101.

6   Rosenshield, *Crime and Punishment*, 118-21.

suffers *because he does not feel guilt!* The narrator emphasizes this: "If only fate had sent him repentance—burning repentance, that breaks the heart, that drives sleep away, such repentance as torments one into dreaming of the noose or the watery deeps! Oh, he would have been glad of it! Torments and tears—that, too, was life. But he did not repent of his crime" (Epilogue 2.544). We are left to infer that repentance would bring relief. Guilt is easier to bear than shame.

In the Epilogue, Dostoevsky uses scriptural shorthand to signal the possibility of change. He sets the final scenes in the season of Lent and the coming of Easter. Like the narration of the Epilogue, Raskolnikov's illness and daydreams of the trichinae are more abstract, more cognitive. The trichinae act out the pride of individualism and rationalism. Their cognitive nature reflects Raskolnikov's state: he is distanced from emotional pain. Like his unconscious dreams, these daydreams represent a return of the repressed. Acting out of self-interest, the trichinae kill one another.

While the Epilogue recapitulates, it does so with a difference. In part 1, Raskolnikov feels compelled by a mechanical external force. After hearing that the pawnbroker will be alone, "he suddenly felt with his whole being that he no longer had any freedom either of mind or of will, and that everything had suddenly and finally been decided" (1.5.62). In the Epilogue, Raskolnikov seeks Sonya and, "How it happened he himself did not know, but suddenly something seemed to pick him up and throw him down at her feet" (Epilogue 2.549). In both cases, Raskolnikov is gripped by forces beyond his control. In part 1, Raskolnikov returns to his coffin-room like a man "condemned to death." In the biblical landscape of the final Epilogue scene, he is resurrected "into a new life." Most significantly, Raskolnikov is no longer alone. He has traveled the painful road from self-enclosure to self-sacrificing love: "He knew by what infinite love he would now redeem all her sufferings" (Epilogue 2.550). Raskolnikov has finally embraced the guilt script: he has repented and longs to expiate his sins. He has been resurrected. On the last pages of *Crime and Punishment*, Dostoevsky gives readers the guilt script we have long been expecting.

12

Text and Philosophy

Notes from a Cave: Teaching *Notes from Underground* in a Philosophy Class

Nancy Workman

I.

> Yet another thing tormented me then: namely, the fact that nobody was like me, and I wasn't like anyone. 'I am one, but they are everyone,' I would think, and—and get lost in thought.
>
> —*Notes from Underground*, Part II, Section I[1]

Some time ago, feeling I needed a change of pace from many years of teaching Literature Humanities, a year-long Western literature survey course that Columbia College freshmen take as part of the Core Curriculum, I decided to teach the companion year-long survey course usually taken by sophomores, Contemporary Civilization, commonly referred to simply as CC. Students in CC read a series of texts including philosophical works; Jewish, Christian, and Muslim scriptures; manifestos and documents pertaining to the French, American, and Haitian revolutions; and an assortment of other texts including the occasional economic or biological treatise. What ties all these disparate texts together is the perception that they all have something important to contribute to a discussion about the shape of a good human life. Before classes began, I thought it might make sense to ask two basic questions about each text: "If what this asserts is true, how should we live?," and "Is what it asserts actually true?" Excellent class discussions would, I hoped, ensue.

---

[1] F. M. Dostoevskii, *Polnoe sobranie sochinenii v tridtsati tomakh* (Leningrad: Nauka, 1972-90), 5:125. The translation is mine.

In practice, as someone whose background is in literature, I found deciding what to do with the material in class quite disorienting; I was used to teasing out interpretations by paying close attention to tone or patterns of imagery or alliteration, and here I was apparently dealing with texts in which some writer just said exactly what he or she meant. What do you do with *that*? Once the syllabus advanced past Plato's Allegory of the Cave, a vast ocean of ideas seemed to stretch ahead of me without so much as a vivid metaphor to cling to (and analyze).

For the spring term, I decided to include a piece of fiction, something with both philosophical and literary concerns, for the interpretation of which my own expertise might be a real asset. Among the Russians, Dostoevsky seemed the best candidate. Without being reducible to sermons or lectures, his works feature characters passionately concerned with how to live a good human life in their own time and place. Conveniently for the purposes of my class, his works frequently critiqued schools of thought with which my students were about to become familiar. Time considerations made *Notes from Underground* the most attractive option. I was eager to have a different kind of discussion about it than the sort I would have had in a literature class, a discussion that would take seriously the *ideas* with which part 1 is so thickly larded. In fact, I considered assigning part 1 in isolation so we could focus on the *ideas*, a notion that in hindsight—I ended up assigning both parts—seems to undercut my whole purpose in including a work of fiction and, more seriously, to misunderstand how fiction, and Dostoevsky's fiction in particular, actually works as a way of thinking about "the good life."

I'm especially glad I decided to assign part 2 as well because our class discussion of part 1 didn't seem to go particularly well. In talking about its philosophical underpinnings, we did duly note that the underground man found Utilitarian concepts distasteful (the students had read Mill); that he felt touchy about being told he was descended from a monkey (they had just read Darwin); that he would no doubt have sneered at Hegel's concept of the relentless teleological march of history toward ultimate freedom by means of a mechanism Hegel himself refers to as a "slaughter-bench," culminating in an ideal State run on the Prussian model; that determinism provoked him; that references to Rousseau, whose "Discourse on the Origin of Inequality" and "On the Social Contract" they had read, were everywhere.[2] After this enumeration of influences, however, the discussion of *ideas* petered out far more quickly than I had imagined it would, and for the remainder of the two-hour class I was thrown back on my old friends, "plot" and "character."

In that time, we touched on issues for which my background in Russian literature was helpful in interpreting the text: what "type" the underground man was meant to represent, why Dostoevsky set the story in St. Petersburg, the obligatory plot summary of *What Is to Be Done?* Our discussion of the plot of part 2 turned largely around the underground man's self-absorption: his inability, for example, to understand that Liza's suffering was far greater than his own. The one moment I remember vividly from the session occurred, however, when I asked the class a different kind of question, not concerned with *ideas*, historical background, or literary technique: "Who has ever felt like this character?" I raised my own hand with some trepidation—was I exposing something shameful about myself? But it turned out I was in good company: over the course of about twenty long seconds, everyone eventually raised a hand.

When the class was over, I was dissatisfied with the way it had gone. I wondered if I had simply mishandled the material— perhaps that was why no intellectually engaging discussion about free will, utopian thinking, history, or the place of the individual in society had emerged. In pondering this question afterwards, I kept coming back to the very first text we had read in CC, Plato's

---

2   For a very informative discussion of the importance of Rousseau's "On the Social Contract" and *Second Discourse* in *Notes from Underground*, see Olga Stuchebrukhov, "'Ridiculous' Dreams versus Social Contract: Dostoevskij, Rousseau, and the Problem of Ideal Society," in *Studies in Eastern European Thought* 59 (2007): 101-17. This very erudite and useful article suffers from one flaw: it treats the ideas of the underground man as if they accurately expressed the beliefs of Dostoevsky himself.

Republic. Hadn't Plato already warned me that, because it bypasses reason to work through the emotions, imaginative literature is a distraction in the pursuit of both truth and a well-lived life? Had I been wrong to let Dostoevsky into my Republic?

II.

> Who was it that first said that man does nasty things only because he doesn't know where his real interests lie...?
>
> —*Notes from Underground*, Part I, Section VII[3]

As depicted in the *Republic*, Plato's character Socrates finds many occasions to denigrate art. Perhaps most importantly, in *Republic* 10, Plato has Socrates say that there has long been a quarrel between poetry—by which he surely means all imaginative literature—and philosophy.[4] Sometimes what bothers Socrates, and probably his author as well, about "poetry" is its distant relationship to truth, the fact that it is merely the imitation of an imitation of the Really Real. It should be pointed out, however, that untrue stories sometimes come in handy for the Socrates of the *Republic*. At the end of book 10, Plato has Socrates produce an exemplary didactic tale, the Myth of Er, whose instructive value remains whether it refers to reality or not; elsewhere, Socrates (like the Grand Inquisitor) positively asserts

---

[3]   Dostoevsky, *Notes*, 105. Gary Saul Morson answers this question: "The one who 'first proclaimed' this theory, or a version of it, was, of course, Socrates: and the underground man here seems to be answering both the *Republic* and a contemporary utopian target, *What Is to Be Done?*, which outlines a similar theory" (Gary Saul Morson, "Anti-Utopianism in *Notes from Underground*," repr. in *Notes from Underground: A New Translation* [New York: Norton, 1989], 189-90).

[4]   Plato, *Republic*, trans. Alan Bloom, second ed. (New York: Basic Books, 1991), book 10:607b, 290. Hereafter, citations from the *Republic* will be given in the text, and will be identified by both book number and "Stephanus number" (i.e., the number and letter designating a specific section of the text, commonly used in scholarly discourse on Plato), rather than by the page number in Bloom's translation.

the utility of the so-called "Noble Lie" (3:414c and following). With these types of untruth, utility is all that matters.

At two points in the *Republic*, in books 2 and 10, however, Socrates discusses a kind of poetic fiction which he claims is not merely untrue and not useful but positively harmful to the human community and the human soul: the work of the "imitative" poet, who would have no place in a city run according to the principles of justice. The second time he closes the door on these poets, however, he leaves the window open: "[I]f poetry directed to pleasure and imitation have any argument to give showing that they should be in a city with good laws, we should be delighted to receive them back from exile, since we are aware that we ourselves are charmed by them" (10:607c). Aha, I thought when I reread this: a potential way back in for Dostoevsky.

But it would not be easy to get a passport that would allow *Notes from Underground* into the Republic. One of Socrates's major complaints about "imitative poets" is that they are naturally drawn to depicting things that are already full of color and variety, easily perceived by an audience, and he mentions as a particular favorite of these imitators "the irritable and various disposition" (10:605a). This is a problem, according to Socrates, because audiences take in the portrayal of any human type, no matter how unattractive— especially the "direct" portrayal, through quoting that character's own words—as if it were permission or even a very tempting invitation to become like him or (even worse) her. Immersing ourselves in the mind of an "irritable" character is liable to seduce us away from the finest kind of life, that in which the emotions are kept under strict control by the rational part of the soul, by strengthening the "foolish" part. For my purposes, Plato might just as well have had *Notes from Underground* in mind when he wrote this part of the *Republic*, for what is the novella but a prolonged near-total immersion in the mind of an "irritable character"? My question to my students about whether or not they felt they resembled the underground man had been met, as you recall, with a unanimous "Yes," and a later conversation with a couple of them proved that reading *Notes from Underground* had enabled them to recognize and give a fun label to a certain unattractive state of mind they sometimes found themselves in on the subway, for example, but had not motivated them to extirpate it.

So Plato has his character Socrates exclude imaginative literature that engages strong emotions and immerses us in the minds of less-than-ideal others from his imaginary Republic. Of course, he does so *within* a written narrative account made up almost entirely of quoted speech. In other words, Plato uses the techniques of fiction to put forward a condemnation of—or at the very least, a highly suspicious attitude toward—fiction. The fiction that is *Republic* (which takes the form of a monologue: "I went down to the Piraeus yesterday with Glaucon..." [1:327a]), however, is apparently at least potentially salutary. In his introduction to Plato's complete works, John Cooper points out the truth readers sometimes forget, that

> you must work hard even to find out what the author of a Platonic dialogue is saying to the reader—it is in the writing as a whole that the author speaks, not in the words of any single speaker—and the dialogue form demands that you think for yourself in deciding what, if anything, in it or suggested by it is really the truth.... Plato is only inviting others to do their own intellectual work, in cooperation with him in thinking through the issues that he is addressing.[5]

When Dostoevsky crows, referring to readers of *Poor Folk*, "They have become accustomed to seeing the author's mug in everything; I didn't show mine,"[6] he could just as well be talking about Plato's habitual practice: Plato is the original non-mug-showing author, and the genre he chooses to write in, the monologue in the voice of a character quoting a remembered dialogue, means that every apparent "word" comes with its own built-in Bakhtinian "loophole."

---

5 John M. Cooper, introduction to *Plato: Complete Works*, ed. John M. Cooper (Indianapolis, IN: Hackett Publishing, 1997), xx.

6 Quoted in Mikhail Bakhtin, *Problems of Dostoevsky's Poetics*, ed. and trans. Caryl Emerson (Minneapolis, MN: University of Minnesota Press, 1984), 209. The line occurs in a letter to his brother Mikhail Dostoevsky, written on February 1, 1846.

But even if we grant that the message of any of Plato's Socratic dialogues about the true nature of justice, piety, or love is not nearly as clear as it may seem at first glance, that his texts are, like Dostoevsky's, "unfinalizable" in Bakhtin's sense of the word, the most important, basic function of Plato's Socratic dialogues is to promote "philosophizing" in their readers. Thus for the reading of a Socratic dialogue to lead to a classroom discussion about the nature of justice makes perfect sense. But what do we "get" from Dostoevsky's monologue, and what, if anything, does or should it prompt its readers to do, or even to discuss? Clearly it doesn't do for its audience what a Socratic dialogue does for *its* audience: provide, in an efficient form, both a positive model of how to pursue truth through the deployment of logical argumentation and a stimulus to do so. Is it really an adequate or logical response to reading *Notes from Underground* to start a discussion about the pros and cons of Utopian thinking or Utilitarianism? Among other things, we are given notice by the very first paragraph, as well as by the fictional "editor's" label for the underground man, "paradoxalist," at the end, that the underground man does not really represent a position with which we can argue—firstly, because he isn't a "position" but a man, and secondly, because he is not capable of being persuaded by logic, as the characters in a Socratic dialogue are. His ideas are internally self-contradictory. For example, in part 1, section 10, he claims both that the horror of the Crystal Palace idea lies in its unmockability and that Crystal Palace designers have never produced a structure that's unmockable. There's another problem with him as well: Dostoevsky goes to great lengths to insist that we see the underground man as a reader, someone who gets his obviously inadequate ideas about life from books and consequently, as Liza says in part 2, "talks like a book." What does that say about what we can hope to get out of *this* book? Is our situation as readers of *Notes from Underground* a *mise en abîme* in which a bad character who "talks like a book" is presented as writing a book from which we in turn will learn to talk like books? In Plato's dialogue *Phaedrus*, Socrates complains about the destructive effects of interacting with a book rather than with a human being: books, he says, are frozen and fixed; you can ask them questions, but they'll never give you a new answer, always the same one. That Plato himself must have felt that this was not necessarily true is implied by the fact that he *wrote it down*. That Dostoevsky wrote the writings of the underground man, that he invited us to marinate ourselves in that irritable consciousness, suggests in itself that there is some value to this activity—but what is it?

If Dostoevsky's goal were the opposite of Plato's—to provide a negative model we should be sure not to imitate—it's clear that he could have used a technique Plato has Socrates suggest in *Republic* 10, for dealing with the necessity of sometimes depicting bad people and actions: he could have written a very external, third-person account of a thoroughly despicable character, with no quoted speech; after all, that's basically what he did do when he created Luzhin in *Crime and Punishment*.[7] Luzhin's thoughts upon being refused and sent away by Dunya in part 5, chapter 1 are—with minor exceptions—not quoted but given in *erlebte Rede* so drenched in sarcasm that the dullest reader couldn't miss the idea that this is a BAD MAN. But our experience of reading the words of the underground man is quite different. Dostoevsky seems to insist upon precisely what Plato forbids: that the reader try on the persona of the underground man, and that he or she recognize that it corresponds to some degree with what is already inside him or her.

What do we gain by this recognition? If I teach Core Curriculum again, and teach *Notes from Underground* within it, I will address that problem head-on. I will spend some time discussing the

---

[7]   See *Republic* 396d: "'In my opinion,' I said, 'when the sensible man comes in his narrative to some speech or deed of a good man, he will be willing to report it as though he himself were that man and won't be ashamed of such an imitation. ... But when he meets with someone unworthy of himself, he won't be willing seriously to represent himself as an inferior, unless, of course, it's brief, when the man does something good; rather, he'll be ashamed, both because he's unpracticed at imitating such men and because he can't stand forming himself according to, and fitting himself into, the models of worse men" (trans. Bloom, 75). Of course, Dostoevsky doesn't literally carry out this strategy, but he does very markedly distance himself from Luzhin's thoughts in a way he seldom or never does with other characters.

implications of having precisely this character (an "irritable" man), depicted in precisely this way (through immersing the reader in his consciousness and creating an identification), discussing precisely this subject matter (Utopian thinking, the "Crystal Palace"), and I will bring in Plato's *Republic* for explicit comparison. In the *Republic*, Socrates has one "irritable" interlocutor, Thrasymachus, who enters the dialogue in this manner:

> Now Thrasymachus had many times started out to take over the argument in the midst of our discussion, but he had been restrained by the men sitting near him, who wanted to hear the argument out. But when we paused … he could no longer keep quiet; hunched up like a wild beast, he flung himself at us as if to tear us to pieces. … And he shouted out into our midst and said, "What is this nonsense that has possessed you for so long, Socrates? And why do you act like fools making way for one another?" (336b-c)

But over the course of a few pages, using a series of questions, Socrates tames Thrasymachus, first making him blush (350d) and finally getting him to concede explicitly that he has been convinced that "injustice is never more profitable than justice" (354a). In other words, Thrasymachus, who may represent the reader's own suspicion that unjust behavior is, if nothing else, more profitable than just, shows himself to be susceptible to the persuasive powers of philosophy, and stops obstructing the discussion that will continue to map out the Kallipolis, the completely just city. In his monologue in part 1 of *Notes from Underground*, however, the underground man is an untamable Thrasymachus who totally controls the discussion and prevents it from going anywhere meaningful. His discussion is interior (though with Bakhtin's perpetual "sideways glance"), but it's difficult to imagine any Socrates who could persuade him. He doesn't need someone like the philosopher to lead him to a state of *aporia*, an understanding of the fact that his own previously unexamined beliefs are actually self-contradictory; he is in such a state from the very beginning of the piece, and not only aware but proud of it. His irritable, internal dialogue, an eternal chewing-over of a cud that never gets digested, doesn't form a chain of logical argumentation but a Mobius strip, the twisting of a two-sided piece of material into a paradoxically one-sided loop around which one can trace an endless path without ever getting anywhere.

When we recognize at least part of ourselves in this extreme, concentrated character, something happens to our attitude toward his discussion of the Crystal Palace that a straightforward argument would have difficulty eliciting: the perversity of this character as embodied not in some particular argument but in the totality of everything he says (and, later, everything he does) simply demolishes the Crystal Palace idea and makes it look not illogical but silly and untenable. If our identification with the character, achieved by immersion in his consciousness, causes us to think, "Yes, this is (sometimes) what it *feels like* to be a person," then we grasp something important about what a human self is, in all its bottomless complexity, that competes tacitly with the view of human nature put forth by "the philosophers" in general and, I would insist, not merely the Rational Egoists.[8] Dostoevsky makes immediately palpable the futility of speaking about human beings as if they were abstract units. If this man exists—and if *we* feel like him when we read *Notes*, he must—how can any Utopia be possible, whether it is Plato's just city, the Kallipolis; Rousseau's republic of individuals transformed into citizens "forced to be free" in "On the Social Contract"; or Hegel's "goal of world history"? Creation of a recognizable underground man says that the philosophers *as a group* are simply insufficiently attentive to the characteristics of the experience of being human. If they can't factor all this perversity into their accounts, how can we trust them to explain how we should live?

---

[8] See James Scanlan, "The Case against Rational Egoism," in *Dostoevsky the Thinker* (Ithaca, NY: Cornell University Press, 2002), 57-80, for a very helpful interpretation of *Notes from Underground* as a philosophically coherent response to *What Is to Be Done?*

III.

> Lord, we know what we are, but know not what
> we may be.
>
> —*Hamlet* IV:v:43-44

It now seems to me that *Notes from Underground*, dialogic as its style may be, is not designed to foster a conversation about, for example, utopian thinking, but precisely to shut such a conversation down and direct the reader's attention elsewhere. It turns out to be completely necessary to Dostoevsky's project that we do precisely what Plato considers so dangerous: that we see ourselves in an "undesirable" character, or see him in ourselves. Though thinking about Dostoevsky in light of Plato's *Republic* hasn't convinced me that my unsatisfactory class was actually a success, in the end I do believe that the question, "How many of you have felt like this character?" was the right one to ask in a course intended to foster inquiry into the nature of the good human life. In writing *Notes from Underground* as—among other things—an anti-utopian response to *What Is to Be Done?*, Dostoevsky implicitly claims to be a more profound thinker about the human condition than Chernyshevsky. If we were to make this tacit assertion explicit, however, Dostoevsky would be saying not, "I am a better thinker *and* a better novelist than you, Nikolai Gavrilovich," but precisely, "I am a better thinker *because* I am a better novelist than you." Dostoevsky would hold that the imaginative power of a novelist is perhaps the single most important tool a thinker can have; it is the sympathetic imagination, not logic, that gives us at least a chance of knowing what human beings really are, and not just what we "may be" were the world to be organized otherwise.

13

TEXT AND CONTEXT II

Dostoevsky's *Notes from Underground* Revisited, Plus a Few Thoughts about Winnie-the-Pooh

Ellen Chances

Dedicated to Bob Belknap

> [S]ome lived in trees and some lived underground....[1]
>
> —A. A. Milne, *Winnie-the-Pooh*

In *The House at Pooh Corner*, Pooh, Rabbit, and Piglet can't find their way from the sand-pit home, and they keep ending up at the Pit again. Finally Pooh asks,

> "How would it be, ... if, as soon as we're out of sight of this Pit, we try to find it again?"
>
> "What's the good of that?" said Rabbit.
>
> "Well," said Pooh, "we keep looking for Home and not finding it, so I thought that if we looked for this Pit, we'd be sure not to find it, which would be a Good Thing, because then we might find something that we *weren't* looking for, which might be just what we *were* looking for, really."[2]

Introduction

When I began to write this article on teaching *Notes from Underground*, I considered the above passage from *The House at Pooh Corner* as

---

[1] A. A. Milne, *Winnie-the-Pooh* (New York: Dutton Children's Books, 2001), 29.

[2] A. A. Milne, *The House at Pooh Corner* (New York: Dutton Children's Books, 2001), 123-24.

relevant to teaching that novel. It then seemed as if this was not the case. As I finished working on the article, I concluded that what I call the "Pooh principle" was, in fact, connected to Dostoevsky's novel. Thus, I first focus on Dostoevsky, and near the end, I bring Winnie-the-Pooh into the discussion.

My article is in two parts, in honor of the division of *Notes from Underground* into two parts. In honor of Robert Belknap, I call them "Genesis" and "Structure," because his books are called *The Genesis of "The Brothers Karamazov"* and *The Structure of "The Brothers Karamazov."* The first part of the article discusses the background that I give students, and the second part, the structure of the novel.

Part One: The "Genesis" of *Notes from Underground*: Background

In *Genesis*, Belknap writes that scholars should treat letters, memoirs, or manifestos as equals of fiction.[3] Extending Belknap's statement to different areas, I explain some of the novel's background and context. I tell students that *Notes from Underground* came out in *Epoch* (Эпоха), the thick journal that opened after the censors had closed *Time* (Время).[4] These were the journals that Dostoevsky founded, contributed to, and edited, together with his brother Mikhail. I talk about "concept of the soil" (*pochvennichestvo*), the ideology that they, together with Apollon Grigoriev, Nikolai Strakhov, and others, espoused in the journals. Educated Russians had become cut off from the soil, from the simple Russian people, through Western ideas and rational thinking. It was up to the educated to learn the people's spiritual values. I then explain that the ideology shifted from a belief in laws as a way to solve Russia's problems to a belief in the spiritual transformation of each individual as the only way to effect change. The only way to change, according to the

---

[3]   Robert L. Belknap, *The Genesis of "The Brothers Karamazov": The Aesthetics, Ideology, and Psychology of Making a Text* (Evanston, IL: Northwestern University Press, 1990), 11.

[4]   The novel was published in *Epokha*, nos. 1, 2, and 4 (1864).

ideology, was through the spontaneous love of one human being for another.[5]

Notes from Underground, I tell students, can be read as a fictionalized version of the ideology of "the concept of the soil" (*pochvennichestvo*). The underground man can be seen as "sick and spiteful" precisely because he suffers from the disease of consciousness, which derives from Western European rational thought. He describes the "nasty, despicable" moans of an educated man suffering from a toothache: "He begins ... to moan ... like a man who's 'renounced both the soil and the common people,' as they say nowadays." ("Он начинает ... стонать ... как человек 'отрешившийся от почвы и народных начал, как теперь выражаются'").[6] In contrast to Liza, who shows spontaneous compassion toward and love for the underground man, the underground man is not capable of compassion. The censored part of *Notes from Underground* would have shown the alternative to the underground that the "men of the soil" (*pochvenniki*) advocated.

Another aspect of the background to the novel has to do with Grigoriev, also a *pochvennik*. Both his life and his ideas are important to the novel. Once, he tried to rescue a fallen woman from a brothel. Belknap, in *The Genesis of "The Brothers Karamazov,"* states that we

---

5   For a detailed analysis of the ideology of *pochvennichestvo* and its evolution on the pages of *Time* and *Epoch,* see Ellen Chances, "Pochvennichestvo: Ideology in Dostoevsky's Periodicals," *Mosaic* 7, no. 2 (1974): 71-88; Chances, "Literary Criticism and the Ideology of Pochvennichestvo in Dostoevsky's Thick Journals *Vremia* and *Epokha,*" *Russian Review* 34, no. 2 (1975): 151-64; and Chances, "Pochvennichestvo: Evolution of an Ideology," *Modern Fiction Studies* 20, no. 4 (1974-75): 543-51. For more on *pochvennichestvo,* see Wayne Dowler, *Dostoevsky, Grigor'ev and Native Soil Conservatism* (Toronto: University of Toronto Press, 1982); and Andzhej de Lazari, *V krugu Fedora Dostoevskogo: Pochvennichestvo* (Moscow: Nauka, 2004), trans. M. V. Leskinen and N. M. Filatova (originally published as Andrzej de Lazari, *W kręgu Fiodora Dostojewskiego. Poczwiennictwo* [Łodz, Ibidem, 2000]). For more on *Vremia* and *Epokha,* see V. S. Nechaeva, *Zhurnal M. M. i F. M. Dostoevskikh "Vremia" 1861-1863* (Moscow: Nauka, 1972) and V. S. Nechaeva, *Zhurnal M. M. i F. M. Dostoevskikh "Epokha" 1864-1865* (Moscow: Nauka, 1975).

6   Fyodor Dostoevsky, *Notes from Underground,* trans. and ed. Michael R. Katz (New York: Norton, 1989), 11. F. M. Dostoevskii, *Zapiski iz podpol'ia,* in *Polnoe sobranie sochinenii v tridtsati tomakh* (Leningrad: Nauka, 1972-90), 5:106-7.

have to note what Dostoevsky did, not only what he said.[7] Here, in telling the students about a detail of Grigoriev's life—that he tried to rescue a fallen woman from a brothel—, I note what Dostoevsky knew. I also note what Dostoevsky did not write. Thus, in the epigraph to part 2 of *Notes from Underground*, he quotes lines from the Nekrasov poem, "When Out of the Darkness of Delusion" ("Когда из мрака заблужденья").[8] Significantly, the poem's next stanza, not quoted by Dostoevsky, stresses the narrator's capacity to empathize: "Believe me: I listened not without concern,/I fervently tried to grasp every sound.../I understood everything, child of misfortune!/I forgave everything and forgot everything" ("Верь: я внимал не без участья,/Я жадно каждый звук ловил.../Я понял все, дитя несчастья!/Я все простил и все забыл").[9] I tell my students that Dostoevsky in *Notes from Underground* was combining a reworking of the redemption of the fallen woman theme with the facts of Grigoriev's life. Not only Grigoriev's life, but also his ideas, are important to the novel. In his contributions to Dostoevsky's journals, Grigoriev wrote about his concept of "organic criticism" (*organicheskaia kritika*). For instance, he divided Russian literary characters, such as Lermontov's Pechorin and Maksim Maksimych, into "predatory" (*khishchnye*) types, cut off from reality and the soil; and "meek" (*smirnye*) types, striving toward the soil.[10] We can add

---

7 Belknap, *Genesis*, 13.

8 For the entire poem, see N. A. Nekrasov, *Polnoe sobranie stikhotvorenii v trekh tomakh*, ed. and introd. K. I. Chukovskii (Leningrad, Sovetskii pisatel', 1967), 1:101-2.

9 Ibid., 102.

10 See, for example, A. Grigor'ev, "Lermontov i ego napravlenie," *Vremia*, no. 12 (1862): 1-33. For more on Grigoriev, "organic criticism," and its importance for *pochvennichestvo*, see Ellen Chances, "Literary Criticism." For relevant material on Grigoriev and these points, also see B. F. Egorov, "Apollon Grigor'ev: poet," in Apollon Grigor'ev, *Stikhotvoreniia. Poemy. Dramy* (St. Petersburg: Akademicheskii Proekt, 2001), 5-47; B. F. Egorov, "Materialy ob Ap. Grigor'eve iz arkhiva N. N. Strakhova," *Uchenye zapiski Tartuskogo gosudarstvennogo universiteta* 139 (1963): 343-50; and Wayne Dowler, *An Unnecessary Man: The Life of Apollon Grigor'ev* (Toronto: University of Toronto Press, 1995).

to Grigoriev's list. What, I ask my students, if not a "predatory" type, is the underground man? And what, if not a "meek" type, is Liza?

I also talk about scholarship that has been written connecting *Notes from Underground* to Chernyshevsky.[11] I speak about Joseph Frank's explanation of parody, with part 1 considered as a "parody of determinism," and part 2 as a "parody of vanity." I tell the students about Frank's hypothesis that the ideas of the 1860s, reflected in part 1 of *Notes from Underground*, stem from the egoism of the 1840s, illustrated in part 2.[12]

I then tell my students about the tradition of the "superfluous man" (лишний человек) in Russian literature. In different forms, this type of figure existed in many portrayals of literary characters from the nineteenth century (such as Pushkin's *Eugene Onegin*, Lermontov's *A Hero of Our Time*) through the works of Turgenev, Tolstoy, Chekhov, and beyond, even into the twenty-first century. Furthermore, I explain, a strong, grounded character, often a woman, is frequently juxtaposed to the intellectual, alienated "superfluous man," either a societal and/or metaphysical misfit or a rebel against the cycles of nature or God.

I then explain the ways that Dostoevsky's novel, it seems to me, fits into that tradition. The non-conformist underground

---

[11] N. L. Brodskii, "Chernyshevskii i ego chitateli 60-kh godov," *Vestnik vospitaniia*, no. 9 (1914): 155-79; V. Komarovich, "Mirovaia garmoniia Dostoevskogo," *Atenei*, nos. 1, 2 (1924): 122-30; A. Skaftymov, "*Zapiski iz podpol'ia* sredi publitsistiki Dostoevskogo," in A. Skaftymov, *Nravstvennye iskaniia russkikh pisatelei* (Moscow: Khudozhestvennaia literatura, 1972), 88-133; Joseph Frank, "Nihilism and *Notes from Underground*," *Sewanee Review* 69 (1961): 1-33; and Joseph Frank, *Dostoevsky: The Stir of Liberation 1860-1865* (Princeton, NJ: Princeton University Press, 1986), 310-47. Skaftymov sees a key role, in *Notes from Underground*, not only for Chernyshevsky's *What Is to Be Done?* (*Что делать?*), but also for his earlier writings, such as "The Anthropological Principle in Philosophy" ("Антропологический принцип в философии"), in *Sovremennik*, nos. 4, 5 (1860). Skaftymov suggests that Dostoevsky's acquaintance with ideas (such as the "Crystal Palace" ["хрустальный дворец"]) of Chernyshevsky against which he protested, came earlier than *What Is to Be Done*, and that Dostoevsky also knew the ideas "directly from Western European sources." Skaftymov, "*Zapiski iz podpol'ia* sredi publitsistiki Dostoevskogo," 128.

[12] See Frank, *Stir of Liberation*.

man—who himself is part of Petersburg, "the most abstract and premeditated city" ("самый отвлеченный и умышленный город") in the world, the city that does not fit into Russia—does not fit into the world of Christian morality. He is diseased precisely because the city is diseased with the germs of Western European ideas. The underground man does not conform to, he is superfluous to, God's law. In contrast, Liza, despite being a prostitute, conforms to higher spiritual values.[13]

Examining the possibilities of multi-dimensional approaches to *Notes from Underground*, I focus students' attention on important scholarly works that deal with various interpretations of the novel. I discuss Belknap's ideas about the "unrepentant confession."[14] I speak about Robert Jackson's metaphysical analysis of the novel.[15] I speak about the work of three other scholars, Liza Knapp, Deborah Martinsen, and Robin Miller.[16] I talk about Knapp's analysis of the underground man in terms of Dostoevsky's metaphysics, in terms of inertia, and in terms of science and religion.[17] I speak about Martinsen's work on the underground narrator.[18] I talk about the underground man's lying to himself and to others. In that context,

---

[13] For more on the superfluous man and ideas of nonconformity and conformity, see Ellen Chances, *Conformity's Children: An Approach to the Superfluous Man in Russian Literature* (Columbus, OH: Slavica Publishers, 1978). For a discussion of *Notes from Underground*, see 96-98.

[14] Robert L. Belknap, "The Unrepentant Confession," in *Russianness: Studies on a Nation's Identity: In Honor of Rufus Mathewson 1918-1978*, ed. Robert L. Belknap (Ann Arbor, MI: Ardis, 1990), 113-23.

[15] Robert Louis Jackson, *Dostoevsky's Underground Man in Russian Literature* ('s-Gravenhage: Mouton, 1958). For the chapters on the novel itself, see 13-64.

[16] Knapp, Martinsen, and Miller are all former students of Belknap's.

[17] Liza Knapp, *The Annihilation of Inertia: Dostoevsky and Metaphysics* (Evanston, IL: Northwestern University Press, 1996), 1-36.

[18] Deborah Martinsen, "Narrators from Underground," *Dostoevskii's Overcoat: Influence, Comparison, and Transposition*, volume II (Rodopi, Amsterdam-New York, 2013), 261-74.

I bring up books by Miller and by Martinsen that include discussions of Dostoevsky and lying.[19]

As the background section of this article demonstrates, I present to students ideas that scholars have already worked out. After providing them with those multiple scholarly perspectives on contexts into which to place *Notes from Underground*, I turn to other issues that are relevant to understanding the novel. For example, I introduce questions that I myself have not resolved, so that together my students and I can explore them.

Part Two: Pondering the Structure of *Notes from Underground*

I have been haunted, for years, by this work's structure. Why does Dostoevsky use the chronology that he does, with the first part taking place in the 1860s and the second part in the 1840s? Why is part 1 mostly an essay-diatribe, and part 2 mostly a story? Of course, one *can* see a coherence. The same narrator presents the whole work as a confession as he narrates ideas and events, as he tells the readers his story in both part 1 and part 2. I tell the students about the highly intelligent explanations that scholars have offered—such as defining part 1 as ideas, "theory," and part 2 as action, "practice." For instance, Frank emphasizes the underground man's attacks on Chernyshevsky in part 1, and characterizes part 2 as mocking sentimental romantic stories. Frank explains that Dostoevsky demonstrates that the "vanity" and "egoism" of the 1840s led to the condition in which the underground man finds himself twenty years later.[20] These explanations are excellent, but I am still haunted by the question, "Why that particular structure?" In fact, Dostoevsky, unsatisfied with this form for a novel, never went back to it.

So why did he use that chronology—part 1 in the 1860s, and part 2 in the 1840s? I ask students to consider with me what is left

---

[19] Robin Feuer Miller, *Dostoevsky and "The Idiot": Author, Narrator, and Reader* (Cambridge, MA: Harvard University Press, 1981); and Deborah A. Martinsen, *Surprised by Shame: Dostoevsky's Liars and Narrative Exposure* (Columbus, OH: The Ohio State University Press, 2003).

[20] Frank, *Stir of Liberation*, 310-47.

out of the novel: the 1850s. *Notes from Underground* reflects, however indirectly, events in Dostoevsky's life in the 1850s and early 1860s in both his personal and political lives. Dostoevsky spent the 1850s in prison and exile, and, as scholars have noted, the underground man is tormented by his imprisoned consciousness. During his exile, Dostoevsky was in a relationship—he admitted that it was against his own self-interest—with his future first wife, who, he felt, tortured him. He had described abusive relationships in previous works. Perhaps, though, his awareness of the pain he inflicted on himself in this relationship was one of the many factors contributing to his focus, in *Notes from Underground*, on people's acting against their own self-interest. In the early 1860s, Dostoevsky was rejected by his mistress, Apollinaria Suslova, when he went to see her in Paris, leaving his seriously ill wife in Russia. I ask my students to consider that in portraying the underground man's behavior toward Liza, Dostoevsky is indirectly reversing his wife's painful treatment of and Suslova's cruel rejection of him. Thus, as we can see, the novel contains indirect echoes of Dostoevsky's 1850s and early 1860s experiences.

As we ponder the form of *Notes from Underground*, I tell students about work, including that of Jackson, Miller, and Gary Saul Morson, on *Notes from the House of the Dead* (Записки из мертвого дома). Jackson sees it as a "prologue" to *Notes from Underground*, "in its psychological and philosophical insights into the problem of beleaguered man."[21]

I then talk about the structure of *Notes from the House of the Dead*, with its story, in two parts (one very short), of the protagonist Goryanchikov's experiences. The chronology is backwards. In the first brief section, the narrator introduces Goryanchikov and describes recent events. The rest of the novel consists of

---

[21] Robert Louis Jackson, *The Art of Dostoevsky: Deliriums and Nocturnes* (Princeton, NJ: Princeton University Press, 1981), 160. For compelling evidence for his claim that the philosophical and psychological insights that Dostoevsky presents in *Notes from the House of the Dead* are highly significant for *Notes from Underground*, see chapter 5, "Freedom in the Shadow of the Dead House," 144-70.

Goryanchikov's description of his entire labor camp experience, from beginning to end. I also tell my students that we would have expected, from Goryanchikov's words upon his release—"Freedom, a new life, resurrection from the dead... What a glorious moment!" ("Свобода, новая жизнь, воскресенье из мертвых... Экая славная минута!")[22]—that he would be happy. Instead, after he is free, Goryanchikov isolates and thus imprisons himself. Freedom has not led to inner freedom: he creates his own self-imprisonment in his own tormented consciousness. I then tell students that Morson says that this is a tale of "despair" or "hope," depending on which of the narrators one follows.[23] I tell students about the parallel structure of imprisoned consciousness of *Notes from Underground* and *Notes from the House of the Dead*. Jackson asks whether *Notes from Underground* might, "in the figurative sense," be the "strange horrible pages" that comprise the other part of Goryanchikov's notebook.[24]

Next I discuss the genre of *Notes from the House of the Dead*. I tell my students that Miller describes it as "hover[ing] at the boundaries of several genres."[25] In this connection, she points out Morson's focus on its "double narrative identity—a compound of the voice of the fictional wife-murderer and a representation of Dostoevsky's autobiographical experience in prison."[26] In Morson's writings, he characterizes this work as a memoir and novel.[27] He also speaks about mixed genres in later Dostoevsky works. Thus, he speaks about *Diary of a Writer* as an artistic work, a "semifiction"

---

[22] F. M. Dostoevskii, *Zapiski iz mertvogo doma*, in *Polnoe sobranie sochinenii v tridtsati tomakh*, 4:232.

[23] Gary Saul Morson, "Introductory Study," in Fyodor Dostoevsky, *A Writer's Diary*, vol. 1: *1873-1876*, trans. and annot. Kenneth Lantz (Evanston, IL: Northwestern University Press, 1994), 24-25.

[24] Jackson, *Art of Dostoevsky*, 170.

[25] Robin Feuer Miller, *Dostoevsky's Unfinished Journey* (New Haven, CT: Yale University Press, 2007), 22.

[26] Ibid., 197.

[27] Morson, "Introductory Study," 24-25.

including fiction, journalism, etc.[28] He sees the form of that work as affecting the shape of *Brothers Karamazov*.[29]

I ask students to consider the shape of *Notes from Underground*, a hybrid genre, not quite fiction and not quite reportage. Part 1 has an almost journal-article-like texture, and part 2 has a short-story-like texture. I ask students to think about the relationship between the form of a journal, a journal article, and *Notes from Underground*. Dostoevsky had been writing feuilletons since the 1840s. He had been reading journals and writing journalism for the same length of time. He wrote a "feuilleton novel" (фельетонный роман) *The Insulted and the Injured* (*Униженные и оскорбленные*), which appeared in *Time*. During all of his writing life, he wrote articles, fiction, and essays. He edited and shaped journals in the 1860s and beyond. In one way, then, the structure of parts 1 and 2 of *Notes from Underground* reflects Dostoevsky's lifelong interest in journalism and fiction. Part 1 is the equivalent of journalism (current events), and part 2 is presented as a story. I explain to students that the book has the shape of a thick journal, which contained fact and fiction.

I tell students about Skaftymov, who has shown parallels between Dostoevsky's *Time* and *Epoch* articles and the ideas of the underground man.[30] We have seen the ways in which *Notes from Underground* can be interpreted as a fictionalized reflection of *pochvennichestvo*. In *Notes from Underground*, Dostoevsky uses the same polemic tone as he does in his polemical journal articles.

I tell students that sometimes I see the book as a coherent whole when I turn to some of its psychological dimensions. In part 1, the underground man says that "some things … a man is afraid to reveal even to himself" ("такие [вещи], которые даже и себе человек открывать боится"),[31] and he asks whether one can be open with oneself and not fear the whole truth. Martinsen has spoken

---

[28] Ibid., 10.

[29] Ibid, 70-71.

[30] Skaftymov, "*Zapiski iz podpol'ia* sredi publitsistiki Dostoevskogo," 88-139. On *Time* and *Epoch*, and *Notes from Underground*, see 113-28.

[31] Dostoevskii, *Zapiski iz podpol'ia*, 122.

about the ways in which the underground man uses his circuitous thinking as a defense against vulnerability—for her, because of shame at his own identity.[32] "The structure of his text reflects the structure of his thought," she writes.[33] She convincingly argues that "the narrative ... mirrors his psychological self-enclosure."[34]

I tell students that I have been thinking about a key scene, as I contemplate the structure of the book as one huge defense against feeling. When the underground man is at the brothel, he tells Liza that he would not be as he is—"without feeling" (бесчувственный)[35]—if he had had a family. When he tells her about her life, he uses words that describe his own existence: "cellar" (подвал [for him, it is подполье—underground—of course]), "chains" (цепи), "slavery" (рабство), "in the corner" (в углу).[36] He cannot face his truth, so he projects it onto her—the cellar, chains, slavery, life in a corner. When she tells him that he talks like a book, he detects mockery in her voice. He says that he had not understood that mockery can be a mask for people "whose pride will not let them yield until the last minute, and who are afraid to express their feelings in front of you" ("которые до последней минуты не сдаются от гордости, и боятся перед вами высказать свое чувство").[37]

I ask students whether they agree that this describes the underground man, who puts on a mask, who mocks the world, who hides his vulnerability. To me, this speech reveals the core of his pain. To me, the focus in part 1 is on a person whose brain intellectually spins; and in part 2, the focus is on a person who distances himself from feeling by labeling even his reminiscences a *story*, "Apropos of Wet Snow" ("По поводу мокрого снега"), and by adding an epigraph to his story. Thus, he distances himself from

---

[32] Martinsen, "Narrators," 4.

[33] Ibid., 5.

[34] Ibid., 4.

[35] Dostoevskii, *Zapiski iz podpol'ia*, 156.

[36] Ibid., 153, 155, 160.

[37] Fyodor Dostoevsky, *Notes from Underground. The Double*, trans. Jesse Coulson (London: Penguin Books, 1972), 95; Dostoevskii, *Zapiski iz podpol'ia*, 159.

the painful memories of his abuse of Liza, and from memories of his painful childhood and present condition. We recall that Martinsen wrote that he built walls because of his sense of vulnerability.

The tragedy of the underground man is that he *tries* to make contact with other people and cannot. He does not even admit to himself that that is what he is trying to do. He says that he is writing notes for himself, yet almost everything he talks about has something to do with a connection with other people. It is true that he cruelly breaks the connections—with Zverkov and company, and with Liza. He goes where there are other people, for instance to the tavern. He wants attention. Even as he writes, he anticipates other people's responses. Tragically, he cannot make real steps toward real life. He cannot emerge from his mouse hole of lack of true feeling toward another person.

In the *Epoch* version of *Notes from Underground*, the footnote at the beginning of part 1, signed by Dostoevsky, conceived of the book as having more than two parts. What would these "next excerpts" (следующие отрывки) have been? Since we have the chronology going backwards—the 1860s in part 1 and the 1840s in part 2—could Dostoevsky have been contemplating something about the underground man's miserable childhood? That part is hidden from the underground man because he only hints at that piece of his loveless past. It is hidden from us because Dostoevsky never wrote those extra sections.

By exploring the highways and byways of the novel and of scholarship, I finally have an answer to my question about why *Notes from Underground* is shaped as it is. By following the circuitous route of the question mark, I landed right back where I had started, with a focus on Dostoevsky's journals and beyond.

Winnie-the-Pooh and *Notes from Underground*

In thinking about the theme of this volume, "Teaching Russian Literature," I thought about my approach to teaching. I have certain points I want to cover by the end of a class session. In addition, I give students questions to think about, and I ask them to bring their own questions to class. The discussion veers off in directions

I do not anticipate, yet the points I want to cover somehow get covered.

As I thought about this non-linear method of teaching, I realized that it is very much like the path "home" described in the passage from *The House at Pooh Corner* that is quoted at the beginning of this article. The non-linear approach to life, this "Pooh principle," is precisely what Dostoevsky advocates. The underground man rails against the linear in his cries for a 2x2=5 approach to life. For example, he says that one can say anything about history except one thing: one cannot say that it is "reasonable" (благоразумно).[38]

Other Dostoevsky works display the Pooh way of non-linear thinking that gets you home when you are not looking for home. That is what we learn in *Brothers Karamazov*. You never know what comes out of what, says Father Zosima. The rational path will not lead to truth; only the irrational path will get you home. And that is exactly what Winnie-the-Pooh was talking about.

Afterword

One more thing about Pooh. Piglet says, "Pooh does silly things, and they turn out right."[39] The underground man does cruel things, and they turn out wrong. Pooh is a "Bear of Very Little Brain," but he is all heart. The underground man has too much brain and not enough heart.

For a moment, let us envision the underground man in a utopian future. He removes his mask of spite, emerges from the underground, lives in a tree, and hangs out with his new friend, Winnie-the-Pooh.

---

[38] Dostoevskii, *Zapiski iz podpol'ia*, 116.

[39] Milne, *Winnie-the-Pooh*, 13.

14

TEXT AND PRINTING

The Birth of a Novel from the Work of Journalism: Teaching Saltykov-Shchedrin's *Golovlyovs*

William Mills Todd III

Saltykov-Schedrin and his most famous novel present interrelated challenges and opportunities in our current moment of renewed interest in how we might teach imaginative literature, challenges and opportunities arising from a series of paradoxes which can readily be shared in a classroom as an introduction to the novel.

The first such paradox is biographical and is embodied in the writer's hyphenated surname, the "Saltykov" part of which derives from his distinguished noble lineage, the "Shchedrin" part of which is the penname he assumed in the mid-1850s, as he became one of Russia's most successful and highly remunerated writers—which he remained for decades. Under the first name he read the Bible at his childhood estate, attended the imperial lyceum at Tsarskoe Selo, and rose through the civil service to become a vice-governor of two provinces and a specialist on administration, finances, and taxation. But an antithetical career, represented by his penname, made him a participant in Utopian Socialist circles, a translator (of Byron and Heine), a trenchant satirist, and a contributor first to the radical journal *The Contemporary*, closed by the government in 1866, then to the left-of-center journal *The Fatherland Notes*, closed in 1884, which he also edited. He resolved this paradoxical stance only when he resigned from government service in 1868, but this rich set of roles and occupations left him with an understanding of the imperial order unmatched by any of his contemporaries and with a full toolkit of literary techniques for giving form to his experiences.

This background, in turn, occasions a second paradox of his career, one which raises an important literary issue to discuss with students of any level, namely that although Saltykov-Shchedrin was one of the most highly esteemed writers of his time, the qualities of his writing—their satiric power, their illusive topicality, their stylistic grittiness—have made his works unappealing or inaccessible, in subsequent times, to all but specialized readers. This is true not only of his many sketches, articles, and reviews, but also of most of the larger works into which he gathered them, works such as *The History of a Town* or *Pompadours and Pompadouresses*. These longer works are absolutely relentless in their negative analysis of Russian history, serfdom, bureaucracy, and incipient capitalism, and as such they gave comfort and encouragement to Russia's critical intelligentsia, much as radio political commentators inspire their listeners in early twenty-first-century America. But their very wealth of detail and commentary, combined with a paucity of plot and characterization, leaves little room for a readerly imagination and makes them difficult to process as integral texts for all but those who have a deep commitment to studying the history, politics, and social order of the period. Few are available in Russia in separate editions—this was true even in Soviet times—and few have been translated into English. They have failed to acquire that degree of canonicity which, as Frank Kermode argues, requires readers to view confusing "muddle" as a potentially comprehensible "enigma" to attack with all possible hermeneutic resources.[1]

The exception to this neglect of Saltykov-Shchedrin's works has been his novel *The Golovlyovs*, translated at least eight times into English. But here one confronts a third paradox, one which offers an insight not only into the author's writing process, but into the literary process of the post-Emancipation period: namely that his greatest novel was not conceived and begun as a novel at all, but rather emerged from a series of sketches, *Well-Intentioned Speeches*, which he had started publishing in *Notes of the Fatherland* in October 1872. The fifteenth of these sketches, published in October 1875, became a chapter of the future novel, as did three other installments

---

[1]   Frank Kermode, *The Genesis of Secrecy: On the Interpretation of Narrative* (Cambridge, MA: Harvard University Press, 1979), 57.

in the *Well-Intentioned Speeches* cycle, which Saltykov-Shchedrin subsequently published as a whole three times as a separate edition (1876, 1880, 1883). Not all of the installments of this cycle entered into *The Golovlyovs*, and there is not even an uninterrupted sequence of them. Shorter than the seven chapters of the subsequent novel, these installments do feature dialogue and events, and some focus on the family as one of the topics of hypocritical discourse, but the sketches do not feature a consistent set of characters nor an engaging plot, as they are organized around a self-described "Russian Frondeur's" series of visits and conversations with various "liars" and "hypocrites," conscious and unconscious.[2] Here, as in Saltykov-Shchedrin's other cycles of sketches, culture's "hum and buzz of implication" — to borrow a phrase from Lionel Trilling — become so loud that they drown out the collection for readers of subsequent times and different places.[3]

But the fifteenth of the *Well-Intentioned Speeches*, entitled "A Family Court," although it featured some of the set elements (e.g., estate visits, nasty familial relations) and the brutal dialogue of the other installments in the series, grew beyond the others in its number and depth of characters, in the range of its plot, and in the detail of its setting, as a contemporary newspaper reviewer, Skabichevsky, immediately noticed:

> Here we see passing before us not the pompadours, Tashkentians, wheelers and dealers, plutocrats, lawyers, and other such heroes of our contemporary life... Here to the fore is not that stinging salt of witty, well-targeted derision and exposé by caricature of the more absurd aspects of life, not, in short, those qualities of Mr. Shchedrin's satire to which we are accustomed; no, we have before us here a masterly sketch

---

[2]   M. E. Saltykov-Shchedrin, *Sobranie sochinenii v dvadtsati tomakh*, ed. A. S. Bushmin et al. (Moscow: Khudozhestvennaia literatura, 1965-77), 11:7-12. Subsequent references to this edition will appear in the text. All translations are my own unless otherwise indicated.

[3]   Lionel Trilling, "Manners, Morals, and the Novel," in his *The Liberal Imagination: Essays on Literature and Society* (Garden City, NY: Anchor Books, 1953), 200.

of types of the now bygone past, a profound, psychological analysis, and satire in the narrow sense has been replaced by a bitter humor which, by the end, is transformed into stunning tragedy of a very particular kind.[4]

By the end of the novel, Saltykov-Shchedrin would bring the action forward from the 1850s to the 1870s, but Skabichevsky's categories — psychology, humor, and tragedy — remain appropriate for the subsequent installments, as the novel emerged from the sketches in the months following this first installment.

Saltykov-Shchedrin, who was growing weary of the *Well-Intentioned Speeches*, recognized that he had hit upon something worth pursuing and devoted a number of the ensuing "Well-Intentioned Speeches" to his Golovlyov family, as the chart on the next page illustrates.

The family principle, clear enough even in the journal entries, moves more to the foreground in the novel's chapter titles, involving all of them but the last. Saltykov-Shchedrin endows five of these titles with the legal and financial considerations that he made inseparable from the personal relationships of the land-owning family.

This third paradox, that the novel grew from the middle of a set of journal sketches, can serve several teaching moments. One, for courses more oriented toward Russian culture or history, would be to locate *The Golovlyovs* in a discussion of its journalistic context, amid debates over Russian history, Russian society, Russian governance, or Russian national consciousness in general. The pages of Saltykov-Shchedrin's own *Notes of the Fatherland* and rival thick journals, such as *The Russian Herald* and *The Herald of Europe*, would offer ample material for such discussions, as would novels

---

[4] A. M. Skabichevskii, "Blagonamerennye rechi g. Shchedrina," *Sankt-Peterburgskie vedomosti* 307 (1875), quoted in I. P. Foote, ed., *Saltykov-Shchedrin's The Golovlyovs* (Evanston, IL: Northwestern University Press, 1997), 47. Foote's companion is an invaluable teaching aide with its selections from nineteenth-century critiques, modern articles, and Saltykov-Shchedrin's own comments on the novel.

SERIALIZATION OF *THE GOLOVLYOVS* IN NOTES OF THE FATHERLAND		
Issue	**Title in the Journal**	**Title in *The Golovlyovs***
Oct. 1875	Well-Intentioned Speeches XIII: Family Court	Family Court
Dec. 1875	Well-Intentioned Speeches XVII: A United Family	A United Family
March 1876	Well-Intentioned Speeches XVIII: Family Accounts	Family Accounts
June 1876	Well-Intentioned Speeches. Before Escheatment	The Little Niece
August 1876	Escheated	Escheated (Ch. 6)
Dec. 1876	Family Joys	Forbidden Family Joys (Ch. 5)
May 1880		The Reckoning The Resolution (The Last Episode of the Golovlyov Chronicle)
Separate editions of the novel were published in 1880 and 1883.		

that appeared in these journals while *The Golovlyovs* was being serialized, such as Tolstoy's *Anna Karenina* and Dostoevsky's *Brothers Karamazov*, novels which themselves thematized not only these issues but Russian journalism itself. Readily available journalistic texts for comparison would include ones by Saltykov-Shchedrin's old rival, Dostoevsky, such as the *Diary of a Writer* or *Winter Notes on Summer Impressions*.

A classroom context better able to illuminate the particular qualities which Skabichevsky and other contemporary readers immediately sensed, however, would be one which paid closer attention to the ways in which Saltykov-Shchedrin crafted the memorable world of *The Golovlyovs*. For reasons I will suggest, the novel is most effectively assigned toward the end of a semester of readings, as it provides—in parodic reduction—an encyclopedic summary of the themes, plots, and characterizations in Russian nineteenth-century fiction. The novel is not rich in explicit literary references—its characters inhabit much too low a cultural level for them to get much beyond the Bible, the catechism, and the erotic Barkovian poetry beloved of provincial landowners. The primary narrator, with few exceptions, does not rise above this level of cultural literacy. But *The Golovlyovs* abounds in parallels to a growing tradition of novelistic subgenres—the family chronicle, the pastoral novel, the confessional novel, the novel of spiritual rebirth—and a well-constructed syllabus can bring the students to illuminating recognition of these literary resources, from which Saltykov-Shchedrin has constructed his novel.

Before attempting such overviews, however, a class can build inductively a sense of the novel, establishing what Robert Belknap has called "inherent relationships," i.e., recurring persons, places, things, thoughts, and emotions which echo through the work, inviting readers to compare and contrast situations in the novel, to see change and development, or lack thereof, and to feel the working of relentless, destructive fate.[5] Such relationships become mnemonically crucial to the reader's ability to join together the novel's five years of serial installments.

The novel offers ample opportunity for discovering patterns because of its absolutely relentless pursuit of the Golovlyov's

---

[5] Robert L. Belknap, *The Structure of "The Brothers Karamazov"* (Evanston, IL: Northwestern University Press, 1989), 14-15, 42-45.

cyclical family catastrophe, with its sixteen deaths in three generations. Four deaths receive primary attention: those of the matriarch Arina Petrovna and her three sons (Stepan, Pavel, and Porfiry or "Yudushka"). Further removed from the main action are the deaths of her husband Vladimir, her daughter Anna, five more of her children in childbirth, and three grandchildren (Vladimir and Lyubinka by suicide, Pyotr in prison). One illegitimate grandchild, Vladimir, is buried alive in a Moscow foundling home; the final grandchild, Anninka, lies fatally ill at the novel's end.

Every aspect of the novel recapitulates this pattern of death and sterility. Each description of the estate and its surroundings, its dead stillness and monochromatic gray, suggests qualities of eternal winter. A close reading of one such passage in class would illustrate these qualities. The following perversion of the season of growth and fruition accompanies the death of Pavel in the second chapter:

> A hot July noon. It was as if everything had died on the Dubrovino manor. Not only the idle people, but those who normally worked hard had scattered to various corners and settled down in the shade. The dogs had sprawled under the curtain of a huge willow, and they snapped their teeth audibly as, half asleep, they swatted at flies. Even the trees stood downcast and motionless, as if in torment.... The heat poured down in a scalding wave; the earth, covered with short, scorched grass, was burning hot. An unbearable light, like a golden veil, covered the environs, so that objects could be distinguished only with difficulty.... Everything was drowning in a luminous haze. All kinds of smells, beginning with the fragrant flowering limes and ending with the miasma of the cattle-yard, hung in the air in a thick mass. Not a sound. Except the staccato chopping of the cooks' knives, which carried from the kitchen, presaging the invariable cold soup and meatballs for dinner. (13:54-55)

Human, plant, and animal are joined in a mutual stupor. The only activity centers around basic creatural functions: sleeping and eating. Virtually all of the novel's natural settings, including this one, are veiled by some sort of mist, haze, or fog—emblems of the characters' muddled thoughts and perceptions.

The indoor settings repeat the pattern of tormenting, unyielding sameness, and here, too, close reading shows the relentlessness of the novel's vision. In one of the book's most painful passages, Anninka recalls her service to "holy art," a romantic delusion which leads ultimately to drunkenness, debauchery, and prostitution:

> Here was the dressing room, decorated with cheap wallpaper along the wooden partition with its inevitable bouquet from some lieutenant; here was the stage with its smoke-darkened, fingerprint-soiled decorations, slimy from the moisture; here she herself gyrated on the stage, yes, merely gyrated, imagining that she was acting; here was the auditorium, which seemed so elegant, even brilliant, from the stage, but was in reality so squalid, dark, with motley furniture and with boxes, covered in worn crimson velveteen. And, in conclusion, officers, officers, officers without end. Then the hotel with its stinking corridors, weakly illuminated by the smoking kerosene lamp; then her room to which she hurried after the performance, in order to change for further triumphs, a room with an unmade bed, a washbasin filled with dirty water, a sheet falling onto the floor, and a pair of men's underpants forgotten on the back of the armchair; then the dining room, full of kitchen odors, with a table in the middle. Supper—cutlets with peas, tobacco smoke, noise, crowding, drunkenness, debauchery... And, again, officers, officers, officers without end...
>
> Such were the memories which related to that time which she called the time of her successes, her victories, her happiness...
>
> After these memories began a series of others. In them the chief role was played by a coaching inn, now completely stinking, with walls frozen through by winter, with shaky floors, with board partitions, from between the chinks in which the shiny bodies of bedbugs peeped out. Drunken, quarrelsome nights; traveling landowners, hurriedly pulling three-ruble notes out of their wallets; prosperous merchants, encouraging the "actresses," virtually with whip in hand.

> And in the morning—headache, nausea, and grief, endless grief. In conclusion—the estate at Golovlyovo...
> If only she could forget it all! If only, even in a dream, she could create something else, some magic world which would hide her past and present. But, alas!, the reality which she had experienced was endowed with such iron tenacity that under its weight all of her flashes of imagination died out by themselves. In vain did her dream thrive to create little angels with silver wings—from behind these little angels peeped her former keepers... (13:248-50)

The estate, the scenes of her "triumphs," the dens of her degradation, her dreams—all merge into one recurring nightmare from which there is no escape. At home the village priest and her uncle Porfiry treat her with the same lack of respect as the officers. Her servants' suggestion that acting is no better than prostitution becomes all too true.

Saltykov-Shchedrin links the chapters with a series of *retours des personages*, a technique which further conveys the irony of a futile, changeless existence. Old Vladimir lives out his years of pornographic fantasy as his son Porfiry dispossesses him; then another Vladimir must be eliminated, and Porfiry manages to drive him to suicide through miserly casuistry, only to be confronted by another son named Vladimir, whom he buries in a foundling home, but not before guilt over the child's illegitimate conception begins to unwind his life-sustaining web of aphorisms. In another recurrence of names we see Arina ridding herself of one Anna only to be left with her daughter Anninka and Anninka's twin sister besides. Not only names but types recur endlessly. In each of the novel's seven chapters Porfiry is faced with the problem of dispossessing his mother. She finally dies in the third chapter, but memory of the property which she had given to others haunts him in the fourth and sixth chapters, and a time reversal by the author brings her back to life, cheerful and coarse, in the fifth. In the novel's last paragraph, a figure similar to her appears to take possession of Porfiry's estate, and the action has passed full circle, from one creature of prey to another.

In this world of unmitigated gloom, every fear, bad dream, or ominous prediction is realized. Stepan fears that his mother will oppress him; she does. She in turn fears that Porfiry will take her carriage; he does. Porfiry dreams that his cousin will seize the estate; she is on the verge of doing so as he dies. A curse in this world blasts the one who utters it, not the intended victim: Stepan remembers a curse that would send his mother into convulsions, but it is he who dies in agony. His mother levels her parental curse against Porfiry, but it is she who dies soon afterwards. An aura of supernatural expectation replaces serious effort for the characters, and the novel turns all such fantasies to naught. Foreshadowing and backshadowing are unrelieved by any sense that the Golovlyovs can take responsibility for their actions or change the course of events.[6]

The novel's "inherent relationships" encompass the major institutions and social groups of Russian life, reducing them to a common denominator of mindlessness and futility. During the period the novel spans, approximately 1856-76, the most radical governmental reforms of the century were promulgated. However, only the most negative aspects of these changes find reflection in Saltykov-Shchedrin's crooked mirror. The emancipation of the serfs is barely recorded. Fedulych may be able to resign from Porfiry's tyranny, but he cannot free himself from the contagion of his master's "verbal rot" (13:174).

Of all the institutions the novel tracks, religion and the family are most thoroughly undermined by their inseparable ties to economic exploitation, gluttony, lechery, and meaningless ritual. It was one of the contentions of Saltykov-Shchedrin's beloved Belinsky that the Russian scratches himself even as he utters the name of God, and the deacon's daughter Evpraksiya dutifully follows the script: "Yawning she uttered the words, 'Lord! Merciful Savior! Mother of the Dormition!' as she diligently scratched her backside" (13:206). She herself had been rented to Porfiry by her father in return for

---

6   *The Golovlyovs* is, not unsurprisingly, absent from Gary Saul Morson's innovative study of this issue, *Narrative and Freedom: The Shadows of Time* (New Haven, CT: Yale University Press, 1994).

a monthly food ration. The clergy never appear except in connection with food, and they are totally submissive to Porfiry, who holds the purse strings for their churches. When Porfiry's sons spread butter on communion bread, they provide the perfect emblem for the novel's reduction of spiritual values to animal functions.

Inherent relationships of futility, travesty, and recurrence finally obliterate distinctions between human and animal, human and food, human and environment. One member of the family is forced to eat out of a dog's dish. Anninka kisses a calf, whose slimy mouth is reminiscent of the officers who press their attentions upon her. Old Vladimir spends his time imitating bird calls. The rottenness of the food which Arina feeds her children and servants becomes their moral essence. Finally, by careful manipulation of the passive voice and impersonal constructions, Saltykov-Shchedrin makes human agency nearly disappear. The rich yield of the estate appears to produce and harvest itself (13:44). As if to emphasize his characters' primitive existence, throughout the narrative Saltykov-Shchedrin dwells on those products of nature which are not cultivated but merely hunted or gathered—mushrooms, carp, snipe, berries.

Human capability sinks so low in the novel—especially by comparison with its position in contemporary novels by Dostoevsky, Tolstoy, Turgenev, and Khvoshchinskaya—that even hypocrisy is almost impossible. The narrator distinguishes Russian hypocrisy from French by its virtual lack of consciousness: the French bourgeoisie has firm social principles to support its hypocrisy and to maintain social distinctions, but a Russian grows up without such clear, positive principles as would support proper hypocrisy and hold society together. Porfiry differs from Molière's Tartuffe, the narrator suggests, not in his desires or tactics, but in the extent to which he is barely conscious of what he is doing (13:101-4).

Close reading for style will show that Saltykov-Shchedrin reinforces this low capability, this absence, with negative descriptions and the use of compound words for emptiness, idleness, absence, or negation (in Russian, "*pusto-*..." or "*prazdno-*..."). The style of his characters illustrates Bakhtin's notions of heteroglossia, loopholes, and the polyphonic speech as the Golovlyovs mimic each other and use language evasively or automatically. The closest Porfiry (nicknamed "Yudushka"—little Judas) comes to self-realization before the novel's end occurs in the fifth chapter, when he is confronted with the fact that he has impregnated Evpraksiya on a fast day. The word "adultery" ("прелюбодеяние") brings him up short, but only for a moment:

> In these inner conversations with himself, however confused their content, could be noted something similar to the awakening of conscience. But the question arises: will Yudushka go further along this path, or will his empty thinking [пустомыслие] here serve him as a new loophole [лазейка], thanks to which he, as always, will emerge dry from the water. (13:185-86)

The answer is, indeed, that he uses his religious drivel to escape contemplating the moral consequences of his actions.

Once such patterns are established, one can open the discussion of the novel to the author's use of macro-literary patterns, relating *The Golovlyovs* to other works the students may have read. This can reveal the "literariness" of the novel on a new level of integration, enabling one to see its characters' thoughts and actions not merely as absences, but as negations, parodistic ones, of novelistic writing.[7] Saltykov-Shchedrin, a man of the journals like Dostoevsky, kept his eye closely on the fiction that was being written and translated for the thick journals. As with his famous satire of Dostoevsky's *Notes from Underground*, "The Swallows" ("Стрижи,"

---

[7] Kark D. Kramer, "Satiric Form in Saltykov's *Gospoda Golovlevy*," *Slavic and East European Journal* 14, no. 4 (1970): 453-64, sees the novel as a parody of some novelistic motifs: the return of the prodigal son, the family novel, love intrigue, dramatic conflict, hypocrisy. I differ in more specifically identifying texts which Saltykov-Shchedrin may have used as sources for the satiric use of parody. Russian studies of Saltykov-Shchedrin have tended to neglect the intrinsic aspects of literary change and have looked for reflections of socio-historical reality, largely ignoring the possibilities for parody within *The Golovlyovs*. This is true even of I. T. Ishchenko, *Parodii Saltykova-Shchedrina* (Minsk: Izd. BGU, 1973) and Z. S. Borshchevskii, *Shchedrin i Dostoevskii* (Moscow: Goslitizdat, 1956).

1864), Saltykov would sometimes use parody as a critical device. However, as Robert Belknap has shown with his book *The Genesis of "The Brothers Karamazov,"* it is not enough to show what a writer may have picked up along the way; it is important to show how he transformed it in passing it on, making his sources an important rhetorical instrument. Classroom discussion can bring out the ways in which such citation may function in the work's rhetoric.

Frequently throughout *The Golovlyovs* one recognizes episodes, themes, and characters which have been parodistically borrowed from specific works and traditions. The author, whose satire thrusts against flawed social institutions and against travesties of human potential, now turns against the literary decorum which shielded such institutions and travesties from treatment as bleak as his own. We have already seen how the narrator invokes Tartuffe to illuminate Porfiry's limited consciousness and lack of firm principles about which to be hypocritical. It is possible that there are many more. From among them I shall limit myself to a few clear examples: Rousseau's *Confessions*, Sergei Aksakov's *Family Chronicle*, and Dostoevsky's *Crime and Punishment*.

Rousseau's *Confessions* will only seem incongruous in this list at first glance. One of the major sources of the modern novel in general, it proved a model for explaining the crippling pressure of society on the individual and thus for excusing individual flaws. The confessor demonstrates his moral sensitivity by expressing feelings of guilt, then uses social science or philosophy to assuage that guilt. Rarely are we allowed to forget the alibi: "I as a responsible person was somewhere else; something else (inexperience, society) is to blame." He gets to be both a moral being and the product of his milieu. Confession becomes, as Paul de Man has argued, apology.[8]

In one of his most famous evasions, Rousseau, a best-selling author of educational novels, justifies sending his five children to

---

[8] Paul de Man, "Excuses (Confessions)," in his *Allegories of Reading: Figural Language in Rousseau, Nietzsche, Rilke, and Proust* (New Haven, CT: Yale University Press, 1979), 278-301.

a foundling home. He first takes the alibi of social custom, then turns to philosophy in the following feat of rhetorical heroism:

> Too sincere with myself, too proud to contradict my principles by my deeds, I set myself to examining the destiny of my children and my relationship with their mother in light of the laws of nature, of justice, and of reason, and in light of those laws of that religion which is as pure, holy, and eternal as its author, and which men have sullied in feigning to wish to purify it, and of which they have made nothing more by their formulae than a religion of words.... In handing my children over to public education instead of raising them myself, in fating them to be workers and peasants instead of adventurers and soldiers of fortune, I believed that I had done a deed worthy of a citizen and father, and I considered myself worthy of membership in Plato's republic.... I would have wished, I still wish, to have been raised as they were.[9]

When Porfiry comes to send his infant son to a foundling home, his justification is almost identical, although much less rhetorically orchestrated and couched in a lower stylistic register. Indeed, his syntax falls apart under the strain of justifying himself. He presents the same suggestion that the peasant's life can be a happy one, the same "protesting too much" about Christian and civic virtue, and a similar concluding remark about the desirability of being sent away:

> First of all, we must take pity on Evpraksiya, and, second, we must make a man out of him.... And I want all to go well for us. So that in time little Vladimir will become a real man, both a servant of God and a subject of the Tsar. If God blesses him with a peasant's estate, so that he will know how to work the land.... If another calling is his fate, so that he will know a trade.... They raise them superbly there! ... And if he turns up in the country as a foster child—Christ be with him.

---

[9] Jean-Jacques Rousseau, *Les Confessions* (Paris: Garnier, 1964), 404.

> He will get used to labor from childhood, and labor is also
> a form of prayer! As for us—we do it the real way! We stand
> before the icon, make the sign of the Cross, and if our prayer
> pleases God, he rewards us for it. But a peasant—he must
> work! ... God sees his labors and rewards him for them as he
> does us for prayer.... Ah, Vladimir, Vladimir! ... You yourself
> will see the benefits of it later and will be thankful for it!
> (13:198-99)

Saltykov-Shchedrin parodies Rousseau's infamous passage by
injecting the servant Ulita, the mother of Porfiry's other child,
who Porfiry has already sent to the foundling home. Her cynical
expression and practical questions accompany Porfiry's drivel and
force him to realize what he is actually doing. Ulita's presence ensures
that there will be no harmonious accommodation between Porfiry's
role as "adulterer" and his role as observer of and commentator
on the results of his fornication (13:184). This transplant from
Rousseau provides a striking contribution to the novel's themes
of tyranny, sterility, and social fragmentation. And we experience
a rare moment of humor in the novel in learning that a hypocrite as
callous as Porfiry falls short of the great *philosophe* in the antiheroic
subversion of values.[10]

Moving closer to his gentry roots, Saltykov-Shchedrin
launches his attacks on the Russian family and landowning system
by parodying Sergei Aksakov's *Family Chronicle*. Although it records
certain unpleasant aspects of the seigneurial system, *A Family
Chronicle* nevertheless treats its patriarchal family, the Bagrovs,
with considerable sympathy. It became a virtual *Aeneid* for Russian

---

[10] Although he was revered by Tolstoy, the author of the *Confessions* had
a reputation in nineteenth-century Russia for concealing and manipulating
the truth which he attempted to tell, as we can see from comments in
Dostoevsky's *Notes from Underground* and Lermontov's *A Hero of Our
Time*. Because of their daring revelations, the *Confessions* was seen by
some readers as verging on pornography. Indeed, Saltykov-Shchedrin
reviewed in 1868 a Boborykin novel in which one of the characters seduces
a woman by reading her *Les Liaisons dangereuses* and the *Confessions*
(9:42, 476).

conservative nationalists, a story of the establishment of Russian civilization in the shadow of the Urals. *The Golovlyovs* provides a near mirror-image of this beloved work in that it depicts a process of literal decivilization, if we consider the root of that noun, *civitas* (city), since the novel's characters all move away from the city and then (in the case of Arina, Anna, and Pavel) from the central manor house. *A Family Chronicle* ends with the birth of a son to continue the family. The "Golovlyov Chronicle," as Saltykov called it in his last journal installment, ends with the death of the family's last male child. He turns the patriarchal system upside down; the Golovlyovs prosper only under the matriarch Arina's tyranny. Aksakov's heroic patriarch yields his place to Vladimir Golovlyov—fragile, senile, obscene; Arina Bagrova—timid, passive, dim-witted— becomes Arina Golovlyova, who increases the family property tenfold and single-handedly manages an estate of four thousand serfs.

The most complete parodic transformation, however, is that which reduces Aksakov's Stepan Bagrov into Porfiry. Stepan fully realizes the heroic possibilities of the Russian estate, which permitted the landowner to perfect himself, reform his territories (socially and economically), and achieve a sort of pastoral utopia. The landowner's existence could be virtually uncircumscribed by law and social contract, and Stepan uses this freedom to tame the wilderness, establish a well-ordered estate, rescue a cousin from her depraved husband, and populate the surrounding area with his offspring. Such elevation made him an inviting target for Saltykov-Shchedrin's parodic gifts, and there is no part of Stepan's heroic image which Porfiry does not travesty. Porfiry's freedom, unlike Stepan's, serves no heroic, civilizing purpose: "Shut off in the country, he immediately felt himself at liberty; for nowhere, in no other sphere could his inclinations find such range of movement as here.... A limitless slovenliness became the dominant trait of his relationship to himself" (13:103-4).

The powerful Bagrov degenerates into decrepit Porfiry; his values become the stuff of Porfiry's hypocrisy. Rescue of the cousin is replaced by attempted incest. Stepan's strong moral instincts fade into Porfiry's moral helplessness: "Neither in the past nor in the present did a single moral buttress turn up for him to latch onto" (13:255). Stepan's efforts to build the estate are travestied by Porfiry's sterile, bureaucratic fantasies.

The parody of *Confessions* shapes the presentation of Porfiry's hypocrisy, and the parody of *A Family Chronicle* serves as an armature for Saltykov-Shchedrin's devastating presentation of the Russian countryside. In the novel's final installment, Saltykov-Shchedrin turns again to the values which failed to sustain a viable culture and which, in his critique, served as the material for dim-witted, half-conscious hypocrisy. This concerns religion and the Russian novel, and it brought him back to his long antagonism with Dostoevsky, with whom he had begun his career as a utopian socialist, and with whom he shared visions of a heroic, golden age, visions they developed differently as their paths diverged. For Dostoevsky, whose writing on contemporary France focused on conscious hypocrisy, as did Saltykov-Shchedrin's, his mature vision demanded, as he put it in *Winter Notes on Summer Impressions* (1863), the highest development of the human personality: whole-hearted, unconditional submersion of the individual will into the general will.[11] As is well known, Dostoevsky sought this ideal in Christian belief, and he plotted his major novels on attempts by his intellectual heroes to achieve an existence outside this belief, by negating it or by substituting other visions of a Golden Age (secular, nationalist, socialist) for it. But as his intellectual heroes attempt this, they find that calculated, individual heroism degenerates into vile travesty. The clearest example is Raskolnikov, who defines the historical hero (conqueror, law-giver) as one who has the right to use force and violence to achieve his ends. Working with this perverted, Napoleonic definition of historical heroism, Raskolnikov finds himself committing the messy, useless murder of the old pawnbroker and her pregnant sister. The conclusion, in which Dostoevsky's hero moves toward regeneration and the transcendence of his criminal

---

[11]   F. M. Dostoevskii, *Polnoe sobranie sochinenii v tridtsati tomakh* (Leningrad: Nauka, 1972-90), 5:79. Subsequent references to this edition will appear in the text.

will, continues to arouse charges of improbability a century and a half after it was written.

Raskolnikov is aided in his regeneration by the persuasion of a gentle prostitute, Sonya, who reads him the story of Lazarus and whom the novel never shows practicing her profession. "Kiss the earth, which you have defiled," she urges (6:322). In Siberian exile Raskolnikov has a lucid vision during Easter week, a vision which reveals the magnitude of his crime and the catastrophic consequences of Napoleonic will and reason. Shortly thereafter, on a warm sunny day in a pastoral setting, he falls to the ground, overwhelmed by love for the prostitute, who has just recovered from a serious illness. "Love had resurrected them, the heart of one contained infinite sources of life for the heart of the other" (6:421). He is resurrected ("он воскрес"), and a whole new reality opens up for him. Grace and harmony stretch before him, if not on the pages of this novel.

A child of the child of the age of utopian, universal solutions, Saltykov-Shchedrin praised Dostoevsky for looking beyond social problems of local, immediate interest to humanity's ultimate quest for harmony and equilibrium, but he accused Dostoevsky of undermining his lofty aspirations by cheap mockery of the radicals who were also striving for them (9:412). Predictably, he defended innovation against Raskolnikov's definition of it in terms of force and violence: "Innovators have never been prone to force and violence, for one of the most essential principles of any innovation consists precisely in the negation of force and violence" (9:120). Force and violence to Saltykov-Shchedrin resided precisely in the old forms of life—religion, the patriarchal family, the land-owning system— which he so persistently satirized in his works. Raskolnikov's incipient acceptance of a religious solution made him a tempting target, and the conclusion of *The Golovlyovs* closely parallels that of *Crime and Punishment*.

Rebirth, as Raskolnikov was to experience it, cannot occur in Saltykov-Shchedrin's fictional world. The values which Dostoevsky's hero must accept (humility, love) are those by which Porfiry has deceived himself and destroyed his family. And so Saltykov-Shchedrin recasts Dostoevsky's resurrection myth in an ironic mode.

He seizes upon the images and incidents of Dostoevsky's account (cerebral criminal, sick prostitute, exemplary narrative, festival of rebirth, new reality) and depicts them on the lowest possible level. After hearing endless accounts of Lyubinka's suicide, after hateful quarrels with a most corporeal, most debauched prostitute, Porfiry's conscience dimly awakens. For the first time he thinks he understands Good Friday, and a desperate confusion stirs within him. He rushes out to throw himself on the grave of his mother (cf. Sonya and the earth), whom he had offended—but, ironically, never reaches it. On Easter Sunday the prostitute lies fatally ill—no happy recoveries here—and Porfiry's frozen body is discovered. As a new Arina figure takes over the estate, travesty proves the only transformation of the resurrection motif in *The Golovlyovs*.

Paying attention to these intertextual instances—and there may, of course, be other ones—offers a way to step back from the novel's relentless detail to study some of the larger patterns which helped Saltykov-Shchedrin to give it its enduring power. They help modern readers, as they helped the readers of Saltykov-Shchedrin's time, appreciate the power of the novel's eventful uneventfulness, psychologically crushed characters, and spirit-crushing setting. There remains much to debate and interpret about the author-narrator's position in the novel, the precise meaning of the ending, and the extent to which one can join those contemporary critics who called the novel tragic. That these require debate and interpretation in turn makes the novel endlessly teachable.

15

TEXT AND HISTORY

An Inconvenient Footnote: Lermontov's "Bela" and the Circassian Expulsion

Jefferson J. A. Gatrall

> Circassians, my warrior people,
> Be ready at any hour
> For death's sacrifice...
>
> Черкесы, мой народ военный,
> Готовы будьте всякий час
> На жертву смерти...
>
> —Lermontov, "Circassians"[1]

I've taught Lermontov's *Hero of Our Time* many times, both in Russian and in translation. Each October at Montclair State University I introduce a new group of students to the novel in a course on Russian prose and drama. This course is not only a requirement for the Russian minors in my department, Modern Languages and Literatures, it is also one of a handful of general education courses that satisfy the world literature requirement for all undergraduates at the university. As it turns out, this cross-listing was approved only a few years prior to my arrival. The proposal had met with considerable resistance from other departments on the curriculum committee. The argument that finally won over the committee was as follows: Russian literature counts as world literature because Russia is West and East *simultaneously*. I wholeheartedly agree with this tidy resolution to a centuries-old debate. Nowhere on my current syllabus is the need for a cross-cultural approach to teaching

---

[1]   M. Iu. Lermontov, "Cherkesy," in *Polnoe sobranie sochinenii*, 10 vols., ed. G. N. Seleznev et al. (Moscow: Voskresen'e, 1999-2002), 3:7, lines 71-73.

more evident than in the case of "Bela," the opening section of Lermontov's novel.

This is easier said than done, however. My students generally like reading and discussing "Bela." From a pedagogical perspective, they are immediately drawn to the dark and mysterious Pechorin, and it does not require undue effort on my part to nudge class discussion away from his callous deeds and toward the intricate levels of narration through which they unfold. Yet despite being a crowd-pleaser, "Bela" has always proven a challenging text to teach. This is especially true in seminars, my preferred format for literature courses. The difficulty lies with the connection, at once tenuous and pressing, between the fictional tale "Bela" and a certain series of extra-literary events. On the one hand, these events — which may be provisionally termed the Caucasian War (1817-64) — involve exceptional levels of historical violence that remain a matter of contention to the descendants of all parties involved.[2] On the other hand, this entire history is virtually unknown to North American students. As a non-specialist in the region, I myself do not feel qualified to speak about, let alone speak for, all of the peoples to which Lermontov alludes in "Bela": Circassians, Ossetians, Georgians, Tatars, Chechens, and so on. In terms of classroom dynamics, I'm faced with the task of presenting a makeshift lecture on a brutal war that not only eats into student discussion of Lermontov's text but also threatens to predetermine how that text should be discussed. In teaching "Bela" I'm always anxious that this inconvenient footnote, once pointed out to students, will end up rendering the text above it moot, or worse, mute.

In short, my pedagogical dilemma is whether to lecture or not to lecture. There is certainly much to be said in defense of the latter option. Even without a lecture, "Bela" offers more than enough

---

[2] For a classic account of the Caucasian War, see Willis Brooks, "Nicholas I as Reformer: Russian Attempts to Conquer the Caucasus," in *Nation and Ideology: Essays in Honor of Wayne S. Vucinich*, ed. Ivo Banac, John G. Ackerman, and Roman Szporluk (New York: East European Monographs, 1981), 227-63. See also Charles King, *The Ghost of Freedom: A History of the Caucasus* (Oxford: Oxford University Press, 2008).

formal and thematic material to fill a productive seminar session. This includes discussion of the rhetoric of empire. My better students are able to identify and analyze "Bela" in terms of stock elements from such genres as the "travelogue" or the "oriental tale" (terms I slip early into conversation). By way of analogy with, say, popular films about native Americans (or, more recently, the blockbuster *Avatar*), the characters Pechorin and Bela can be approached through familiar oppositions: settler and native, civilized and savage. Students who are conversant with Said's Orientalism from English or French literature courses have likewise been struck with similarities in the ways that gender, religion, and ethnicity are thematized in "Bela." Such analogies across different imperial contexts, superficial though they may be, serve as convenient points of departure for a close examination of Lermontov's text. Thus cross-cultural issues arise as students and I walk through each step in the tale's central love plot, from Pechorin's attendance at a Circassian wedding to Bela's deathbed lament that she and her husband, as Muslim and Christian, will not reunite in Paradise. Such discussion usually takes on a political dimension, moreover, as students pick up on Maxim Maximych's ethnic slurs or tease out the allegorical possibilities suggested by a soldier's abduction of a woman from occupied territory. There are ways to avoid even having to pause for mini-lectures on foreign terms. On a few occasions, for example, I've solicited volunteers to do a quick online search on the different ethnic groups named in "Bela." In the following class session, each volunteer is usually able to say a few meaningful things about their assigned group's culture, which is better than my saying these same things in lecture. Yet none of this information tends to generate much class discussion. More importantly, the complex history between these groups and the Russian empire passes unnoticed.

The one exception occurred in the Fall 2009 semester, when I had the exceeding good fortune of having a Circassian-American student on my class roster. She jumped at the chance to inform her classmates about the expulsion of her ancestors from imperial Russia. After the capture of the Chechen leader Imam Shamil in August 1859, tsarist forces pursued aggressive policies to pacify Western Circassia, the last front of the Caucasian War. These policies ranged from the systematic destruction of mountain villages, or auls, to a negotiated arrangement with the Ottoman Empire to absorb the region's predominantly Muslim populace. Administrative efforts on both sides of this coordinated effort were nevertheless unprepared for the sheer numbers of refugees involved. Indeed, the human costs at the close of the Caucasian War extended well beyond the pragmatics of military necessity. By 1865, at least 370,000 inhabitants of Western Circassia—to take a conservative estimate—migrated to the Ottoman Empire. Of those remaining in Russia, another 100,000 were forced to relocate to the Kuban lowlands.[3] Estimates on the numbers of Circassians who perished, whether due to massacre, hunger, disease, or drowning, are more speculative and vary widely, from a few hundred thousand to as many as a million and a half.[4] At the end of this mass migration—one of the century's largest—the vast majority of surviving Circassians no longer lived in Circassia. As one British observer summed up the situation in May 1864, "Circassia is gone."[5]

As we talked after class, my student explained that her friends never know anything about the Circassians and their history, but that when she tells them, "They are blown away." This is the crux of my dilemma. The tragic fate of the groups known collectively as Circassians is a compelling and even urgent story in its own right. This story extends long before, and long after, the few months in 1837-38 between the stationing of the dragoon officer Lermontov at the Caucasian front and the writing of "Bela" on his return to St. Petersburg. Descendants of the Circassian women who would have been Bela's contemporaries now live in Turkey, Syria, Jordan, Israel, and even New Jersey, which did receive a belated wave of

---

[3]   Dana Sherry, "Social Alchemy on the Black Sea Coast, 1860-65," *Kritika: Explorations in Russian and Eurasian History* 10, no. 1 (2009): 7.

[4]   Stephen D. Shenfield, "The Circassians: A Forgotten Genocide?," in *The Massacre in History*, ed. Mark Levene and Penny Roberts (Oxford: Berghahn Books, 1999), 154.

[5]   Henry Bulwer, quoted in Paul B. Henze, "Circassian Resistance to Russia," in *The North Caucasus Barrier*, ed. Marie Bennigsen Broxup (New York: St. Martin's Press, 1992), 101.

Circassian refugees (who had until that point been living in the Middle East) in the wake of the Six-Day War.[6] Yet such a formulation of the problem already risks being too reductive. Ultimately, the thin line that connects Bela's story and the story of the *muhajirs*, or "migrants," is at least as much intertextual as it is historical. Either way, the connection hinges on an unstable term: Circassian (черкес). In the case of "Bela," it is hardly clear that the eponymous heroine is Circassian at all. Kamennyi Brod, the fortress on the Aksai River where the story is set, lies to the west of the territory demarcated as "Circassia" (Черкессия) on imperial Russian maps. Literary critics, sifting through the ethnographic *realia* that the multiple narrators deploy, have proposed that Bela may be Kabardian, Chechen, or Kumyk—only the first of which represents a Circassian group.[7]

Be that as it may, Pechorin and Maxim Maximych identify Bela and her female companions throughout the story as "Circassian" (черкешенка). Far from being scientific, this ethnic label suggests the influence of a conventional literary figure—the Circassian beauty. The Circassian beauty appears in Turkish and Arabic folklore, in the poetry of Byron and Pushkin, in the critical reviews of Belinsky, and in the poster art of the P. T. Barnum circus.[8] The Circassian beauty

---

6   See Rieks Smeets, "Circassia," *Central Asian Survey* 14, no. 1 (1995): 107, 125.

7   On Bela's possible ethnicity, see S. N. Durylin, *"Geroi nashego vremeni"* *M. Iu. Lermontova* (Moscow: Gosudarstvennoe uchebno-pedagogicheskoe izdatel'stvo, 1940), 49-50; B. S. Vinogradov, "Gortsy v romane Lermontova 'Geroi nashego vremeni' (Tezisy doklada)," in *M. Iu. Lermontov: Voprosy zhizni i tvorchestva*, ed. A. N. Sokolov and D. A. Gireev (Ordzhonikidze: Severo-osetinskoe knizhnoe izdatel'stvo, 1963), 55-56; and V. A. Manuilov, *"Geroi nashego vremeni"* *M. Iu. Lermontova: Kommentarii* (Leningrad: Prosveshchenie, 1966), 91-93.

8   For non-Russian treatments of this figure, see Linda Frost, "The Circassian Beauty and the Circassian Slave: Gender, Imperialism, and American Popular Entertainment," in *Freakery: Cultural Spectacles of the Extraordinary Body*, ed. Rosemarie Garland Thomson (New York: New York University Press, 1996), 248-62; Thomas McLean, "Arms and the Circassian Woman: Frances Browne's 'The Star of Attéghéi,'" *Victorian Poetry* 41, no. 3 (2003): 301-5; Setenay Nil Doğan, "From National Humiliation to Difference: The Image of the Circassian Beauty in the Discourses of Circassian Diaspora Nationalists," *New Perspectives on Turkey* 42 (2010), 77-102.

may be a princess, or a slave, or a princess sold into slavery. As Voltaire explained as early as 1734, "The Circassians are poor, their daughters are beautiful, and indeed it is in them they chiefly trade."[9] Lermontov's tale "Bela" playfully reworks these clichés, down to the macaronic pun in the heroine's name ("beautiful woman" in Italian; "misfortune" in Turkish). It is not the sultan but a Russian officer who trades goods for a Circassian beauty. Pechorin himself seems aware of these traditions; before seeing Bela at the wedding, he is unimpressed: "I had a much higher opinion of Circassian women" (Я имел гораздо лучшее мнение о черкешенках).[10] In defending his abduction of Bela to Maxim Maximych, Pechorin repeatedly appeals to the supposed marriage customs of her people. A stolen wife is still a wife "among them" (по-ихнему).[11] Later he explains that if they return Bela to her father, that "savage" will "stab her or sell her" (если отдадим дочь этому дикарю, он ее зарежет или продаст).[12] For her part, Bela insists that she is "not a slave" but "a prince's daughter" (я не раба ... я княжеская дочь!).[13]

The term "Circassian" is also an unstable term in the history of the Caucasus. The term, perhaps of Turkish provenance, was not originally the self-identification of any particular ethnic group. In the nineteenth century, "Circassian" served in Russian state documents as an umbrella category for a number of linguistically-related groups in the Northwest Caucasus, including the Adyghe, Kabardin, and Shapsug. The Abkhaz, Ubykhs, and other groups were also usually included.[14] In the twentieth century, terminological practice diverged significantly between the minority of Circassians remaining in the Soviet Union and those living in the diaspora. Stalin broke the Circassians into four individual groups, as well as into

---

[9] Voltaire, *Letters on the English or Lettres philosophiques* (Whitefish, MT: Kessinger Publishing, 2004), letter 11, p. 28.

[10] Lermontov, *Geroi nashego vremeni*, in *Polnoe sobranie sochinenii*, 6:220.

[11] Ibid., 228. Maxim Maximych here paraphrases Pechorin's words.

[12] Ibid., 230.

[13] Ibid., 241.

[14] Smeets, "Circassia," 111; Shenfield, "The Circassians," 162n2.

different geographical regions, so as to forestall any formation of a unified national identity. The Russian Federation has inherited these regions and ethnic categories. Outside of Russia, however, especially in Turkey, the term Circassian came to refer to a broad number of ethnic groups that migrated from the Caucasus.[15] Indeed, memory of the expulsion helped underwrite this usage. Since the breakup of the Soviet Union, the term Circassian, as an identity position, has been increasingly embraced by organizations in Russia, the Middle East, and the United States in a coordinated effort to gain global recognition.[16] Thus the phrase "Circassian genocide," or "геноцид черкесского народа," occurs in recent petitions to the Russian Duma, the UN, the European Parliament, and the US Congress.[17] The issue of Circassian genocide gained further traction in the international press during the approach to the 2014 Winter Olympics in Sochi, where skiing events were scheduled on site of the Caucasian War's final battle.[18] In the early months of 1864, thousands of Ubykhs, native to the area, were either massacred or deported from Sochi, the same port through which so many other Circassian groups had already passed. The Ubykh language has since become extinct. The last stand of the Ubykhs, by contrast, is still commemorated annually on May 21 by the world Circassian community.[19]

---

[15] See Zeynel Abidin Besleney, "Circassian Nationalism and the Internet," openDemocracy, May 21, 2010, http://www.opendemocracy.net/od-russia/zeynel-abidin-besleney/circassian-nationalism-and-internet.

[16] See, for instance, Paul Goble, "Circassian Diaspora Calls on Circassians in Russia to Declare Themselves Members of a Single People," *Window on Eurasia* (blog), September 15, 2010, http://windowoneurasia.blogspot.com/2010/09/window-on-eurasia-circassian-diaspora.html.

[17] "Caucasus Report," *Radio Free Europe: Radio Liberty* 8, no. 23 (July 15, 2005), http://www.rferl.org/content/article/1341730.html.

[18] Sufian Zhemukhov, "The Circassian Dimension of the 2014 Sochi Olympics," PONARS, Policy Memo No. 65, Georgetown University, September 2009, http://ceres.georgetown.edu/esp/ponarsmemos/page/78357.html; Ekaterina Sokirianskaia, "Winter Games, Circassian Misery," *The New York Times*, 5 December 2013.

[19] A day of mourning is observed on May 21, the date of a large Russian

In the classroom, the Russian conquest of Circassia represents one of those occasions—serfdom is another—on which I feel compelled to step beyond the literary imaginary and into the "nightmare" of history (to rework Stephen Dedalus's metaphor). If there is a moral imperative at work here, it is not a categorical one. There are too many historical narratives intersecting with each fictional text on my syllabus for all of them to be brought to the attention of students. One of the most dominant narratives surrounding *A Hero of Our Time*—especially in the classroom— remains Lermontov's biography. This is somewhat ironic. On the one occasion that Lermontov does speak in his own voice—that is, in the foreword—he insists that the novel is not a self-portrait. From the point of view of literary analysis, Lermontov's personal ties to the region—childhood trips, military exile, fateful duel—constitute historical digressions no more or less than do other potential Caucasian narratives. This is true as well of his posthumous canonization as the "poet of the Caucasus," a legacy that extends to multiple national traditions within and beyond the Russian Federation.

Even in matters of the Caucasus, some narratives have only recently attained currency in Russian literature courses. In 1992, Peter Scotto noted with some justice that the historical connection between "Russia's literary engagement with the Caucasus" and the "discourse and practice of imperialism" had not received adequate scholarly attention in either North America or the Soviet Union.[20] Twenty years later, and after several more wars in the Caucasus, this connection between literature and empire has been much more thoroughly established, thanks in large part to the work of such scholars as Susan Layton, Katya Hokanson, and Harsha Ram. As Layton observes, the formative works of the "literary Caucasus"— those of Pushkin, Bestuzhev-Marlinsky, Lermontov, and Tolstoy—

---

victory parade in 1864. Armed fighting between Russian and Ubykh forces ended a few days earlier.

[20] Peter Scotto, "Prisoners of the Caucasus: Ideologies of Imperialism in Lermontov's 'Bela,'" *PMLA* 107, no. 2 (1992): 246-47.

were written between 1822 and 1863.[21] Hokanson likewise emphasizes Pushkin's constitutive role in "defining the narrative of the conquest of the Caucasus" for subsequent Russian culture.[22] The heyday of the Caucasian tale, in both prose and narrative poetry, thus coincides with the standard timeline of the Caucasian War. This coincidence of historiography is more conspicuous than it might appear at first sight. The Caucasian War, vastly underreported in comparison with the Patriotic War (1812-13) or the Crimean War (1853-56), was a protracted and non-continuous conflict fought under three tsars over multiple fronts. In the case of Circassia, the Russian Empire intervened militarily in the region from the beginning of Catherine II's reign, long before General Alexei Ermolov's early fortifications along the Sunzha River in 1817-18. In terms of literary history, Ram traces an imperial poetics as far back as the 1730s in Russian poetry. Yet he, too, concurs that Pushkin's *Prisoner of the Caucasus* proved instrumental in "consolidating" a specifically Caucasian theme.[23]

How much the Caucasian tale sustained the tsarist project of empire-building, or led its critique, represents a related and more controversial subject. Pushkin and Lermontov in particular have had critical pressures brought to bear on their literary reputations in light of their letters, poems, and fiction relating to the early stages of the Caucasian War. The long-term ideological consequences of the Caucasian tale constitute a legitimate line of inquiry. In 1995, to note just one well-publicized example, Jacques Chirac, defending Russian policy in a French presidential debate, referred to the "vicious Chechen" of Lermontov's "Cossack Lullaby." As Layton rightly observes, Chirac's citation reflects both a historical continuity in certain stereotypes about Chechens and a crude misreading of

---

[21] Tolstoy's *Hadji Murat* (1912) is the key exception. Susan Layton, *Russian Literature and Empire: Conquest of the Caucasus from Pushkin to Tolstoy* (Cambridge: Cambridge University Press, 1994), 6.

[22] Katya Hokanson, "Literary Imperialism, Narodnost' and Pushkin's Invention of the Caucasus," *Russian Review* 53, no. 3 (1994): 336.

[23] Harsha Ram, *The Imperial Sublime: A Russian Poetics of Empire* (Madison, WI: University of Wisconsin Press, 2003), 25-26, 160.

Lermontov's Chechnya.[24] I've encountered similar misreadings of this poem in the comments sections of various Russian blogs and newspapers.

For students in search of essay topics, I often recommend that they explore this vibrant scholarship on empire and literature. The gap between this scholarship and the classroom is nevertheless difficult to bridge. In my annual class on "Bela," students, almost without exception, are introduced to the Caucasian tale and the Caucasian War for the first time. The situation differs somewhat between students with Russian backgrounds and those without. The former tend to know more about the Caucasus in general and to have a greater stake in how events from Russian history are perceived in class. In the case of the latter, lack of familiarity and a third-party perspective present challenges that set the topic of the Caucasian War apart from many analogous teaching contexts. When I was an instructor for Columbia's Contemporary Civilization seminar, for example, my students were all too aware of subsequent German history when reading about the "slave mentality" of Jews in Nietzsche's *Genealogy of Morals*. Their initial unease became a productive starting point for open dialogue on the relationship between words and events, ideology and its aftermath. (To what extent do ideas shape the course of history?; is an author responsible for the ways that others later use his or her words?, and so on.) There is no comparable background upon which to draw for the Caucasian War. Even the Second Chechen War, now over a decade old, occurred too early to inform the collective memory that my current students bring with them to the classroom.

Ultimately, my decision to address the Caucasian War in the classroom, right or wrong, arises from a desire to make this history better known, to fill a silence with a counter-story. Here Chinua Achebe's famous critique of Conrad's *Heart of Darkness* offers a useful pedagogical parallel. At the time Achebe delivered his 1975 lecture, *Heart of Darkness* was, as he put it, "the most commonly

---

[24] Susan Layton, "A Russian Reverie: Chechnya's Literary Legacy," *History Today* 47, no. 2 (1997), 6.

prescribed novel in twentieth-century literature courses in English Departments of American universities."[25] Yet somehow Conrad's racially fraught representations of Africans had escaped serious discussion either in scholarship or in the classroom. In attacking Conrad over the issue of racism, Achebe aimed to diminish the place of *Heart of Darkness* in the canon of English literature. Whatever the merits of his attack, it has had a lasting impact in the classroom, which is no small feat in itself. In retrospect, Achebe's influential essay did not so much prevent *Heart of Darkness* from appearing on North American syllabi as it altered the terms under which the novel was discussed. The essay and the novel are now indeed often assigned in tandem.[26] After Achebe, it was no longer feasible to reduce Africa, with all of its history and peoples, to the level of a footnote in Conrad's novel or Kurtz's psyche—or, as Achebe writes, to assign Africa "the role of props for the break-up of one petty European mind." Moreover, whether or not Conrad was a "thoroughgoing racist,"[27] as Achebe notoriously alleged, became a question that demanded close reading of the novel's rhetorical strategies. On the one hand, Achebe's provocations, when handled with balance and in a spirit of open-ended dialogue, provided an exemplary opportunity for "teaching the conflict," to borrow a catchphrase from the 1990s culture wars.[28] On the other hand, the novel, for all its formal virtuosity, became entangled in a web of competing narratives deriving from European interventions in

---

[25] Chinua Achebe, "An Image of Africa: Racism in Conrad's 'Heart of Darkness,'" in *Hopes and Impediments: Selected Essays* (New York: Doubleday, 1989), 14-15.

[26] Padmini Mongia, "Why I Teach Conrad and Achebe," in *Approaches to Teaching Conrad's "Heart of Darkness" and "The Secret Sharer,"* ed. Hunt Hawkins and Brian W. Shaffer (New York: Modern Languages Association of America, 2003), 105.

[27] Achebe, "An Image of Africa," 11, 12.

[28] The phrase was popularized by Gerald Graff's *Beyond the Culture Wars: How Teaching the Conflicts Can Revitalize American Education* (New York: Norton, 1992).

central Africa at the turn of the twentieth century. New Criticism, in other words, had given way to New Historicism in the classroom.

It is this second shift that presents the greater pedagogical burden in the case of "Bela." Like *Heart of Darkness* in English curricula, Lermontov's *Hero of Our Time* is one of the most commonly assigned texts in North American Slavic departments. It is usually the first full-length novel that students read in my survey on Russian prose. The point is not that it should not be there, but rather that Lermontov, or rather his novel's characters and narrators, should not emerge as the first and last word that students ever hear in a classroom about the Circassians. The peoples represented in the novel have greater claims on the attention of students than as mere background for the understanding of Lermontov's art, Pechorin's psychology, or the Russian *zeitgeist*—the "our time" in the novel's title. If students have heard nothing about Circassian history or culture beforehand, they will not learn much discussing the novel among themselves in class.

In the past, I've considered including other texts for counterbalance: Tolstoy's *Hadji Murat*, for instance, or a scholarly article. Students could read a Circassian Nart saga, thanks to John Colarusso's invaluable anthology,[29] or watch a video clip of a Circassian wedding dance, one that could be compared to the dance that Pechorin observes in the novel. As in all syllabus revision, however, adding one text means dropping another. Over the past few iterations of the course, the text I've chosen to add is a brief lecture. The advantage to this approach lies in its minimized opportunity costs; namely, expanded class discussion or lectures on other topics. The attempt to balance a novel with a lecture is nevertheless not readily reconciled with those twin pillars of contemporary pedagogy in the humanities: open dialogue and close reading. Both are central to my own approach. In contrast to modern seminars, the tradition of lecturing carries connotations of

---

[29] John Colarusso, ed. and trans., *Nart Sagas from the Caucasus: Myths and Legends from the Circassians, Abazas, Abkhaz, and Ubykhs* (Princeton, NJ: Princeton University Press, 2002).

learning by rote, professional privilege, and a rhetoric of authority. In an age in which students have online access to the classics, there is no longer any need for a lectern, that medieval contraption for mounting rare books. Yet in practice, the lecture remains an integral component of the seminar method. What has been legitimately deemed obsolete is not the lecture per se but its monopoly on class time. In Chekhov's *A Boring Story,* the protagonist embarks on his own physiology lectures without a "single prepared thought in [his] head"; yet he strives throughout to keep his speech "literary," his definitions "short and precise," and his phrasing "simple and elegant": "Each minute I must sit back and remember that I have at my disposal *only an hour and forty minutes.*"[30] Twenty minutes is my upper limit for lectures in seminar sessions.

In classes on "Bela," I postpone my lecture on the Caucasian War until the end of a class session, so that students have ample time to work through the text on terms unrelated to my own preoccupations. I begin the lecture with a few words about the war's origins. The rationale for the war can be illustrated with a map of the region, such that students can see how its diverse peoples are situated between seas on the east and west and between an expanding Russian empire on the north and south. I discuss the initial stages of the war under the direction of General Ermolov, a person whom Maxim Maximych mentions fondly,[31] as well as the resistance movement led by Imam Shamil. As my lecture is an oral text, delivered from minimal notes, the details change each time round. I do prepare a more thorough description of the war's conclusion, however, discussing General Nikolai Evdokimov's scorched-earth campaign from the late 1850s to 1864, which left scores dead in burned-out villages, and the severe hardships that Circassian refugees faced as they migrated over land and water to the Ottoman Empire. I provide conflicting statistics on the numbers of dead and

---

[30] Emphasis added. A. P. Chekhov, "Skuchnaia istoriia (iz zapisok starogo cheloveka)," in *Polnoe sobranie sochinenii i pisem v tridtsati tomakh,* (Moscow: Nauka, 1974-83), part 1: *Sochineniia,* 7:261, 262.

[31] Lermontov, *Geroi nashego vremeni,* 238.

displaced, so as to give some sense that this history, hardly set in stone, is still deeply contested. There is continuing debate over the extent to which the migration was forced, coerced, or voluntary, as well as over how large a role deportation assumed in official tsarist policy.[32] Among the most controversial questions is what to call this movement of people. *Makhadzhirstvo*,[33] which appears frequently in Russian scholarship, is an Arabic-derived term that evokes the migration of Muhammad and his followers from Mecca to Medina. As for common nouns, "expulsion," "emigration," "genocide," and "ethnic cleansing" are leading contenders. The last two terms, which derive from a twentieth-century lexicon, I introduce only as an afterword to my own narrative, if at all.

A lecture, of course, is by nature a monologue. Yet I hope that my lecture is not monologic, a finalizing word about either Circassian history or Lermontov's text, and that my retelling of the *muhajirs'* story, although Lermontov plays only a tertiary role in it, never ceases to be in dialogue with the story "Bela." My primary teaching objective is to defamiliarize "Bela" by juxtaposing to it a radically different example of a Circassian tale. This second story is not meant as a "key" to Lermontov's text, yet neither is it, in the end, a mere "footnote." How these two Circassian stories relate is, in fact, my final question for students. Does our understanding of Lermontov's novel change when viewed alongside this second story? Some students respond that little changes; for example, the second story helps clarify that the novel is set at a time of war. This is not always obvious to students on first reading, a point that has

---

[32] For diverging opinions on this controversy, see Sherry, "Social Alchemy on the Black Sea Coast," 7-30; James H. Meyer, "Immigration, Return, and the Politics of Citizenship: Russian Muslims in the Ottoman Empire, 1860-1914," *International Journal of Middle East Studies* 39, no. 1 (2007): 15-32; Justin McCarthy, *Death and Exile: The Ethnic Cleansing of Ottoman Muslims, 1821-1922* (Princeton, NJ: Darwin Press, 1995), 23-58; Shenfield, "The Circassians," 149-62; A. Kh. Kasumov and Kh. A. Kasumov, *Genotsid adygov: iz istorii bor'by adygov za nezavisimost' v XIX veke* (Nal'chik: Logos, 1992).

[33] G. A. Dzidzariia appears to have popularized this term through the monograph *Makhadzhirstvo i problemy istorii Abkhazii XIX stoletiia* (Sukhumi: Alashara, 1975).

prompted debate about Pechorin's personal stake in, or indifference to, the war and its conduct. Other students tackle the question of authorial intent. If, as one student put it, Lermontov intended to present a "realistic" portrait of the Caucasus, then he bears some responsibility to "represent" the people living there in an accurate manner. This formulation generated discussion about the kinds of truth claims that the narrators make about the region's peoples and landscapes. Finally, it is worth noting that, in response to my lecture, I cannot remember a single student turning on Lermontov personally, or liking his novel any more or less than before.

Aside from spurring such discussions, which sometimes spill over into the next class, this particular lecture is designed with longer-term pedagogical goals in mind. In the last two weeks of the course, students present on topics of their own, by which point they will have heard almost two dozen short lectures from me. As a group, these lectures are meant to model particular types of reading practices, from formalism and genre analysis to feminism and cultural history. In lecturing on Circassia in a class on "Bela," I hope to give students license and even encouragement to step outside the texts we read, so as to see from perspectives that these texts preclude. These perspectives, in turn, open onto new texts and new stories. Whether students ever return to Lermontov's novel, or to the North Caucasus, is not crucial. We read "Bela" early in the course. Later in the same novel we'll see a Tatar boatman, Ukrainian smugglers, and a Serbian gambler—not to mention the ritual of a duel, a Western export that Russian officers smuggle with them to the Caucasus.[34] All of these textual figures offer potential openings into history. It is not possible to prepare a lecture in each case, yet after expanding one such footnote into a story of its own, I hope that my students sense that there are always other narratives beyond what we're reading, and that a few of them will follow the document trail, on- or offline, necessary to reach them.

---

[34] On the foreign roots of dueling in Russia, see Irina Reyfman, *Ritualized Violence Russian Style: The Duel in Russian Culture and Literature* (Stanford, CA: Stanford University Press, 1999), 45-96.

16

TEXT IN SYLLABUS I

Teaching "Literature and Empire": The Case for *Anna Karenina*

Cathy Popkin

If a Slavic department's basic survey of the nineteenth-century Russian novel is designed as a course on "Literature and Empire," what should the syllabus include? *A Hero of our Time* is an obvious candidate, since Lermontov's celebrated work of prose features the Caucasus and other conquests and simultaneously aspires to novelhood. But what about a selection by Pushkin? Will *Eugene Onegin* do, or does the course call for something more manifestly on topic, such as *The Prisoner of the Caucasus*? The latter, admittedly, is not nineteenth-century prose, but, then again, neither is the former. And must we cast about for a work by Turgenev that explicitly takes on the imperial project, or does the conjunction in Literature *and* Empire broaden the inquiry sufficiently to accommodate, say, *Fathers and Sons*?

The question is particularly vexed in the case of Tolstoy. When I was compiling the syllabus for "Literature and Empire: The Reign of the Novel in Russia (19th Century)," it seemed self-evident that I should teach *Hadji Murat* (its 1904 completion notwithstanding) and welcome the opportunity to do so: Tolstoy's last novel is a great one; it is also significantly shorter than the rest; as a treatment of Russian aggression in Chechnya, its contemporary resonance is unmistakable, and it is unquestionably right on topic.[1] But for

---

[1] As many have remarked, the lion's share of nineteenth-century Russian literature on Russian imperialism was preoccupied with the annexation of one region in particular — the Caucasus — despite the fact that, in the process of becoming the largest contiguous empire in history, Russia extended itself in all available directions. Having reached east to the Sea of Japan

some reason I resisted the topical imperative, and as is no doubt obvious from my title, I indulged my desire to read *Anna Karenina*. My purpose here is to report the results of that self-indulgence, both for what it illuminates in Tolstoy's novel and for what it suggests about the selection of course material in general, especially in topic courses.

For a serious examination of the dyad *literature* and *empire*, is it necessary (or desirable, preferable, or sensible) to identify texts that are expressly concerned with the expansion and retention of the Russian empire? Or is it possible (or desirable, preferable, sensible, or profitable) to consider any substantial text written in the context of the Russian imperial project on the assumption that that text will somehow be informed by those aspirations—the political, historical, and imaginative urgencies of empire?

As it turns out, though far from an obvious choice for a discussion of imperialism, *Anna Karenina* not only has much to say on the specific subject of empire but it also has a lot to teach us about the way political, historical, and cultural issues can be appropriated to address the most existential, personal, and aesthetic problems. In this respect, the question of empire works at the very center, not just at the periphery, of Tolstoy's novel.

How might one begin to study "Literature and Empire" absent an explicit treatment of imperialist expansion? One suggestion is to address the expansiveness of the text itself. Not to be glib about

---

by 1700 and west to encompass most of Poland, Belarus, eastern Ukraine, and the territories on the Baltic and Black Seas by 1800, the Russian empire continued to expand on multiple fronts in the nineteenth century as well, staking claims in the Central Asian steppes to the south, annexing Finland to the north, extending its western borders beyond Warsaw, and, most famously, annexing the violently contested land beyond the Caucasus mountains and between the Black and Caspian Seas to the southwest. The brutality of the Caucasian campaign, the passion of the resistance it encountered, the charisma of the tribal leaders, the growth of nationalist sentiment in Russia itself, and the perceived exoticism of these colonial subjects (by analogy with the subject peoples in the orientalist endeavors of European colonial powers) seem to have conspired to make the conquest of the Caucasus the literary focal point through the Romantic period and beyond.

some putative connection between vast territory and fat books, but a novel's capaciousness might be viewed as a mark of an analogous sort of authorial ambition, an aspiration to encompass more and more world, to assimilate it to one's own purposes, to subsume it under one's own vision, and to project sovereign authority over that enormous universe. How much space does a writer need, after all? The occupation of artistic space *is* an assertion of a kind of territorial prerogative, and a smallish plot obviously does not suffice for Tolstoy. Monika Greenleaf and Stephen Moeller-Sally identify in the literary projects of the Golden Age what they call "cultural analogues to imperial power," pointing to those earlier writers' attempts to compete with the state's narratives and to arrogate to themselves the right to expatiate on Russianness and produce "Russian subjects."[2] It may not be amiss to look at the monumental prose forms of the latter half of the nineteenth century as an index of a subsequent effort toward literary sovereignty, the impulse to establish the "reign" of the novel, and to consolidate its power beyond dispute.

The amplitude of the Tolstoyan novel notwithstanding, though, the apparent boundlessness of its dimensions and its reach is only that—apparent. Moreover, even in a novel as commodious as *War and Peace*, what's at stake is not merely the occupation of space, but its delineation: not only size, but shape. Otherwise all fat novels would be alike, when in fact each is skinny in its own way. And in *Anna Karenina*, the novel that begins not only with this famous articulation of sameness and difference, but also with a reassurance that everything will "shape itself" or "shape up" (образуется; 1:2),[3]

---

[2] Monika Greenleaf and Stephen Moeller-Sally, "Introduction," in *Russian Subjects: Empire, Nation, and the Culture of the Golden Age*, eds. Greenleaf and Moeller-Sally (Evanston, IL: Northwestern University Press, 1998), 2.

[3] In the parenthetical references, the first number refers to the part, the second to the chapter, of *Anna Karenina*. This should enable readers to locate the passages in any Russian edition or in the translation of their choice. I have drawn translations from the English version of Louise and Aylmer Maude (New York: Oxford University Press, 1980), revising them as needed.

we would be advised to look precisely at what is being shaped, what shape it is being given, and how the contours that define that shape mark the boundary precisely between the same and the different.

Classically a boundary recognizes the frontier between one's own territory and what lies beyond it, distinguishing between self and other, own and alien, свой and чужой, the place of residency and the locus of strangerhood.[4] It separates what something is from what it is not. Indeed, it has by now become something of a commonplace to note that this form of mapping—the stark juxtaposition of "us" and "not us"—is an oblique but effective way of delimiting and situating the elusive self. How rich, then, the imaginative possibilities of the multiethnic Russian empire, with its mandate of conquest and annexation, its shifting frontier, and its lexicon of integration, acculturation, assimilation, incorporation, and conversion of non-Slavic ethnic groups—how rich for an examination of the Russian subject in terms of all the things it emphatically is not! And had we been reading *Hadji Murat*, we would no doubt have been justified in framing our analysis in terms of a juxtaposition of self and exotic other. But *Anna Karenina* is emphatically not *Hadji Murat*.

In *Anna Karenina* the study of the инородцы (literally, those "of other race")[5] is explicitly the province of Karenin, the novel's living representative of state and empire, who commissions "an investigation of every aspect—political, administrative, economic, ethnographic, material, and religious—of the lives of these ethnic others," chiefly to outmaneuver local political rivals (3:14). The novel further undermines our confidence in the contrastive model of self-definition in its swipe at the visiting (western European) "foreign prince" (иностранный принц)—the one who is said to resemble

---

4   This final opposition stems from Richard Gustafson's magisterial treatment of Tolstoy, *Leo Tolstoy: Resident and Stranger* (Princeton, NJ: Princeton University Press, 1986).

5   The legal status "of other race" was formally created in 1822 to apply to the nomadic ethnic groups of Siberia. By the second half of the nineteenth century it was used more broadly to refer to other non-Russian ethnic groups throughout the Asian part of Russia.

a cucumber. This man's fieldwork in nationality studies is driven by a taste for exotica, and his quest to uncover the quintessential Russian spirit consists of the juxtaposition of a harem in Turkey, an elephant in India, and some comparable Russian depredations (4:1). On the novel's own terms, then, the confrontation with the exotic other (as titillating as it is for the prince and as urgent as it seems to Karenin) is not the most productive juxtaposition, and the boundary between the same and the very different is not the crucial one. Indeed, what makes *Anna Karenina* far more interesting is that the delineations it seeks are more complicated.

To cut straight to the chase at long last, I will propose that *Anna Karenina* attempts to locate the self, not in the starker terms of cultural *difference*, but in the hazier realm of *similarity*. Its painful discriminations are between likes; its boundaries chart a painstaking path through territories that are expressly contiguous and related, and whose propinquity is powerful. To invoke, but to realign, the novel's opening gambit, I might say that Tolstoy makes paramount the distinction not between sameness and difference, but between sameness and resemblance—between things that are "похожи" (similar).

It is thus fitting that the novel's principal paradigm of foreign policy is neither Russia's earlier conquest of the colorful Caucasus nor its ongoing annexation of sizable chunks of exotic Central Asia, but rather the Pan-Slavic enterprise.[6] In positing a transcendent community of Slavs whose common Slavdom trumps nations and states, in imagining a mapping of territory in which sameness overrides political boundaries, Pan-Slavism represents the logical complement to the multiethnic model of empire, where expanding borders run roughshod over difference. Not that Pan-Slavism

---

[6] The Pan-Slavic movement, which arose mid-century, posited the unity of all Slavic peoples. In Tolstoy's novel it takes the form of a popular identification on the part of many Russians with their suffering "brother Slavs" in the Balkans, who were struggling for independence from the Ottoman Empire. When Serbia declared war on Turkey in 1876, Russian volunteers joined that war effort in solidarity. When Russia formally declared war on Turkey itself a year later, Pan-Slavism provided an excellent justification for Russia's own imperial aspirations.

in practice was any less imperialistically motivated than other modes of empire building; in essence it represents an alternate way of disregarding existing borders. But the treatment of the Slavonic question in the novel also helps foreground Tolstoy's keen interest in the potential pitfalls entailed in negotiating relations of *resemblance*. For even if all Slavs are in some sense "похожи друг на друга" ("resemble one another"; 1:1), they can hardly be said to be identical with the Russian self. Balkan Slavs are *not* Russian, though they are "единоверцы" ("of the same religion"; 8:15). The Roman Catholic Poles are not even that. The "Russification of Poland" is an undertaking—and a lively topic for Oblonsky's dinner parties— precisely because the sameness of all Slavs cannot be assumed.

Pan-Slavism is rendered—and handily dismantled—in the novel in terms of three propositions, three assertions of едино-родство—ethnic sameness—that complement the multiethnic rhetoric of ино-родство—ethnic otherness:

1. Identity statements about BEING. Being "of the same religion" and "of the same blood" (единокровцы) converts all Slavs into "brothers." They are similar; therefore they are us. But that identity statement is flawed. Brothers are proximate and similar others, not selves. Indeed, the evidence of the whole novel makes it clear that even literal brothers are not the self, a fact emphasized by the varying degrees of proximity and distance between Levin and his half- and full-brothers. Even full brothers, who are genuinely "of the same blood," are ultimately once removed. Nikolai is not equal to or the same as Levin.

2. Assertions about FEELING. The contention that this "identity to" implies inexorable "identification with," giving rise to an intuitive, visceral sensation, a condition of perfect—even unavoidable—access to the pain of the other—especially, the novel tells us, when "единокровцы," our "blood brothers," are being killed. But this construction of empathy is pathology; the experience of dying, as evidenced in the account of the drawn-out death of Levin's blood brother Nikolai, serves mainly to isolate the sufferer. The body of the other in pain—no matter how proximate that other—presents a spectacle inexorably alien to the self, and Levin can no more vicariously feel the suffering of his dying brother than he is in a position to experience the pain of Kitty's giving birth.

3. The proposition that this condition of BEING identical and FEELING someone's pain culminates in luminous SPEAKING. The Pan-Slavic justification for the declaration of war on behalf of our suffering blood brothers and co-religionists is the repeated assertion that "the people have spoken" — "народ выразил свою волю" (8:15) — an act of speech both gloriously unanimous and perfectly expressive. Levin is understandably flummoxed by this image of the entire nation rising up at once and speaking with a single voice, and his private thoughts about the essential diversity of the Russian nation (after all, we have carpenters and cooks, peasants and teachers, and those are not all one thing!) easily counter the plausibility of a single will, let alone a single expression of that will. Even more powerfully than in such direct counterarguments, though, the novel undermines this grand assertion of voicing and articulation in its insistence that the truest feelings are marked by aphasia. We recall the famous wordless diplomacy between Kitty and Levin that initiates their union, much as we are led, in the end, to assent to the fact that Levin's final insights remain unspoken.

The abject identification of sameness, then, comes across as being equally misguided as the abject infatuation with difference we saw in the case of the cucumber prince. And yet surely Tolstoy need not have gone to all this trouble just to expose the falseness of Pan-Slavism, the status of which is undercut from the start by the character of its proponents, with Vronsky's departure by train to the Serbian war figuring as no less an act of self-extinction than Anna's throwing herself under one does. The Balkan conflict per se does not even intrude upon the action until Part 8, once Anna is dead and other characters have taken up the Pan-Slavic cause. Thanks to Tolstoy's undisguised disdain for the war effort, this final installment never made it into the novel in its original serialized form;[7] but while the publisher's refusal to print Part 8 kept the

---

[7]   *Anna Karenina* — or the first 7/8 of it — appeared serially in thirteen installments over twenty-eight months: from January to April 1875, from

most problematic ideology off the pages of the *Russian Herald*, the segment on the Slavonic question is only the novel's most overtly political treatment of similarity and relatedness.

The whole Pan-Slavic nexus reflects, rather, a broader, more profound, and much more compelling exploration of sameness and difference in the novel. It is part of Tolstoy's translation of the binary logic of "едино–"/"ино–," of "свой" and "чужой" (of "same" and "different," of self and other), into the less starkly delineated terrain of similarity, where differences are not so obvious and relatedness is not tantamount to identity.

It is common currency to think of Russian culture as a hybrid beast and to see its nineteenth-century variant in particular as informed by two somewhat antithetical impulses. One, the imperial paradigm, foregrounds absorption, expansion, the annexing of neighboring or even distant territory, and the concomitant appropriation (or suppression) of a multiplicity of cultural modes. The second—the nationalist myth—stresses instead organic generation from within, finding its origin in what is native, natural, and indigenous, and thus imagining an essential and unified self. In ham-handedly positing and then easily dismissing the myth of an organic and unified Slavdom, Tolstoy takes the first, if not entirely subtle, step toward discrediting the myth of organic unity that underlies the spurious vision of a perfectly unanimous Russian nation rising up to speak for the collective Slavs, suggesting that the indigenous and national may be no more monolithic than the multiethnic. Difference between is more immediately palpable; difference within is much harder to negotiate. The novel thus

---

January to April 1876, and from December 1876 to April 1877. Tolstoy published Part 8 on its own. The novel we now take for granted as an eight-part structure assumed its familiar form only once Tolstoy had revised and assembled all the pieces for publication as a freestanding edition. For a succinct and suggestive treatment of the differences between that separate edition and the original serial publication, see William Mills Todd III, "The Responsibilities of (Co-)Authorship: Notes on Revising the Serialized Version of *Anna Karenina*," in *Freedom and Responsibility in Russian Literature: Essays in Honor of Robert Louis Jackson*, ed. Elizabeth Cheresh Allen and Gary Saul Morson (Evanston, IL: Northwestern University Press, 1995), 159-69.

looks for a way to map out a world of relatedness in which one can find one's place amidst beings that are not starkly different but nonetheless not the self.

This more subtle engagement with the conceptual difficulties of similarity is palpable in the novel's positioning of Levin, whose painstaking delineation of the self can be viewed as an act of discrimination between the most proximate kinds of others. Levin's *Bildung* can be viewed as a series of potential identifications with beings he feels affinity for and propinquity with—emphatically not the exotic other, who is clearly other—but closer, more indigenous, and hence more confusing ones. If he rejects the identification with his fellow Slavs, he nevertheless revels in the similarity and closeness he (temporarily) feels, for instance, with both the Russian peasantry and the adherents of the Russian Orthodox Church. And yet similarity only goes so far, and principally we get a series of portraits of what Levin is not quite. Levin can mow until he is blue in the face and feel a tremendous sense of brotherhood with his laborers, but in the final analysis he is no peasant. Ultimately, the novel posits a *division* of labor. And while he is briefly attracted to the idea of a community of co-religionists, pleased by the thought that it is easier to believe in an existing living church that compounds the belief of all men, struck by the proposition that it is not given to an isolated man to discover truth, Levin's serial epiphanies are finally the product of his individual discriminations, of his separating himself from the articulation of any generalized will or belief system. And while his beliefs do not diverge from Christianity—they are truly похожи, the resemblance is strong—clearly Levin is Christian "по-своему," "in his own way." He has begun to negotiate the delicate boundary between what is "similar" and what is genuinely his own (свой).

For that matter, is Tolstoy's hero Levin or Lëvin (Lyovin)? Despite assurances on the part of the author's daughter that "In our home everyone pronounced it 'Levin'" (у нас дома все говорили 'Лёвин'),[8] scholars continue to use both. While the names are so

---

[8]   Cited by Alexis Klimoff in "Is it 'Lévin' or 'Lëvin'?" *Tolstoy Studies Journal*

similar that orthography declines to distinguish between them, the two constructions of the name are distinct, one perhaps invoking a closer relationship with the author Lëva Tolstoy, who, while similar to his character in many ways, is still by no means identical to him. Or perhaps the essential difference between the two names that resemble one another suggests the distance between a Christian Levin (i.e., Lëvin) and a "Jewish" one (Levin). On this particular point, on the essential similarity or ultimate difference between creeds—the question of whether Jews or Muslims, who have similar beliefs in God, have identical relationships with Him, whether they are свои or just похожи (truly one's own or just strong in resemblance)—Levin declares himself unable to declare. So much for the capacity to speak definitively (the people have spoken!). About what is really important, Levin cannot speak at all.[9]

Thus, it can hardly be an accident that the text's most radiant and most essential moment comes to us courtesy of the entirely pre-linguistic Mitya. At the very end of the novel, on the heels of literally hundreds of pages of Levin's labored attempts to locate himself on a variety of continua, amidst people of various social classes, religious affiliations, and blood relations, Mitya, to the enormous excitement of his parents, that day "obviously, undoubtedly had begun to recognize his own people" ("очевидно, несомненно уже сознавал всех своих"; 8:18). This is where I see the question posed

---

11 (1999): 110. The two dots over the "e," which change the pronunciation from "ye" to "yo," are omitted in print.

[9] We recall, from Roman Jakobson's discussion of aphasia, that there are two types of being at a loss for words. In the first, the capacity for selection and substitution is disturbed; in the second, it is the power of combination and contiguity that is impaired. Jakobson famously cites *Anna Karenina*, not because of its silences, but as an example of realist prose that spurns substitution (metaphor) in favor of combination (metonymy). But if for Jakobson similarity is what allows for substitution, for Tolstoy similarity is what precludes it. Similarity demands relations. It does not authorize substitution. It establishes relations not of identity, but rather of contiguity. Jakobson develops his theory of aphasia in "Two Aspects of Language and Two Types of Aphasic Disturbances," in Roman Jakobson, *Language in Literature*, eds. Krystyna Pomorska and Stephen Rudy (Cambridge, MA: The Belknap Press of Harvard University Press, 1987), 95-114.

by empire to be at the very heart of this novel: in the difficulty, yet possibility—and maybe even the necessity—of recognizing one's own people. Levin may spurn his Serbian "brothers," but it is imperative that he recognize his own son. This modality is marked at the end of Tolstoy's novel with Levin's newborn ability to feel the swell of emotion occasioned by the wigglings of his no-longer newborn child, an intuitive upsurge of *feeling* that contrasts sharply with the national sentiment ostensibly occasioned by his Slavic "kin."

And yet I do not mean to suggest merely that the personal trumps the national, that identifying "one's own" is simply a matter of staying home with one's family. Rather, the terms of the novel's personal discriminations dovetail with the discriminative urgencies—such as the problem of national identity—created by the expansive embrace of empire. Which people *are* one's own?

This powerful resonance between the problems of foreign policy and the arena of domestic affairs, this imaginative assimilation of the mandates of empire to the operations of home territory, is palpable in the novel's own version of manifest destiny. Tolstoy's open hostility to the imperial project notwithstanding, Levin's repeated assertion of a sort of Russian "mission" never seems to be undercut in the novel: Levin contemplates the Russian people, "whose mission it is to occupy and cultivate enormous unoccupied tracts of land, deliberately, as long as any land remains unoccupied" (3:29). If Russians are destined and driven to occupy space, at least the imperative here seems to be to occupy not foreign terrain, but one's own land, not to occupy and acculturate, but to occupy and cultivate, in pursuit not of the dominance of Russian culture but of the triumph of Russian agriculture.[10] Notably the same passage specifies that one must cultivate one's own land "свойственным образом"—not only in a way that suits the land but also по-своему—in one's own way.

---

[10] Admittedly, depending on where this "unoccupied land" that Tolstoy arrogates to the peasants is located, the expansion of Russian agriculture might well turn out to be about spreading Russian culture after all.

The problem of identifying what is one's own makes the novel's chief epistemological achievement not *discovery* (of something new and alien, whether territory or precept), but *recognition*; recognizing one's own, as Mitya does, is also the task of the adults, who sometimes do and sometimes do not recognize their own children; it is accomplished by Levin and Kitty, who recognize each other across a crowded skating rink; it is also the achievement of Levin's final, silent epiphany, which is essentially a recognition of what was within him all along.

This same (or, rather, a *related*) question about how far afield one has to go to learn something brings me back to the question I began with about putting together a syllabus. The evidence of Tolstoy's novel suggests that Levin gains a lot more by focusing on the familiar than the cucumber prince does in his experience of the exotic. Perhaps, by analogy, it should not be a foregone conclusion that it will *necessarily* be more mind-expanding to include a work by an ethnic or racial or socioeconomic or geographical "other" than to read a canonical text. Not that Tolstoy should be invoked as an alibi for curricular conservatism, but it is probably worth recognizing the *difficulty* of truly understanding what one's own consists of, how much harder it is, in a way, to stake out a place of one's own in a range of contiguous places than to do so in contrast to palpably alien ones, to identify one's own place amidst proximate positions that may be similar (похожи) but will never be the same (свои). (The issue of "other voices" is one that arises more often in the context of Columbia's Core Curriculum, which desperately does not want to be insular, but which is sometimes uncertain about how multicultural its embrace should be.) For that matter, it is not entirely clear in Tolstoy's novel either what the unit of selfhood might be: the individual self? One's family? One's "circle"? One's class? One's nation? All of God's people?

What *is* clear to me, though, is that Tolstoy's preoccupation with these questions makes it absolutely appropriate to read *Anna Karenina* in the context of a course on literature and empire, a recognition that knocks up against the prevalent wisdom that we need to dismantle the canon in order to engage urgent issues like race, gender, and imperialism. I have come to believe fairly strongly that a text need not be explicitly about racial identity to be inhabited by positions that demand interrogation, all the more so as they reign unchallenged and often undetected, and that it is just as important and powerful and fruitful to recognize the silently assumed as to join the general outcry against injustices explicitly (and properly) exposed. I have no objection to works or whole courses that do the latter, but we ought not to forget to see what's lurking in the texts that we readily embrace as "our own."

Do we need to jettison our traditional reading lists in order to assign books that take us where we need to go? Do we need to assign a book that explicitly addresses the theme of imperialism or post-colonialism in order to discuss literary treatments of empire? I don't think so. Moreover, I don't think that discussions of empire are ancillary even to the most traditional domestic concerns and configurations of novelistic space. To talk about *Anna Karenina* and empire is neither to make light of the imperialist project nor to betray the novel's most intimate and very own terms.

17

TEXT IN SYLLABUS II

Reading for the Self:
Unwrapping the Nested Autobiographies
in Lermontov's *A Hero of Our Time*

Rebecca Stanton

I teach Lermontov's *A Hero of Our Time* not in its usual context of the nineteenth-century Russian prose canon, but in my comparative literature courses on self-narrative: a graduate seminar that pairs key Russian and Western narratives of the self along thematic lines, and an undergraduate class that explores a wide variety of first-person narratives, from that of Odysseus in Homer's *Odyssey* to that of Rigoberta Menchú in her controversial memoir. Both courses take as their point of departure the premise that autobiography is inherently impossible—since narrative is by its nature fictional, and autobiography is defined by the correspondence between a narrative and objective truth, which can never be firmly established. At the same time, the idea of this correspondence, which is the central idea of autobiography, forces us to read all "autobiographical" narratives *as if* they were true. This tension, between the confessional and testimonial force of the first-person voice and the reader's consciousness of the constructedness of the narrative, creates a kind of paradox that close reading can examine and appreciate but never fully resolve.[1] The multiplicity of first-person narrative voices in *A Hero of Our Time* makes it a particularly tempting target for such a reading.

---

[1]   The irresolvable tension between "truth" and "design" in autobiographical narrative has been axiomatic to autobiography scholarship since the publication of Roy Pascal's seminal *Design and Truth in Autobiography* (Cambridge, MA: Harvard University Press, 1960). My courses extend the destabilizing influence of this tension into the study of fictional first-person narratives.

Abstracted from its traditional place in the Russian canon, between Pushkin's "novel in verse" *Eugene Onegin* and Gogol's "*poema*" in prose *Dead Souls*, Lermontov's novel-in-tales changes shape. Some of its most celebrated features fade into relative insignificance: Pechorin no longer embodies the literary type of the "superfluous man," the Caucasus no longer exemplifies a cliché of Russian orientalism. And the novel's famously "involute structure"[2] reads less as a chapter in the history of Russian literature's rather complicated approach to the novel as a genre, and more as a function of the story's multiplicity of tellers, each one a self-asserting "I" who shapes the narrative, to the extent of his ability, in his own image.

Depending on the reader's approach and on the edition of the text assigned, there are at least four, if not five or even six, of these autobiographical narrators. In reverse order of appearance, these are (1) the novel's central character Pechorin, who is introduced into the narrative by (2) Maxim Maximych, who is in turn introduced by (3) an unnamed traveler, who in *his* turn is framed by (4) the "Author," purveyor of the "Author's Preface." Somewhere behind the persona of the "Author"—and indeed, behind all the narrators—lurks a fifth figure: Lermontov himself, inaccessible through the medium of the text, and seemingly confined to that unknowable territory of "authorial intention" from which sophisticated readers, forewarned about the "intentional fallacy" and the "death of the author," know themselves to be debarred.[3] But, as Vladimir Nabokov notes in his "Translator's Foreword" to the novel, "For the emotional type of reader, much of the novel's poignancy and fascination resides in

---

2   Vladimir Nabokov, "Translator's Foreword," in Mikhail Lermontov, *A Hero of Our Time*, trans. Vladimir Nabokov in collaboration with Dmitri Nabokov (Ann Arbor, MI: Ardis, 1988), vii. Quotations from Nabokov's notes and from Lermontov's novel itself are also taken from this edition.

3   See William K. Wimsatt and Monroe C. Beardsley, "The Intentional Fallacy," in *The Verbal Icon: Studies in the Meaning of Poetry* (Lexington, KY: University of Kentucky Press, 1954), 3-18; and Roland Barthes, "The Death of the Author," in *Image—Music—Text*, trans. Stephen Heath (New York: Hill and Wang, 1977), 142-48.

the fact that Lermontov's own tragic fate is somehow superimposed upon that of Pechorin."[4]

In fact, the circumstances of Pechorin's death are left obscure in Lermontov's text (though Nabokov, apparently a bit of an "emotional type" himself, attempts in endnotes to conjecture the outline of the story), but the duel Pechorin stages in the novel's fourth installment, "Princess Mary," and which kills his "grotesque shadow" Grushnitsky,[5] bears notable similarities to the one in which Lermontov would die a year or two later.[6] (The "emotional type of reader" could therefore go so far as to contend that Pechorin, in some figurative and uncanny sense, kills his own creator.) A reader even vaguely familiar with the particulars of Lermontov's life and death can easily use these to fill in the missing details of Pechorin's biography, such as his reasons for being in the Caucasus (exile as a punishment for dueling?) and the cause of his premature demise (another duel?). The impression of identity between Pechorin and his creator is heightened by the fact that the text captures both author and hero in their mid-twenties, and that both die young in exotic locales. Under the influence of these circumstantial coincidences, more "literary" features of the text, such as Pechorin's incurable melancholy and the orientalist clichés of the setting, detach themselves from their native context of Russian romantic writing and attach themselves to Lermontov's own authorial persona.[7]

---

4   Nabokov, xix. In other words, Lermontov's literal death in a duel rescues him from "death" in the Barthesian sense; Nabokov, writing ten years before Barthes' "Death of the Author," could not enjoy the irony of this observation, but modern readers, and students, can.

5   Nabokov, xviii.

6   Both duels are fought at Pyatigorsk, between Russian soldiers serving in the Caucasus, and end with a corpse lying at the foot of a mountain; both arise from one party's mockery of the other's Romantic posturing in the presence of ladies. See David Powelstock, "Mikhail Iur'evich Lermontov," in *Russian Literature in the Age of Pushkin and Gogol: Poetry and Drama*, ed. Christine Rydel (Detroit: Gale Group, 1999), 202.

7   This process works in both directions: as Irina Reyfman notes, "Pushkin's and Lermontov's passion for dueling and especially their deaths in duels added significantly to the duel's lofty status." Reyfman, *Ritualized Violence*

For Nabokov, the "emotional type of reader" who looks for Lermontov in the text stands in disadvantageous contrast to the "good reader" who is repeatedly invoked elsewhere in his Foreword and in the copious annotations he appears compelled to append to his translation. The creation of this invidious opposition, and its subsequent use as a tool with which to discipline the reader, is just one of the many ways in which Nabokov imposes himself on Lermontov's text as an uninvited *sixth* narrator—an endeavor that attracts minute scrutiny in my comparative literature classes, where we read the novel in Nabokov's translation, and follow it with his own *Speak, Memory* and *Lolita*. As Nicholas Warner has observed, Nabokov's annotations not only "emerge as a text paralleling and mocking Lermontov's own," but even presume to reshape Lermontov's text into a form more closely resembling Nabokov's original works, sending the reader on a treasure hunt through interlinked endnotes and "creat[ing] a shadow story ... that goes beyond what Lermontov gives us."[8] Moreover, in his constantly interrupting notes, his upstaging Foreword, and his efforts to discipline the reader into "good" modes of interpretation, Nabokov engages in a project strikingly similar to that of Narrator 4 (the "Author") and Narrator 3 (the traveler), both of whom seek in their respective "Introductions" (to the book as a whole, and to the excerpts from Pechorin's journal) to shape and control the reader's response to the texts they frame.[9]

This strategy is not without risk, since it exposes Nabokov himself to the same skeptical reading he imposes on the novel's internal narrators. Indeed, a "good reader" of Nabokov's translation can hardly fail to notice the translator's resemblance to the very narrator (number 3, the traveler) whose "romanticist

---

Russian Style: The Duel in Russian Culture and Literature (Stanford, CA: Stanford University Press, 1999), 84.

8   Nicholas O. Warner, "The Footnote as Literary Genre: Nabokov's Commentaries to Lermontov and Puškin," *Slavic and East European Journal* 30, no. 2 (1986): 172.

9   Warner, 170.

notions" he goes out of his way to disparage.[10] Both set themselves up as editors, framers, and interpreters of a text whose author is conveniently deceased; one could even, uncharitably, suggest that Nabokov follows the traveling narrator's lead in taking "advantage of the opportunity to sign another man's work with my own name." (The traveling narrator characterizes this as an "innocent forgery"; notably, Nabokov forbears in this instance to insert a contradicting footnote.) Taking note of these resemblances leads students to detect further parallels, not only between Nabokov and the traveler but among the rest of the novel's narrators as well; as the students quickly discover, the effort to take possession of others' words and stories—and to control the reader's response to them—is not confined to the writers of prefaces, but is common to all six of the narrators they have identified. This in turn alerts them to a central ethical dilemma of autobiographical narrative: it necessarily subordinates all "other" characters to the subjectivity of the narrator, making them mere pawns in his story of himself, objects or instruments of his self-realization rather than subjects in their own right.[11]

Considering the novel in this way, as the product of a competition among multiple autobiographical narrators who vie for control of the text and of each other, certainly represents a more sophisticated approach to its autobiographical dimensions than the "emotional type" of reading Nabokov disparages. What, though, does it do for us to read this text as belonging to a canon of writings about the self, and to bring to bear on it some of the tools that

---

[10] For a more extensive analysis of these parallels, and of Nabokov's risky choice to join Lermontov's text as a sixth narrator, see my article "Talking Back to Nabokov: A Commentary on a Commentary," *Ulbandus, the Slavic Review of Columbia University* 10 (2007): 212-21.

[11] David Powelstock sees the characters of *A Hero* as gripped simultaneously by a "subjective fallacy," which causes them to "imagine themselves [as] wholly the authors of their own fates *and the fates of others*," and by an "objective fallacy," which causes them to "convince themselves of their own goodness by forming attractive images of themselves, *and unattractive images of others*." See Powelstock, *Becoming Mikhail Lermontov: The Ironies of Romantic Individualism in Nicholas I's Russia* (Evanston, IL: Northwestern University Press, 2005), 331-32 (my italics).

critics have developed for analyzing autobiography? Leaving aside
the additional layer of self-narration superimposed by Nabokov,
and considering only Lermontov's original text, I think examining
A Hero of Our Time from this autobiographical perspective does two
main things:

1) It invites us to consider on equal terms *all* of the selves
   who take a hand in the narration, or in other words to
   take account of Maxim Maximych, the traveling narrator,
   and the author as something more than just a series of
   lenses through which to view Pechorin; even, perhaps, to
   contemplate the possibility that there is more than one
   candidate for the title of "A Hero of Our Time."

2) It raises the question of just what model of selfhood that
   Lermontov puts forward, or, as I prefer to formulate the
   question for my students, what is the *problem of the self*
   that the text sets out to solve.

In the remainder of this chapter I will touch upon some of the
implications of these two effects.

The Novel as a Set of Nested Autobiographies: Reconsidering the "Hero"

The peculiarity of autobiographical discourse is that it collapses
three usually distinct entities—protagonist, narrator, and author—
into one. As these three story-*producing* figures converge, however,
the autobiographical story's *audience* diverges into three distinct
entities: the "coaxer" or coercer who provokes the narrator to
narrate (this role is sometimes performed not by an individual but
by an internalized cultural imperative); the "addressee" to whom
the narrator directs his story; and the "consumer" who, finally,
sits down with the book—and over whom the narrator can exert
only indirect influence.[12] Each of the three main autobiographical

---

[12] For a more detailed explanation of these three audience positions, see
Sidonie Smith and Julia Watson, *Reading Autobiography: A Guide for*

narrators in *A Hero of Our Time* finds himself vis-à-vis the others, at one time or another, in the various positions of coaxer, addressee, or consumer: they are not only one another's narrators, but also one another's audiences, in the multiple senses of the word that autobiography entails.

Similarly, given that a commonplace of self-narratives from the *Odyssey* on is the motif of the journey, during which the self comes to know itself through a series of encounters with significant "others," it seems useful to recognize that each of the narrators in *A Hero of Our Time* is both a traveling self and, in relation to the text's other traveling selves, a significant "other." In this sense, Pechorin is no more privileged than any of the other narrators; while he does seem to make a much greater impression on both Maxim Maximych and the unnamed traveler than they make on him, the latter two narrators nonetheless have a very significant impact on Pechorin's self-fashioning—at the editorial level. Each takes a turn at controlling the plotting of the novel—what is told and what is not, in what order and with what bias—and the traveling narrator even triumphantly declares his authorship by "sign[ing] another man's work with my own name."

The traveling narrator's falsification of the "signature" on the autobiographical text brazenly violates what Philippe Lejeune has called the autobiographical pact.[13] Under the terms of this pact, autobiography is defined as a contract between writer and reader, whereby the truth of the events depicted—that is, the correspon-

---

Interpreting Life Narratives (Minneapolis, MN: University of Minnesota Press, 2001), 50, and Ken Plummer, *Telling Sexual Stories: Power, Change, and Social Worlds* (London: Routledge, 1995), 21.

[13] See Philippe Lejeune, *Le pacte autobiographique* (Paris: Seuil, 1975). David A. Goldfarb, in his article "Lermontov and the Omniscience of Narrators" (*Philosophy and Literature* 20 [1996], 61-74), also invokes Lejeune in relation to Pechorin's journal, but casts Pechorin as the signatory of the pact, which remains in his view wholly contained within the bounds of the text (that is, it is a pact between the imaginary Pechorin and his imaginary readers). Whereas Goldfarb is concerned chiefly with epistemological issues, I am concerned with the ethical (and quasi-legal) implications of breaking the pact in the flagrant way the traveling narrator does here, and the impact of this contractual breach on our reception of the text.

dence between the narrated experience on the page and the actual experience of the author—is guaranteed precisely by the name that appears on the title page of the work, and which refers simultaneously to its narrator, protagonist, and author. The traveling narrator's announcement that he has "sign[ed] another man's work with my own name," in defiant breach of the pact throws into sharp relief the extreme extent to which Pechorin's autobiographical narrative has been hijacked. Perhaps "Pechorin" is not the name of the stories' original protagonist at all, but the name of the (hitherto presumed nameless) traveler who has "signed" them! To entertain this idea is to realize how fully Pechorin has been supplanted in—even erased from—his own narrative, replaced by the editor who controls the shape of the text.

Scholars have traditionally viewed the "nested" narrative structure of the novel as a "structural trick [that] consists in bringing Pechorin gradually nearer and nearer until he takes over," even though "by the time he takes over he is dead."[14] But in what sense does Pechorin "take over"? Several scholars have written intriguingly about the exercise of narrative power in the text: who exercises it over whom, and when, and how it is wrested away. Lewis Bagby sees a power struggle in the efforts of the traveling narrator to impose Romantic literary genre on Maxim Maximych's narrative, and the latter's equally determined efforts to resist this imposition; both of them, and Pechorin too, are "manipulators" who "distort their material (*fabula*)" in the service of their own literary assumptions.[15] David Goldfarb argues that all three of the main narrators recognize, and negotiate, a trade-off between "power" (the ability to shape the story's action directly, usually reserved for first-person narrators who are also participants) and "knowledge"

---

[14] Nabokov, vii. Nabokov here follows the orthodoxy established in 1840 by one of the novel's first reviewers, the influential critic Vissarion Belinsky; see V. G. Belinskii, "*Geroi nashego vremeni*: Sochinenie M. Lermontova," *Polnoe sobranie sochinenii v dvenadtsati tomakh*, ed. S. A. Vengerov (St. Petersburg: Tip. M.M. Stasiulevicha, 1900), 290-372, especially 297, 303.

[15] Lewis Bagby, "Narrative Double-Voicing in Lermontov's *A Hero of Our Time*," *Slavic and East European Journal* 22, no. 3 (1978): 265-86.

(the ability to narrate authoritatively everything that "really happened" in the story, usually reserved for third-person narrators located outside the story). In Goldfarb's interpretation, however, Pechorin wangles the best of both worlds (and breaks the bounds of autobiographical discourse) by adopting a genre for the final story that allows him to set himself up as "a first-person omniscient narrator" — a feat that should be impossible, and that surely signals a victory for Pechorin over the normal constraints of narrative.[16] David Powelstock goes even further, contending that "Even after his death, Pechorin controls the narrative of his life, wrenching it away from Maxim, the Editor, and the reader, relentlessly breaking the narrative frames that arise out of others' desires to contain and reify him."[17]

While these interpretations of *A Hero*'s narrative structure add much to our understanding of the novel, and accurately describe its unfolding as experienced by a Pechorin-centric reader, they are perhaps a bit too optimistic on Pechorin's behalf about the degree of narrative autonomy he truly enjoys. A reader approaching the text from the perspective of autobiography and its constraints — in particular, the tension between "truth" and "design" that I alluded to in my opening paragraph — will immediately see Pechorin's experimentation with different genres for the self-narrated portions of his story as evidence that, far from "breaking the narrative frames" constructed for him by others, Pechorin is intent upon adding to them. As Elizabeth Cheresh Allen puts it: "When [Pechorin] tries to imagine an identity for himself that he can act upon, he winds up playing roles that he has derived from characters in Romantic literature … becom[ing] so immersed in them that they serve as almost the only identity he has."[18]

---

[16] Goldfarb, 61-73.

[17] Powelstock, *Becoming*, 359. Elsewhere, Powelstock also notes how the multiple-first-person narrative structure threatens the very existence of the novel, since the premature death of any one of its three main narrators would prevent the text from reaching the reader — a point worth bringing to students' attention (*Becoming*, 347-48).

[18] Elizabeth Cheresh Allen, *A Fallen Idol Is Still a God: Lermontov and the*

In this reading, even Pechorin's accession to the position of first-person narrator ("omniscient" or otherwise) doesn't so much break down the walls of his narrative prison as rearrange the bricks. As Emma Lieber argues, Pechorin's very dedication to genre—his seeming desire to understand himself precisely as the source and hero of a Romantic narrative, and to work at perfecting the form of the narrative in which he stars—means that the closer we get to Pechorin's direct narrative of himself, the more he actually *recedes* from view: "Pechorin's writing locks him even deeper into the multi-layered fiction in which he is located.... [His] self, rather than being revealed and made eminently present by the process of self-narration, disappears."[19] Precisely at the moment of his (ostensibly) most intimate self-revelation, the "hero" vanishes.

But even as the reader grasps in vain for Pechorin, a still more sinister narrative game is afoot, signaled by the traveling narrator's brazen violation of the autobiographical pact. The fact is that while the frames around Pechorin are allegedly being stripped away—as we go from Maxim Maximych's second-hand tales about Pechorin to the traveling narrator's first-hand encounter with him and thence to Pechorin's direct account of himself—what is actually happening

---

Quandaries of Cultural Transition (Stanford, CA: Stanford University Press, 2006), 151. For a catalogue of the genres employed by the novel's various narrators, see Herbert Eagle, "Lermontov's 'Play' with Romantic Genre Expectations in *A Hero of Our Time*," *Russian Literature Triquarterly* 10 (1974): 299-315. Goldfarb (66-67, 69-71) and Powelstock (360) comment on some of the intriguing implications of these changes of genre. Lending some support to Powelstock's characterization of Pechorin as a *breaker* of narrative frames, Vladimir Golstein argues that he invokes these genres only to frustrate the expectations they create (Golstein, *Lermontov's Narratives of Heroism* [Evanston, IL: Northwestern University Press, 1998], 151-53). On the other hand, Allen argues that the adherence of individual chapters to different literary genres is an aspect of the novel's "structural fragmentation," which is also manifested through its "narratorial, temporal, and spatial disjunctures," and which in turn "refracts Pechorin's elementally fragmented personality"; in other words, it's not just that the fragments prevent us from fully accessing Pechorin's self: they reveal that there *is* no unified self there for us to find (Allen, *Fallen Idol*, 143-150).

19   Emma Lieber, "The Vanishing Self in Lermontov's *Hero of Our Time*," unpublished course paper, Columbia University, 2004.

is that the traveling narrator is gradually *tightening* his control over Pechorin's story. At first, he is rather mutinously limited to relaying whatever he can get out of Maxim Maximych; then he gets to give us his own impressions; and finally he enjoys complete ownership of Pechorin's personal papers, which he edits freely, publishing only "excerpts," announcing that he has "altered all proper names," and referring tantalizingly to the "fat notebook" which he has opted *not* to publish. Under these circumstances, Pechorin can never be anything other than the character the traveling narrator wants him to be: the character whose life and thoughts he has appropriated and published under a fraudulent autobiographical pact as the story of "A Hero of Our Time." If we read the novel as the story of just one self—Pechorin's—then, as Lieber argues, the object of our quest disappears from view just when we think we are getting close to it. But if we read it as a nested set of competing self-narratives, the traveling narrator's successful assertion of himself—and subordination of Pechorin's story to his own—becomes apparent. The "disappearance" of Pechorin is the necessary condition for the ascendancy of a rival "hero," the traveling narrator—the one character whose *lack* of a self (or what Allen calls a "true and autonomous identity"[20]) is even more marked than Pechorin's own.

The Problem of the Self: Reconsidering "Time"

To turn to the second of the questions generated by considering *A Hero of Our Time* from an autobiographical perspective: if we are reading Lermontov's novel as an exercise in self-narrative, what is its project, the problem of the self that it sets out to solve? By the time we get to this text in the classroom, students have read a variety of autobiographical works in both the confessional and the testimonial modes, and they are well positioned to recognize that Lermontov's autobiographical narrators walk a fine line between the two. That is, on the one hand, these narrators use their experience in the world to explain the inner workings of their own personalities:

---

[20] Allen, *Fallen Idol*, 151.

the landscape through which they travel, the others they encounter, the events that occur, all become "all about them." On the other hand, the power of this confessional self-revelation is harnessed as a means of authenticating their account of reality—and, significantly, of each other—so that the confession actually underwrites the testimony, even as the testimony is subordinated to the confession. We may speculate, then, that one aspect of the "problem" addressed in Lermontov's complex self-narrative machine is the difficulty of reconciling one's own view of oneself with the perspectives contributed by others, which are, in their own right, valid evidence about the self; or, to put it in Bakhtinian terms, the conundrum that a person's "consciousness of himself is constantly perceived against the background of the other's consciousness of him—'I for myself' against the background of 'I for another.'"[21]

While *A Hero of Our Time* as a whole amply illustrates the complex ways in which internal and external views of a given self might collide, it is the supposed *absence* of such a split consciousness that the traveling narrator claims as the unique asset of Pechorin's journal, and cites as the justification for his decision to publish parts of it, prompted "solely [by] the desire to be useful."[22] This claim of utility—echoed by Lermontov's authorial persona in the "Author's Preface," who likens himself to a doctor administering bitter medicine for our own good—is based on Rousseau, who had called his own *Confessions* "a unique and useful work, which may serve as a first point of comparison in the study of man that is certainly yet to be begun."[23] Unlike Rousseau's *Confessions* (which "have already

---

21 Mikhail Bakhtin, *Problems of Dostoevsky's Poetics*, ed. and trans. Caryl Emerson (Minneapolis, MN: University of Minnesota Press, 1984), 207. Bakhtin is talking specifically about Dostoevsky's heroes, but his point holds true for any individual living in society; indeed, he argues here that it is precisely this aspect of Dostoevsky's works, their interest in "the orientation of one person to another person's discourse and consciousness," that makes them particularly true to life.

22 Lermontov, 64.

23 Lermontov, 2; Jean-Jacques Rousseau, *Confessions*, trans. Angela Scholar, ed. and intro. Patrick Coleman (Oxford: Oxford World's Classics, 2000), 3.

the defect of his having read them to his friends"), Pechorin's text is supposed to be written "without the ambitious desire to provoke sympathy or amazement," and the traveling narrator assures us that he is "convinced of the sincerity of this man who so mercilessly exhibited his own failings and vices."[24]

This remarkable statement, ignoring both the inherent fallibility of first-person narrative and the concrete evidence of serial duplicity presented in the stories that follow, represents either an extremely fatuous misreading of Pechorin's journal, or a brazen piece of misdirection on the part of the traveling narrator. Students at this juncture will be irresistibly reminded of the protestations of Alkinoös, the king of Phaiakia, who after hearing Odysseus's first-person account of his wanderings—including all the various trickeries to which the teller has resorted along the way— exclaims:

> "Odysseus, we as we look upon you do not imagine
> that you are a deceptive or thievish man, the sort that the black earth
> breeds in great numbers, people who wander widely, making up
> lying stories...."[25]

This is a moment where we really feel the gap between the "addressee" of the narrative and ourselves as its final "consumers": has Alkinoös, we ask ourselves incredulously, been listening to the same story we just read?[26] Similarly, while there may be many "failings and vices" on display in Pechorin's narrative, it is far from obvious to a reader of ordinary perspicacity that Pechorin "mercilessly exhibits" these; rather, to an even greater extent than Rousseau (or Odysseus), he is at pains to evade responsibility for

---

24 Lermontov, 63-64.

25 Homer, *The Odyssey*, trans. Richmond Lattimore (New York: Harper Perennial Classics, 2007), 177 (11.363-6).

26 Scholars of Homer differ on whether Alkinoös is to be taken at his word here. Some argue that his expression of trust is sincere, others that it is intended ironically, as a warning to Odysseus that Alkinoös does, indeed, have his number.

anything bad that happens in his vicinity, chalking it up to "Fate," ill-fortune, or the stupidity of others.

It seems, then, that the traveling narrator's bid to rival Rousseau's *Confessions* in both utility and "sincerity" is doomed to failure. The comparison with Rousseau, however, may prompt students to consider Lermontov's contribution to a different, though related, philosophical problem, one Rousseau inherits from an autobiographical tradition stretching all the way back to the *Confessions* of St. Augustine: the difficulty of reassembling the fragments of the self that are scattered across time and space into a single, simultaneous picture. If the first "problem of the self" tackled by Lermontov involves reconciling internal and external perspectives on the self, the second involves reconciling "former" and "current" versions of the self—some of which may be imperfectly remembered, or wholly forgotten—into a unified identity.

Augustine, in the *Confessions*, seems to feel especially keenly the distortion of the self that results from its attenuation over time— a problem of human perspective, which lacks the deity's ability to perceive all moments simultaneously. He addresses the problem by carefully gathering every moment of his own life into his book, compensating for those that predate his own earliest memories by assembling a kind of composite picture from infants he has observed as an adult.[27] Rousseau engages in a similar kind of reconstruction, beginning his narrative from before his own birth and attempting to complete "the only portrait of a man, painted exactly according to nature and in all its truth, that exists and will probably ever exist." Lermontov seems to combine the two approaches: "*A Hero of Our Time*, gentlemen, is indeed a portrait, but not of a single individual."[28]

The metaphor of the portrait becomes a model for overcoming time. "What I am engaged on here," Rousseau writes, "is ...

---

[27] Saint Augustine, *Confessions*, trans. and intro. Henry Chadwick (Oxford: Oxford University Press, 1991), 6-7. Augustine's detailed philosophical discussion of time, which appears to exist for humans but not for God, occupies Book XI of the *Confessions*.

[28] Rousseau, 3; Lermontov, 2.

a double portrait of my state of mind, at the moment when the event happened and at the moment when I described it."[29] The portrait summarizes these two "moments" (and all the moments in between) into a single simultaneous instant; it takes time to create, but—unlike a written narrative—once finished it can be "read" and appraised instantaneously, erasing the element of time and providing a perspective on human life akin to the one Augustine ascribes to God alone.[30] Lermontov enacts a similar "instantaneous" quality in his portrait of Pechorin by ending the narrative just at the moment where it is poised to begin.

Having concluded the text with a discussion between Maxim Maximych and Pechorin about the existence, or not, of predestination, Lermontov leaves these two characters—now "safely solipsized" by the traveling narrator[31]—precisely where we first found them: at the moment just before Pechorin's abduction of Bela. Of course, predestination or no predestination, we know exactly how the remainder of the narrative will unfold. Although we have seen Pechorin reveal himself over time, there is no possibility that he will ever change; he is trapped in a moment that is simultaneously the end and the beginning. It turns out, then, that both the terms in the novel's title denote absences: *A Hero of Our Time* is not only devoid of a definite "hero," it is also devoid of "time."

---

[29] Rousseau, 648.

[30] See note 27 above and Augustine, *Confessions*, Book XI.

[31] The expression "safely solipsized" is borrowed from another complexly-framed first-person narrator, Nabokov's Humbert Humbert. Vladimir Nabokov, *Lolita* (New York: Vintage, 1997), 60.

18

TEXT AND GENRE

Unsettling Students: Road Rage and the Quest for Fixity in *Dead Souls*

Marcia A. Morris

One of the most challenging reads for undergraduate students is Gogol's *Dead Souls*. While undergrads characteristically respond to the novel with great enthusiasm, they nevertheless find it difficult to move beyond interpretations of it as social parody. This essay will argue that genre-inflected considerations can go a long way toward enhancing their reading of *Dead Souls*.

The use of genre as an interpretive tool seems somewhat old-fashioned today; it was also viewed with scant sympathy by any number of nineteenth-century Russian writers. Leo Tolstoy, for example, famously described *War and Peace* as "not a novel, much less ... a poem, and even less a historical chronicle. *War and Peace* is what the author wanted to and was able to express in the form in which it is expressed,"[1] a formulation that, on the one hand, discouraged his audience from reading his masterpiece through the lens of genre and, on the other, offered no explicit suggestions for doing otherwise. Significantly, Tolstoy voiced this disapprobation of genre so negatively and yet so prominently ("not," "much less," "even less") that he ended up, in effect, privileging it. It is difficult to escape the conclusion, then, that Tolstoy was actually quite interested in problems of categorization, even if in apophatic fashion.

Undergraduate students are generally quite relieved to learn of Tolstoy's quirky pronouncement, since it reassures them that

---

[1]   Initially published in *Russkii arkhiv*, in 1868. Quoted here from L. N. Tolstoi, *Polnoe sobranie sochinenii v devianosta tt.* (Moscow, 1955), 16:7.

the novel's taxonomical challenges are a function of the author's conscious design at least as much as they are a result of their own potentially imperfect interpretive skills. Gogol, by contrast, offers his readers considerably less explicit interpretive comfort. However, by subtitling *Dead Souls* a *poema*, he does serve notice of a subversive intention vis-à-vis generic boundaries. And it is not merely his subtitle that causes generic confusion; the entire ensuing text baffles its readers by looking sometimes like one kind of work, and sometimes like quite another.

On the principle that the things Russian authors most vigorously and explicitly abjure sometimes turn out to be precisely the things that are most important to them, this essay will consider a strategy for teaching *Dead Souls* that takes genre into consideration, not as a prescriptive category but rather as an interpretive lens, the application of which sometimes focuses and sometimes distorts our reading. I will suggest ways in which we can situate the novel not *in* a given genre but, rather, *vis-à-vis* a number of its most proximate generic intertexts. I will, in other words, hew to a middle line somewhere between the Tolstoyan approach and the neo-classical.

The incautious application of specific genre categories to texts is, as we all know, fraught with peril. In Tzvetan Todorov's words: "The major work creates, in a sense, a new genre and at the same time transgresses the previously valid rules of the genre."[2] Accordingly, while the formulaic work incarnates genre, the major work transcends it. Nevertheless, genre, when understood less as a rigid array of rules and more as an "invitation to form,"[3] offers us a fruitful way to discuss literature with undergraduate students. Our initial task, then, must be to shift our students' understanding

---

[2]   Tzvetan Todorov, *The Poetics of Prose*, trans. Richard Howard (Ithaca, NY: Cornell University Press, 1977), 43.

[3]   Claudio Guillén, "On the Uses of Literary Genre," in *Literature as System: Essays toward the Theory of Literary History* (Princeton, NJ: Princeton University Press, 1971), 109. This is very much the approach taken by Ronald D. LeBlanc in *The Russianization of Gil Blas: A Study in Literary Appropriation* (Columbus, OH: Slavica, 1986).

of genre away from prescriptive norms and toward the "horizon of expectations" that underpins the sophisticated reader's experience of the text.[4]

What, then, is the horizon of expectations that we bring to a reading of *Dead Souls*? Like all great originals, *Dead Souls* represents something new under the sun. Even so, however, Gogol's great novel *does* occur within a literary context. For the purposes of this essay, I will focus on five intertexts that help us to frame that context: Homer's *Odyssey*, Dante's *Inferno*, and the anonymous *Life of Lazarillo de Tormes* from the western European tradition; and F. V. Bulgarin's *Ivan Vyzhigin* and the seventeenth-century anonymous *Tale of Ruff, Son of Ruff* from the Russian. I do not mean to suggest that these texts constitute a uniquely authoritative set of intertexts, much less to imply that they exhaust the potential universe of Gogol's sources. Rather, my five texts comprise one among many coherent backgrounds against which to read *Dead Souls*. If we hope to teach the novel effectively at an undergraduate level, we must posit boundaries to the universe of our student-readers' expectations.

Of the five texts I have just identified, only two, *Lazarillo* and *Ivan Vyzhigin*, could be said to represent examples of the same genre category (the picaresque), and even these two diverge in significant ways.[5] Accordingly, genre as traditionally formulated is not a sufficient common denominator. Rather, what binds these works to each

---

4   "The new text evokes for the reader (listener) the horizon of expectations and 'rules of the game' familiar to him from earlier texts, which as such can then be varied, extended, corrected but also transformed, crossed out, or simply reproduced." Hans Robert Jauss, *Toward an Aesthetic of Reception*, trans. Timothy Bahti (Minneapolis, MN: University of Minnesota Press, 1982), 88.

5   Indeed, Ronald D. LeBlanc considers *Ivan Vyzhigin* to be a prime example of the moral-satirical novel rather than the picaresque (*Russianization of Gil Blas*, 213). V. T. Narezhny's *A Russian Gil Blas or the Adventures of Prince Gavrila Simonovich Chistiakov* might seem, for a variety of reasons, to be an even closer intertext for *Dead Souls*. Unfortunately, Narezhny's initial chapters were seized almost immediately after they were published, and the remaining chapters appeared in print only in the Soviet period. Thus, Narezhny's novel was largely unknown in the nineteenth century.

other as well as to *Dead Souls* is the chronotope of the road. But the road is an ancient and frequently encountered structuring device,[6] and while it constitutes a necessary shared feature for the texts under discussion, it, like genre, is an insufficient one.

Among *Dead Souls* and its intertexts, however, there are additional commonalities that argue for the existence of a loosely conceived travel genre whose distinctive features range across a spectrum of possible realizations. In all six works, the road itself becomes a formal manifestation of two opposing, mirror-imaged functions: on the one hand, it both constitutes a trial of the protagonists and provides a locus for that trial; on the other, it offers multiple occasions for the protagonists to spy on the lives of the strangers they encounter. As a result, our protagonists-on-the-road exist on the margins of normal societal structures, be it by virtue of their urge to observe others from the outside (the spying function), or by virtue of being judged themselves by the inside (the trial function).[7] The road's spying and judging opportunities doubly estrange our protagonists from their community, making them at one and the same time alienated, observing subjects and marginalized, observed objects. Moreover, with the exception of Dante, these estranged protagonists are, to a greater or lesser extent, rogues who are thwarted in their search for the consolations of the private life. For the majority of their fictive existences they fail to achieve or re-achieve integration into their communities.[8]

---

[6]   On this question, see M. M. Bakhtin, "Forms of Time and of the Chronotope in the Novel," in *The Dialogic Imagination: Four Essays*, trans. Caryl Emerson and Michael Holquist (Austin, TX: University of Texas Press, 1981), 98.

[7]   Bakhtin suggests that the co-occurrence of the devices of the road, the trial, and spying on others define the chronotope of the picaresque novel ("Forms of Time," 125). Although we might consider the *Odyssey* a distant ancestor of the picaresque, the *Divine Comedy* is a greater stretch, and I do not propose to ally it with the genre.

[8]   Of the rogue protagonist, Bakhtin writes: "This is the philosophy of a person who knows only private life and craves it alone, but who does not participate in it, who has no place in it—and therefore sees it in sharp focus, as a whole, in all its nakedness, playing out all its roles but not fusing his identity with any one of them" (ibid., 126).

Why do these protagonists embark on the road to begin with? Odysseus and Dante freely choose the road as a necessary means to a desirable end. Lazarillo de Tormes and Ivan Vyzhigin, by contrast, have no choice; they are forced to take to the road. Odysseus, of course, returns to his beloved Ithaca to set his affairs in order, while Dante ascends to more spiritual heights. Somewhat unexpectedly, the reluctant travelers, Lazarillo and Vyzhigin, also prosper. Lazarillo obtains a modest position, marries, and settles down; Ivan Vyzhigin ultimately comes into the inheritance that has been perfidiously withheld from him.

A rather different view of the road obtains in the seventeenth-century Russian *Tale of Ruff, Son of Ruff* (Повесть о Ерше Ершовиче). We first meet Ruff, a fish, in a Lake Rostov courtroom. The wily protagonist's days on the road are now past, and he is being tried for his alleged attempts to appropriate someone else's prosperity. We learn through testimony at the trial that at an earlier point Ruff set off from the Volga with his wife and children, hoping to discover richer feeding grounds. Recently he has fed in Lake Rostov and, according to the other fish, bamboozled them out of their patrimony. Additionally, he has affected a much more illustrious pedigree than he is actually entitled to. Ruff counterclaims that Lake Rostov really *is* his patrimony, that the other fish are by rights his serfs, and that he is a high-born, respectable fish whose kin are known and savored in fish soup by wealthy Moscow boyars.

This tale, for all its artlessness, offers us more of a puzzle than the better-articulated works we have just examined. Who among all its characters, for example, should we believe: Ruff or his many accusers? Why does Ruff set out on the road to begin with—to recapture what is rightfully his, or to swindle others out of what is properly theirs? What do his wife and children, who are often invoked but never seen, have to do with his plans/machinations?

The question of motivation, thus, is both over-sufficiently and insufficiently answered. If we believe Ruff, then he, like Odysseus, has taken to the road in order to return to the place where he belongs. If we believe some of Ruff's accusers, then he, like Lazarillo, has set out with the explicit intention of stealing from others. If we believe yet others, then Ruff, like Vyzhigin, has come down in life and has embarked on his journey with the understandable—if maddening—intention of improving his and his family's fortunes. *Ruff, Son of Ruff* takes the form of a battle of words, and no authoritative answer emerges as to who Ruff truly is or what he is seeking.

Like the motivations for taking to the road, the nature of the life experienced on it varies from one text to another. It is incumbent on Odysseus, for example, to prove his own worth; unless he survives his many ordeals, he will never see home. Thus, the trial outweighs the spying function in the *Odyssey*. In the *Inferno*, by contrast, Dante repeatedly judges and encounters men and women like himself, while his own occasional trepidations, which constitute the moments when he himself is judged, are short-lived and easily overlooked. In the *Inferno*, then, the spying function takes the upper hand.

In our two examples from the picaresque tradition, we encounter a less polarized allocation of the trial and spying functions. In *The Life of Lazarillo de Tormes*, the notion of reciprocal judgment is established explicitly and early. Lazarillo's first master, the blind man, tries the boy's gullibility by inviting him to listen to a putative noise inside the statue of a bull and then slamming his head into it. When, some time later, Lazarillo decides to leave the blind man, he pays him back in kind, proving that he has spied on him long enough to understand how he will react in any given situation.

> I lined him up so that he was facing the pillar. Then I gave a jump and got in back of the column, like somebody waiting for a bull to charge, and I said to him:
> "Come on! Jump with all your might and you'll land clear of the water."
> I'd hardly finished saying it when the poor blind man hurled himself forward, charging like a billy-goat. He had even taken a step back so as to get a running start and jump better, and he flung himself into the air with all his strength and hit the pillar head-first.[9]

---

[9] *The Life and Adventures of Lazarillo de Tormes: His Fortunes and Adversities,*

Although *Ivan Vyzhigin* lacks a similar, neatly mirrored example of tit-for-tat, the macro-effect of the novel as a whole is the same. We repeatedly watch the protagonist commit follies and be judged for them, but we also watch others persecute him, for which he, in turn, judges them. In both picaresques the trial and spying functions are distributed roughly equally, on the principle of both/and.

The Tale of Ruff, Son of Ruff might seem to offer us a situation like the one we find in the *Odyssey*. After all, the narrative frame of the tale takes the form of a trial—in this case, literal—of the peripatetic protagonist. Once again, however, *Ruff* sets us a puzzle, for we must ask ourselves whether the role of defendant in the trial more properly pertains to its chief protagonist or to his accusers. In point of fact, the fish who come forward to testify against Ruff also end up unwittingly testifying to their own naïveté. Sturgeon, for example, explains how he listened to Ruff's sad tale of woe and then foolishly sanctioned Ruff's invasion of his feeding grounds. In like fashion and each in his turn, the other victimized fish indict themselves on charges of extraordinary credulity, leaving us to wonder whether the court should be trying Ruff for his depredations or the other fish for their stupidity. Accordingly, *Ruff, Son of Ruff*'s judgment function occurs in an either/or universe in which the predominating function is either the fishes' trial of Ruff or Ruff's trial of them. Our heuristic difficulty as readers lies in deciding which choice is "correct"—or, perhaps, even in determining whether in *Ruff, Son of Ruff* any choice can be correct.

This brief review of the distribution of trial and spying functions across the five works we have been examining offers students an insight into plotting strategies in fictions of the road. Specifically, they can now see how repeated iterations of these two basic functions constitute much of the works' plots. Ultimately, however, textual endings, not middles, offer readers the richest food for intertextual thought. In Yury Lotman's words, the opening episodes of a text make it a specific narration about a specific subject. Closing episodes, by contrast, function on the mythologizing level

---

trans. W. S. Merwin (Garden City, NY: Doubleday, 1962), 65.

and generalize the text's meaning.[10] Thus, if we are looking for where *Dead Souls* has engaged most fruitfully in dialogue with other texts, its concluding chapters should prove particularly useful.

The conclusions of the journeys featured in our five chosen texts vary among themselves at the level of detail, but the protagonists, at least in four instances, attain what they originally sought. Unsurprisingly, however, *Ruff, Son of Ruff* offers a somewhat more ambiguous outcome. Since the preponderance of the evidence tells against Ruff and since he has made no particular effort to dispose the court in his favor, he is found guilty of invading Lake Rostov and is handed over for punishment to the chief complainant, Bream. Bream intends to make a dramatic end to Ruff's criminal antics by eating him, but Ruff refuses to turn his head toward his executioner, leaving Bream to devour him from behind, tail-to-head. Ruff is covered with prickly spikes, and Bream quickly realizes that swallowing from the wrong direction will be very painful. Accordingly, he leaves Ruff at large and unrepentant, ready to continue his much-resented feeding in Lake Rostov. This, of course, constitutes a victory from Ruff's perspective, but it leaves the *Tale's* readers disquieted, wondering whether improvement, be it moral or material, is possible. It offers a grim concluding myth, one that features neither heroic return nor progress.

And what of *Dead Souls*? How do the texts we have been discussing help our students situate themselves vis-à-vis Gogol's novel? How do earlier protagonists' realizations of travel on the road create a horizon of expectations against which they can measure their understanding of Chichikov's adventures? Answering these questions is not easy. To quote Robert A. Maguire: "[T]here is a plethora of 'ideas' in any work by Gogol, together with a polyvalence of detail, which make for an always rich, sometimes baffling complexity."[11] Gavriel Shapiro offers a similar view,

---

[10] Iurii Lotman, *Struktura khudozestvennogo teksta* (Providence, RI: Brown University Press, 1971), 265.

[11] Robert A. Maguire, *Exploring Gogol* (Stanford, CA: Stanford University Press, 1994), 351.

likening Gogol's syncretic achievement in *Dead Souls* to that of his landowner Kostanzhoglo, whose profit comes from refashioning and repurposing "all sorts of rubbish."[12]

I have identified several different road-related threads in this essay. When woven together, these threads create a motley tapestry of life-as-journey. Gogol picks this tapestry apart, rearranges the threads, and then re-weaves them into *Dead Souls*. If we encourage our students to read part 1 of *Dead Souls* in terms of our hypothetical tapestry—and, again, I readily admit that this is only one of the many possible horizons of expectation that we might choose—then the warp of Gogol's creation, the largely invisible thread that forms a structure across which to weave the fabric, owes much to *Ivan Vyzhigin* and *Ruff, Son of Ruff*. The weft, or crosswise thread, derives from our other works. If, however, we take into consideration evidence from the surviving chapters of part 2, then we come to a somewhat different conclusion. If we attempt to reconstruct the second part from the fragments that remain—if, in other words, we do that unfashionable thing and try to reconstruct Gogol's authorial intentions for the novel—then another pattern emerges. The *Odyssey*, *Inferno*, and *Lazarillo* become more prominent, taking up the structure-giving function of the novel's warp, while *Ivan Vyzhigin* and *Ruff* recede into a more decorative place in the weft.

Part 1 of *Dead Souls* introduces us to Chichikov in the rank and quality of traveler. He literally rolls into the novel in a carriage; he takes a room in a hotel, thereby intimating that his visit will be brief and that he will eventually move on; and he reifies these intimations by very quickly embarking on a series of short trips to local landowners' estates. The problem is, however, that small, seemingly trivial details insistently point in another direction. Even before Chichikov's carriage has managed to pull up to the hotel, two peasants speculate on its roadworthiness:

> "Hey," said one to the other, "look at that there wheel! You think that wheel could make it as far as Moscow if it had to,

---

[12] Gavriel Shapiro, *Nikolai Gogol and the Baroque Cultural Heritage* (University Park, PA: Pennsylvania State University Press, 1993), 235.

or couldn't it?" "It could," replied the other. "But not as far as Kazan, I bet?" "Not as far as Kazan it couldn't," replied the other.[13]

Chichikov himself adds to the doubt that the peasants have subtly sown. His first foray onto the streets yields a playbill, torn from a wall and bearing witness to the settled life of a town; it anchors him imperceptibly to a particular place. He also takes a calculating look at a young lady in the street and offers us a morsel of evidence concerning his ultimate goal—matrimony and the sedentary life.

Evidence of stasis continues to accrue: Chichikov's carriage runs off the road; it is stuck in the mud; his horses can go nowhere until they have been re-shod. The landowners Chichikov visits offer him a vision of what domesticity might mean; by providing him with the opportunity to focus his attention both on the defects of their estate management and on the ways in which those defects might be remedied, they implicate him in the fixed, rooted life of the countryside.

The town, too, attempts to fix Chichikov in place through its "Tale of Captain Kopeikin." For one brief moment, everyone becomes convinced that Chichikov is an ill-used, one-armed, one-legged veteran of the campaign of 1812. It is only when they focus explicitly on Kopeikin's lack of limbs, the characteristic that binds him to one, narrowly-delimited space, that they realize that he cannot be Chichikov. Nothing daunted, however, they shift gears and immediately move on to consider whether Chichikov might not, in point of fact, be Napoleon-in-disguise. The small fact of Napoleon's immobilization on a distant, isolated island does not deter them.

Of course, Chichikov rides about the province, giving the lie to any notion of immobility. Or does he? After visiting landowners, Chichikov always returns to the town, his point of departure. He cultivates acquaintances; he attends the Governor's ball; he flirts

---

[13] N. V. Gogol, *Dead Souls*, trans. Robert A. Maguire (London: Penguin, 2004), 5. All subsequent page references are listed in the text.

with the ladies. He develops an abscessed tooth and determines "that it was better to keep to his room for three days or so" (239). The town begins to look like a fixed abode, *from* which short visits might be mounted but *in* which a comfortable life is lived.

All of this argues for a certain resistance to the novel's chronotope: both landowners and townsfolk want to bind Chichikov to a particular place, and he himself seems perfectly happy to be bound. This notion of false fixity, achieved in middle age after a lifetime of vicissitudes, reminds us of *Ruff, Son of Ruff*, whose protagonist may be unregenerate but is nevertheless settled in a particular place at the time that the tale begins. In both *Dead Souls* and *Ruff*, the motivation for the protagonist's earlier travels was the search for a home, for a place in which to settle with his family. Once he finds a potential home, however, he is subjected to the scrutiny and condemnation of its original denizens.

Dead Souls additionally reflects certain structural patterns activated in *Ivan Vyzhigin*. In each novel, bouts of misfortune occur somewhere in the provinces, while amelioration occurs in town. Movement initially ebbs outward from a fixed point and then flows back toward it again; misadventures occur on the road while reconciliation takes place in town.

In *Ivan Vyzhigin* as well as *Ruff, Son of Ruff*, we sense the protagonist's need for a place of quiet and safety. In Edward Wasiolek's words, "The Russian vision, as it is embodied in the novel, oscillates between the conviction that reality is design-haunted and the fear that there is no design, the belief that the world is continuity and the fear that it is rupture, the conviction that there is a place for everything and everyone and a place for nothing and no one."[14] Maguire, looking more particularly at the implications of place for Gogol, suggests that, "For Russians, one of the most powerful and enduring imperatives has been a fear of disorder or placelessness, and a corresponding need for structure

---

[14] Edward Wasiolek, "Design in the Russian Novel," in *The Russian Novel from Pushkin to Pasternak*, ed. John Garrard (New Haven, CT: Yale University Press, 1983), 54.

and discipline."[15] He views Chichikov's arrival in the provincial town as an intrusion "into a tightly bounded space, and therefore ... a threat."[16] Chichikov, in effect, represents the forces of disorder and placelessness, and he must, therefore, be tried. In my reading, however, Chichikov himself feels the need for a tightly bounded space and thus ineluctably inserts himself into the town.

The end of part 1 of *Dead Souls* takes us back again to *Ruff*. The protagonist's machinations have been uncovered, and he has been excoriated by the townsfolk. But although he has been convicted of unseemly behavior, Gogol has set him loose. He cannot be swallowed; he must not be assimilated; he will not mend his ways. What can be done with him?

Part 2 of the novel—the more puzzling part for students— attempts to answer that question. The extant chapters suggest that Gogol may have partially adapted a plotting model similar to that of *Lazarillo de Tormes*. Chichikov travels from one estate to the next, mindful of his need to learn how to survive in the world. In a sense, the landowners he meets become his masters; they show him, whether by good example or bad, how life should be lived. Lazarillo's ultimate fate is far too modest for Chichikov, though, so *Lazarillo de Tormes*'s applicability is limited.

This pattern derives, in part, from the *Odyssey*. Odysseus's encounters with grotesque beings are demythologized and humanized in *Lazarillo*, but they remain at heart grotesque. Chichikov's acquaintances in part 2 become ever more grotesque as well. Again, however, the analogy between works ultimately fails to hold. Odysseus's present encounters with grotesque beings steadies him for future encounters with humans like himself; they prepare him for his return home. Gogol has given us to believe that Chichikov, by contrast, was well advised to abandon his home, and that return to it would constitute defeat. Chichikov can hardly "return" to the ways of righteousness when he never experienced them to begin with.

---

[15]   Maguire, *Exploring Gogol*, 3.

[16]   Ibid., 234.

A final possibility—that Gogol hoped to guide his hero upward on Dante's path to moral improvement—proves to be equally problematic. In the surviving episodes of part 2, Chichikov takes one step forward only to follow it up with one step back. Some new scheme, some ephemeral, indefensible plan, always drags him back into his quest for unearned material gain. Thus, Dante's self-embraced moral education cannot be expected to help the worldly, acquisitive Chichikov.

I would suggest that in the texts we have examined there are subtle differences between Russian and Western treatments of the road. In the Russian tradition pre-dating Gogol, the adventures encountered on the road are the stuff of superficial plot; they are generally comical and are originally intended to amuse readers. Yes, the protagonist is tried by his adventures, but even so he ultimately contrives to wiggle out of his culpability. In our Western examples, particularly in the *Odyssey* and the *Inferno*, the road teaches a critical lesson. If the protagonist ends up where he hoped to be, it is because he has learned from his experience. In *Dead Souls*, Gogol confronted and attempted to negotiate these bivalent traditions of the road. Much of the novel's ambiguity can be traced to the difficulties inherent in the task. Our students need to discover that the different traditions Gogol relied upon shared significant generic features but that, even so, they were only partly compatible among themselves.

19

TEXT, GENRE, AND MORALITY I

Searching for Freedom in *Eugene Onegin**

Svetlana Grenier

One of the important things students can "get" out of reading nineteenth-century novels is moral education.[1] When I teach my Russian Novel of Adultery course as part of Georgetown's Humanities and Writing program, one of my goals is to guide my students into confronting and questioning their own assumptions about romantic love. Early in the semester I present Denis de Rougemont's understanding of romantic passion as illustrated in the story of Tristan and Iseult. I encourage my students to read excerpts from de Rougemont's *Love in the Western World*, which I put on library reserve. In reading the three novels that constitute the core of my course, Pushkin's *Eugene Onegin*, Herzen's *Who Is to Blame?*, and Tolstoy's *Anna Karenina*, students encounter both romantic and anti-romantic points of view. They soon discover that the stories told in these novels are relevant to their own lives and endlessly thought-provoking. Some students eventually conclude

---

*   I teach *Eugene Onegin* in translation in my Humanities and Writing course (primarily for first-year students), and in Russian in an upper-level course dedicated to this single text. I use the strategies described in this essay in both courses. When teaching the novel in English, I have students read a rhymed translation by Walter Arndt and Nabokov's unrhymed version. I refer to both translations in class, sometimes providing my own translation and the necessary information on particularly significant rhymes.

[1]   For someone who spent her formative years in the Soviet Union of the 1960s-1970s, when "communist morality" inspired little respect, and no other morality or philosophy was easily accessible, Tolstoy's and Dostoevsky's novels functioned indeed as "textbooks of life" (in the words of a popular Soviet slogan).

that these books in fact pose questions about the meaning of life, which has been my intention all along.

When a fictional family is destroyed, readers are bound to ask, with Herzen, "Who is to blame?" In order to be able to hold someone responsible for some wrongdoing, the "judge" (in this case, the reader) must consider that particular "someone" to be a free agent, to a greater or lesser extent. An individual cannot be held responsible if she has no choice. My students and I thus examine issues of personal freedom and free will throughout the semester. I challenge my students to investigate Pushkin's, Herzen's, and Tolstoy's concepts of freedom and free will and to question their own concept(s), both in dialogue with the authors and with one another. As is typical in Russian, when I say "freedom" (свобода), I mean both external freedom, i.e., the ability to carry out one's decisions and wishes unencumbered by external obstacles, and internal freedom, i.e., the ability to make choices and to acknowledge one's responsibility for making them, which is closer to "free will."[2] The theme of freedom unites the three novels. Some characters actively seek freedom and make it their highest priority. For most of *Eugene Onegin*, for example, Pushkin's Eugene values his external freedom above everything else. Herzen's Lyubonka seeks to be freed from "childhood/childish beliefs" and from society's interference in her private life. Tolstoy's Anna wants "freedom to love." Other characters, such as Pushkin's Tatyana and Tolstoy's Levin, Kitty, and Dolly, have different priorities and are less concerned with freedom.

---

[2]   Critic Apollon Grigoriev used this second Russian meaning when he wrote about Herzen's novel in a letter to Gogol on November 29 (17), 1848: "How much intellect expended in order to deny the **highest mover of human activity, i.e., freedom—and the responsibility linked with it** ... [and to] demonstrate [t]hat no one is to blame for anything, that everything is conditioned by preexisting facts and that those facts entangle [опутывать] a man in such a way that he has no release [выход] from them." *Apollon Apollonovich Grigor'ev: Materialy dlia biografii*, ed. Vladimir Kniazhnin (Petrograd, [Tipografiia Ministerstva Zemledeliia], 1917), 113; quoted in G. G. Elizavetina, "'Kto vinovat?' Gertsena v vospriiatii russkikh chitatelei i kritiki XIX veka," in *Literaturnye proizvedeniia v dvizhenii epokh* (Moscow: Nauka, 1979), 8.

I teach these novels by focusing on how various characters and authors define freedom and how authors portray their protagonists: as free agents—in other words, responsible *subjects*—or as helpless victims—*objects* of their circumstances and passions. By using the terms "subject" and "subjecthood" to indicate agency, I enlist grammar as a pedagogical tool.

By the end of the course, the following pattern emerges: characters who pursue external freedom, i.e., those who prioritize not being "bound" (связан) and being able to do what they want, end up as unhappy "slaves," as objects of their own passions, living in a severely circumscribed world with few meaningful choices (Onegin, Anna).[3] Characters who value and seek meaning (смысл) derived from connections or ties (связь), end up as free subjects (Tatyana, Levin).[4]

The three novels can be read as variations of a single plot. In all three, a married heroine faces the temptation of an illicit affair with the unmarried man pursuing her; she falls in love with him; and "illicit" conversations, in which the man confesses his love, take

---

[3]   Tatyana calls Onegin "a slave to a petty feeling" ("чувства мелкого раб"). A. S. Pushkin, *Evgenii Onegin*, chap. 8, stanza XLV, line 14 (my translation), in *Polnoe sobranie sochinenii*, 10 vols., 2nd ed. (Moscow: Izd. AN SSSR, 1957), 5:188. When quoting from *Eugene Onegin*, I will hereafter give reference, in parentheses in the text, to the chapter, stanza, and line number followed by the page number from Alexander Pushkin, *Eugene Onegin*, trans. Walter Arndt, 2nd rev. ed. (New York: E. P. Dutton, 1981), e.g., 8:XLV:14; Arndt 219. Anna speaks of herself as a "slave" in part 6, chapter 23. See L. N. Tolstoi, *Sobranie sochinenii*, 20 vols. (Moscow: GIKhL, 1960-65), 9:239.

[4]   One would naturally ask, "What about Anna, who apparently also seeks meaning based on a connection—liaison (связь)—with Vronsky?" Tolstoy, it seems, considers an adulterous liaison a simulacrum rather than a true, or meaning-producing, connection. The affair starts with cutting the external and internal ties that bind Anna's various impulses and feelings together into a single personality (see Richard Gustafson's interpretation of the paper knife on her ride to St. Petersburg, in his *Leo Tolstoy: Resident and Stranger* [Princeton, NJ: Princeton University Press, 1986], 303-9). The affair then leads to the complete estrangement of the two lovers, and eventually, for both Anna and Vronsky, to the loss of all meaning and to cutting all connections with life—in an echo of the first two train scenes, by means of trains.

place. The plots diverge in what happens after the crucial confession, as Herzen and Tolstoy both experiment with Pushkin's ending. Both seem to ask, "What would have happened had Tatyana not left the room after her speech to Onegin in chapter 8?" Tolstoy, writing after Herzen, adds, "What would have happened had Beltov continued to pursue Lyubonka instead of leaving the town of N. at the end of *Who Is to Blame?*" Each consecutive novel thus represents an affair that goes one step further than the previous one.

My students and I focus on the moral questions that arise for the characters (and consequently, for the reader) in situations of potential or actual adultery. The three female protagonists face the same dilemma: how to deal with their feelings for men other than their husbands. They make different decisions in the end, but they all have to consider the same factors: their own feelings; their husbands; their children, in the case of Anna and Lyubonka; their pursuers; other people in their "inner circles," such as their close friends and extended families; and the broader societies in which they live (small-town society, in the case of Lyubonka, and Petersburg high society, in the case of Anna and Tatyana). Last but not least, each must deal with her conscience before and after making her decisions.

In writing *Eugene Onegin*, Pushkin lays the foundation not only for the Russian novel as a whole but also specifically for the novel of adultery. I thus ask my students to explore the "terms" in which Pushkin first poses this moral dilemma, i.e., what concepts and values he brings to bear on it, such as love, passion, freedom, happiness, fulfillment, honor, career, and poetry. I invite them to define each concept's meaning in the text by using the structural approach, that is, through binary oppositions. How do these various terms interact: are they synonymous or antonymous to one another? For example, together we look for the opposites of freedom that appear in a given text. What entities encroach on each character's freedom and limit it? These questions teach my students to focus on how an individual author's language encodes his or her worldview and system of values. In the process, they learn an important lesson: words do not always mean the same thing, and readers must be careful not to impose their own understanding of a particular word on the text at hand. (Students can then use this approach to analyze any text, including contemporary economic and political discourse, and discover its rhetorical, and often enough propagandistic, purposes.)

I show students how to find various definitions of freedom in *Eugene Onegin* by examining Pushkin's images of freedom and un-freedom. We attempt to define freedom based on its opposites in several passages of chapter 1, which abounds with references to freedom, on the one hand, and to literal and metaphorical captivity and oppression, on the other (e.g., 1:XXXI:12; XV:13; XXV:4; XXXVIII:5; XLV:1; L:1-7; LIV:12-14). First we examine how Pushkin's narrator compares himself and Onegin to prisoners (колодник[и]): "Aware again in recollection/Of love gone by, romance of yore;/.../ As some fair dream from **prison** night/The sleeping **convict** may deliver/To verdant forests—fancy-lorn/We reveled there at life's young morn" (1:XLVII:6-7, 11-14; Arndt 25).[5] What are they prisoners of? Next we examine how the narrator becomes "free": "The Muse appeared, past Love's intrusion,/It cleared the mind in darkness **bound**,/And **free** once more, I seek the fusion/Of feeling, dream, and magic sound./I write…." (1:LIX:1-4; Arndt 31).[6] What is freedom associated with? How is lack of freedom represented? The narrator becomes "dumb and mute" (глуп и нем; 1:LVIII:14) when he is in love, and he sees the passing of love as liberation. (The opposition between freedom and love comes as a big shock to many students!) Exploring this passage, we discover how for Pushkin freedom is inextricably connected with creating poetry and with the mastery of one's faculties that is necessary for writing.

Just as poetry itself is not a formless "free for all" but an intricate formal structure, so Pushkin's "poetic" freedom requires discipline and commitment, two things that Onegin cannot abide

---

5   "Воспомня прежних лет романы,/Воспомня прежнюю любовь,/ Чувствительны, беспечны вновь,/.../Как в лес зеленый из тюрьмы/ Перенесен колодник сонный,/Так уносились мы мечтой/К началу жизни молодой".

6   "Прошла любовь, явилась Муза,/И прояснился темный ум./Свободен, вновь ищу союза/Волшебных звуков, чувств и дум;/Пишу…"

but that the narrator loves, as he discloses in the novel's penultimate stanza: "Farewell…, my true ideal,/And you, my unremitting, heady,/Though modest toil. You let me feel/All bliss that ever poets covet:/Life in world's storm, yet heedless of it,/And friends' sweet converse by my side" (8:L:1-7; Arndt 221).[7] The parallelism of these two farewells in consecutive lines creates a connection between the author's "true [верный] ideal," i.e., Tatyana, and his "unremitting [постоянный] toil." By pairing in this parallel the words "верный," which also means "faithful, unfailing, reliable," and "постоянный," which means "constant," Pushkin relates faithfulness and constancy to one another and to his ideal. This connection in turn draws a parallel between Tatyana's faithfulness (both to her youthful love and to her marital vows), and the narrator's faithfulness (to his Muse and his work).[8] The result of the author-narrator's constancy and faithfulness is a "free novel" (свободный роман) (8:L:12), a gift that has made the author, and he hopes, the reader, both happy and, in some sense, free.

This is all well and good, many students object, but what about people who are not poets? Can they, according to Pushkin, achieve freedom or happiness? And which should they strive for? Pushkin's protagonists apparently achieve neither. A captive of her loveless marriage and of Petersburg high society, Tatyana seems neither happy nor free. Onegin may be as "free" as he ever was,

---

[7] "Прости ж …/И ты, мой верный Идеал,/И ты, живой и постоянный,/ Хоть малый труд. Я с вами знал/Всё, что завидно для поэта:/Забвенье жизни в бурях света,/Беседу сладкую друзей". Cf. Onegin: "He tried to write—from such tenacious/Endeavor, though, his mind recoiled;/And so the paper stayed unsoiled" ("Хотел писать—но труд упорный/Ему был тошен; ничего/Не вышло из пера его" (1:XLIII:9-11; Arndt 23); "[Afraid of love lest it] betray me/Of that chilled freedom that was mine./…/All ties cast off,…/I thought detachment, calm, would pass/In place of happiness" ("Свою постылую свободу/Я потерять не захотел. …/Чужой для всех, ничем не связан,/Я думал: вольность и покой/Замена счастью"; 8, Onegin's Letter to Tatyana; Arndt 211).

[8] I usually also point out the idea of Onegin as Tatyana's Muse, discussed by Olga Peters Hasty in *Pushkin's Tatiana* (Madison, WI: University of Wisconsin Press, 1999), 96 and passim, which reinforces the final pairing of the two fidelities.

but he has now changed his mind and would, he claims, gladly exchange his now "stale" (постылая) freedom for "happiness" and the "bliss" (блаженство) of Tatyana's love. What is it that Pushkin is telling us about freedom and happiness through these characters? To answer that, we trace the two protagonists' stories and each one's relationship with freedom.

Onegin pursues freedom throughout his life, eschewing all commitments, which he sees as limitations on his freedom. He never attempts civil or military service; he is "sickened" by the "persistent work" required of writers; he especially avoids marriage: he tells Tatyana that he is not "captivated" (пленился) by the idea of "limiting" (ограничить) his life by "the family circle" (4:XIII:1-2, 6). By the novel's end, however, he disowns his pursuit of "freedom and peace" (вольность и покой) (8, Onegin's Letter to Tatyana) as erroneous and gives up his will and self-control, becoming what Tatyana calls a "slave" to his emotions.

In discussing Onegin I draw my students' attention to how Pushkin, through the use of grammar and rhyme, regularly portrays his protagonist as an object of outside circumstances or internal states. Onegin is frequently either the grammatical object (direct or indirect) of various verbs or the subject of passive constructions. I try to make students realize that Pushkin uses grammar in such a way as to define freedom as "subjecthood": he juxtaposes active and passive language structures, thereby dramatizing various characters' positions as subjects of their own actions, decisions, and choices or as objects and "victims" of their emotional states and external influences. At the same time, Pushkin describes the subjects as "free" and the objects, as un-free (slaves or captives).

The first time one of the Russian words for "freedom" (свобода) occurs in the novel, it immediately introduces the ironic paradoxes of the notion of freedom in Onegin's life.[9] First of all,

---

[9] When I teach the monograph course on *Eugene Onegin* in Russian, I usually assign an excerpt on freedom from Anna Wierzbicka's book *Understanding Cultures through Their Key Words: English, Russian, Polish, German, Japanese* (New York: Oxford University Press, 1997), 125-55. In that course we spend some time discussing the differences between the three Russian words

Pushkin rhymes "freedom" (*svoboda*) with "fashion" (*moda*). This rhyme suggests that Onegin's freedom translates into becoming a slave to fashion and societal conventions. Pushkin also employs two passive participles to accompany the word "freedom," thereby underscoring the situational irony of these lines: "This left Eugene in free possession;/Clad in a London dandy's fashion,/With hair style of the latest cast,/He joined Society at last" (1:IV:5-8; Arndt 6). Because our translation does not reflect the original's grammar and rhyme, I supply my own prose version, including Russian rhymes where necessary: "Now my Onegin is **free**;/His hair **cut** in the latest **fashion**;/Like a London dandy **dressed**—/He has finally seen **the World**" (1:IV).[10] I show the students how parallelism creates additional connotations: since the second and third lines are grammatically and semantically parallel, the parallelism indirectly transfers to their rhyming lines, ultimately connecting the notions of freedom (свобода) and high society (свет).[11] The last line ("And finally…") suggests that subjecting oneself to the two rituals ("hair cut," "dressed") is the prerequisite for "seeing the World" (свет [also meaning "light" in Russian]), which casts further doubt on the whole notion of Onegin's "freedom," or at least his understanding of it. Onegin also obeys his "watchful repeater," which tells him, for instance, when to go to dinner, to the theater, etc. ("Drives out and joins the promenading,/Till the repeater's watchful peal/Recalls him to the midday meal./…/But the repeater's jingling hammers/Bid them to the new ballet piece" [1:XV:13-14; 1:XVII:3-4; Arndt 10, 11].[12] Pushkin reinforces the idea of submitting to something external by repeating the same rhyme: *odet/svet* [dressed/World]; *odet/razdet/ vnov' odet* [dressed/undressed/newly dressed]; *breget/obed* [repeater/

---

translated as "freedom" or "liberty": свобода, воля and вольность.

[10] "Вот мой Онегин **на свободе**;/**Острижен** по последней **моде**;/Как *dandy* лондонский **одет**—/И наконец увидел **свет**".

[11] When time permits, I also draw students' attention to the semantic echo of this rhyme in 1:XV:9, 12: "в утреннем уборе"/"на просторе" ("morning trim/freely, in a free space").

[12] "И там гуляет на просторе,/Пока недремлющий брегет/Не прозвонит ему обед ... Но звон брегета им доносит,/Что новый начался балет".

dinner]; *kotlet/breget[a]/balet* [cutlets/repeater/ballet]). By paying attention to grammar, students can see that, although "free," Onegin has become the pawn of society and its rituals. Onegin's submission to society takes its tragic toll when, in his duel with Lensky, he finds himself unable to resist "public opinion" (6:XI:13) and becomes a "helpless play-ball of convention" ("мячик предрассуждений" [6:X; Arndt 143]), an object of the "duel-machine," and almost mechanically kills his young friend.

Next my students and I may wrestle with the question of how Onegin's use of freedom in order to subjugate himself to society's fashions compares to the poet's decision to subordinate his inspiration to poetry's strict forms. Students easily observe that both have an aesthetic dimension, but we must ask whether there are significant differences. Does the individual's goal matter? How much freedom does each subject find within the chosen strictures? How much of the decision derives from conscious choice?

The contrast between characters as truly free subjects and as seemingly free objects becomes clear when we compare Onegin to Tatyana. Tatyana seems to undergo an opposite evolution: while Onegin's pursuit of freedom transforms him from an active subject into an object, Tatyana follows a no-less paradoxical trajectory from subject to object and back to subject.

Initially, Tatyana has both external and internal freedom. When she falls in love with Onegin, Pushkin's language shows her as both subject and object: the subject of her choice and her creative imagination on the one hand, and the object of her feelings and impersonal states on the other.[13] In chapter 7 Tatyana loses her external freedom when she is transported to Moscow and dragged from one salon to the next there (she becomes largely a grammatical

---

[13] She appears as subject many times in chapter 3, stanzas VII-X, e.g., "Heart thirsting for … it knew not whom//Now found him" ("Душа ждала … кого-нибудь//И дождалась…" [3:VII:14, 3:VIII:1; Arndt 64]); later, "She proves … trustful of the dream she chose" ("Она … верит избранной мечте" [3:XXIV:3-4; Arndt 72]). She appears as object also a number of times, e.g., "Dreams haunt you everywhere you go" ("Тебя преследуют мечты" [3:XV:10; Arndt 68]); "Love's languorous unease assails her" ("Тоска любви Татьяну гонит" [3:XVI:1; Arndt 69]). There are more examples of both.

object once in Moscow, e.g., "So from one luncheon to another/They haul Tatyana day by day" [7:XLIV:1-2; Arndt 185]).[14] When Onegin sees her again in Petersburg in chapter 8, she appears to him to be the opposite of her younger self, whose feelings were "out, at liberty" (наруже, на воле) in her letter (8:XX:9). And yet, Pushkin saturates descriptions of Tatyana with words denoting freedom: "[S]he/ Remains superbly poised and free" (8:XXII:13-14; Arndt 205); "At home receives him unembarrassed [freely]" (8:XXXI:3; Arndt 210); in her salon "free liveliness" rules the conversation (8:XXIII:11-14).[15]

In chapter 8, Pushkin also completes Tatyana's transformation from the object of her emotions into the subject of her behavior. In this chapter, she becomes the unquestionable subject of her actions. Here Tatyana is the grammatical subject of practically every active voice sentence in which she appears. The only exceptions occur in the last stanza of Tatyana's speech. Here Tatyana twice uses passive constructions when speaking about herself. First, she says, "But now my lot/Is cast for good" (8:XLVII:2-3; Arndt 220).[16] This can be read as if Tatyana were "blaming fate" for the current situation and absolving herself of responsibility. Tatyana's next sentence disabuses the reader of such an interpretation, however: "If—let me face it—/ I acted rashly" (8:XLVII:3-4; Arndt 220).[17] She acknowledges that she herself had ultimately decided her fate. Tatyana continues in the active voice except for the famous penultimate line—"But I was pledged another's wife" (8:XLVII:13; Arndt 220)[18]—in which she uses the passive about which Belinsky raged, "'Was given away,' not 'gave myself'!"[19] The context, which has established Tatyana's

---

[14] "И вот: по родственным обедам/Развозят Таню каждый день". See also 7:XLVI, 7:XLIX-LI, 7:LIV.

[15] "[О]на/Сидит покойна и вольна", "Свободно дома принимает"; "Разумный толк без пошлых тем,/Без вечных истин, без педанства,/… не пугал ничьих ушей/Свободной живостью своей".

[16] "Но судьба моя,/Уж решена".

[17] "Неосторожно,/Быть может, поступила я".

[18] "Но я другому отдана…"

[19] "Here is the true boast of feminine virtue! But I *became* another's wife—

responsibility for her actions—"I acted,"[20] "I married," "I beg of you," "I know," "I love you" (8:XLVII:4, 8, 9, 10, 12)—shows this passive to be just a statement of fact, of the resulting situation, that is, of the fate that has been decided at least in part by Tatyana's own action. Tatyana's position is unequivocal: "I have married" (note the different construction used about her mother: "But presently they set her bridal/And never asked for her advice" [2:XXXI:3-4]).[21] The final rhyme: "я ... отдана/Я буду ... верна" (8:XLVII:13-14) emphasizes the antinomy inherent in Tatyana's position. Tatyana has accepted as a subject the limitations of freedom that life has gradually imposed on her. As a subject of her decisions, she will not use the circumstances unfavorable to her feelings ("given away" ["отдана"]) as an excuse to abandon her commitments and her agency.[22] Tatyana, unlike Onegin, has learned that actions have consequences.

When reading *Eugene Onegin*, many students become fascinated with the question of fate versus free will. Pushkin's narrator and his characters often refer to Fate ("Fate treated young Onegin gently" [1:III:5; Arndt 6]; "My friend Onegin had decided/ On foreign travel with me soon;/But presently we were divided/ By destiny for many a moon" [1:LI:1-4; Arndt 27]).[23] Some students ask whether the notion of Fate negates the existence of free will. We

---

precisely *became* and *not gave myself!* Eternal fidelity—*to whom* and *in what?* Fidelity to relations which are a desecration to feelings and to the chasteness of femininity, for there are certain relations which, unsanctified by love, are supremely immoral... A woman's life is chiefly centered in the life of the heart: for her to love means to live, and to sacrifice means to love. It was for this role nature created Tatiana; but society remade her...." V. G. Belinsky, *Selected Philosophical Works* (Moscow: Foreign Languages Publishing House, 1956), 291-92. The original is in V. G. Belinskii, *Polnoe sobranie sochinenii*, 13 vols. (Moscow: Izd. AN SSSR, 1953-59), 7:501.

[20] *"Postupila ia"*: this phrase rhymes with *"sud'ba moia,"* again stressing Tatyana's own contribution to her "lot" or fate.

[21] "Но, не спросясь ее совета,/Девицу повезли к венцу".

[22] Note that the same rhyme occurs in *"ona/Sidit pokina i vol'na."*

[23] "Судьба Евгения хранила"; "Онегин был готов со мною/Увидеть чуждые страны;/Но скоро были мы судьбою/На долгий срок разведены".

discuss the role of Fate in the protagonists' stories and attempt to trace the cause of various events either to Fate or to the protagonists' own decisions. In the process we discover that whenever Onegin invokes Fate (or an impersonal "something"), he does so to deny his responsibility for his own actions (e.g., "Is this to be the sad estate/ Assigned you [Tatyana] by the savage Fate?" [4:XV:13-14; Arndt 93]; "Then a dark shadow fell to blight us:/When Lensky, luckless fate! Succumbed" [8, Onegin's letter to Tatyana; Arndt 211]).[24] He always presumes to know what Fate holds for him (the narrator speaks of his "foreboding vision" [тот, кто все предвидит] in 4:LI:9), while Tatyana humbly tries to divine what Fate has planned for her and tries to interact with Fate, which she identifies with Providence. For example, she asks herself in her letter to Onegin: "All this, it may be, is misguided/Delusion of a callow heart,/And Fate has otherwise decided" (3: Tatyana's Letter to Onegin; Arndt 78).[25] She chooses to love Onegin, and accepts this choice as an action of Fate, not caring whether this love will have a happy ending or not ("She murmurs: 'I shall be undone;/Undone by him, I will be cheerful,/Nor rail at Fate's decree. Why live?/He has no happiness to give'" [6:III:11-14; Arndt 140]; "The man for whom she has been yearning/By willful destiny's decree" [7:XXIV:5; Arndt 175]).[26] She is conscious of her own choices (such as her love for Onegin and her decision to marry her husband) and takes responsibility for them after the fact.

Pushkin's concept of freedom is clearly paradoxical and strongly tied to poetry, whose formal discipline makes the free flight of thought possible. In Pushkin, one can find freedom in remaining faithful, in being "bound" to something, whether one's work or marriage, provided one accepts these limitations as a subject (like Tatyana, who has "grown into her role,/The weary pomp of her

---

[24] "Ужели жребий вам такой/Назначен строгою судьбой?"; "Еще одно нас разлучило…/Несчастной жертвой Ленский пал…"

[25] "Быть может, это всё пустое,/Обман неопытной души!/И суждено совсем иное…"

[26] "'Погибну', Таня говорит,/'Но гибель от него любезна./Я не ропщу: зачем роптать?/Не может он мне счастья дать'"; "Того, по ком она вздыхать/Осуждена судьбою властной…"

position/Fused with the substance of her soul" [lit. "taken on the ways of her constricting rank"]; 8:XXVIII:2-4).[27] My students and I discuss various reasons why Pushkin focuses so much on inner freedom and appears to celebrate Tatyana's decision to reject an illicit affair. I remind students of the biographical background: Pushkin was engaged to be married when he was finishing the novel. Is it possible that Tatyana's faithfulness reflects his hope that his own bride would be faithful too? Perhaps Pushkin's focus on inner freedom reflects the situation of a person whose external freedom was severely circumscribed by the power of the state and society? The inner, "secret freedom" was the only freedom available to Pushkin by 1830, and he had given up striving for the other kind (for example, political freedom), since he considered it unattainable.[28]

Whatever psychological and political factors underlie the outcome of Pushkin's plot, he does not broadcast them to the reader. Above everything, his message is poetic: the antinomy and balance of freedom and limitation, of poetry and prose in the "free novel" in verse, are the prerequisites for creating beauty in art—and quite possibly in life. To his prose-writing progeny, Pushkin bequeaths a balancing act that is difficult to follow.

---

[27] "[Т]вердо в роль свою вошла!/... утеснительного сана/Приемы ... приняла!"

[28] "Secret freedom" (тайная свобода) is the phrase from Pushkin, "К Н. Я. Плюсковой," in his *Polnoe sobranie sochinenii,* 1:340. Here I draw on Roman Jakobson's discussion of the finale of the novel in "Marginal Notes on *Eugene Onegin,*" in Pushkin, *Eugene Onegin,* trans. Arndt, xliv-xlv.

20

Text, Genre, and Morality II

Examining Lensky's Body:
Forensic Pedagogy

Catharine Theimer Nepomnyashchy

But Pushkin was deliberately writing a novel about nothing. In *Evgeny Onegin* he could think of nothing but shirking his responsibilities as narrator. The novel is made up of poor excuses that draw our attention away to the margins of the verse page and hinder the development of the plot line selected by the writer. The action is just barely held together by the two letters and two monologues of amorous quid pro quo, which lead to absolutely nothing, and by a nonentity elevated to the status of hero, and almost every sentence comes close to drowning in distracting secondary material. No less than three balls are held in it, and taking advantage of the attendant fuss, the author loses the thread of his narration, wanders off, marks time, beats around the bush and sits it out in the underbrush, in the background of his own story. For example, Onegin's quarrel with Lensky, which should play first fiddle in the conflict, almost comes to nothing, crowded out by the pies baked for the heroine's nameday party.[1]

The extreme simplicity of Pushkin's story has been proclaimed many times—by critics. Boy meets girl; boy rebuffs girl; boy re-meets girl; girl rebuffs boy. Finis. But such a precis is not only a crude oversimplification of this multifaceted novel-in-verse, it mutilates by omission the very plot it purports to summarize. For the overlooked Lenskii-Olga courtship is more than a decorative frieze for—or

---

1   Abram Tertz (Andrei Sinyavsky), *Strolls with Pushkin*, trans. Catharine Theimer Nepomnyashchy and Slava Yastremski, intro. Catharine Theimer Nepomnyashchy (New Haven, CT: Yale University Press, 1993), 92.

a contrapuntal obbligato to—the Onegin-Tatyana affair. Intimately intertwined with the lives of both hero and heroine, it exercises a crucial influence on their destinies.[2]

Thus, the body of Lensky, slain by his friend, stimulates the process of transformation, in the course of which Onegin and Tatyana radically switch roles, and the whole dynamics of life gains much in death.

> Zaretsky carefully laid
> The frozen corpse upon the sleigh;
> He drove the awful treasure home.
> Scenting the corpse, the horses
> Snorted and struggled,
> Wet the steel bit with white foam,
> And flew as swiftly as an arrow.[3]

After years of teaching *Eugene Onegin*—with all the attendant challenges of translation, stanzaic structure, digressive narrator, and quizzical hero—to students most of whom are younger than Pushkin was himself when he began writing his "novel in verse," I have come to believe that the most fruitful approach to Pushkin's masterwork resides in an examination of the complex mechanisms through which the poet embeds, or perhaps more precisely weaves into the very texture of his novel in verse, the passage of time. As Richard Gustafson observes in his discussion of the famous digression on feet in the first book of *Onegin* in his seminal article, "The Metaphor of the Seasons in *Evgenij Onegin*": "So in this digression Puškin not only suggests the plot of his story—the crushing of the spring flower—but he also introduces his great theme of the work: the constant and inevitable passage of time."[4]

---

[2]   Richard Gregg, "Stanza and Plot in *Evgenii Onegin*: A Symbiosis?," *Slavonic and East European Review* 72, no. 4 (Oct. 1994): 617.

[3]   Abram Tertz, *Strolls with Pushkin*, 86. Translation of *Eugene Onegin*, chapter 6, stanza 35, is Yastremski's and mine.

[4]   Richard F. Gustafson, "The Metaphor of the Seasons in *Evgenij Onegin*," *Slavic and East European Journal* 6, no. 1 (Spring 1962): 8.

In this vein, Gustafson outlines in the course of his article how the use of the seasons in Pushkin's novel in verse revolves around the contrapuntal metaphorization of spring and winter to convey the fatal passage of time in the novel. I build on Gustafson's argument by taking as my point of departure Lensky's dead body, which lies in a structurally central position two-thirds of the way through the text of *Eugene Onegin*; Lensky's corpse figures the irrevocability of loss as the essence of time as it infects all aspects of Pushkin's masterwork from plot to structure to the very nature of the Onegin stanza. This infection of the poem by time as loss culminates in—and elucidates the significance of—Tatyana's final response to Onegin in book eight and the abrupt "in medias res" ending of the novel in a narrative digression.

Before turning to Lensky's cadaver, however, let us dwell for a moment on the fact that the poet's untimely demise is foreshadowed by another dead body that confronts us in the very first stanza of the poem. The looming corpse is highlighted by the wish for death attributed to the title character in the concluding lines of the stanza— one of the snappiest of Pushkin's whiplash couplet-punchlines.

> My uncle, man of firm convictions…
> By falling gravely ill, he's won
> A due respect for his afflictions—
> The only clever thing he's done.
> May his example profit others;
> But God, what deadly boredom, brothers,
> Not daring once to steal away!
> And, oh, how base to pamper grossly
> And entertain the nearly dead,
> To fluff the pillows for his head,
> And pass him medicines morosely—
> While thinking under every sigh:
> The devil take you, Uncle, Die!" (EO I.1; p. 15)[5]

---

5   Translations throughout are taken from *Eugene Onegin: A Novel in Verse by Alexander Pushkin*, trans. James E. Falen (Carbondale, IL: Southern Illinois University Press, 1990). Henceforth page numbers to this edition will be given, along with the canto and stanza, in parentheses in the text. Whenever

This opening stanza is separated by some fifty stanzas, almost an eighth of the entire work, from stanza 53, in which we learn after the fact that Pushkin's text indeed began with a corpse, that Onegin's uncle may well have already been dead just as he was wishing him so. Most important here is the fact that the intervening stanzas of the first canto, aside from giving us a rudimentary account of Onegin's early education, are primarily devoted to chronicling "a day in the life of a Petersburg dandy," that is, the mad and pointless race of the social calendar which drives the eponymous protagonist and his peers into a futile cycle of social engagements, which (like the enduring image of the squirrel in a wheel) simultaneously enslaves Petersburg high society to time marked by the "unsleeping Breguet" (EO I.15[6]) watch and denies the fatal progression of time to old age and death:

> Some mornings still abed he drowses,
> Until his valet brings his tray.
> What? Invitations? Yes, three houses
> Have asked him to a grand soirée.
> There'll be a ball, a children's party;
> Where will he dash to, my good hearty?
> Where will he make the night's first call?

---

the issue of teaching *Eugene Onegin* to American students comes up, the problem of translation seems unavoidable: how can we possibly convey the greatness of the original when that greatness lies first and foremost in the extraordinary marriage of fluid language and rigid form, a feat impossible to duplicate in translation? Ever since the appearance of the James Falen translation I have, while never ceasing to encourage students to learn Russian so that they can read *Onegin* in the original, never worried— or encouraged my students to worry—that reading *Eugene Onegin* in translation is any more or less problematical than reading any other great work of literature in translation. Because I consider the Falen translation of *Eugene Onegin* so successful in conveying the spirit and the sense of the work to undergraduates, I have cited his translation throughout this article.

6   See also I.17:
> Another round would hardly hurt them,
> To wash those sizzling cutlets down;
> But now the chime and watch [*breguet*] alert them:
> The brand new ballet's on in town!
> (EO I.17; p. 21)

> Oh, never mind—he'll make them all.
> But meanwhile, dressed for morning pleasure.
> And smart in wide-brimmed *Bolívar*,
> He drives to Nevsky Boulevard,
> To stroll around at total leisure,
> Until Bréguet's unsleeping chime
> Reminds him that it's dinnertime.
> (EO I.12; p. 20)

As I will suggest below, this counterpoint between the frivolous and the rigid as a manifestation of temporal paradox motivates both the function of the Onegin stanza and the narrative digressions in the poem (digressions that simultaneously delay—Shklovskian замедление—and meditate on the passage of time).

When Onegin arrives in the country, confronted by his uncle's corpse, the rhythm of the "novel" fundamentally changes. Time in the countryside, closely tied to the progression of the seasons, differs in essence from the artificially constructed Petersburg round; if Petersburg time seems a pointlessly spinning wheel, country time is measured by the cycle of tradition bound by ritual. Onegin's first brush with the life cycle in the country is in fact the natural death of his uncle, whose funeral the country dwellers view as business as usual:

> He found the manor fairly bustling
> With those who'd known the now deceased;
> Both friends and foes had come ahustling,
> True lovers of a funeral feast.
> They laid to rest the dead departed;
> Then, wined and dined and heavy-hearted,
> But pleased to have their duty done,
> The priests and guests left one by one.
> (EO I.53; p. 38)[7]

In the same fashion, once she has given up the whirl of Moscow and the lure of sentimental novels, Tatyana's mother devotes herself

---

[7] The last line of the Russian, translated literally, is a bit more pointed: "And importantly took their leave as if they had taken care of business."

to the running of husband and household, until her husband passes on and is laid to rest under a grave marker which presages an analogous stone under which the youthful body of Lensky will soon—far too soon—come to lie:

> Amid this peaceful life they cherished,
> They held all ancient customs dear;
> At Shrovetide feasts their table flourished
> With Russian pancakes, Russian cheer;
> Twice yearly too they did their fasting;
> Were fond of songs for fortune-casting.
> Of choral dances, garden swings.
> At Trinity, when service brings
> The people, yawning, in for prayer,
> They'd shed a tender tear or two
> Upon their buttercups of rue.
> They needed kvas no less than air.
> And at their table guests were served
> By rank in turn as each deserved.
>
> And thus they aged, as do all mortals.
> Until at last the husband found
> That death had opened wide its portals,
> Through which he entered, newly crowned.
> He died at midday's break from labor,
> Lamented much by friend and neighbor,
> By children and by faithful wife—
> Far more than some who part this life.
> He was a kind and simple *barin*,
> And there where now his ashes lie
> A tombstone tells the passerby:
> *The humble sinner Dmitry Larin*
> *A slave of God and brigadier*
> *Beneath this stone now resteth here.*
> (EO II.35-36; p. 62, Pushkin's emphasis)[8]

---

8   In tracing the central role of Lensky's corpse in the text, it is telling to note that the stanza immediately following this introduces Lensky's return home along with a visit to Larin's grave:

Into this bucolic backwater, Onegin's arrival—along with Lensky's return from abroad—introduces plot.[9] Specifically, these events seem to set in motion the comedic convention of the (double) marriage plot.[10] In fact *Eugene Onegin* does, in a sense, end in a double marriage—at least to the extent that both "heroines" end up married in the end. However, from the point of view of the conventional expectations—notably shared by the inhabitants of the surrounding countryside who quickly settle the issue of the marriages of Lensky and Olga and Onegin and Tatyana in local gossip—the two women end up married to the "wrong" men. And it is Lensky's death that

> Restored to home and its safekeeping,
> Young Lensky came to cast an eye
> Upon his neighbor's place of sleeping,
> And mourned his ashes with a sigh.
> And long he stood in sorrow aching;
> "Poor Yorick!" then he murmured, shaking,
> "How oft within his arms I lay,
> How oft in childhood days I'd play
> With his Ochakov decoration!
> He destined Olga for my wife
> And used to say: 'Oh grant me, life,
> To see the day!'" ... In lamentation,
> Right then and there Vladimir penned
> A funeral verse for his old friend.
> (EO II.37; p. 63)

[9] My thoughts about plot convention were recently invigorated by a rich series of lectures on the workings of plot delivered by Bob Belknap as the 2011 Leonard Hastings Schoff Memorial Lectures at Columbia University. Meir Sternberg's *Expositional Modes and Temporal Ordering in Fiction* has also played a seminal role in my thinking about plot.

[10] I have made this argument specifically in relation to Jane Austen's *Pride and Prejudice* in my article, "Jane Austen in Russia: Hidden Presence and Belated Boom," in *The Reception of Jane Austen in Europe*, ed. Anthony Mandal and Brian Southam (London: Continuum, 2007), 334-49. Richard Gregg makes a related argument: "And yet a surprise—and a tragic one at that—is precisely what awaits the poet who writes in clichés and the fiancée who is one. Reversing the stereotypical courtship of popular fiction (*amor omnia vincit*), Lenskii and Ol'ga's idyllic betrothal is free of impediments but ends in disaster: he is killed in a fortuitous duel; she, 'the funeral baked meats' barely cold, marries another. All of which is to say that Pushkin's juxtaposition of predictable characters produces a denouement which it would be impossible to foresee." Gregg, "Stanza and Plot," 614.

derails the unfolding of the course of the plot as would be expected from this novelistic set-up, which leads the reader to anticipate that Lensky will marry Olga as desired by her father, and that the "hero" Onegin will marry the "heroine" Tatyana.

We are, however, alerted that something has "gone wrong" almost from the outset, when Onegin, after his first visit to the Larins' domicile, remarks that—again from the point of view of literary convention—Lensky has paired himself against type, as Onegin observes:

> "And really you prefer the other?"
> "Why not?"—"Were I the poet, brother,
> I'd choose the elder one instead—
> Your Olga's look is cold and dead." (EO III.5; p. 69)

Pushkin's narrator sets up Onegin's dismissal of Olga in the preceding canto:

> Oh, Olga's every trait…. But glance
> In any novel—you'll discover
> Her portrait there. (EO III.23; p. 56)

Thus the poet falls for the stereotypical heroine of an implicitly hackneyed novel, while Onegin, who is early on associated with prose,[11] appreciates, at least in theory, the poetic appeal of Tatyana— "A wild creature, sad and pensive" (EO II.25; p. 57). This should alert us that the famous symmetries of Pushkin's plot overshadow fateful deviations from symmetry, deviations that mark the conventional plot—and traditional time—gone awry.

---

[11] Here we should remember:
> But Lensky, having no desire
> For marriage bonds or wedding bell,
> Had cordial hopes that he'd acquire
> The chance to know Onegin well.
> And so they met—like wave and mountain,
> Like verse and prose, like flame and fountain;
> Their natures distant and apart. (EO II.13, p. 51)

One significant, if oft-overlooked, asymmetry is implanted in the core plot skeleton of letter and response. After all, Tatyana makes Onegin cool his heels waiting for her answer much longer, a whole winter—and in fact apparently plans no response at all until Onegin surprises her weeping over his missive. Here we should note that the much-vaunted symmetry of Tatyana's and Onegin's letters and responses is undercut quite clearly in Canto VIII, verse 333:

> No answer came. Eugene elected
> To write again… and then once more—
> With no reply. (213)

I do not think it is going too far to suggest that Tatyana mourns Lensky as she mourns her now impossible love for Onegin—and that viewing the equivalence here helps us to understand that in her final conversation with Onegin what Tatyana is really lecturing him about is the nature of time, and the slipperiness of literary genre as well. More surprising still, a close reading of the second half of the work reveals that Onegin himself is haunted by the dead Lensky.

In this context, let us note Tatyana's and Onegin's recurring preoccupation with Lensky's death throughout the second half of the novel in verse. Thus, when Tatyana is left alone in her country home by Olga's departure after her marriage, the narrative has this to say of her thoughts of Onegin:

> She finds brother's slayer hateful
> And loathes the awful thing he's done.
> (EO VII.14; p. 172)

Tellingly, the stanza ends with a reference to Lensky:

> Two hearts, perhaps, remain forlorn
> And mourn him yet... But wherefore mourn?..
> (EO VII.14; p. 172)

We can only assume that the second sad heart belongs to Onegin (rather than to the flighty Olga, who has already married and moved on), and in fact we learn when Onegin reappears in the final canto that it is precisely the death of Lensky that has driven him from the countryside to aimless wandering:

> He left his home in disillusion
> And fled the woods' and fields' seclusion,
> Where every day before his eyes
> A bloody specter seemed to rise;
> He took up travel for distraction. (EO VIII.13; p. 201)[12]

Moreover, in his letter to Tatyana, Onegin makes explicit the fact that they are separated by Lensky's death:

> And had, it's true, no inclination
> To lose my hateful freedom then.
> What's more; poor guiltless Lensky perished,
> And his sad fate drew us apart...
> From all that I had ever cherished
> I tore away my grieving heart;
> Estranged from men and discontented,
> I thought in freedom, peace of mind,
> A substitute for joy I'd find,
> How wrong I've been! And now tormented!
> (EO VIII; p. 211)

And when Onegin receives no response from Tatyana, he falls into a sort of delirium, and what appears to his imagination first, as listed in the narrative, is Lensky's corpse:

> He sees a youth, quite still, reposing
> On melting snow — as if he's dozing
> On bivouac; then hears with dread
> A voice proclaim: "Well then, he's dead!"
> (EO VIII.37; p. 215)

This train of hallucinations leads him, by the flow of narrative, to Tatyana as we first saw her in the country before she met Onegin:

---

[12] Here the Falen translation does take a liberty worth flagging for students, since Pushkin's text specifies that Onegin sets off on his travels not "for distraction," but rather "without a goal."

> A country house… a windowsill…
> Where she sits waiting… waiting still!..
> (EO VIII.37; p. 215)

> And oftentimes she'd sit all day
> In silence at the window bay.
> (EO II.25; p. 57)

Yet Onegin's fateful dilemma lies in the very fact that time cannot go backward, that Tatyana is not "waiting still," that he cannot retreat into poetry from the inexorable flow of novelistic time. As the narrator remarks, the prosaic Onegin is reduced to such a state that he almost becomes a poet:

> He got so lost in his depression,
> He just about went mad, I fear,
> Or else turned poet.
> (EO VIII.38; p. 215)

By the time he does go to see Tatyana for their final meeting, Onegin himself resembles a corpse: "He enters like a dead man" (EO VIII.40; p. 216).

It is necessary to read Tatyana's response to Onegin in the context of the repeated references to Lensky's body as an unyielding marker of the irreversible passage of time, a memento mori that determines the shape of the plot. More than once not only my students, but I myself, have raised the issue of what is so awful about Onegin's "lecture" to Tatyana that it makes her "lecture" him in return so harshly? After all, Onegin speaks honestly from a position of greater experience and does not take advantage of the situation. In short, he acts like a "gentleman." Over the years, I have come to believe that the most telling lines in Tatyana's speech at the end are:

> And happiness was ours… so nearly!
> It came so close!.. But now my fate
> Has been decreed. (EO VIII.47; p. 220)

I take Tatyana's true reproach to be that Onegin is guilty of missing his time, and the chance will never recur. They cannot step back over Lensky's corpse; there is no way back to the past.[13] In this most symmetrical of literary structures, the hero and heroine are out of sync.

If we read Pushkin's "novel in verse" as a meditation and instantiation of the passage of time, the narrator's abrupt abandonment of the plot and concluding digression on time follow organically from the very structure of *Eugene Onegin*. The final lines read:

> Oh, many, many days have fled
> Since young Tatyana with her lover,
> As in a misty dream at night,
> First floated dimly into sight—
> And I as yet could not uncover
> Or through the magic crystal see
> My novel's shape or what would be.
>
> But those to whom, as friends and brothers,
> My first few stanzas I once read—
> "Some are no more, and distant… others."
> As Sadi long before us said.
> Without them my Onegin's fashioned,
> And she from whom I drew, impassioned,
> My fair Tatyana's noblest trait…
> *But blest is he who rightly gauges*
> *The time to quit the feast and fly,*
> *Who never drained life's chalice dry,*
> *Nor read its novel's final pages;*
> *But all at once for good withdrew—*
> *As I from my Onegin do.*
> (EO VIII.50-51; pp. 221-22)

---

[13]   We should also remark here that Tatyana notes in her final speech to Onegin that her Nanny is now dead as well.

I have italicized the final lines to underscore what seems to be an inescapable echo of Lensky's untimely death in the narrator's concluding words announcing his timely exit. And I will bring my own remarks to a close here, by raising two questions and answers to which an instructor might well devote a final class on *Eugene Onegin*. The first has to do with how reading *Eugene Onegin* in the light of Lensky's bloody corpse might enrich our understanding of the relationship between the novel's plot and its structure. The second, related, question has to do with whether Pushkin's generic anxiety about poetry vs. prose is also revealed to be more complex and profound when we view his masterwork from this perspective.

Lensky's intractable corpse marks the final, defining limit. Here the stanzas devoted to Lensky's death are apt:

> He lays a hand, as in confusion,
> On breast and falls. His misted eyes
> Express not pain, but death's intrusion.
> Thus, slowly, down a sloping rise,
> And sparkling in the sunlight's shimmer,
> A clump of snow will fall and glimmer.
> Eugene, in sudden chill, despairs.
> Runs to the stricken youth... and stares!
> Calls out his name! — No earthly power
> Can bring him back: the singer's gone,
> Cut down by fate at break of dawn!
> The storm has blown; the lovely flower
> Has withered with the rising sun;
> The altar fire is out and done!...
>
> He lay quite still and past all feeling;
> His languid brow looked strange at rest.
> The steaming blood poured forth, revealing
> The gaping wound beneath his breast.
> *One moment back — a breath's duration —*
> *This heart still throbbed with inspiration;*
> Its hatreds, hopes, and loves still beat.
> Its blood ran hot with life's own heat.
> But now, as in a house deserted,
> Inside it — all is hushed and stark,

> Gone silent and forever dark.
> The window boards have been inserted,
> The panes chalked white. The owner's fled;
> But where, God knows. All trace is dead.
> (EO VI.31-32; p. 157)

Again I have italicized the most telling lines, those that register the fatal moment which cannot be reclaimed, the death of imagination. I would suggest that the finality of Lensky's death signifies the limits of verbal play and would go even further to maintain that the digressive narrative in which the symmetrical plot is clothed and the rigid formula of the Onegin stanza in which Pushkin's verbal ebullience is confined correspond to this tension between potential and mortality that constitutes the essence of *Eugene Onegin*. Much has been written about the unPushkinian saturation in metaphor of these passages devoted to Lensky's death. I would argue that metaphor in and of itself serves as a trope for the limit of communication which inheres in the inexorable flow of time. Metaphor constitutes an attempt—potentially rich in the possibility of generating signification, but ultimately doomed to failure—to staunch the slippage between word and referent, to halt the deferral of time Derrida labeled "différance." To put this point in what might be more "undergraduate-friendly" terms, metaphor—most simply the substitution of one word for another—signals the death of the myth of the language's straightforward, "one-to-one" relationship to the "body" of reality. Onegin desperately tries, but Lensky's name will no longer bring him back to life.

It is a cliché of *Onegin* criticism that Lensky's death "symbolizes" the death of poetry. However, like many critical truisms, this one, while containing a grain of truth, threatens to trivialize a more complicated opposition that subsumes the arguments that I have made thus far. Pushkin's "novel in verse" does indeed hover between novel and verse from start to finish, haunted as much by Pushkin's anxiety about falling prey to novelistic convention as it is by Lensky's corpse—thus, Lensky's corpse stands as the ultimate test of Pushkin's hybrid masterpiece. The ordered complexity of the Onegin Stanza, the free-wheeling chatter of the narrator, and the stunning and sparkling rhyme all continually distract from the minimalist plot, which, as I have attempted to show—most obviously in the intervention of Lensky's death—carries within itself a certain ambivalence, an insecurity about the very genre of the novel itself. Playing with the limits of poetry, Pushkin is loathe to commit to the "hackneyed" form of the novel, the predictability of plot. Like Lensky (however, unwittingly), Pushkin's narrator "rightly gauges/The time to quit the feast and fly," refusing to give us a conventional "happy ending"—or any real ending at all. In the final analysis, what is perhaps most important to convey to students when teaching *Eugene Onegin* is Pushkin's extraordinary achievement in melding life and art, in creating a work of literature that is so obviously carefully crafted and deviously plotted, on the one hand, and so full of the throbbing pulse of life exposed most vividly by its untimely end, on the other.

21

TEXT AND PERFORMANCE

The Power of Pedagogy: Dispelling the Darkness in Tolstoy's Drama

Maude Meisel

When introducing a discussion of some particularly shattering Dostoevskian passage, Robert Belknap sometimes reminds us that literature can tell you things, show you things, and/or do things to you. Tolstoy's first full-length dramatic work, *The Power of Darkness* (Власть тьмы), employs all three of these tactics, any one of which can change a spectator or reader forever. In the third category in particular, the play's reaching-right-inside-you effect helps make *The Power of Darkness* Tolstoy's most Dostoevskian work, and the first thing to cope with in presenting it to an audience (reading or viewing) is shell-shock.

The play's traditional religious motifs of temptation, crime, punishment, and redemption also evoke Dostoevsky, but Tolstoy intensifies the visceral impact of his tale first by making it a worst-case scenario and second by presenting it in the most three-dimensional of literary genres. As demonstrated by Martin Meisel in *How Plays Work*, awareness of a play's performative aspects is essential to understanding and teaching it.[1] In discussing *The Power of Darkness*, one thing I hope to show is how consideration of what the audience sees and hears enhances literary approaches for readers in a classroom.

Of course, the three-dimensional perspective immediately exposes the host of arresting contradictions, both real and apparent, that riddle Tolstoy's play in every dimension and on all levels, and another thing I hope to show is how examining these contradictions

---

[1]   Martin Meisel, *How Plays Work* (New York: Oxford University Press, 2007).

elucidates the play's meaning very effectively. Areas of contradiction range from original conception and purpose to reception and production history to the text's language, themes, and imagery to its realization in performance.

To begin with the play's conception, the first great contradiction is the very fact of its existence, and any discussion of Tolstoy's drama must start with a brief reminder that even before his religious conversion his opinion of theater in general, and of his contemporary theater in particular, was extremely low. Both his essays and his fiction make it clear that he considered the theater elitist, unnatural, and morally suspect. "The drama," he wrote in 1906, "has become in our time merely an empty and immoral amusement for the empty and immoral crowd." [2]

Despite these views, however, Tolstoy wrote some sixteen dramatic pieces of varying length and seriousness, which suggests that he also saw how this medium could enhance his artistic and/or didactic endeavor. Disliking and distrusting contemporary theater, he claimed with *The Power of Darkness* to be employing the same hated genre to do something different, genuine, and useful: to write something that would be both popular and natural as well as informed by a higher moral purpose. [3] This brings me to the last thing

---

[2] From Tolstoy, "Shakespeare and the Drama," in *Recollections and Essays*, trans. Aylmer Maude (London: Oxford University Press, 1961), 380-81. The passage continues: "The drama in our time is like a great man fallen to the lowest stage of degradation, who yet continues to pride himself on his past, of which nothing now remains. And the public of our time is like those who pitilessly get amusement out of this once great man, now descended to the lowest depths." See also Tolstoy, *What is Art?*, trans. Richard Pevear and Larissa Volokhonsky (1898; London: Penguin Books, 1995), 8: "For a cultivated man it [opera, ballet, etc.] is unbearable, tiresome; to a real working man it is totally incomprehensible. It might be pleasing, and then just barely, to some depraved artisans who have picked up a gentlemanly spirit but have not yet been satiated with gentlemanly pleasures, and who want to give testimony of their civilization, or else to young lackeys. And all this vile stupidity is produced not only with no kindly merriment, with no simplicity, but with spite and beastly cruelty."

[3] See Aylmer Maude, *Tolstoy on Art* (London: Oxford University Press, 1924), 459-60; see also Paul T. Nolan's opening summary of earlier critics on

I would like to show, which is that although the term "didactic" is generally used to disparage a work of art, didacticism need not rule out quality, such as when, like a good teacher, Tolstoy uses his skill to move us, shatter preconceptions, and change our lives.

As Tolstoy explained in a newspaper interview, he took his plot largely from the Tula court case of the peasant Efrem Koloskov, who confessed at his stepdaughter's wedding feast to having previously seduced her and murdered their child.[4] However, Tolstoy added threads to the story line, such as the poisoning of Anisya's husband, that fill out the three-fold structure of the play's dramatic action.

The play's five acts consist of three overlapping and progressively intensifying cycles of temptation, crime, and retribution. The first cycle is presented complete in act 1 as a kind of foretaste when Nikita, encouraged by Matryona, his mother, gives way to the temptation to slough off the poor orphan Marina (seduced by him earlier that year with a false promise of marriage) by swearing on an icon that he never touched her. Afterwards, he feels uncomfortable with what he's done but makes no move to repair the injury to Marina. At the same time, the second cycle is beginning, with Nikita's adulterous paramour Anisya tempted to hasten her ailing husband's death by using poison. With Matryona once again acting as *agent provocateur*, Anisya gives in to temptation and commits the crime in act 2. Act 3 presents retribution for Anisya, as Nikita, now her husband, drinks heavily, despises her, and abuses her. At the same time, the third cycle begins as Nikita indulges in the temptation of relations with his stepdaughter Akulina. This transgression culminates in act 4 when, under pressure from his mother and his wife, Nikita murders Akulina's and his own baby by crushing it under a plank. In act 5, the degradation of Nikita's life

---

Tolstoy's didactic approach in this play, followed by his own discussion of how the different dramatic styles employed in different scenes of the play are unified by a central controlling religious purpose. "Tolstoy's *Power of Darkness*: Genre as Meaning," *Educational Theatre Journal* 17, no. 1 (March 1965): 1-3.

[4]   See L. N. Tolstoi, *Polnoe sobranie sochinenii* (Moscow: Khudozhestvennaia literatura, 1946-53), 26:706, for the article in *Novosti* (January 1896).

and the haunted horror of his psyche (tormented by the phantom sound of "crunching baby bones") represent the terrible retribution that drives him to the brink of suicide. However, the play ends with a powerful image of redemption when, instead of hanging himself as he intends, Nikita finds the strength at Akulina's hurriedly-arranged wedding to break his downward spiral with a public confession.

As a result of censorial objection, *The Power of Darkness* has two different versions of the fourth act's infanticide. Most interesting, however, and contrary to what one might expect, Tolstoy's censor-driven rewrite works very well on its own terms and is arguably just as effective and horrifying (though in a different way) as the original.[5] In the original version, we watch the murder unfold in the courtyard space between the shed where Akulina has just given birth and the cottage where her suitor's matchmakers have just been hustled into an agreement and sent off without seeing her. Matryona and Anisya superstitiously baptize the baby, then toss it into a cellar through an onstage hatch, goading Nikita into killing it, which he does as mentioned above. The women claim the murder is his job since the baby is his, and they feel he has to "take responsibility" for his actions. As witnesses to this terrifyingly plausible evil, the audience hears everything. For the full effect, readers must continue to hear the crying and crunching in their own haunted imaginations as well.

The alternative version moves the murder offstage so that we no longer experience this evil directly as eyewitnesses. Nonetheless, the new scene creates almost as great a sense of horror through our identification with the still naïve and innocent ten-year-old Anyutka, daughter of Anisya and her murdered first husband. In this version, Nikita's hired hand, an old soldier and mostly reformed drunkard named Mitrich, is looking after Anyutka inside the cottage while the murder is taking place out in the courtyard.

---

5   Some have even argued that the rewrite is "a far more superior artistic product than the original, grossly naturalistic scene." See Peter Rudy, "Introduction" to *Darkness and Light: Three Short Works by Tolstoy*, ed. Peter Rudy (New York: Holt, Rinehart and Winston, 1965), xxviii.

The other characters, Nikita, Anisya, and Matryona, appear briefly several times, in states of great agitation, to fetch some implement or take a drink, and enough is said for the audience and Mitrich to understand what is happening. Mitrich ineptly tries to shield Anyutka from too much awareness, but she hears enough to start feeling deeply uneasy. Gradually she is overwhelmed by shocking suspicions she can neither confront nor shake off. In side-stepping Anyutka's increasingly direct questions, Mitrich delivers a diatribe on the evil nature of the peasant women that all sweet young peasant girls inevitably become. Anyutka asks if she herself will one day be like them and expresses the wish to be dead too (like the baby); finally, she starts hallucinating in terror. Though generating horror in quite different ways, both the death of the baby and the death of Anyutka's innocence are excruciating scenes to watch—as even a reader can tell.

The play was first written in 1886 in response to Mikhail Lentovsky's request for something for the people's theater in Moscow (Skoromokh). However, Mariya Savina, the powerful leading lady of the Alexandrinsky Theater in St. Petersburg, heard about it and persuaded Tolstoy to let her use it (sight unseen) for her benefice instead.[6] When news of *The Power of Darkness* first began to circulate in 1886, it excited huge interest in society, which anticipated something that would "revolutionize" theater. Unfortunately, even with the alternative fourth act, the censor passed the play only for publication (in a multivolume collected works in 1887), not for performance. With hard work, Savina and other prominent theater figures managed to impress the tsar (Alexander III) and gain his approval for a production at the Alexandrinsky Theater, but when the play was already in dress rehearsal, the strong objections of Synod Ober-procurator Konstantin Pobedonostsev caused the tsar to change his mind. As a result, public production and further publication were forbidden in Russia until 1895, and the first public performances took place abroad: in Paris (Antoine, 1888),

---

6   Iulia Petrovna Rybakova, "Kommentarii," in L. N. Tolstoi, *Sobranie sochinenii v 22 tomakh* (Moscow: Khudozhestvennaia literatura, 1982), 11:492.

Berlin (Brahm, 1890), Italy, Switzerland, and Holland.[7] The first staging in Russia is believed to have occurred in 1890 in a private home in Tsarskoe Selo, with amateur actors under the direction of Alexandrinsky actor/director V. N. Davydov. The performance caused a sensation, and many artistic and literary figures were present, including Anton Chekhov.[8]

When the official ban was lifted in Russia in 1895, productions followed immediately in St. Petersburg and Moscow at both imperial (Alexandrinsky, Malyi) and private (Literaturno-artisticheskii kruzhok, Korsh, Skomorokh, and eventually Moscow Art) theaters, as well as in dozens of provincial venues,[9] but after the furor of that first decade, productions have generally been few and far between. Later productions include one at the Malyi in 1956 with Igor Ilinsky as Akim,[10] and in the past ten years there have been revivals at the Bolshoi Dramaticheskii Teatr in St. Petersburg, the Malyi in Moscow, and the Mint Theater in New York in 2007.

The play's most striking aspect for early audiences was the revolutionary use of peasant language not just for comic effect, local color, or naturalism for its own sake, but as the language of serious tragic drama with spiritual depth. The sense of sin's inexorable, implacable consequences that makes the play tragic (in a manner reminiscent of *Macbeth*) is reflected in the folk saying used as a subtitle: "If a claw is caught, the whole bird is lost." To contemporary audiences, the tragic action and the peasant language clashed dramatically, and this innovation puts Tolstoy at the forefront of similar theatrical experiments throughout Europe, which include *Cathleen ni Houlihan* by Lady Gregory and W. B. Yeats in Ireland and Gerhart Hauptmann's *The Weavers* in Germany.[11] Also innovative

---

[7]   For more production history details, see "Spektakli: Anons," Bol'shoi Dramaticheskii Teatr imeni F. A. Tovstonogova, St. Petersburg, 2005, http://bdt.infobox.ru/plays/vlasttmi.html.

[8]   Rybakova, "Kommentarii," 11:493-94.

[9]   Ibid., 11:494.

[10]   See Igor' Il'inskii, *Sam o sebe* (Moscow: Iskusstvo, 1973).

[11]   Martin Meisel, *How Plays Work*, 248n4.

was Tolstoy's attempt to let strong feeling emerge through the ordinary dialogue and inarticulate flounderings of everyday life. It is worth repeating here that Chekhov attended the 1890 private staging in Tsarskoe Selo.

In an attempt to do justice to Tolstoy's achievement, Stanislavsky prepared for the 1902 Moscow Art Theater production by taking his troupe to Tula province so they could live in a village for two weeks. They brought back artifacts (dishes, etc.) and two genuine peasants as consultants: an old man and an old woman. The old woman turned out to have stage presence, and Stanislavsky tried casting her in the role of Matryona; however, he couldn't get her to remember the censor and refrain from swearing when she was supposed to be annoyed or upset. Next, he tried using her in crowd scenes or as a background singer, but he observed that she was so real she made the rest of the troupe look fake. In concluding his account, he judges the production to have been a failure, explaining that, in striving for "ethnographic naturalism," he lost sight of the play's spiritual content.[12] This is a telling story in many ways, particularly as it demonstrates that Tolstoy's momentous creative leap with authentic peasant language was not entirely without artistry and compromise.

Understanding the proportions of artistry and innovation in Tolstoy's use of language is particularly important when working in translation. The use of folk aphorisms and the motif of inarticulateness are not so difficult to render, but translating the effect of using ordinary peasant idiom offers quite a challenge. Louise and Aylmer Maude's translation of the play for the 1904 London production (by G. B. Shaw's Stage Society) spurred Max Beerbohm's substantive article on the art of translation. The Maudes had tried to find equivalents for Tolstoy's Tula dialect expressions in English Cockney, and, although he liked the play, Beerbohm complained bitterly about this approach.[13] To elucidate his position

---

[12] Konstantin Stanislavsky, *My Life in Art*, trans. J. J. Robbins (New York: Meridian Books, 1956), 400-03.

[13] Max Beerbohm, "The Stage Society," in *Last Theatres 1904-1910* (New York:

(in response to public requests from both Maude and Shaw), he wrote a fine article on the problems and pitfalls of dramatic translation with *The Power of Darkness* as his main illustration. His essential premise is that translation, although worth the effort, is basically impossible and inevitably entails huge compromises. Nevertheless, not all compromises are equal, and Beerbohm concludes that the best compromise in translating local dialect is to write the English version in simple ordinary language that does not jerk the audience out of the dramatic illusion with strange conflicts of culture.[14] His approach has been the norm in more recent English language productions.

Examining aspects of the language and/or staging, we quickly uncover the play's basic theme: the opposition of material and spiritual. For instance, if a close look at the use of the term "covering [прикрывать] sin" shows that for Akim in act 1, it means atonement and involves confession (too hard for Nikita at that time), for Matryona and those who follow her in later acts, it means keeping one's crimes a secret. These two characters (Nikita's parents) and their contrasting relationships with language express most fundamentally the spirit/matter conflict at the play's heart. Matryona is glib, full of self-interested arguments and excuses for evil, while Akim, the principle of good, cannot apply pressure, argue, or even speak clearly. Both parents care for their son, but Matryona focuses on his material well-being, Akim on his spiritual health—and there is no overlap whatsoever.

Other characters are less pure in their make-up. For the most part they fall into temptation and sin to pursue what seems like material comfort or an easy life, sometimes entailing "covering sin" in order to maintain a comfortable social position. For Nikita, Anisya, and Akulina, money is only a means to an end: they are motivated mainly by lust. This shows a seriously ailing spirituality, but they are not so thoroughly soulless as Matryona, who is

---

Taplinger Publishing, 1970), 115-16 (originally published in *The Saturday Review*, December 31, 1904).

[14] Max Beerbohm, "Dramatic Translation" in *Last Theatres*, 121-22 (originally published in *The Saturday Review*, January 21, 1905).

motivated entirely by the quest for wealth and ends up the only irredeemable character.

Matryona and Akim also exemplify the thematic male/ female opposition, which is a secondary manifestation of the play's spirit/matter opposition. All the adult female characters with one exception (Marina) are on the material side, and this connection is not accidental. Mitrich's diatribe on peasant women's lack of spiritual values in the alternate fourth act illuminates the play's view on the subject, but Mitrich concedes that the women's venality may not be entirely their fault. Nevertheless, when Savina first read the play she had requested for her benefice, she went to visit Tolstoy and asked if he would increase ten-year-old Anyutka's age since none of the adult female roles appealed to her at all. Tolstoy declared her charming but refused to change the play. (At the 1895 St. Petersburg premiere, Savina played Akulina to good reviews.)[15] Of course the spirit/matter opposition, with its gendered associations, figures prominently in Tolstoy's biography as well, but the well-known conflict between himself and his wife over his spiritual vocation and the material expectations of family life, culminating in his famous final escape attempt, is not our topic here.

In *The Power of Darkness*, the spirit/matter opposition manifests itself in contradictions at every level of what we see and hear. Tolstoy dispenses with description and uses the theatrical medium to communicate these contradictions as experience. For example, glib and compulsively observed traditional religious or folk rituals, presented on stage to the audience, repeatedly contradict the reality of the play's situation. Characters with entirely non-spiritual motives bow ritualistically to icons when they enter the scene; Matryona speaks for parental love while pushing her son to murder his child; Nikita ritually forgives the dying Pyotr although Nikita is sleeping with Pyotr's wife; Anisya ritually bewails her husband's death even though she killed him; Anisya and Matryona baptize

---

[15] Iulia Petrovna Rybakova, "Pervye postanovki *Vlasti t'my* v Rossii," in *Lev Tolstoi: Problemy dramaturgii i stsenichskoi interpretatsii* (Leningrad, LGITMiK, 1978), 64.

the child they intend to murder; and finally, Akulina's traditional wedding feast covers an abyss of lies and sin including adultery, incest, and murder.

Marriage, in particular, figures as an empty ritual bond, and nearly all the marriages we see are oppositional. The marriage of Matryona and Akim is the most extreme example, but the marriages of Pyotr and Anisya, Nikita and Anisya, and Mitrich and his wife (whom we hear about from him) are similarly characterized by moral conflict. Only Marina and her husband's marriage has some truth and harmony in it since, as we learn, it was established on a foundation of full confession and forgiveness. The absurd emptiness of the religious rituals featured in the play can be connected to Tolstoy's much noted antipathy to formalist ritual in any form, whether in high society, among the freemasons, in the church (from which he was excommunicated in 1901), or, ironically, in the theatrical arts.

Nevertheless (and most contradictory of all), despite its clear contempt for ritual religion, this is a deeply religious play. It turns out that on-stage religious rituals, however divorced from the play's reality, still represent the possibility of redemption by existing in characters' lives as place markers for missing spiritual content.[16] This is because sin, like darkness, is, in fact, an absence, a vacuum. Matryona seems an active persuasive force, and Akim seems passive, inarticulate, and powerless, but this is deceptive. Evil happens in the play by weakness, failure of will, yielding to material comfort. Not much effort is needed for characters to fall into the vacuum of sin, which catches a claw and then sucks in the rest (just like a bank with a debtor, as Mitrich describes it). Without God, as the critic Innokenty Annensky explains, even the ultimate good—maternal love—becomes darkness.[17] Conversely, perceiving

---

[16] Although *King Lear* was famously disparaged by Tolstoy in "Shakespeare and the Drama" (1906), something similar happens there: Edmund is the only one of the many villains ever to mention gods, even facetiously, and he alone experiences repentance.

[17] Innokentii Annenskii, "Tri sotsial'nykh dramy: Vlast' t'my," in *Knigi otrazhenii* (Moscow: Nauka, 1979), http://Annensky.lib.ru/otr/otr1-7.htm.

and following spiritual truth needs active vigilance, standing firm, making gestures, and good in this play leads by example rather than by verbal argument. In Act 3, Akim dramatically walks out on his son's immoral household and returns his gift of money. Later Mitrich encourages Nikita with the story of his own reformation, and when Nikita finally takes the plunge, his confession inspires another from Akulina.

The false reality of evil makes good seem passive and weak, but escaping from sin once you've fallen takes drastic and heroic action, in line with discarding/plucking out/cutting off the offending member, as suggested in the play's epigraph from Matthew 5:28-29. For someone in Nikita's position, redemption requires a genuine reconnection with spiritual values and with the community (мир), and public confession is his only way out of the darkness. When Mitrich helps Nikita finally see what has been motivating him ("what people think"), the seemingly insurmountable barrier to salvation vanishes—an empty illusion generated in the spiritual vacuum of evil is dispelled into nothing by confession. The play's title suddenly becomes ironic, with evil exposed as weakness in thrall to illusion, and the so-called "non-resistance to evil" practiced by the likes of Akim emerges as an expression of moral strength.

Tolstoy could not have chosen a better medium to demonstrate this vacuum and shining reemergence than the multi-dimensional theatrical one. As audience members, we feel ourselves sucked into the void as well—until the electrifying theatrical coup of Nikita's public confession gives meaning to the previously empty rituals and saves us all from the terrifying dark. The blackness of Nikita's sin and the depth of his inhuman degradation magnify the impact of the transcendent spiritual victory at the end. The last act shows the illusion-making negative vacuum of darkness triumphed over by the void-filling illusion-banishing positive power of light. And since, as the play teaches us, good leads by example, there is hope that it will act on us as Nikita's confession does on Akulina, leading us all to salvation along with its protagonist. Thus, by channeling the power of light for moral instruction, Tolstoy reaches inside of us, changes our perception, and simultaneously fills the void he perceived under the ritual surface of his contemporary theater.

22

Unperformable Text

"Visible Only in Very Clear Weather": Teaching Chekhov's Second Acts

Elizabeth Klosty Beaujour

How does one make students in a literature class really aware of the relationship between the printed text of a play and its implicit additional function as a script for performance? It does, of course, happen that an author uses the dramatic form without ever intending that the text be staged — for examples, consider W. H. Auden's "The Sea and the Mirror," his dramatized commentary on Shakespeare's *Tempest*, or Herman Ivanovich Busch's disastrous "Philosophical Tragedy" in Nabokov's *The Gift*.[1] But Chekhov did intend his plays to be staged. We have ample evidence in his correspondence and in the memoirs of members of the Moscow Art Theatre that he not only expected his plays, especially his two last plays, to be performed,

---

[1]   "From the very beginning it was apparent that the road led to disaster. The Rigan's farcical accent and bizarre solecisms were incompatible with the obscurity of his meaning. When already in the Prologue, there appeared a 'Lone Companion' (*odinokii sputnik* instead of *odinokii putnik*, lone wayfarer) walking along that road, Fyodor still hoped against hope that this was a metaphysical paradox and not a traitorous *lapsus*. The Chief of the Town Guard, not admitting the traveler, repeated several times that he 'would not pass definitely' (rhyming with 'nightly'). ... There were also two choruses, one of which somehow managed to represent the de Broglie's waves and the logic of history, while the other chorus, the good one, argued with it. 'First Sailor, Second Sailor, Third Sailor' continued Busch, enumerating the conversing characters in his nervous bass voice edged with moisture. There also appeared three flower vendors: a 'Lilies' Woman,' a 'Violets' Woman,' and a 'Woman of Different Flowers.' Suddenly something gave: little landslides began among the audience." Vladimir Nabokov, *The Gift*, trans. Michael Scammell with the collaboration of the author (New York: G. P. Putnam's Sons, 1963), 78-79.

but also that he was even willing to make changes to the texts in consideration of which actors would play which roles.

If *The Three Sisters* and *The Cherry Orchard* are meant to be performed, then what is one to make of these stage directions for the second act of *The Cherry Orchard*?

> A field. An old, long abandoned chapel, leaning to one side, and beside it a well, large slabs that were apparently once tombstones, and an old bench. A road leading to Gaev's estate can be seen. At one side, towering poplars cast their shadows; there, the cherry orchard begins. Further off there are telegraph poles and way, way off, in the distance, dimly sketched on the horizon is the outline of a large town, visible only in the best and clearest weather [который бывает виден только в очень хорошую ясную погоду]. Soon the sun will set.[2]

How can one possibly stage that? The leaning tombstones, the crumbling chapel, the old bench, even the line of telegraph poles are easy enough to reproduce in a set, but what about that large town, way off in the distance and visible only in very clear weather? How do you do that? These directions would seem to be primarily a text to set the *reader's* mood, rather than instructions to a set designer. The last two sentences especially resemble the atmosphere-creating descriptions in Chekhov's stories, such as the one that closes "The Man in the Case," much more than a usable set description.[3]

---

[2] The translation here, and all following citations from Chekhov, are essentially those of Laurence Senelick, in his *Anton Chekhov's Selected Plays*, Norton Critical Edition (New York: Norton, 2005).

[3] "It was midnight. On the right could be seen the whole village, a long street stretching far away for four miles. All was buried in deep silent slumber; not a movement, not a sound; one could hardly believe that nature could be so still. When on a moonlit night you see a broad village street, with its cottages, haystacks, and slumbering willows, a feeling of calm comes over the soul; in this peace, wrapped away from care, toil, and sorrow in the darkness of night, it is mild, melancholy, beautiful, and it seems as though the stars look down upon it kindly and with tenderness, and as though there were no evil on earth and all were well. On the left the open country

So how do you deal in a classroom with these stage directions, which students tend to skip as unimportant prefatory material, while they may sometimes be more important to the play than the actual dialogue? Perhaps the best angle of approach in a classroom is to first ask the students to describe the mood evoked for them by this "setting" in their *reading* of the opening of the second act. They must be led to see, if they have not already seen, that this poetic introductory text, full of descriptions of neglect and decay, is about change and contrast, about the decline of the old and the threat of the new. If they look at the passage again, as a stage direction this time, it is easier for them to see that the contrast indicated in the text is going to be carried in performance by changes in light almost as much as it is by the interactions of the characters on stage. The statement at the end of the description that the sun is about to set is crucial, but it is precisely the kind of thing that the *reader* forgets, as the action proceeds. Technically, it is for this reason that Gaev says a few minutes before the act ends, "The sun has set, ladies and gentlemen." The students, insofar as they have been *readers*, will probably have forgotten this. Of course a theatre audience in a decent production cannot forget the changing light. The gradual lowering of light in front of their eyes is crucial, and the students will now keep this in mind, if and when they see *The Cherry Orchard* staged.

Getting the light right in Chekhov's second acts is one of the most important signs of whether a director is attuned to Chekhov. In *The Cherry Orchard*, as the light on the stage lowers, the setting sun may, in fact should, still shine on that large town, visible only in very clear weather. The characters dither in gradually lowering light on the forestage, in the waning of one of those very clear days,[4]

---

began from the end of the village; it could be seen stretching far away to the horizon, and there was no movement, no sound in that whole expanse bathed in moonlight." Anton Chekhov, 201 Stories by Anton Chekhov, no translator indicated, accessed January 23, 2009, http://chekhov2.tripod.com/189.htm.

[4] Of course one solution would be for the director to decide that, on that day, it was not very clear weather, and so the town wasn't visible—problem solved.

and at the end of the act, they are almost in the dark. Looming over the characters is that town, which should, in contrast, become increasingly visible high up in the rear of the stage as the light on the forestage dims. In a modern theater, this can be done in several ways. The town can become black on the horizon, as the buildings on Central Park West do when the sun sets behind them. Or, if the sun is setting opposite the town, the windows can blaze. Whatever the director's choice to increase the looming presence of the town, visible only in very clear weather, the characters on the stage have not been paying attention to the falling darkness, as they have not been paying attention to the problems that the darkness symbolizes. If it is properly done, a theatre audience will subtly, gradually, increasingly, be aware of the interaction of light, looming modernization, and urbanization (those summer dachas!).[5] By the end of the act, both the readers and the viewers have been reminded, in the case of the *reader* by Gaev's comment, or in the case of a theatre audience by the physical change on stage, that time is passing and so is everything else: the essential Chekhovian realization.

In fact, as is also the case in *Three Sisters*, the second act of *The Cherry Orchard* contains the whole play in miniature (including the sound of the breaking string, about which more later). The only characters who don't care that it has grown dark in the field are Anya and Trofimov; they are the ones who don't care at the final curtain either.

But if you are teaching *The Cherry Orchard* in a literature class, be it a class on Chekhov as a whole or one on the history of the Russian Drama, and if you do not have access to a sophisticated production of the play, how, beyond simply telling them, can you convince your students of the significance of the increasingly looming city and of the dying of the light? The obvious option is to show them DVDs (obligatorily more than one) of productions of

---

[5]   An interesting complement to my emphasis on light is Boris Zingerman's "Space in Chekhov's Plays," an extract from Zingerman's *Teatr Chekhova i ego mirovoe znachenie*, ed. A. A. Anikst (Moscow: Nauka, 1988). This excerpt was chosen and translated by Laurence Senelick and is included in his *Anton Chekhov's Selected Plays*, 491-99.

the play, or at a minimum, to show them a variety of realizations of act 2. There are at least four English language versions of *The Cherry Orchard* currently available on DVD. However, DVDs bring with them their own nefarious distortions of Chekhov's intentions. So, of course, may theatrical productions,[6] but the distortions of DVDs are different. Either they treat *The Cherry Orchard* as a movie script, and the action takes place in "real" houses and "real" nature,[7] as

---

6 Stanislavsky himself described his set as follows in a letter to Chekhov (November 19, 1903):

"Please God the set will work. A little chapel, a small gully, a neglected cemetery in an oasis of trees amid the Steppes. The left part of the stage and the centre without masking flats — just the distant horizon. This will be done with a continuous semi-circular backdrop with supports to take it into the distance. In one place a stream glistens, on a hillock a country house can be seen. Telegraph poles and a railway bridge. Allow us, during one of the pauses, to bring a train with little puffs of smoke across. That could work splendidly [a "real" bridge. Even a "real" train! **How, how? EKB**]. Before the sunset the town is briefly visible [**How, how? EKB**]. Towards the end of the act, mist; it will rise especially thick from the canal downstage. The concert of frogs and the corncrake at the end of the act likewise. On the left downstage, a hayfield with a small stook, in which the scene with the group of walkers will take place. This is for the actors to help them live their roles. The general tone of the set in the style of Levitan. Countryside — like [around] Orel, but not further south than the Kursk district." (Cited in Jean Benedetti, trans. and ed., *The Moscow Art Theatre Letters* [New York: Routledge, 1991], 185.)

Chekhov told Olga Knipper that he thought they would have to try to stop Stanislavsky from bringing on the train as well as the corncrakes and frogs. So he wrote to Stanislavsky on November 23:

"Haymaking normally takes place 20-25 June, at that time the corncrake does not cry; frogs also are silent at that time. Only the oriole is heard. No churchyard, there was one a very long time ago. Two or three slabs lying scattered about, that's all that remains. A bridge, that's very good. If the train can make its appearance without any noise, not a sound, then go ahead." (Ibid., 186)

7 Meyerhold rightly chastises Stanislavsky and his heirs for attempting to put "real" nature and "real" scenery on stage:

"Following Stanislavsky's dictum that one day it will be possible to show the audience a real sky in the theatre, every director has racked his brains to raise the roof as high as possible over the stage. Nobody realizes that instead of rebuilding the stage (a most expensive undertaking) it is the fundamental principle of the naturalistic theatre, which needs to be broken

in the case of Michael Cacoyannis's film,[8] or, in the (few) instances when the video is a record of a stage production, it inevitably succumbs to the temptations of changing camera angles and shifting perspectives, indulging in close-ups, etc. Anything to avoid Chekhovian "boredom" and to make the play more "accessible" and lively. Close-ups are the most problematic. They falsify everything, particularly the ensemble relation of characters and the groupings in space and light. So although videos of performances do make the text *visible*, they violate the essence of the theatrical experience, in which each individual member of the audience sees the full stage from a single, unchanging perspective and distance. This cannot have been what Chekhov had in mind. If you show a class DVDs of productions of Chekhov's plays, you must, at appropriate moments during the screenings, comment about the particular problems posed by DVDs and films.

Another inescapable non-verbal element of act 2 of *The Cherry Orchard*, and one that recurs just before the final curtain of the play, is the "Sound of the Breaking String."[9] The stage directions read: "Everyone sits, absorbed in thought. Silence. The only sound is Firs, softly muttering. Suddenly a distant sound is heard, as if from the sky; the sound of a breaking string, dying away, mournfully."[10]

---

down. It is this principle alone which has caused the theatre to commit such absurdities…. The characters in Act Two of *The Cherry Orchard* walk through "real" ravines, across "real" bridges, past a "real" chapel, yet from the sky are suspended two big pieces of blue-painted canvas with tulle frills, which bear no resemblance at all either to sky or clouds." (*Meyerhold on Theatre*, ed. and trans. Edward Braun [New York: Hill and Wang, 1969], 51.)

[8]   In the visually stunning film by Michael Cacoyannis, Charlotte Rampling is the most touching and sympathetic Lyubov Andreevna I have ever seen. But it is no longer Chekhov's play, even if it is still Chekhov's story. *The Cherry Orchard*, directed by Michael Cacoyannis, performances by Charlotte Rampling, Alan Bates, et al. (Melanda films, 1999; King Video, 2001), DVD.

[9]   Maurice Valency, *The Breaking String: The Plays of Anton Chekhov* (New York: Oxford University Press, 1966).

[10] Senelick, *Anton Chekhov's Selected Plays*, 591. I have put back the word "silence" in Chekhov's directions, which Senelick has dropped.

(Все сидят, задумались. Тишина. Слышно только, как тихо бормочет Фирс. Вдруг раздается отдаленный звук, точно с неба, звук лопнувшей струны, замирающий, печальный.) Each character who tries to identify the sound does so in a way appropriate to his or her persona. Lopakhin thinks of an industrial accident: a rope breaking in a mineshaft, somewhere far away. Gaev thinks it is perhaps a bird, a heron. Trofimov proposes an owl, and Firs is reminded of signs of disaster just before the "troubles" — the emancipation of the serfs. Lyubov Andreevna may come closest to what the sound should convey when she says, with a shiver, "unpleasant, somehow" (Неприятно почему-то). All this works very well in the text, leaving the sound undefined, for the reader to imagine. But how does one stage this scene? One would think this would be relatively easy. The sound is clearly described as the sound of a breaking string. We are also told that the sound, like the city, is far off. Here too, DVDs of productions can be helpful in the classroom, but primarily because they are always disappointing, and the comparison with the evocative power of the text favors the latter. In the Cacoyannis film, the sound is a rumbling, like a minor earthquake or a plane taking off from LaGuardia. In a 1962 Royal Shakespeare Company production, directed by Michel Saint-Denis, with Peggy Ashcroft, John Gielgud, and with the young Judi Dench playing Anya,[11] the sound is a two-tone metallic one, as if a pipe had been struck in two different spots. It does fade away nicely, however. In a 1981 BBC production, with Judi Dench playing Ranevskaya this time,[12] the sound is very low, as though one of the lowest strings in a piano had been plucked, with the pedal depressed to make the

---

[11] Anton Chekhov, *The Cherry Orchard*, directed by Michel Saint-Denis, directed for TV by Michael Eliot, performances by Peggy Ashcroft, John Gielgud, Dorothy Tutin, Judi Dench, Ian Holm, Paul Hardwick (BBC, 1962; BBC Video, 1996), DVD. Gielgud is given credit for the English version.

[12] Anton Chekhov, *The Cherry Orchard*, English version by Trevor Griffiths from a translation by Helen Rappaport, directed by Richard Eyre, performances by Judi Dench, Bill Paterson, Anton Lesser, et al. (BBC, 1981; BBC Video, 1996), DVD.

sound linger. None of these are the sound of a breaking string.[13] One wonders if it would not be best to leave the sound to the imagination, which, of course, is what happens when one reads the play, but it would pose serious problems to do so in performance. I have never seen a production where the director dared not to use a real sound at all, to leave it to the audience's imagination as is the case for the reader, although eminent director Giorgio Strehler argues for just this solution, a solution which is persuasive for act 2, but less so for act 4.[14] While one can get away with a sound unheard in staging act

---

[13] Stanislavsky planned a fairly complex setup to produce the "Sound of the Breaking String," which he identifies with Lopakhin's explanation: it is a mine accident. Donald Rayfield quotes Stanislavsky's instructions for creating the sound as follows:

"Stretch from the beams to the floor three wires (probably the sound will depend on the metal the wire is made from), one thick wire (and the density of the sound will depend on the thickness), a second thinner wire, and a third still thinner (perhaps made of different metals). Pass a thick piece of rope over these wires. The first sound denotes the mine bucket falling. The others are the echo, i.e., the sound wandering over the steppe. To accompany or finish this scale of sounds, a light tremolo on the big drum (thunder)." (Donald Rayfield, *Understanding Chekhov* [Madison, WI: University of Wisconsin Press, 1999], 255.)

One wonders if Evreinov was aware of this project when he designed the set for "Theater of the Soul" a few years later. There, the vertical wires represent nerves, which are strained, and plucked until the poor divided protagonist shoots himself, and red ribbons pour out of the huge heart that beats in the rear of the stage. In Evreinov's play, it is the heart that breaks, not the strings.

[14] Senelick translates the relevant section from Strehler's *Per un teatro unamo* (Milan: Feltrinelli, 1974) as follows:

"In the second act, for the first time we register the famous "sound" of the snapped string—a problem against which all stage directors have banged their heads. I do not believe that the demystifying solution of certain directors nowadays—striking a little gong to change "the atmosphere"—is a good one. Better nothing, courageously. And why not? Why couldn't this sonic symbol be something the characters hear in the twilight—"they" hear it, and we, the audience looking on, do not?.. Today, until someone proves the contrary, I believe this famous sound to be a literary illusion, sediment of writing to evoke a sonorous fact, which has the aspect of an objective theatricality. I believe that no one can refuse the idea according to which the same sound heard in the second act, repeated in the last, when

2, in the final scene of the play the sound of the breaking string is a necessary contrast to the sound of the axe in the cherry orchard. You can't have one without the other. Here again, a teacher needs to be sure the students have understood the difficulties of concretizing elements of the text other than the dialogue. And here again, there is much to be said for the solution of working only with the text of the play in the classroom. Each reader can imagine the sound to his or her satisfaction. All members of an audience are submitted to the director's generally unsatisfactory choice in a theatrical production, and Lyubov Andreevna's response, "Unpleasant, somehow," is deprived of its resonance.

While *The Cherry Orchard*, Chekhov's last play, is the most problematic to "realize" in performance, there are similar difficulties in earlier plays, and they increase with each play. I will limit myself here to *The Three Sisters*, the play that immediately precedes *The Cherry Orchard*; I will discuss only the second act there too, because second acts in Chekhov generally pose problems different from those that appear in other moments in the plays' rhythms. In a traditional play, of course, the second act is when the action really takes off. In a Chekhov play, the second act is the one in which least of all happens; it is the act which relies the most on mood, a mood created by conversation certainly, but even more so by sounds, laughter, pauses, and changing light.

Act 2 of *The Three Sisters* takes place in the same space as does act 1. This is relatively unusual for a Chekhov play in which changes of setting (outside to inside, inside to outside, one room to another) are an important element of composition. But as the curtain rises on act 2, it might as well be somewhere else, and in a sense, it *is* somewhere else, so much has the passage of time changed the nature of the space. Act 1 has taken place on a sunny morning in spring,

---

the stage is empty, with Firs motionless in his real and apparent death, is not necessary—is even superfluous. All the more so since with this sound there are the famous axe blows on the cherry trees. So much so that I do not believe in realizing it with a "sound," but instead with a "silent sound," more sonorous than a blade or a gunshot." (Strehler, in Senelick, *Anton Chekhov's Selected Plays*, 618-19.)

a time of hope and renewal at the end of a year of mourning for the sisters' father. Act 2 opens in the dark. Here are the scenic directions: "Same set as Act One. Eight o'clock at night. From offstage, as if from the street, one can faintly hear a concertina playing. No lights. Enter Natalya Ivanovna in a housecoat and carrying a candle; she walks around and stops by the door leading to Andrei's room."

No lights. A candle arrives in the hands of Natasha in a housecoat, who clearly now belongs here. That she is making sure that no one has left a light on sets the mood of the act, which will be all about killing the light, in all senses. She leaves her own candle on the table. It is the only source of light on the stage where Andrei remains alone after his conversation with Natasha. Ferapont enters. The two men huddle over the candle in the otherwise empty stage, a conspiratorial duo which is motivated by the fact that Andrei is trying to read the papers Ferapont has brought by the light of the single candle.[15] The intimacy of the small circle of light in the large dark stage also helps Andrei confess his disappointment in his marriage and his life to the deaf Ferapont, giving a feeling of secretiveness to what is in fact a non-conversation. They both exit and then the stage is left empty for a moment.

The whole movement of the act forward from this second moment of emptiness goes from this darkness and void and hopelessness, through gradually increasing light illuminating a real, heard, confession of love this time, to a well-lit room with comfortable company, through the subsequent introduction of

---

[15] One wonders if perhaps Chekhov was remembering here the scene in *Crime and Punishment* when Raskolnikov asks Sonya to read the Gospel passage about the raising of Lazarus: "He took the book over to the candle and began leafing through it. … The candle-end had long been burning out in the bent candlestick, casting a dim light in this destitute room upon the murderer and the harlot strangely come together over the reading of the eternal book" (Fyodor Dostoevsky, *Crime and Punishment*, trans. Richard Pevear and Larissa Volokhonsky [New York: Vintage Classics, 1992], 324, 328. Even more curiously, when Sonya reads, her voice cracks: "At the third word, her voice rose and broke like an overtightened string" (326).

tension in the form of the two "spoiler" characters, Natasha and Solyony, and then back to dark and emptiness once again, with the breaking up of what was supposed to be a festive gathering. Students who have read the play tend to focus on the dialogue, but here again it is essential for the teacher to make sure that students pay attention to the stage directions as they read, which they rarely do spontaneously. Toward the beginning of the act, after Andrei and Ferapont exit, a lullaby is heard off-stage, reasserting the presence of Natasha's child, and then Masha and Vershinin arrive. Here Chekhov's instructions say: "Enter Masha and Vershinin. Later, during their dialogue, the parlor maid lights a lamp and candles." These candles are placed in the drawing room and in the reception room, which is usually placed upstage or upstage left. So, the light must gradually rise as the parlor maid lights candles and lamps one after another, and this rising light accompanies the conversation between Masha and Vershinin and greets the arrival of Irina and Tuzenbach. But the stage direction is given only once, at the beginning of the change of atmosphere. The *reader* will have forgotten it, which is why Masha has, rather improbably, to move to another chair and say, "There is more light over here," as Vershinin is declaring his love. The fragile peace is sustained not only by the light, but also by Masha's frequent soft laughter (which, for reasons unclear to me, annoying to Chekhov, and contrary to explicit directions in Chekhov's text, Stanislavsky wanted to be "hysterical laughter"). Even the arrival of Chebutykin, who has not paid his rent, does not destroy the comfort. But the arrival of Natasha and Solyony does begin the break-up, gradually introducing *poshlost'* (vulgarity, cheapness, etc., an almost untranslatable Russian word) and quarrelsomeness, which is brought to something of a head by the note from Vershinin's daughter announcing that his wife has tried to poison herself, obliging him to leave and making Masha uncharacteristically lose her temper with old Anfisa. It is all downhill from there, and people leave, or briefly return and then leave, having been deprived of the enjoyable festivities for which they were all waiting by Natasha's claim that Bobik is not at all well and needs quiet. After the main group leaves, and we hear (or read about) their offstage cheerfulness, Anfisa and the parlor maid clear the table and extinguish the lights.[16] Here again, this is a gradual process in performance. The light gradually dims. The nursemaid sings, and Andrei and Chebutykin sneak out across the darkened stage. Solyony makes his declaration and his threats, then leaves when Natasha makes a brief appearance. Vershinin, Olga, and Kuligin come, and then leave again, having found the party dispersed. Natasha sneaks out across the stage for a sleigh ride with Protopopov, the most important unseen character in the play, leaving Irina alone, on the once-again emptied and still dimmed stage (at the high point of the act, there were more than a dozen people on stage, and lights in both the drawing room and the reception room). So here again, as in the second act of *The Cherry Orchard*, changes in light and sound effects carry the mood at least as much as does the dialogue. It is extraordinarily subtly done, and peace and the possibility of any kind of joy die with the dying of the light.

How does one ensure that the full emotional effects of Chekhov's second acts, and ultimately of his plays in their entireties, are felt by students, since these effects rest not only on dialogue and character relationships but also on silences, pauses, the wind in the chimney, haunting unidentified sounds, nursemaids singing, doorbells ringing, and most of all, in the second acts, on careful, gradual, changes in light? In the end, it is a question of recognizing a feeling, of participating in a mood rather than analyzing, which is the usual activity in a classroom. Oddly enough, it may actually be easier to verbally transmit the feeling of a non-verbal sensation than it is to rely on seeing the feeling "portrayed" on a stage, because only rarely does a production of a Chekhov play give his atmospheric cues their due. In fact, this is probably the most important lesson

---

16 The DVD of *The Three Sisters*, as played by the National Theatre Company of England, a film directed by Laurence Olivier (trans. Moura Budberg, performances by Alan Bates, Laurence Olivier, Joan Plowright, Derek Jacobi, et al. [1970; Kino Video, 2003], DVD), handles the lighting of Chekhov's directions scrupulously. The major flaw in this performance, other than the usual caveats about films of Chekhov plays, is that the recording is old, and occasionally difficult to understand if you do not already know the play well.

to be learned from teaching Chekhov in a literature class. Reading the play may or may not satisfy. Seeing the play produced generally does not.

So, after trying it every which way, I have come to the reluctant and somewhat paradoxical conclusion that the best way to teach Chekhov is to rely primarily on reading and discussing the *texts*,[17] directing the students' attention to the non-dialogic elements in the text, and with only very brief and occasional recourse to what is usually considered "experiencing" the plays: that is, seeing performances, especially on DVD or by a small, semi-professional company, which is rarely in fact a real "company."[18] Leaving mood-creating directions to students' imaginations, once these imaginations have been focused on these directions, which they tend to neglect as unimportant introductory material, may, despite Chekhov's intention to have his plays staged, give a fuller sense of the extraordinary balance of elements that create mood than would seeing an actual performance. Of course there are pitfalls here too, in particular the difficulty for the student uninitiated in reading plays, especially Russian plays, in keeping the characters straight while reading.

To be fair, the solution of focusing primarily on the text still does require a bit of theatricality: the teacher's performance. I would strongly advise against having students read Chekhov's lines aloud,

---

[17] Curiously, John Stokes, in a recent review article in the *Times Literary Supplement* about several books on theater, maintains that this can even be true about old performances. "It is through reading past critics—not through scratchy recordings and fuzzy films—that we truly see and hear dead actors." Stokes, "Something More than a Passing Show," *Times Literary Supplement* (August 14, 2009), 9.

[18] I say this although perhaps the best performance of *The Three Sisters* I ever saw was done by the Vassar Experimental Theatre, with Robert Brustein playing Andrei, Evert Sprinchorn as Tusenbach, C. Gordon Post as Chebutykin, and Robert Kingston as Vershinin. Oddly, I do not remember who played any of the three sisters, perhaps because the men were faculty members and the women were undergraduates, as was I. Of course, the whole thing may have been glorified in memory, given the passage of fifty years and the absence of any documentation beyond a few ratty-edged photos.

however. I know this is, theatrically and pedagogically, a retrograde position, and that class participation is frequently a positive and desirable thing, but in this context, having students read Chekhov out loud can only drive the texts into the ground. Any instructor with some physical presence can handle Chekhov. What I advocate is actually a judicious balance of several methodologies, but the main thing is to ensure that the students, who are your audience, have the sense of lives being frittered away, of cities looming, visible only in very clear weather, of things coming to an end, of the dying of the light and with it, of time going irrevocably by.

INDEX

Milne, A. A. 186; *House at Pooh Corner, The* 186, 198; *Winnie-the-Pooh* 186

Milton, John 145

Mobius, August F. 184

Moeller-Sally, Stephen 235

Molière, Jean B. P. de 209

Mongia, Padmini 228n26

Montaigne, Michel 34

Morris, Marcia xiv; 13

Morson, Gary Saul xv, 9, 10, 69, 178n3, 193, 194, 208n6

Mortimer, Ruth 86n11, 91n23

Nabokov, Dmitri 247n2

Nabokov, Vladimir V. xiii, 97, 247, 247n2, 248, 249, 250, 250n10, 251, 253n14, 260n31, 274, 313, 313n1; "Affair of Honor, An" 97; *Gift, The* 313; *Lolita* 249; *Speak, Memory* 249; "Spring in Fialta" 97

Napoleon 39, 166, 169, 215, 270

Narezhny, V. T. 263n5

Naumov, N. I. 40

Nechaeva, V. S. 188n5

Nekrasov, Nikolai A. 74, 77, 78, 80, 82, 83n4, 189; "Parable, The" 77; *Petersburg Collection* 74; "To the Sowers" 77; "V. G. Belinsky" 77; "When Out of the Darkness of Delusion" 189; *Who Can Be Happy and Free in Russia?* 77

Nemirovsky, Igor ix

Nepomnyashchy, Catharine T. xv, 14, 287n1

Newman, John H. 39; *Apologia pro Vita Sua* 39

Newton, Alice ix

Ngai, Sianne 136n5

Nietzsche, Friedrich 82, 83, 94, 227; *Antichrist, The* 83; *Genealogy of Morals* 227

Nohejl, Regine 119n11

Nolan, Paul T. 303n3

Nussbaum, Martha C. 27, 134

Olivier, Laurence 324n16

Orwell, George 28

Ovid 73n10; "Fasti" 73n10; *Metamorphoses* 73n10

Painter, Kirsten ix

Paperno, Irina 79

Parts, Lyudmilla 89n20

Pascal, Roy 246n1

Paterson, Bill 319n11

Pausanias 73n10

Pavlova, Karolina K. 40; *A Double Life* 40

Paxton, Robert 39

Peace, Richard 98n1

Peirce, Charles S. 45n2

Pelouse, T. J. 142; *Notions générales de chimie* (with E. Frémy) 142

Peter the Great 40

Pevear, Richard 70n4, 86n12, 95n29, 163n1, 303n2, 322n15

Phillips, Adam 136

Pindar 73n10

Pisarev, Dmitry I. 40, 41; "Destruction of Aesthetics" 40

Pisemsky, Aleksei F. 40; *Thousand Souls, A* 40

Plato 10, 34, 35, 176–178, 178n4, 179–185, 212; *Phaedrus* 181; *Republic, The* 10, 178, 178n3n4, 179, 180, 182, 182n7, 183, 185

CPSIA information can be obtained at www.ICGtesting.com
Printed in the USA
BVOW03*1610230214

345678BV00004B/21/P

9 781618 113498